COOPERS & CUSTOMS CUTTERS

Worthingtons of Dover
and Related Families
1560-1906

Mihi pertinent æquoris undæ.

COOPERS &
CUSTOMS CUTTERS

Worthingtons of Dover
and Related Families
1560-1906

Janet Robyn Worthington

N.Z.R.N., Dip. F.H.S., F.S.A.G.

Phillimore

1997

Published by
PHILLIMORE & CO. LTD.
Shopwyke Manor Barn, Chichester, West Sussex

B.WOR

ISBN 1 86077 011 8

Printed and bound in Great Britain by
BOOKCRAFT LTD.
Midsomer Norton, Avon

This book is dedicated to my mother

Barbara May Worthington, née Hills
(1914-1995)

who remembered my father's stories
and passed them on

Sea Song

A wet sheet and a flowing sea,
A wind that follows fast,
And fills the white and rustling sail
And bends the gallant mast–
And bends the gallant mast, my boys,
While, like the eagle free,
Away the good ship flies, and leaves
Old England on the lee.

'Oh for a soft and gentle wind,'
I heard a fair one cry;
But give to me the snoring breeze,
And white waves heaving high–
And white waves heaving high, my boys,
The good ship tight and free;
The world of waters is our home,
And merry men are we.

There's tempest in yon horned moon,
And lightning in yon cloud;
And hark the music, mariners!
The wind is piping loud, my boys,
The lightning flashing free,–
While the hollow oak our palace is,
Our heritage the sea.

A. CUNNINGHAM

Contents

List of Illustrations

Family History Charts

Foreword

My cousin, the authoress (Janet Worthington) has asked me to add a foreword to this biography of her great-great-great-grandfather and my great-great-grandfather, Benjamin Jelly Worthington. I am descended through one of his sons, Dr. William Collins Worthington, who practised in Lowestoft, Suffolk, whilst her line is through his brother, Henry.

After 144 years, I followed in our ancestor's footsteps by joining the Royal Navy in 1918, as a cadet, a few months before the end of the First World War and spent four years in the Royal Naval College at Osborne and Dartmouth. I retired in 1922 at the time of the post-war 'Geddes Axe' economy cuts of the three forces, including the closure of Osborne, when we were all encouraged to resign. I then entered the business world in the City of London and joined my father's firm of rubber brokers.

In April 1940, I rejoined the Royal Navy via the R.N.V.R. after the Second World War had been in progress six months and in May was appointed to a Fleet minesweeper, operating out of Dover Harbour, clearing sea routes to the Belgian and French coasts for the evacuation of the Allied armies. As the ship was not at sea until the following day, I was able to visit St Mary's churchyard to locate the family vault in which the Commander's parents and 12 other relatives were buried. At that time it was enclosed by iron railings as was the churchyard, later removed towards the war-effort and only recently renewed (not around the vault). During 1991 we have renovated these tombs and also those in St Andrew's churchyard nearby, where the Commander, his wife and others were buried. We hope they will remain a visible memorial to our Dover branch of the Worthington family for many more years to come.

John F. Worthington D.S.C.
erstwhile Lieutenant Commander R.N.V.R.

Preface and Acknowledgements

Benjamin Jelly Worthington lived and worked for His Majesty's Customs Service at the height of what was called the 'grand, adventurous epoch of the smugglers which covered little more than a century and a half, beginning about the year 1700 and ending about 1855 or 1860'.[1] Smugglers were a notorious and dangerous band of men who threatened the trade and financial welfare of England.

The sailors who ran backwards and forwards across the English Channel in cutters, yawls, luggers and sometimes open boats were some of the finest seamen in the world. They were certainly the most skilled fore-and-aft sailors and pilots to be found anywhere on the seas which wash the coasts of the United Kingdom. They were sturdy and strong of body, courageous and enterprising of nature. Consequently the English Government wisely determined that in all cases of an encounter with smugglers the first aim of the Preventive Officers should be to capture the smugglers themselves, for they could be promptly impressed into Naval service and be put to the good of the nation instead of to its disadvantage.

The information regarding Benjamin has all been obtained from primary and secondary records and can be verified. The descendants of Benjamin Jelly Worthington are fortunate that Customs and Excise records still survive despite the burning down of the Customs House by the side of the Thames in 1814.

Although I was raised surrounded by family heirlooms and told family stories, my ancestral background was a complete mystery. My mother Barbara May Worthington, née Hills, and my daughter Amanda Jane Clark were interested in their family history long before I was. The family history bug is very catching and any involvement however brief can be fatal. I have them to thank for this!

Over the past 15 years Kathleen Hollingsbee of Tilmanstone, Kent, has regularly sent me gleanings from various Kent sources. Without her assistance this book would not have been possible. Through her astuteness original wills and indentures were discovered for sale at a Sandwich fair.

Bob Hollingsbee has contributed most of the photographs pertaining to Dover. While strolling through a snow-covered churchyard at Charlton near Dover he discovered one of the oldest known Worthington artifacts, John Worthington's headstone dated 1747.

In 1983 I met, initially by correspondence and later in person, the very helpful late Rev. Dr. Edward (Ted) Hughes. He has been known to write me letters on Christmas Eve after spending several hours searching parish registers held in St Mary's Church for Worthington family entries. I am sincerely appreciative of his efforts on my behalf as I have not found all clergymen quite so supportive.

I would not have found my cousin John F. Worthington of Fleet, Hampshire, if Philip M. Worthington, author of *The Worthington Families of Medieval Britain*, had not put me in touch with him. My thanks to John for allowing me to view the family oil paintings hanging in his hallway on several occasions and providing me with copy from an unpublished anonymous Worthington family history *c.*1928. Some of the family photographs were kindly provided by New Zealand and Welsh cousins, Marie Horsfield, Shirley Lamy, Enfys and Huw Spencer Lloyd, Jean Hankey and Ann Facey. Along with David Hill and Lynda Cumming, Ann Facey also revealed another line of Dover Worthingtons who settled in New Zealand. My thanks to my brother, Garth John Worthington and cousin, Kenneth Worthington of New Zealand who have contributed photographs of family heirlooms in their possession.

Dr. David H. Villers, Ph.D., M.A., B.A. (Hons.), historian of South Ealing, London, spent months at the Public Record Office, Kew, searching through Customs Records. I am grateful for his excellent assistance as it would have been very difficult for me to spend the amount of time necessary to research these records myself. His report of 6 September 1986 is reproduced in full as Appendix 1. Permission to reproduce material was obtained from the Controller of Her Majesty's Stationery Office; the National Maritime Museum, Greenwich, London; the Centre for Kentish Studies; and the Department of Pictures & Maps, The National Library of Wales.

Thanks are also due to Michael Hunt, Museum Officer of the Ramsgate Maritime Museum, for donating the photograph of the model of the Revenue cutter *Tartar* and copies of original letters written by Benjamin Worthington displayed at the Museum. Michael Freeman, Curator of the Ceredigion Museum, Aberystwyth introduced me to Alfred Worthington's artwork and generously provided biographical information. Information on Dover Worthingtons was also kindly given by Mark Frost, Assistant Curator of Dover. I am also very grateful to John Algar, Southgate, Wales for his cross country journeys to Aberystwyth in search of my Welsh cousins; and to P.Ll. Gwynn-Jones, M.A., Lancaster Herald, who checked the authenticity of claims to Coats of Arms by ancestors at The College of Arms, London. I would also like to thank my friend and fine artist, Heather D. Smith of Art Power, Sydney for her drawings of the Coats of Arms.

Amanda Jane Clark, B.A., Communications, M.P.R.I.A. and Evan C. Best, M.A., B.A. (Hons.), Dip.F.H.S., F.S.A.G. have assisted me to edit the final manuscript. I am extremely grateful to Amanda who helped research and write the latter part of the book. My husband, Donald John Clark, has been an enthusiastic and encouraging supporter of this project.

I have endeavoured to be as accurate and complete as possible with this research but many errors and omissions can still occur in a work of this kind. Living on the other side of the world has been a disadvantage as I would have liked to have been able to spend more time researching records in England myself. Several family members who are very interested in the contents of this book are now in their eighties and nineties and would like to see it published during their lifetimes.

All corrections, omissions and additional material can be sent to me at P.O. Box 161, Lane Cove, Sydney, New South Wales, Australia 2066 as I may one day find the strength to publish an addendum!

Jan Worthington, N.Z.R.N., Dip.F.H.S., F.S.A.G.

[1] Chatterton, E. Keble, *King's Cutters and Smugglers 1700-1855* (George Allen & Company Ltd., London, 1912), p.1.

Family History Charts—Worthingtons

The following charts have been compiled from information found in parish registers, Freemen records, wills, cemetery transcriptions, apprenticeship and civil registration records.

Worthington Descendants Chart 1

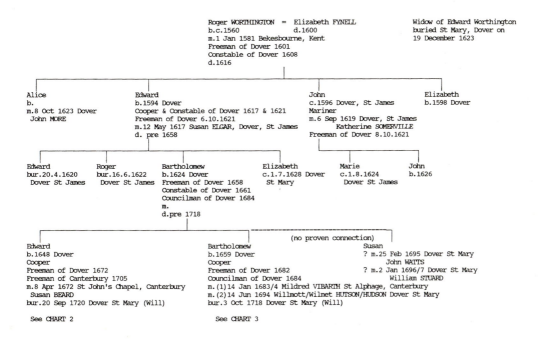

Worthington Descendants Chart 2 (from Chart 1)

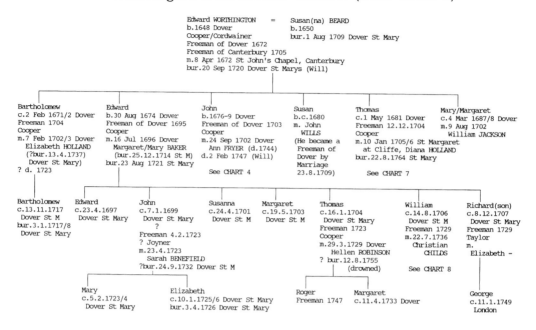

Edward WORTHINGTON = Susan(na) BEARD
b.1648 Dover   b.1650
Cooper/Cordwainer   bur.1 Aug 1709 Dover St Mary
Freeman of Dover 1672
Freeman of Canterbury 1705
m.8 Apr 1672 St John's Chapel, Canterbury
bur.20 Sep 1720 Dover St Marys (Will)

Bartholomew
c.2 Feb 1671/2 Dover
Freeman 1704
Cooper
m.7 Feb 1702/3 Dover
  Elizabeth HOLLAND
  (?bur.13.4.1737)
  Dover St Mary)
? d. 1723

Edward
b.30 Aug 1674 Dover
Freeman of Dover 1695
Cooper
m.16 Jul 1696 Dover
  Margaret/Mary BAKER
  (bur.25.12.1714 St M)
bur.23 Aug 1721 St Mary

John
b.1676-9 Dover
Freeman of Dover 1703
Cooper
m.24 Sep 1702 Dover
  Ann FRYER (d.1744)
d.2 Feb 1747 (Will)

See CHART 4

Susan
b.c.1680
m. John
WILLS
(He became a
Freeman of
Dover by
Marriage
23.8.1709)

Thomas
c.1 May 1681 Dover
Freeman 12.12.1704
Cooper
m.10 Jan 1705/6 St Margaret
  at Cliffe, Diana HOLLAND
bur.22.8.1764 St Mary

See CHART 7

Mary/Margaret
c.4 Mar 1687/8 Dover
m.9 Aug 1702
  William JACKSON

Bartholomew
c.13.11.1717
Dover St M
bur.3.1.1717/8
Dover St Mary

Edward
c.23.4.1697
Dover St Mary

John
c.7.1.1699
Dover St Mary
?
Freeman 4.2.1723
? Joyner
m.23.4.1723
  Sarah BENEFIELD
?bur.24.9.1732 Dover St M

Susanna
c.24.4.1701
Dover St M

Margaret
c.19.5.1703
Dover St M

Thomas
c.16.1.1704
Dover St Mary
Freeman 1723
Cooper
m.29.3.1729 Dover
  Hellen ROBINSON
? bur.12.8.1755
  (drowned)

William
c.14.8.1706
Dover St M
Freeman 1729
m.22.7.1736
  Christian
  CHILDS

See CHART 8

Richard(son)
c.8.12.1707
Dover St Mary
Freeman 1729
Taylor
m.
  Elizabeth -

Mary
c.5.2.1723/4
Dover St Mary

Elizabeth
c.10.1.1725/6 Dover St Mary
bur.3.4.1726 Dover St Mary

Roger
Freeman 1747

Margaret
c.11.4.1733 Dover

George
c.11.1.1749
London

Worthington Descendants Chart 3 (from Chart 1)

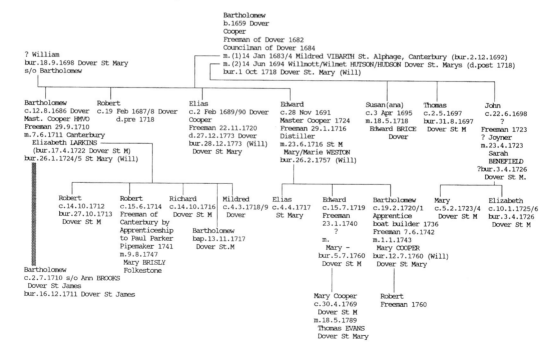

Bartholomew
b.1659 Dover
Cooper
Freeman of Dover 1682
Councilman of Dover 1684
m.(1)14 Jan 1683/4 Mildred VIBARTH St. Alphage, Canterbury (bur.2.12.1692)
m.(2)14 Jun 1694 Willmott/Wilmet HUTSON/HUDSON Dover St. Marys (d.post 1718)
bur.1 Oct 1718 Dover St. Mary (Will)

? William
bur.18.9.1698 Dover St Mary
s/o Bartholomew

Bartholomew
c.12.8.1686 Dover
Mast. Cooper HMVO
Freeman 29.9.1710
m.7.6.1711 Canterbury
  Elizabeth LARKINS
  (bur.17.4.1722 Dover St M)
bur.26.1.1724/5 St Mary (Will)

Robert
c.19 Feb 1687/8 Dover
d.pre 1718

Elias
c.2 Feb 1689/90 Dover
Cooper
Freeman 22.11.1720
d.27.12.1773 Dover
bur.28.12.1773 (Will)
Dover St Mary

Edward
c.28 Nov 1691
Master Cooper 1724
Freeman 29.1.1716
Distiller
m.23.6.1716 St M
  Mary/Marie WESTON
bur.26.2.1757 (Will)

Susan(ana)
c.3 Apr 1695
m.18.5.1718
  Edward BRICE
  Dover

Thomas
c.2.5.1697
bur.31.8.1697
Dover St M

John
c.22.6.1698
?
Freeman 1723
? Joyner
m.23.4.1723
  Sarah
  BENEFIELD
?bur.3.4.1726
  Dover St M.

Bartholomew
c.2.7.1710 s/o Ann BROOKS
Dover St James
bur.16.12.1711 Dover St James

Robert
c.14.10.1712
bur.27.10.1713
Dover St M

Robert
c.15.6.1714
Freeman of
Canterbury by
Apprenticeship
to Paul Parker
Pipemaker 1741
m.9.8.1747
  Mary BRISLY
  Folkestone

Richard
c.14.10.1716
Dover St M

Bartholomew
bap.13.11.1717
Dover St.M

Mildred
c.4.3.1718/9
Dover

Elias
c.4.4.1717
St Mary

Edward
c.15.7.1719
Freeman
23.1.1740
?
m.
  Mary -
  bur.5.7.1760
  Dover St M

Bartholomew
c.19.2.1720/1
Apprentice
boat builder 1736
Freeman 7.6.1742
m.1.1.1743
  Mary COOPER
  bur.12.7.1760 (Will)
  Dover St Mary

Mary
c.5.2.1723/4
Dover St M

Elizabeth
c.10.1.1725/6
bur.3.4.1726
Dover St M

Mary Cooper
c.30.4.1769
Dover St M
m.18.5.1789
  Thomas EVANS
  Dover St Mary

Robert
Freeman 1760

Worthington Descendants Chart 4 (from Chart 2)

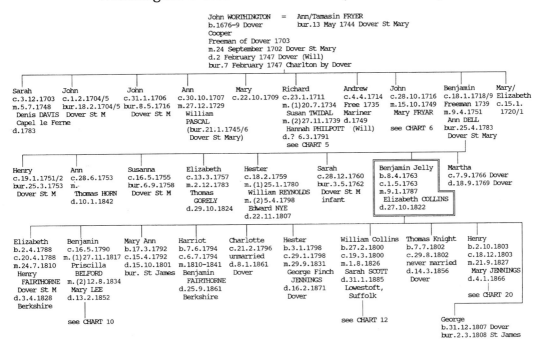

John WORTHINGTON = Ann/Tamasin FRYER
b.1676-9 Dover   bur.13 May 1744 Dover St Mary
Cooper
Freeman of Dover 1703
m.24 September 1702 Dover St Mary
d.2 February 1747 Dover (Will)
bur.7 February 1747 Charlton by Dover

Children (row 1):

Sarah
c.3.12.1703
m.5.7.1748
Denis DAVIS
Capel le Ferne
d.1783

John
c.1.2.1704/5
bur.18.2.1704/5
Dover St M

John
c.31.1.1706
bur.8.5.1716
Dover St M

Ann
c.30.10.1707
m.27.12.1729
William
PASCAL
(bur.21.1.1745/6
Dover St Mary)

Mary
c.22.10.1709

Richard
c.23.1.1711
m.(1)20.7.1734
Susan TWIDAL
Mariner
m.(2)27.11.1739
Hannah PHILPOTT (Will)
d.? 6.3.1791
see CHART 5

Andrew
c.4.4.1714
Free 1735
Mariner
d.1749

John
c.28.10.1716
m.15.10.1749
Mary FRYAR
see CHART 6

Benjamin
c.18.1.1718/9
Freeman 1739
m.9.4.1751
Ann DELL
bur.25.4.1783
Dover St Mary

Mary/
Elizabeth
c.15.1.
1720/1

Children of Benjamin (row 2):

Henry
c.19.1.1751/2
bur.25.3.1753
Dover St M

Ann
c.28.6.1753
m.-
Thomas HORN
d.10.1.1842

Susanna
c.16.5.1755
bur.6.9.1758
Dover St M

Elizabeth
c.13.3.1757
m.2.12.1783
Thomas
GORELY
d.29.10.1824

Hester
c.18.2.1759
m.(1)25.1.1780
William REYNOLDS
m.(2)5.4.1798
Edward NYE
d.22.11.1807

Sarah
c.28.12.1760
bur.3.5.1762
Dover St M
infant

Benjamin Jelly
b.8.4.1763
c.1.5.1763
m.9.1.1787
Elizabeth COLLINS
d.27.10.1822

Martha
c.7.9.1766 Dover
d.18.9.1769 Dover

Children of Benjamin Jelly (row 3):

Elizabeth
b.2.4.1788
c.20.4.1788
m.24.7.1810
Henry
FAIRTHORNE
Dover St M
d.3.4.1828
Berkshire

Benjamin
c.16.5.1790
m.(1)27.11.1817
Priscilla
BELFORD
m.(2)12.8.1834
Mary LEE
d.13.2.1852

see CHART 10

Mary Ann
b.17.3.1792
c.6.7.1794
d.15.10.1801
bur. St James

Harriot
b.7.6.1794
c.6.7.1794
m.1810-1841
Benjamin
FAIRTHORNE
d.25.9.1861
Berkshire

Charlotte
c.21.2.1796
unmarried
d.8.1.1861
Dover

Hester
b.3.1.1798
c.19.3.1798
m.29.9.1831
George Finch
JENNINGS
d.16.2.1871
Dover

William Collins
b.27.2.1800
c.19.3.1800
m.1.8.1826
Sarah SCOTT
d.31.1.1885
Lowestoft,
Suffolk

see CHART 12

Thomas Knight
b.7.7.1802
c.29.8.1802
never married
d.14.3.1856
Dover

Henry
b.2.10.1803
c.18.12.1803
m.21.9.1827
Mary JENNINGS
d.4.1.1866

see CHART 20

George
b.31.12.1807 Dover
bur.2.3.1808 St James

Worthington Descendants Chart 5 (from Chart 4)

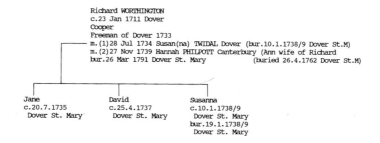

Richard WORTHINGTON
c.23 Jan 1711 Dover
Cooper
Freeman of Dover 1733
m.(1)28 Jul 1734 Susan(na) TWIDAL Dover (bur.10.1.1738/9 Dover St.M)
m.(2)27 Nov 1739 Hannah PHILPOTT Canterbury (Ann wife of Richard
bur.26 Mar 1791 Dover St. Mary   (buried 26.4.1762 Dover St.M)

Jane
c.20.7.1735
Dover St. Mary

David
c.25.4.1737
Dover St. Mary

Susanna
c.10.1.1738/9
Dover St. Mary
bur.19.1.1738/9
Dover St. Mary

Worthington Descendants Chart 6 (from Chart 4)

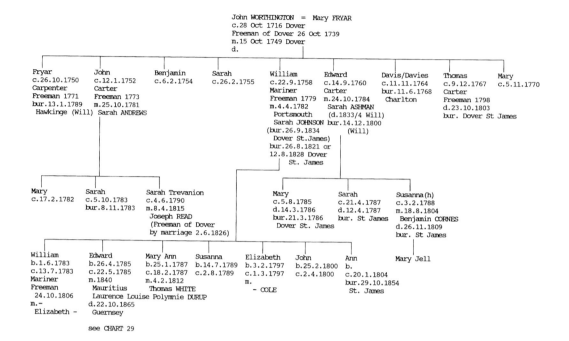

John WORTHINGTON = Mary FRYAR
c.28 Oct 1716 Dover
Freeman of Dover 26 Oct 1739
m.15 Oct 1749 Dover
d.

Fryar
c.26.10.1750
Carpenter
Freeman 1771
bur.13.1.1789
Hawkinge (Will)

John
c.12.1.1752
Carter
Freeman 1773
m.25.10.1781
Sarah ANDREWS

Benjamin
c.6.2.1754

Sarah
c.26.2.1755

William
c.22.9.1758
Mariner
Freeman 1779
m.4.4.1782
Portsmouth
Sarah JOHNSON
(bur.26.9.1834
Dover St.James)
bur.26.8.1821 or
12.8.1828 Dover
St. James

Edward
c.14.9.1760
Carter
m.24.10.1784
Sarah ASHMAN
(d.1833/4 Will)
bur.14.12.1800
(Will)

Davis/Davies
c.11.11.1764
Charlton

Thomas
c.9.12.1767
Carter
Freeman 1798
d.23.10.1803
bur. Dover St James

Mary
c.5.11.1770

Mary
c.17.2.1782

Sarah
c.5.10.1783
bur.8.11.1783

Sarah Trevanion
c.4.6.1790
m.8.4.1815
Joseph READ
(Freeman of Dover
by marriage 2.6.1826)

Mary
c.5.8.1785
d.14.3.1786
bur.21.3.1786
Dover St. James

Sarah
c.21.4.1787
d.12.4.1787
bur. St James

Susanna(h)
c.3.2.1788
m.18.8.1804
Benjamin CORNES
d.26.11.1809
bur. St James

William
b.1.6.1783
c.13.7.1783
Mariner
Freeman
24.10.1806
m.-
Elizabeth -

Edward
b.26.4.1785
c.22.5.1785
Mauritius
m.1840
Laurence Louise Polymnie DURUP
d.22.10.1865
Guernsey

see CHART 29

Mary Ann
b.25.1.1787
c.18.2.1787
m.4.2.1812
Thomas WHITE

Susanna
b.14.7.1789
c.2.8.1789

Elizabeth
b.3.2.1797
c.1.3.1797
m.
- COLE

John
b.25.2.1800
c.2.4.1800

Ann
b.
c.20.1.1804
bur.29.10.1854
St. James

Mary Jell

Worthington Descendants Chart 7 (from Chart 2)

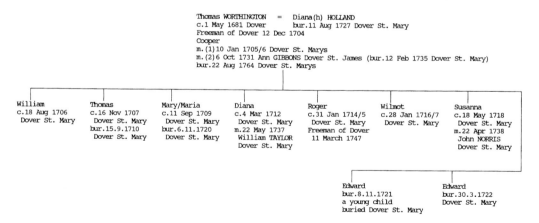

Thomas WORTHINGTON = Diana(h) HOLLAND
c.1 May 1681 Dover   bur.11 Aug 1727 Dover St. Mary
Freeman of Dover 12 Dec 1704
Cooper
m.(1)10 Jan 1705/6 Dover St. Marys
m.(2)6 Oct 1731 Ann GIBBONS Dover St. James (bur.12 Feb 1735 Dover St. Mary)
bur.22 Aug 1764 Dover St. Marys

William
c.18 Aug 1706
Dover St. Mary

Thomas
c.16 Nov 1707
Dover St. Mary
bur.15.9.1710
Dover St. Mary

Mary/Maria
c.11 Sep 1709
Dover St. Mary
bur.6.11.1720
Dover St. Mary

Diana
c.4 Mar 1712
Dover St. Mary
m.22 May 1737
William TAYLOR
Dover St. Mary

Roger
c.31 Jan 1714/5
Dover St. Mary
Freeman of Dover
11 March 1747

Wilmot
c.28 Jan 1716/7
Dover St. Mary

Susanna
c.18 May 1718
Dover St. Mary
m.22 Apr 1738
John NORRIS
Dover St. Mary

Edward
bur.8.11.1721
a young child
buried Dover St. Mary

Edward
bur.30.3.1722
Dover St. Mary

Worthington Descendants Chart 8 (from Chart 2)

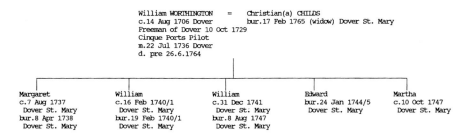

William WORTHINGTON = Christian(a) CHILDS
c.14 Aug 1706 Dover   bur.17 Feb 1765 (widow) Dover St. Mary
Freeman of Dover 10 Oct 1729
Cinque Ports Pilot
m.22 Jul 1736 Dover
d. pre 26.6.1764

Margaret	William	William	Edward	Martha
c.7 Aug 1737	c.16 Feb 1740/1	c.31 Dec 1741	bur.24 Jan 1744/5	c.10 Oct 1747
Dover St. Mary	Dover St. Mary	Dover St. Mary	Dover St. Mary	Dover St. Mary
bur.8 Apr 1738	bur.19 Feb 1740/1	bur.8 Aug 1747		
Dover St. Mary	Dover St. Mary	Dover St. Mary		

Worthington Descendants Chart 9

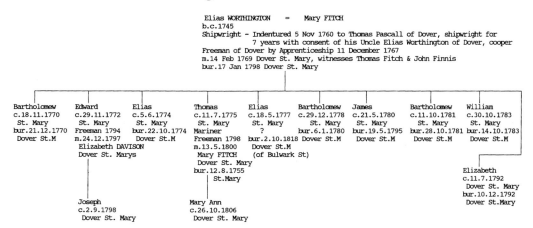

Elias WORTHINGTON = Mary FITCH
b.c.1745
Shipwright - Indentured 5 Nov 1760 to Thomas Pascall of Dover, shipwright for
             7 years with consent of his Uncle Elias Worthington of Dover, cooper
Freeman of Dover by Apprenticeship 11 December 1767
m.14 Feb 1769 Dover St. Mary, witnesses Thomas Fitch & John Finnis
bur.17 Jan 1798 Dover St. Mary

Bartholomew	Edward	Elias	Thomas	Elias	Bartholomew	James	Bartholomew	William
c.18.11.1770	c.29.11.1772	c.5.6.1774	c.11.7.1775	c.18.5.1777	c.29.12.1778	c.21.5.1780	c.11.10.1781	c.30.10.1783
St. Mary	St. Mary	St. Mary	St. Mary	St. Mary	St. Mary	St. Mary	St. Mary	St. Mary
bur.21.12.1770	Freeman 1794	bur.22.10.1774	Mariner	?	bur.6.1.1780	bur.19.5.1795	bur.28.10.1781	bur.14.10.1783
Dover St.M	m.24.12.1797	Dover St.M	Freeman 1798	bur.2.10.1818	Dover St.M	Dover St.M	Dover St.M	Dover St.M
	Elizabeth DAVISON		m.13.5.1800	Dover St.M	(of Bulwark St)			
	Dover St. Marys		Mary FITCH					
			Dover St. Mary					
			bur.12.8.1755					
			St.Mary					

Joseph
c.2.9.1798
Dover St. Mary

Mary Ann
c.26.10.1806
Dover St. Mary

Elizabeth
c.11.7.1792
Dover St. Mary
bur.10.12.1792
Dover St.Mary

Descendants of Lieutenant Benjamin Worthington Chart 10 (from Chart 4)

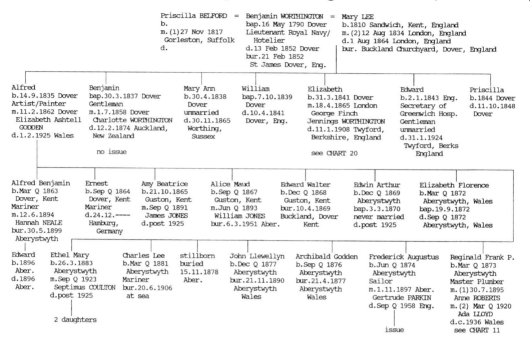

```
Priscilla BELFORD  =  Benjamin WORTHINGTON  =  Mary LEE
b.                     bap.16 May 1790 Dover     b.1810 Sandwich, Kent, England
m.(1)27 Nov 1817       Lieutenant Royal Navy/    m.(2)12 Aug 1834 London, England
Gorleston, Suffolk     Hotelier                  d.1 Aug 1864 London, England
d.                     d.13 Feb 1852 Dover       bur. Buckland Churchyard, Dover, England
                       bur.21 Feb 1852
                       St James Dover, Eng.
```

Alfred	Benjamin	Mary Ann	William	Elizabeth	Edward	Priscilla
b.14.9.1835 Dover	bap.30.3.1837 Dover	b.30.4.1838	bap.7.10.1839	b.31.3.1841 Dover	b.2.1.1843 Eng.	b.1844 Dover
Artist/Painter	Gentleman	Dover	Dover	m.18.4.1865 London	Secretary of	d.11.10.1848
m.11.2.1862 Dover	m.1.7.1858 Dover	unmarried	d.10.4.1841	George Finch	Greenwich Hosp.	Dover
Elizabeth Ashtell	Charlotte WORTHINGTON	d.30.11.1865	Dover, Eng.	Jennings WORTHINGTON	Gentleman	
GODDEN	d.12.2.1874 Auckland,	Worthing,		d.11.1.1908 Twyford,	unmarried	
d.1.2.1925 Wales	New Zealand	Sussex		Berkshire, England	d.31.1.1924	
					Twyford, Berks	
	no issue			see CHART 20	England	

Alfred Benjamin	Ernest	Amy Beatrice	Alice Maud	Edward Walter	Edwin Arthur	Elizabeth Florence
b.Mar Q 1863	b.Sep Q 1864	b.21.10.1865	b.Sep Q 1867	b.Dec Q 1868	b.Dec Q 1869	b.Mar Q 1872
Dover, Kent	Dover, Kent	Guston, Kent	Guston, Kent	Guston, Kent	Aberystwyth	Aberystwyth, Wales
Mariner	Mariner	m.Sep Q 1891	m.Jun Q 1893	bur.10.4.1869	bap.3.3.1870	bap.19.9.1872
m.12.6.1894	d.24.12.----	James JONES	William JONES	Buckland, Dover	never married	d.Sep Q 1872
Hannah NEALE	Hamburg,	d.post 1925	bur.6.3.1951 Aber.	Kent	d.post 1925	Aberystwyth, Wales
bur.30.5.1899	Germany					
Aberystwyth						

Edward	Ethel Mary	Charles Lee	stillborn	John Llewellyn	Archibald Godden	Frederick Augustus	Reginald Frank P.
b.1896	b.26.3.1883	b.Mar Q 1881	buried	b.Dec Q 1877	b.Sep Q 1876	b.Jun Q 1874	b.Mar Q 1873
Aber.	Aberystwyth	Aberystwyth	15.11.1878	Aberystwyth	Aberystwyth	Aberystwyth	Aberystwyth
d.1896	m.Sep Q 1923	Mariner	Aber.	bur.21.11.1890	bur.21.4.1877	Sailor	Master Plumber
Aber.	Septimus COULTON	bur.20.6.1906		Aberystwyth	Aberystwyth	m.1.11.1897 Aber.	m.(1)30.7.1895
	d.post 1925	at sea		Wales	Wales	Gertrude PARKIN	Anne ROBERTS
						d.Sep Q 1958 Eng.	m.(2) Mar Q 1920
	2 daughters						Ada LLOYD
						issue	d.c.1936 Wales
							see CHART 11

Descendants of Lieutenant Benjamin Worthington Chart 11 (from Chart 10)

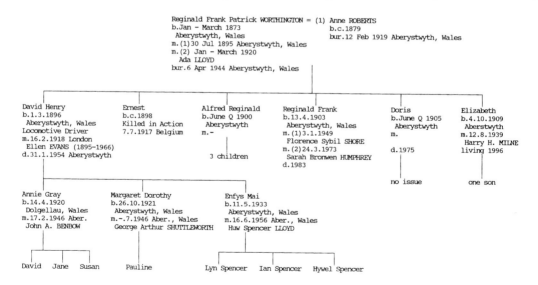

```
Reginald Frank Patrick WORTHINGTON  =  (1) Anne ROBERTS
b.Jan - March 1873                         b.c.1879
Aberystwyth, Wales                         bur.12 Feb 1919 Aberystwyth, Wales
m.(1)30 Jul 1895 Aberystwyth, Wales
m.(2) Jan - March 1920
Ada LLOYD
bur.6 Apr 1944 Aberystwyth, Wales
```

David Henry	Ernest	Alfred Reginald	Reginald Frank	Doris	Elizabeth
b.1.3.1896	b.c.1898	b.June Q 1900	b.13.4.1903	b.June Q 1905	b.4.10.1909
Aberystwyth, Wales	Killed in Action	Aberystwyth	Aberystwyth, Wales	Aberystwyth	Aberstwyth
Locomotive Driver	7.7.1917 Belgium	m.-	m.(1)3.1.1949	m.	m.12.8.1939
m.16.2.1918 London			Florence Sybil SHORE		Harry H. MILNE
Ellen EVANS (1895-1966)		3 children	m.(2)24.3.1973	d.1975	living 1996
d.31.1.1954 Aberystwyth			Sarah Bronwen HUMPHREY		
			d.1983	no issue	one son

Annie Gray	Margaret Dorothy	Enfys Mai
b.14.4.1920	b.26.10.1921	b.11.5.1933
Dolgellau, Wales	Aberystwyth, Wales	Aberystwyth, Wales
m.17.2.1946 Aber.	m.-.7.1946 Aber., Wales	m.16.6.1956 Aber., Wales
John A. BENBOW	George Arthur SHUTTLEWORTH	Huw Spencer LLOYD

David	Jane	Susan	Pauline	Lyn Spencer	Ian Spencer	Hywel Spencer

Descendants of William Collins Worthington Chart 12 (from Chart 4)

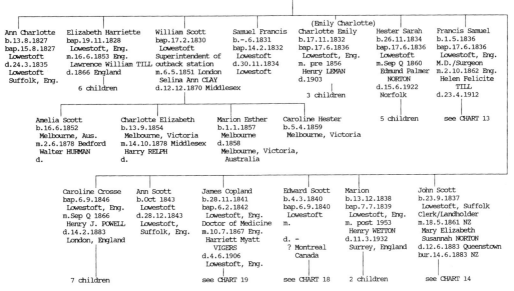

William Collins WORTHINGTON = Sarah SCOTT
b.27 Feb 1800 Dover, Kent   b.c.1802 Bungay, Suffolk, England
Doctor of Medicine/Surgeon   d.1855
m.1 Aug 1826 Bungay, Suffolk, England
d.31 Jan 1885 Lowestoft, Suffolk, England

Ann Charlotte
b.13.8.1827
bap.15.8.1827
Lowestoft
d.24.3.1835
Lowestoft
Suffolk, Eng.

Elizabeth Harriette
bap.19.11.1828
Lowestoft, Eng.
m.16.6.1853 Eng.
Lawrence William TILL
d.1866 England

6 children

William Scott
bap.17.2.1830
Lowestoft
Superintendent of
outback station
m.6.5.1851 London
Selina Ann CLAY
d.12.12.1870 Middlesex

Samuel Francis
b.-.6.1831
bap.14.2.1832
Lowestoft
d.30.11.1834
Lowestoft

(Emily Charlotte)
Charlotte Emily
b.17.11.1832
bap.17.6.1836
Lowestoft, Eng.
m. pre 1856
Henry LEMAN
d.1903

3 children

Hester Sarah
b.26.11.1834
bap.17.6.1836
Lowestoft
m.Sep Q 1860
Edmund Palmer
NORTON
d.15.6.1922
Norfolk

5 children

Francis Samuel
b.1.5.1836
bap.17.6.1836
Lowestoft, Eng.
m.2.10.1862 Eng.
Helen Felicite
TILL
d.23.4.1912

see CHART 13

Amelia Scott
b.16.6.1852
Melbourne, Aus.
m.2.6.1878 Bedford
Walter HURMAN
d.

Charlotte Elizabeth
b.13.9.1854
Melbourne, Victoria
m.14.10.1878 Middlesex
Harry RELPH
d.

Marion Esther
b.1.1.1857
Melbourne
d.1858
Melbourne, Victoria,
Australia

Caroline Hester
b.5.4.1859
Melbourne, Victoria

Caroline Crosse
bap.6.9.1846
Lowestoft, Eng.
m.Sep Q 1866
Henry J. POWELL
d.14.2.1883
London, England

7 children

Ann Scott
b.Oct 1843
Lowestoft
d.28.12.1843
Lowestoft,
Suffolk, Eng.

James Copland
b.28.11.1841
bap.6.2.1842
Lowestoft, Eng.
Doctor of Medicine
m.10.7.1867 Eng.
Harriett Myatt
VIGERS
d.4.6.1906
Lowestoft, Eng.

see CHART 19

Edward Scott
b.4.3.1840
bap.6.9.1840
Lowestoft
m.

d. -
? Montreal
Canada

see CHART 18

Marion
b.13.12.1838
bap.7.7.1839
Lowestoft, Eng.
m. post 1953
Henry WETTON
d.11.3.1932
Surrey, England

2 children

John Scott
b.23.9.1837
Lowestoft, Suffolk
Clerk/Landholder
m.18.5.1861 NZ
Mary Elizabeth
Susannah NORTON
d.12.6.1883 Queenstown
bur.14.6.1883 NZ

see CHART 14

Descendants of William Collins Worthington Chart 13 (from Chart 12)

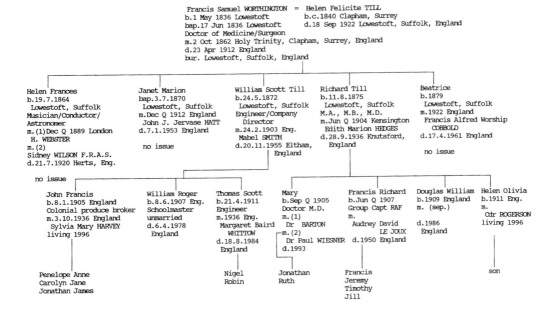

Francis Samuel WORTHINGTON = Helen Felicite TILL
b.1 May 1836 Lowestoft   b.c.1840 Clapham, Surrey
bap.17 Jun 1836 Lowestoft   d.18 Sep 1922 Lowestoft, Suffolk, England
Doctor of Medicine/Surgeon
m.2 Oct 1862 Holy Trinity, Clapham, Surrey, England
d.23 Apr 1912 England
bur. Lowestoft, Suffolk, England

Helen Frances
b.19.7.1864
Lowestoft, Suffolk
Musician/Conductor/
Astronomer
m.(1)Dec Q 1889 London
H. WEBSTER
m.(2)
Sidney WILSON F.R.A.S.
d.21.7.1920 Herts, Eng.

no issue

Janet Marion
bap.3.7.1870
Lowestoft, Suffolk
m.Dec Q 1912 England
John J. Jervase HATT
d.7.1.1953 England

no issue

William Scott Till
b.24.5.1872
Lowestoft, Suffolk
Engineer/Company
Director
m.24.2.1903 Eng.
Mabel SMITH
d.20.11.1955 Eltham,
England

Richard Till
b.11.8.1875
Lowestoft, Suffolk
M.A., M.B., M.D.
m.Jun Q 1904 Kensington
Edith Marion HEDGES
d.28.9.1936 Knutsford,
England

Beatrice
b.1879
Lowestoft, Suffolk
m.1922 England
Francis Alfred Worship
COBBOLD
d.17.4.1961 England

no issue

John Francis
b.8.1.1905 England
Colonial produce broker
m.3.10.1936 England
Sylvia Mary HARVEY
living 1996

William Roger
b.8.6.1907 Eng.
Schoolmaster
unmarried
d.6.4.1978
England

Thomas Scott
b.21.4.1911
Engineer
m.1936 Eng.
Margaret Baird
WHITTOW
d.18.8.1984
England

Mary
b.Sep Q 1905
Doctor M.D.
m.(1)
Dr BARTON
m.(2)
Dr Paul WIESNER
d.1993

Francis Richard
b.Jun Q 1907
Group Capt RAF
m.
Audrey David
LE JOUX
d.1950 England

Douglas William
b.1909 England
m. (sep.)

d.1986
England

Helen Olivia
b.1911 Eng.
m.
Cdr ROGERSON
living 1996

Penelope Anne
Carolyn Jane
Jonathan James

Nigel
Robin

Jonathan
Ruth

Francis
Jeremy
Timothy
Jill

son

Descendants of William Collins Worthington Chart 14 (from Chart 12)

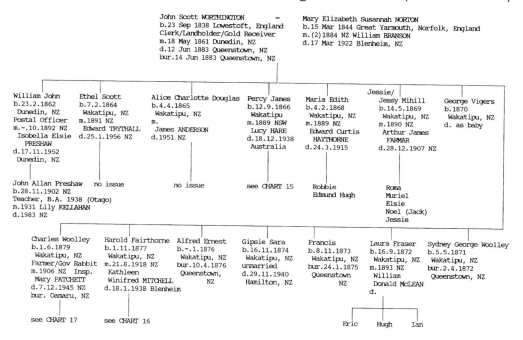

John Scott WORTHINGTON
b.23 Sep 1838 Lowestoft, England
Clerk/Landholder/Gold Receiver
m.18 May 1861 Dunedin, NZ
d.12 Jun 1883 Queenstown, NZ
bur.14 Jun 1883 Queenstown, NZ

=

Mary Elizabeth Susannah NORTON
b.15 Mar 1844 Great Yarmouth, Norfolk, England
m.(2)1884 NZ William BRANSON
d.17 Mar 1922 Blenheim, NZ

William John
b.23.2.1862
Dunedin, NZ
Postal Officer
m.-.10.1892 NZ
Isobella Elsie
PRESHAW
d.17.11.1952
Dunedin, NZ

Ethel Scott
b.7.2.1864
Wakatipu, NZ
m.1891 NZ
Edward TRYTHALL
d.25.1.1956 NZ

Alice Charlotte Douglas
b.4.4.1865
Wakatipu, NZ
m.
James ANDERSON
d.1951 NZ

Percy James
b.12.9.1866
Wakatipu
m.1889 NSW
Lucy HARE
d.18.12.1938
Australia

Maria Edith
b.4.2.1868
Wakatipu, NZ
m.1889 NZ
Edward Curtis
HAYTHORNE
d.24.3.1915

Jessie/
Jessy Mihill
b.14.5.1869
Wakatipu, NZ
m.1890 NZ
Arthur James
FARMAR
d.28.12.1907 NZ

George Vigers
b.1870
Wakatipu, NZ
d. as baby

John Allan Preshaw
b.28.11.1902 NZ
Teacher, B.A. 1938 (Otago)
m.1931 Lily KELLAHAN
d.1983 NZ

no issue

no issue

see CHART 15

Robbie
Edmund Hugh

Roma
Muriel
Elsie
Noel (Jack)
Jessie

Charles Woolley
b.1.6.1879
Wakatipu, NZ
Farmer/Gov Rabbit
m.1906 NZ Insp.
Mary PATCHETT
d.7.12.1945 NZ
bur. Oamaru, NZ

see CHART 17

Harold Fairthorne
b.1.11.1876
Wakatipu, NZ
m.21.8.1918 NZ
Kathleen
Winifred MITCHELL
d.18.1.1938 Blenheim

see CHART 16

Alfred Ernest
b.-.1.1876
Wakatipu, NZ
bur.10.4.1876
Queenstown,
NZ

Gipsie Sara
b.16.11.1874
Wakatipu, NZ
unmarried
d.29.11.1940
Hamilton, NZ

Francis
b.8.11.1873
Wakatipu, NZ
bur.24.1.1875
Queenstown
NZ

Laura Fraser
b.16.9.1872
Wakatipu, NZ
m.1893 NZ
William
Donald McLEAN
d.

Sydney George Woolley
b.5.5.1871
Wakatipu, NZ
bur.2.4.1872
Queenstown, NZ

Eric   Hugh   Ian

Descendants of William Collins Worthington Chart 15 (from Chart 14)

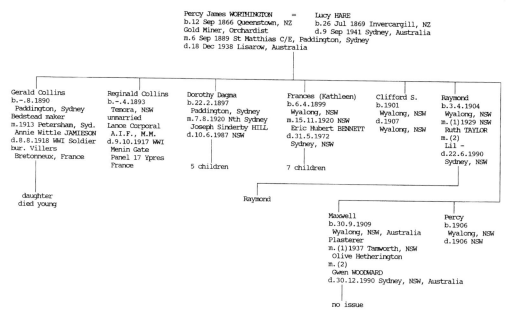

Percy James WORTHINGTON
b.12 Sep 1866 Queenstown, NZ
Gold Miner, Orchardist
m.6 Sep 1889 St Matthias C/E, Paddington, Sydney
d.18 Dec 1938 Lisarow, Australia

=

Lucy HARE
b.26 Jul 1869 Invercargill, NZ
d.9 Sep 1941 Sydney, Australia

Gerald Collins
b.-.8.1890
Paddington, Sydney
Bedstead maker
m.1913 Petersham, Syd.
Annie Wittle JAMIESON
d.8.8.1918 WWI Soldier
bur. Villers
Bretonneux, France

daughter
died young

Reginald Collins
b.-.4.1893
Temora, NSW
unmarried
Lance Corporal
A.I.F., M.M.
d.9.10.1917 WWI
Menin Gate
Panel 17 Ypres
France

Dorothy Dagma
b.22.2.1897
Paddington, Sydney
m.7.8.1920 Nth Sydney
Joseph Sinderby HILL
d.10.6.1987 NSW

5 children

Frances (Kathleen)
b.6.4.1899
Wyalong, NSW
m.15.11.1920 NSW
Eric Hubert BENNETT
d.31.5.1972
Sydney, NSW

7 children

Clifford S.
b.1901
Wyalong, NSW
d.1907
Wyalong, NSW

Raymond
b.3.4.1904
Wyalong, NSW
m.(1)1929 NSW
Ruth TAYLOR
m.(2)
Lil -
d.22.6.1990
Sydney, NSW

Raymond

Maxwell
b.30.9.1909
Wyalong, NSW, Australia
Plasterer
m.(1)1937 Tamworth, NSW
Olive Hetherington
m.(2)
Gwen WOODWARD
d.30.12.1990 Sydney, NSW, Australia

no issue

Percy
b.1906
Wyalong, NSW
d.1906 NSW

Descendants of William Collins Worthington Chart 16 (from Chart 14)

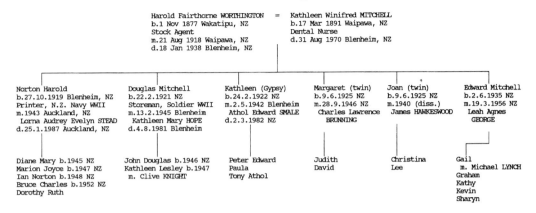

Harold Fairthorne WORTHINGTON   =   Kathleen Winifred MITCHELL
b.1 Nov 1877 Wakatipu, NZ   b.17 Mar 1891 Waipawa, NZ
Stock Agent   Dental Nurse
m.21 Aug 1918 Waipawa, NZ   d.31 Aug 1970 Blenheim, NZ
d.18 Jan 1938 Blenheim, NZ

Norton Harold
b.27.10.1919 Blenheim, NZ
Printer, N.Z. Navy WWII
m.1943 Auckland, NZ
 Lorna Audrey Evelyn STEAD
d.25.1.1987 Auckland, NZ

Diane Mary b.1945 NZ
Marion Joyce b.1947 NZ
Ian Norton b.1948 NZ
Bruce Charles b.1952 NZ
Dorothy Ruth

Douglas Mitchell
b.22.2.1921 NZ
Storeman, Soldier WWII
m.13.2.1945 Blenheim
 Kathleen Mary HOPE
d.4.8.1981 Blenheim

John Douglas b.1946 NZ
Kathleen Lesley b.1947
m. Clive KNIGHT

Kathleen (Gypsy)
b.24.2.1922 NZ
m.2.5.1942 Blenheim
 Athol Edward SMALE
d.2.3.1982 NZ

Peter Edward
Paula
Tony Athol

Margaret (twin)
b.9.6.1925 NZ
m.28.9.1946 NZ
 Charles Lawrence
 BRUNNING

Judith
David

Joan (twin)
b.9.6.1925 NZ
m.1940 (diss.)
 James HAWKESWOOD

Christina
Lee

Edward Mitchell
b.2.6.1935 NZ
m.19.3.1956 NZ
 Leah Agnes
 GEORGE

Gail
m. Michael LYNCH
Graham
Kathy
Kevin
Sharyn

Descendants of William Collins Worthington Chart 17 (from Chart 14)

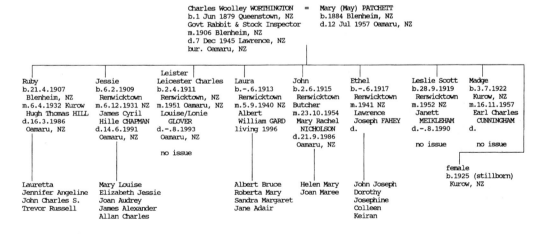

Charles Woolley WORTHINGTON   =   Mary (May) PATCHETT
b.1 Jun 1879 Queenstown, NZ   b.1884 Blenheim, NZ
Govt Rabbit & Stock Inspector   d.12 Jul 1957 Oamaru, NZ
m.1906 Blenheim, NZ
d.7 Dec 1945 Lawrence, NZ
bur. Oamaru, NZ

Ruby
b.21.4.1907
Blenheim, NZ
m.6.4.1932 Kurow
 Hugh Thomas HILL
d.16.3.1986
Oamaru, NZ

Lauretta
Jennifer Angeline
John Charles S.
Trevor Russell

Jessie
b.6.2.1909
Renwicktown
m.6.12.1931 NZ
 James Cyril
 Hille CHAPMAN
d.14.6.1991
Oamaru, NZ

Mary Louise
Elizabeth Jessie
Joan Audrey
James Alexander
Allan Charles

Leister
Leicester Charles
b.2.4.1911
Renwicktown, NZ
m.1951 Oamaru, NZ
 Louise/Lonie
 GLOVER
d.-.8.1993
Oamaru, NZ

no issue

Laura
b.-.6.1913
Renwicktown
m.5.9.1940 NZ
 Albert
 William GARD
living 1996

Albert Bruce
Roberta Mary
Sandra Margaret
Jane Adair

John
b.2.6.1915
Renwicktown
Butcher
m.23.10.1954
 Mary Rachel
 NICHOLSON
d.21.9.1986
Oamaru, NZ

Helen Mary
Joan Maree

Ethel
b.-.6.1917
Renwicktown
m.1941 NZ
 Lawrence
 Joseph FAHEY
d.

John Joseph
Dorothy
Josephine
Colleen
Keiran

Leslie Scott
b.28.9.1919
Renwicktown
m.1952 NZ
 Janett
 MEIKLEHAM
d.-.8.1990

no issue

Madge
b.3.7.1922
Kurow, NZ
m.16.11.1957
 Earl Charles
 CUNNINGHAM
d.

no issue

female
b.1925 (stillborn)
Kurow, NZ

Descendants of William Collins Worthington Chart 18 (from Chart 14)

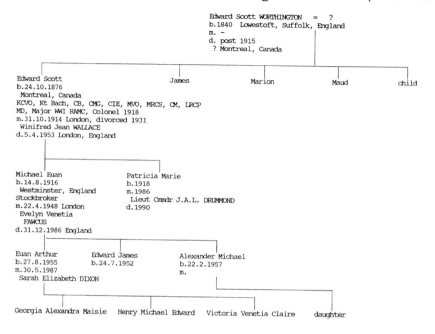

Edward Scott WORTHINGTON = ?
b.1840 Lowestoft, Suffolk, England
m. -
d. post 1915
? Montreal, Canada

Edward Scott
b.24.10.1876
Montreal, Canada
KCVO, Kt Bach, CB, CMG, CIE, MVO, MRCS, CM, LRCP
MD, Major WWI RAMC, Colonel 1918
m.31.10.1914 London, divorced 1931
Winifred Jean WALLACE
d.5.4.1953 London, England

James   Marion   Maud   child

Michael Euan
b.14.8.1916
Westminster, England
Stockbroker
m.22.4.1948 London
Evelyn Venetia
FAWCUS
d.31.12.1986 England

Patricia Marie
b.1918
m.1986
Lieut Cmmdr J.A.L. DRUMMOND
d.1990

Euan Arthur
b.27.8.1955
m.30.5.1987
Sarah Elizabeth DIXON

Edward James
b.24.7.1952

Alexander Michael
b.22.2.1957
m.

Georgia Alexandra Maisie   Henry Michael Edward   Victoria Venetia Claire   daughter

Descendants of William Collins Worthington Chart 19 (from Chart 14)

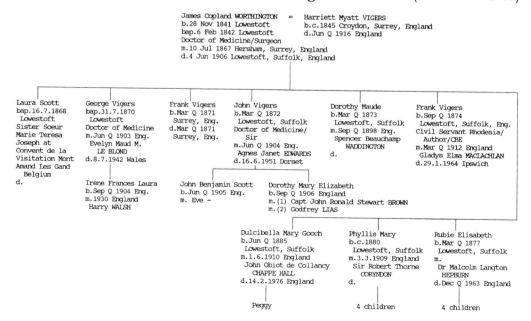

James Copland WORTHINGTON = Harriett Myatt VIGERS
b.28 Nov 1841 Lowestoft   b.c.1845 Croydon, Surrey, England
bap.6 Feb 1842 Lowestoft   d.Jun Q 1916 England
Doctor of Medicine/Surgeon
m.10 Jul 1867 Hersham, Surrey, England
d.4 Jun 1906 Lowestoft, Suffolk, England

Laura Scott
bap.16.7.1868
Lowestoft
Sister Soeur
Marie Teresa
Joseph at
Convent de la
Visitation Mont
Amand Les Gand
Belgium
d.

George Vigers
bap.31.7.1870
Lowestoft
Doctor of Medicine
m.Jun Q 1903 Eng.
Evelyn Maud M.
LE BLOND
d.8.7.1942 Wales

Frank Vigers
b.Mar Q 1871
Surrey, Eng.
d.Mar Q 1871
Surrey, Eng.

John Vigers
b.Mar Q 1872
Lowestoft, Suffolk
Doctor of Medicine/
Sir
m.Jun Q 1904 Eng.
Agnes Janet EDWARDS
d.16.6.1951 Dorset

Dorothy Maude
b.Mar Q 1873
Lowestoft, Suffolk
m.Sep Q 1898 Eng.
Spencer Beauchamp
WADDINGTON
d.

Frank Vigers
b.Sep Q 1874
Lowestoft, Suffolk, Eng.
Civil Servant Rhodesia/
Author/CBE
m.Mar Q 1912 England
Gladys Elma MACLACHLAN
d.29.1.1964 Ipswich

Irene Frances Laura
b.Sep Q 1904 Eng.
m.1930 England
Harry WALSH

John Benjamin Scott
b.Jun Q 1905 Eng.
m. Eve -

Dorothy Mary Elizabeth
b.Sep Q 1906 England
m.(1) Capt John Ronald Stewart BROWN
m.(2) Godfrey LIAS

Dulcibella Mary Gooch
b.Jun Q 1885
Lowestoft, Suffolk
m.1.6.1910 England
John Obiot de Collancy
CHAPPE HALL
d.14.2.1976 England

Phyllis Mary
b.c.1880
Lowestoft, Suffolk
m.3.3.1909 England
Sir Robert Thorne
CORYNDON
d.

Rubie Elisabeth
b.Mar Q 1877
Lowestoft, Suffolk
m.
Dr Malcolm Langton
HEPBURN
d.Dec Q 1963 England

Peggy

4 children

4 children

Descendants of Henry Worthington Chart 20 (from Chart 4)

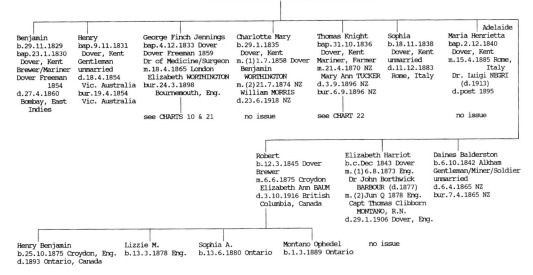

Henry WORTHINGTON = Mary JENNINGS
b.2 Oct 1803 Dover   bap.19 Feb 1806 Dover, Kent
Gentleman, Brewer   d.28 Aug 1865 Chandfontaine, nr Liege, Belgium
m.21 Sep 1827 Dover   bur.1 Sep 1865 St James Dover
d.4 Jan 1866 Worthing, Sussex
bur.10 Jan 1866 St James Church Vault, Dover

Benjamin
b.29.11.1829
bap.23.1.1830
Dover, Kent
Brewer/Mariner
Dover Freeman
1854
d.27.4.1860
Bombay, East
Indies

Henry
bap.9.11.1831
Dover, Kent
Gentleman
unmarried
d.18.4.1854
Vic. Australia
bur.19.4.1854
Vic. Australia

George Finch Jennings
bap.4.12.1833 Dover
Dover Freeman 1859
Dr of Medicine/Surgeon
m.18.4.1865 London
Elizabeth WORTHINGTON
bur.24.3.1898
Bournemouth, Eng.

see CHARTS 10 & 21

Charlotte Mary
b.29.1.1835
Dover, Kent
m.(1)1.7.1858 Dover
Benjamin
WORTHINGTON
m.(2)21.7.1874 NZ
William MORRIS
d.23.6.1918 NZ

no issue

Thomas Knight
bap.31.10.1836
Dover, Kent
Mariner, Farmer
m.21.4.1870 NZ
Mary Ann TUCKER
d.3.9.1896 NZ
bur.6.9.1896 NZ

see CHART 22

Sophia
b.18.11.1838
Dover, Kent
unmarried
d.11.12.1883
Rome, Italy

Maria Henrietta
bap.2.12.1840
Dover, Kent
m.15.4.1885 Rome,
Italy
Dr. Luigi NEGRI
(d.1913)
d.post 1895

Adelaide

no issue

Robert
b.12.3.1845 Dover
Brewer
m.6.6.1875 Croydon
Elizabeth Ann BAUM
d.3.10.1916 British
Columbia, Canada

Elizabeth Harriot
b.c.Dec 1843 Dover
m.(1)6.8.1873 Eng.
Dr John Borthwick
BARBOUR (d.1877)
m.(2)Jun Q 1878 Eng.
Capt Thomas Clibborn
MONTANO, R.N.
d.29.1.1906 Dover, Eng.

Daines Balderston
b.6.10.1842 Alkham
Gentleman/Miner/Soldier
unmarried
d.6.4.1865 NZ
bur.7.4.1865 NZ

Henry Benjamin
b.25.10.1875 Croydon, Eng.
d.1893 Ontario, Canada

Lizzie M.
b.13.3.1878 Eng.

Sophia A.
b.13.6.1880 Ontario

Montano Ophedel
b.1.3.1889 Ontario

no issue

Descendants of Henry Worthington Chart 21 (from Chart 20)

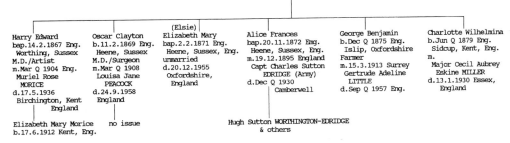

George Finch Jennings WORTHINGTON = Elizabeth WORTHINGTON
bap.4 Dec 1833 Dover, England   bap.31 Mar 1841 Dover, England
Doctor of Medicine/Surgeon   d.6 Jan 1908 Twyford, Berkshire, England
m.18 Apr 1865 London, England   bur.11 Jan 1908 Buckland, Dover, England
d.20 Mar 1898 Bournemouth, England
bur.24 Mar 1898 Buckland, Dover

Harry Edward
bap.14.2.1867 Eng.
Worthing, Sussex
M.D./Artist
m.Mar Q 1904 Eng.
Muriel Rose
MORICE
d.17.5.1936
Birchington, Kent
England

Oscar Clayton
b.11.2.1869 Eng.
Heene, Sussex
M.D./Surgeon
m.Mar Q 1908
Louisa Jane
PEACOCK
d.24.9.1958
England

(Elsie)
Elizabeth Mary
bap.2.2.1871 Eng.
Heene, Sussex, Eng.
unmarried
d.20.12.1955
Oxfordshire,
England

Alice Frances
bap.20.11.1872 Eng.
Heene, Sussex, Eng.
m.19.12.1895 England
Capt Charles Sutton
EDRIDGE (Army)
d.Dec Q 1930
Camberwell

George Benjamin
b.Dec Q 1875 Eng.
Islip, Oxfordshire
Farmer
m.15.3.1913 Surrey
Gertrude Adeline
LITTLE
d.Sep Q 1957 Eng.

Charlotte Wilhelmina
b.Jun Q 1879 Eng.
Sidcup, Kent, Eng.
m.
Major Cecil Aubrey
Eskine MILLER
d.13.1.1930 Essex,
England

Elizabeth Mary Morice
b.17.6.1912 Kent, Eng.

no issue

Hugh Sutton WORTHINGTON-EDRIDGE
& others

Descendants of Henry Worthington Chart 22 (from Chart 20)

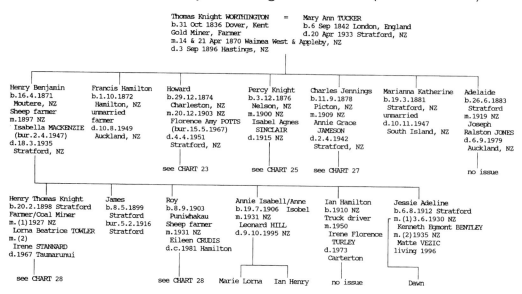

Thomas Knight WORTHINGTON = Mary Ann TUCKER
b.31 Oct 1836 Dover, Kent   b.6 Sep 1842 London, England
Gold Miner, Farmer   d.20 Apr 1933 Stratford, NZ
m.14 & 21 Apr 1870 Waimea West & Appleby, NZ
d.3 Sep 1896 Hastings, NZ

Henry Benjamin	Francis Hamilton	Howard	Percy Knight	Charles Jennings	Marianna Katherine	Adelaide
b.16.4.1871	b.1.10.1872	b.29.12.1874	b.3.12.1876	b.11.9.1878	b.19.3.1881	b.26.6.1883
Moutere, NZ	Hamilton, NZ	Charleston, NZ	Nelson, NZ	Picton, NZ	Stratford, NZ	Stratford
Sheep farmer	unmarried	m.20.12.1903 NZ	m.1900 NZ	m.1909 NZ	unmarried	m.1919 NZ
m.1897 NZ	farmer	Florence Amy POTTS	Isabel Agnes	Annie Grace	d.10.11.1947	Joseph
Isabella MACKENZIE	d.10.8.1949	(bur.15.5.1967)	SINCLAIR	JAMESON	South Island, NZ	Ralston JONES
(bur.2.4.1947)	Auckland, NZ	d.4.4.1951	d.1915 NZ	d.2.4.1942		d.6.9.1979
d.18.3.1935		Stratford, NZ		Stratford, NZ		Auckland, NZ
Stratford, NZ						
		see CHART 23	see CHART 25	see CHART 27		no issue

Henry Thomas Knight	James	Roy	Annie Isabell/Anne	Ian Hamilton	Jessie Adeline
b.20.2.1898 Stratford	b.8.5.1899	b.8.9.1903	b.19.7.1906 Isobel	b.1910 NZ	b.6.8.1912 Stratford
Farmer/Coal Miner	Stratford	Puniwhakau	m.1931 NZ	Truck driver	m.(1)3.6.1930 NZ
m.(1)1927 NZ	bur.5.2.1916	Sheep farmer	Leonard HILL	m.1950	Kenneth Egmont BENTLEY
Lorna Beatrice TOWLER	Stratford	m.1931 NZ	d.9.10.1995 NZ	Irene Florence	m.(2)1935 NZ
m.(2)		Eileen CRUDIS		TURLEY	Matte VEZIC
Irene STANNARD		d.c.1981 Hamilton		d.1973	living 1996
d.1967 Taumarunui				Carterton	

see CHART 28   see CHART 28   Marie Lorna   Ian Henry   no issue   Dawn

Descendants of Henry Worthington Chart 23 (from Chart 22)

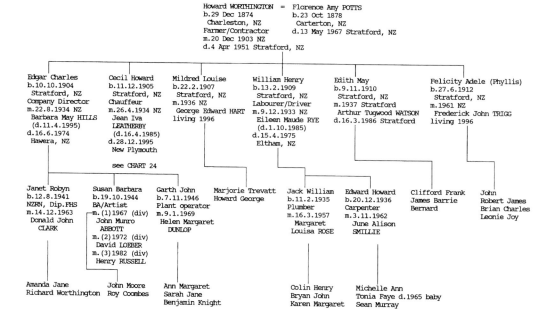

Howard WORTHINGTON = Florence Amy POTTS
b.29 Dec 1874   b.23 Oct 1878
  Charleston, NZ   Carterton, NZ
Farmer/Contractor   d.13 May 1967 Stratford, NZ
m.20 Dec 1903 NZ
d.4 Apr 1951 Stratford, NZ

Edgar Charles	Cecil Howard	Mildred Louise	William Henry	Edith May	Felicity Adele (Phyllis)
b.10.10.1904	b.11.12.1905	b.22.2.1907	b.13.2.1909	b.9.11.1910	b.27.6.1912
Stratford, NZ	Stratford, NZ	Stratford, NZ	Stratford, NZ	Stratford, NZ	Stratford, NZ
Company Director	Chauffeur	m.1936 NZ	Labourer/Driver	m.1937 Stratford	m.1961 NZ
m.22.8.1934 NZ	m.26.4.1934 NZ	George Edward HART	m.9.12.1933 NZ	Arthur Tugwood WATSON	Frederick John TRIGG
Barbara May HILLS	Jean Iva	living 1996	Eileen Maude RYE	d.16.3.1986 Stratford	living 1996
(d.11.4.1995)	LEATHERBY		(d.1.10.1985)		
d.16.6.1974	(d.16.4.1985)		d.15.4.1975		
Hawera, NZ	d.28.12.1995		Eltham, NZ		
	New Plymouth				
	see CHART 24				

Janet Robyn	Susan Barbara	Garth John	Marjorie Trevatt	Jack William	Edward Howard	Clifford Frank	John
b.12.8.1941	b.19.10.1944	b.7.11.1946	Howard George	b.11.2.1935	b.20.12.1936	James Barrie	Robert James
NZRN, Dip.FHS	BA/Artist	Plant operator		Plumber	Carpenter	Bernard	Brian Charles
m.14.12.1963	m.(1)1967 (div)	m.9.1.1969		m.16.3.1957	m.3.11.1962		Leonie Joy
Donald John	John Munro	Helen Margaret		Margaret	June Alison		
CLARK	ABBOTT	DUNLOP		Louisa ROSE	SMILLIE		
	m.(2)1972 (div)						
	David LOEBER						
	m.(3)1982 (div)						
	Henry RUSSELL						

Amanda Jane   John Moore   Ann Margaret   Colin Henry   Michelle Ann
Richard Worthington Roy Coombes   Sarah Jane   Bryan John   Tonia Faye d.1965 baby
                                     Benjamin Knight   Karen Margaret Sean Murray

Descendants of Henry Worthington Chart 24 (from Chart 23)

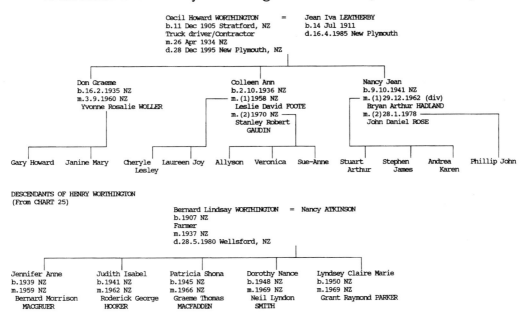

Cecil Howard WORTHINGTON = Jean Iva LEATHERBY
b.11 Dec 1905 Stratford, NZ   b.14 Jul 1911
Truck driver/Contractor   d.16.4.1985 New Plymouth
m.26 Apr 1934 NZ
d.28 Dec 1995 New Plymouth, NZ

Don Graeme
b.16.2.1935 NZ
m.3.9.1960 NZ
Yvonne Rosalie WOLLER

Colleen Ann
b.2.10.1936 NZ
m.(1)1958 NZ
Leslie David FOOTE
m.(2)1970 NZ
Stanley Robert
GAUDIN

Nancy Jean
b.9.10.1941 NZ
m.(1)29.12.1962 (div)
Bryan Arthur HADLAND
m.(2)28.1.1978
John Daniel ROSE

Gary Howard   Janine Mary   Cheryle Lesley   Laureen Joy   Allyson   Veronica   Sue-Anne   Stuart Arthur   Stephen James   Andrea Karen   Phillip John

DESCENDANTS OF HENRY WORTHINGTON
(From CHART 25)

Bernard Lindsay WORTHINGTON = Nancy ATKINSON
b.1907 NZ
Farmer
m.1937 NZ
d.28.5.1980 Wellsford, NZ

Jennifer Anne
b.1939 NZ
m.1959 NZ
Bernard Morrison
MACGRUER

Judith Isabel
b.1941 NZ
m.1962 NZ
Roderick George
HOOKER

Patricia Shona
b.1945 NZ
m.1966 NZ
Graeme Thomas
MACFADDEN

Dorothy Nance
b.1948 NZ
m.1969 NZ
Neil Lyndon
SMITH

Lyndsey Claire Marie
b.1950 NZ
m.1969 NZ
Grant Raymond PARKER

Descendants of Henry Worthington Chart 25 (from Chart 22)

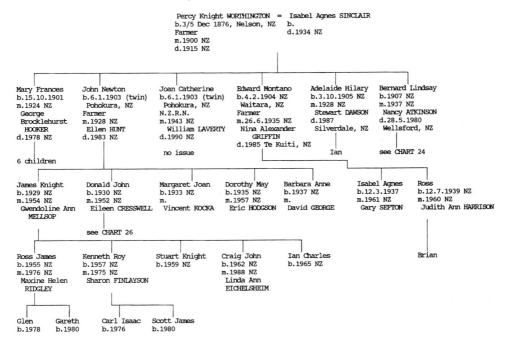

Percy Knight WORTHINGTON = Isabel Agnes SINCLAIR
b.3/5 Dec 1876, Nelson, NZ   b.
Farmer   d.1934 NZ
m.1900 NZ
d.1915 NZ

Mary Frances
b.15.10.1901
m.1924 NZ
George
Brocklehurst
HOOKER
d.1978 NZ

6 children

John Newton
b.6.1.1903 (twin)
Pohokura, NZ
Farmer
m.1928 NZ
Ellen HUNT
d.1983 NZ

Joan Catherine
b.6.1.1903 (twin)
Pohokura, NZ
N.Z.R.N.
m.1943 NZ
William LAVERTY
d.1990 NZ

no issue

Edward Montano
b.4.2.1904 NZ
Waitara, NZ
Farmer
m.26.6.1935 NZ
Nina Alexander
GRIFFIN
d.1985 Te Kuiti, NZ

Adelaide Hilary
b.3.10.1905 NZ
m.1928 NZ
Stewart DAWSON
d.1987
Silverdale, NZ

Ian

Bernard Lindsay
b.1907 NZ
m.1937 NZ
Nancy ATKINSON
d.28.5.1980
Wellsford, NZ

see CHART 24

James Knight
b.1929 NZ
m.1954 NZ
Gwendoline Ann
MELLSOP

Donald John
b.1930 NZ
m.1952 NZ
Eileen CRESSWELL

see CHART 26

Margaret Joan
b.1933 NZ
m.
Vincent KOCKA

Dorothy May
b.1935 NZ
m.1957 NZ
Eric HODGSON

Barbara Anne
b.1937 NZ
m.
David GEORGE

Isabel Agnes
b.12.3.1937
m.1961 NZ
Gary SEFTON

Ross
b.12.7.1939 NZ
m.1960 NZ
Judith Ann HARRISON

Ross James
b.1955 NZ
m.1976 NZ
Maxine Helen
RIDGLEY

Kenneth Roy
b.1957 NZ
m.1975 NZ
Sharon FINLAYSON

Stuart Knight
b.1959 NZ

Craig John
b.1962 NZ
m.1988 NZ
Linda Ann
EICHELSHEIM

Ian Charles
b.1965 NZ

Brian

Glen
b.1978

Gareth
b.1980

Carl Isaac
b.1976

Scott James
b.1980

Descendants of Henry Worthington Chart 26 (from Chart 25)

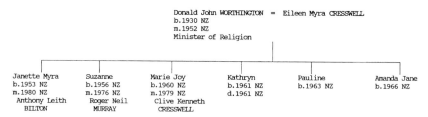

Donald John WORTHINGTON = Eileen Myra CRESSWELL
b.1930 NZ
m.1952 NZ
Minister of Religion

Janette Myra	Suzanne	Marie Joy	Kathryn	Pauline	Amanda Jane
b.1953 NZ	b.1956 NZ	b.1960 NZ	b.1961 NZ	b.1963 NZ	b.1966 NZ
m.1980 NZ	m.1976 NZ	m.1979 NZ	d.1961 NZ		
Anthony Leith	Roger Neil	Clive Kenneth			
BILTON	MURRAY	CRESSWELL			

Descendants of Henry Worthington Chart 27 (from Chart 22)

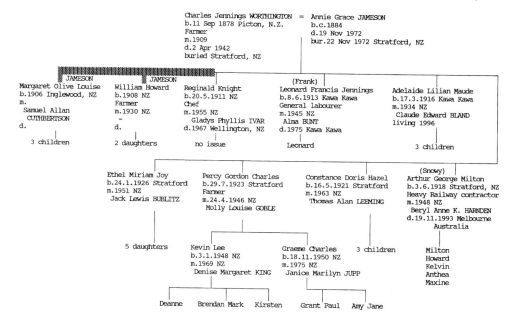

Charles Jennings WORTHINGTON = Annie Grace JAMESON
b.11 Sep 1878 Picton, N.Z.   b.c.1884
Farmer   d.19 Nov 1972
m.1909   bur.22 Nov 1972 Stratford, NZ
d.2 Apr 1942
buried Stratford, NZ

JAMESON   JAMESON

Margaret Olive Louise   William Howard   Reginald Knight   (Frank)   Adelaide Lilian Maude
b.1906 Inglewood, NZ   b.1908 NZ   b.20.5.1911 NZ   Leonard Francis Jennings   b.17.3.1916 Kawa Kawa
m.   Farmer   Chef   b.8.6.1913 Kawa Kawa   m.1934 NZ
  Samuel Allan   m.1930 NZ   m.1955 NZ   General labourer   Claude Edward BLAND
  CUTHBERTSON   -   Gladys Phyllis IVAR   m.1945 NZ   living 1996
d.   d.   d.1967 Wellington, NZ Alma BUNT
                                                              d.1975 Kawa Kawa
  3 children   2 daughters   no issue   Leonard   3 children

Ethel Miriam Joy   Percy Gordon Charles   Constance Doris Hazel   (Snowy)
b.24.1.1926 Stratford   b.29.7.1923 Stratford   b.16.5.1921 Stratford   Arthur George Milton
m.1951 NZ   Farmer   m.1963 NZ   b.3.6.1918 Stratford, NZ
  Jack Lewis BUBLITZ   m.24.4.1946 NZ   Thomas Alan LEEMING   Heavy Railway contractor
                           Molly Louise GOBLE   m.1948 NZ
                                                                            Beryl Anne K. HARNDEN
                                                                          d.19.11.1993 Melbourne
                                                                                Australia

  5 daughters   Kevin Lee   Graeme Charles   3 children   Milton
                         b.3.1.1948 NZ   b.18.11.1950 NZ   Howard
                         m.1969 NZ   m.1975 NZ   Kelvin
                           Denise Margaret KING   Janice Marilyn JUPP   Anthea
                                                                                 Maxine

         Deanne   Brendan Mark   Kirsten   Grant Paul   Amy Jane

XXX

Descendants of Henry Worthington Chart 28 (from Chart 22)

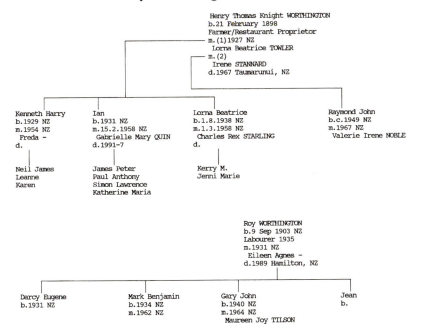

Henry Thomas Knight WORTHINGTON
b.21 February 1898
Farmer/Restaurant Proprietor
m.(1)1927 NZ
Lorna Beatrice TOWLER
m.(2)
Irene STANNARD
d.1967 Taumarunui, NZ

Kenneth Harry
b.1929 NZ
m.1954 NZ
Freda -
d.

Ian
b.1931 NZ
m.15.2.1958 NZ
Gabrielle Mary QUIN
d.1991-7

Lorna Beatrice
b.1.8.1938 NZ
m.1.3.1958 NZ
Charles Rex STARLING
d.

Raymond John
b.c.1949 NZ
m.1967 NZ
Valerie Irene NOBLE

Neil James
Leanne
Karen

James Peter
Paul Anthony
Simon Lawrence
Katherine Maria

Kerry M.
Jenni Marie

Roy WORTHINGTON
b.9 Sep 1903 NZ
Labourer 1935
m.1931 NZ
Eileen Agnes -
d.1989 Hamilton, NZ

Darcy Eugene
b.1931 NZ

Mark Benjamin
b.1934 NZ
m.1962 NZ

Gary John
b.1940 NZ
m.1964 NZ
Maureen Joy TILSON

Jean
b.

Worthington Descendants Chart 29 (from Chart 6)
Information supplied by Ann Facey, New Zealand

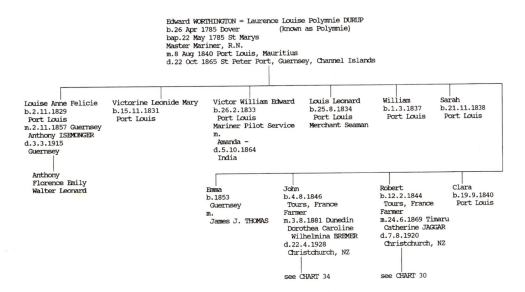

Edward WORTHINGTON = Laurence Louise Polymnie DURUP
b.26 Apr 1785 Dover   (known as Polymnie)
bap.22 May 1785 St Marys
Master Mariner, R.N.
m.8 Aug 1840 Port Louis, Mauritius
d.22 Oct 1865 St Peter Port, Guernsey, Channel Islands

Louise Anne Felicie
b.2.11.1829
Port Louis
m.2.11.1857 Guernsey
Anthony ISEMONGER
d.3.3.1915
Guernsey

Victorine Leonide Mary
b.15.11.1831
Port Louis

Victor William Edward
b.26.2.1833
Port Louis
Mariner Pilot Service
m.
Amanda -
d.5.10.1864
India

Louis Leonard
b.25.8.1834
Port Louis
Merchant Seaman

William
b.1.3.1837
Port Louis

Sarah
b.21.11.1838
Port Louis

Anthony
Florence Emily
Walter Leonard

Emma
b.1853
Guernsey
m.
James J. THOMAS

John
b.4.8.1846
Tours, France
Farmer
m.3.8.1881 Dunedin
Dorothea Caroline
Wilhelmina BREMER
d.22.4.1928
Christchurch, NZ

Robert
b.12.2.1844
Tours, France
Farmer
m.24.6.1869 Timaru
Catherine JAGGAR
d.7.8.1920
Christchurch, NZ

Clara
b.19.9.1840
Port Louis

see CHART 34

see CHART 30

Worthington Descendants Chart 30 (from Chart 29)
Information supplied by Lynda Cumming, New Zealand

PP = Pleasant Point, NZ

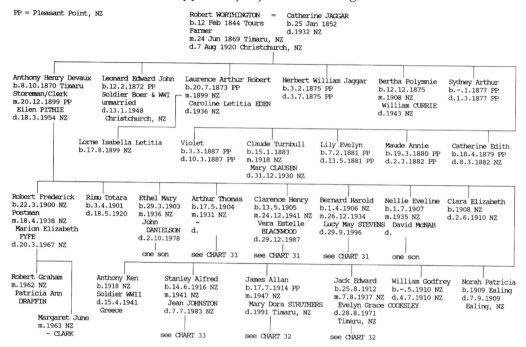

Robert WORTHINGTON = Catherine JAGGAR
b.12 Feb 1844 Tours   b.25 Jan 1852
Farmer   d.1932 NZ
m.24 Jun 1869 Timaru, NZ
d.7 Aug 1920 Christchurch, NZ

Anthony Henry Devaux
b.8.10.1870 Timaru
Storeman/Clerk
m.20.12.1899 PP
Ellen PITHIE
d.18.3.1954 NZ

Leonard Edward John
b.12.2.1872 PP
Soldier Boer & WWI
unmarried
d.13.1.1948
Christchurch, NZ

Laurence Arthur Robert
b.20.7.1873 PP
m.1899 NZ
Caroline Letitia EDEN
d.1936 NZ

Herbert William Jaggar
b.3.2.1875 PP
d.3.7.1875 PP

Bertha Polymnie
b.12.12.1875
m.1908 NZ
William CURRIE
d.1943 NZ

Sydney Arthur
b.-.1.1877 PP
d.1.3.1877 PP

Lorne Isabella Letitia
b.17.8.1899 NZ

Violet
b.3.3.1887 PP
d.10.3.1887 PP

Claude Turnbull
b.15.1.1883
m.1918 NZ
Mary CLAUSEN
d.31.12.1930 NZ

Lily Evelyn
b.7.2.1881 PP
d.13.5.1881 PP

Maude Annie
b.19.3.1880 PP
d.2.3.1882 PP

Catherine Edith
b.18.4.1879 PP
d.8.3.1882 NZ

Robert Frederick
b.22.3.1900 NZ
Postman
m.18.4.1938 NZ
Marion Elizabeth
FYFE
d.20.3.1967 NZ

Rimu Totara
b.3.4.1901
d.18.5.1920

Ethel Mary
b.29.3.1903
m.1936 NZ
John
DANIELSON
d.2.10.1978
|
one son

Arthur Thomas
b.17.5.1904
m.1931 NZ
-
d.
|
see CHART 31

Clarence Henry
b.13.5.1905
m.24.12.1941 NZ
Vera Estelle
BLACKWOOD
d.29.12.1987
|
see CHART 31

Bernard Harold
b.1.4.1906 NZ
m.26.12.1934
Lucy May STEVENS
d.29.9.1996
|
see CHART 31

Nellie Eveline
b.1.7.1907
m.1935 NZ
David McNAB
d.
|
one son

Clara Elizabeth
b.1908 NZ
d.2.6.1910 NZ

Robert Graham
m.1962 NZ
Patricia Ann
DRAFFIN

Margaret June
m.1963 NZ
- CLARK

Anthony Ken
b.1918 NZ
Soldier WWII
d.15.4.1941
Greece

Stanley Alfred
b.14.6.1916 NZ
m.1941 NZ
Jean JOHNSTON
d.7.7.1983 NZ
|
see CHART 33

James Allan
b.17.7.1914 PP
m.1947 NZ
Mary Dora STRUTHERS
d.1991 Timaru, NZ
|
see CHART 32

Jack Edward
b.25.8.1912
m.7.8.1937 NZ
Evelyn Grace
d.28.8.1971
Timaru, NZ
|
see CHART 32

William Godfrey
b.-.5.1910 NZ
d.4.7.1910 NZ
COOKSLEY

Norah Patricia
b.1909 Ealing
d.7.9.1909
Ealing, NZ

Worthington Descendants Chart 31 (from Chart 30)

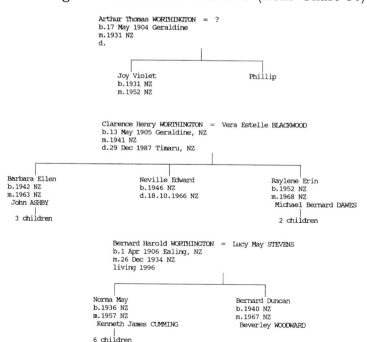

Arthur Thomas WORTHINGTON = ?
b.17 May 1904 Geraldine
m.1931 NZ
d.

Joy Violet
b.1931 NZ
m.1952 NZ

Phillip

Clarence Henry WORTHINGTON = Vera Estelle BLACKWOOD
b.13 May 1905 Geraldine, NZ
m.1941 NZ
d.29 Dec 1987 Timaru, NZ

Barbara Ellen
b.1942 NZ
m.1963 NZ
John ASHBY
|
3 children

Neville Edward
b.1946 NZ
d.18.10.1966 NZ

Raylene Erin
b.1952 NZ
m.1968 NZ
Michael Bernard DAWES
|
2 children

Bernard Harold WORTHINGTON = Lucy May STEVENS
b.1 Apr 1906 Ealing, NZ
m.26 Dec 1934 NZ
living 1996

Norma May
b.1936 NZ
m.1957 NZ
Kenneth James CUMMING
|
6 children

Bernard Duncan
b.1940 NZ
m.1967 NZ
Beverley WOODWARD

Worthington Descendants Chart 32 (from Chart 30)

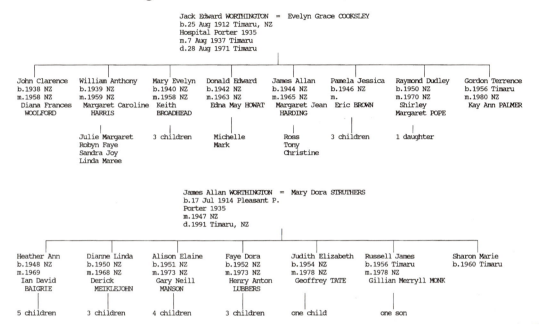

Jack Edward WORTHINGTON = Evelyn Grace COOKSLEY
b.25 Aug 1912 Timaru, NZ
Hospital Porter 1935
m.7 Aug 1937 Timaru
d.28 Aug 1971 Timaru

John Clarence	William Anthony	Mary Evelyn	Donald Edward	James Allan	Pamela Jessica	Raymond Dudley	Gordon Terrence
b.1938 NZ	b.1939 NZ	b.1940 NZ	b.1942 NZ	b.1944 NZ	b.1946 NZ	b.1950 NZ	b.1956 Timaru
m.1958 NZ	m.1959 NZ	m.1958 NZ	m.1963 NZ	m.1965 NZ	m.	m.1970 NZ	m.1980 NZ
Diana Frances	Margaret Caroline	Keith	Edna May HOWAT	Margaret Jean	Eric BROWN	Shirley	Kay Ann PALMER
WOOLFORD	HARRIS	BROADHEAD		HARDING		Margaret POPE	

	Julie Margaret	3 children	Michelle	Ross	3 children	1 daughter	
	Robyn Faye		Mark	Tony			
	Sandra Joy			Christine			
	Linda Maree						

James Allan WORTHINGTON = Mary Dora STRUTHERS
b.17 Jul 1914 Pleasant P.
Porter 1935
m.1947 NZ
d.1991 Timaru, NZ

Heather Ann	Dianne Linda	Alison Elaine	Faye Dora	Judith Elizabeth	Russell James	Sharon Marie
b.1948 NZ	b.1950 NZ	b.1951 NZ	b.1952 NZ	b.1954 NZ	b.1956 Timaru	b.1960 Timaru
m.1969	m.1968 NZ	m.1973 NZ	m.1973 NZ	m.1978 NZ	m.1978 NZ	
Ian David	Derick	Gary Neill	Henry Anton	Geoffrey TATE	Gillian Merryll MONK	
BAIGRIE	MEIKLEJOHN	MANSON	LUBBERS			

| 5 children | 3 children | 4 children | 3 children | one child | one son | |

Worthington Descendants Chart 33 (from Chart 30)

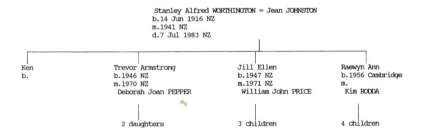

Stanley Alfred WORTHINGTON = Jean JOHNSTON
b.14 Jun 1916 NZ
m.1941 NZ
d.7 Jul 1983 NZ

Ken	Trevor Armstrong	Jill Ellen	Raewyn Ann
b.	b.1946 NZ	b.1947 NZ	b.1956 Cambridge
	m.1970 NZ	m.1971 NZ	m.
	Deborah Joan PEPPER	William John PRICE	Kim RODDA

| | 2 daughters | 3 children | 4 children |

Worthington Descendants Chart 34 (from Chart 29)

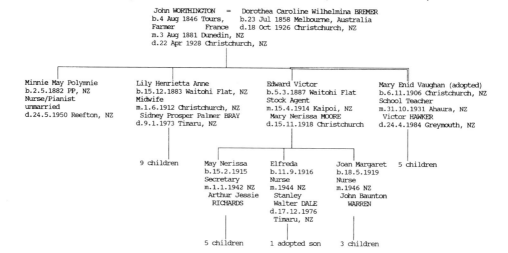

John WORTHINGTON   =   Dorothea Caroline Wilhelmina BREMER
b.4 Aug 1846 Tours,   b.23 Jul 1858 Melbourne, Australia
Farmer   France   d.18 Oct 1926 Christchurch, NZ
m.3 Aug 1881 Dunedin, NZ
d.22 Apr 1928 Christchurch, NZ

Minnie May Polymnie	Lily Henrietta Anne	Edward Victor	Mary Enid Vaughan (adopted)
b.2.5.1882 PP, NZ	b.15.12.1883 Waitohi Flat, NZ	b.5.3.1887 Waitohi Flat	b.6.11.1906 Christchurch, NZ
Nurse/Pianist	Midwife	Stock Agent	School Teacher
unmarried	m.1.6.1912 Christchurch, NZ	m.15.4.1914 Kaipoi, NZ	m.31.10.1931 Ahaura, NZ
d.24.5.1950 Reefton, NZ	Sidney Prosper Palmer BRAY	Mary Nerissa MOORE	Victor HAWKER
	d.9.1.1973 Timaru, NZ	d.15.11.1918 Christchurch	d.24.4.1984 Greymouth, NZ

9 children

5 children

May Nerissa	Elfreda	Joan Margaret
b.15.2.1915	b.11.9.1916	b.18.5.1919
Secretary	Nurse	Nurse
m.1.1.1942 NZ	m.1944 NZ	m.1946 NZ
Arthur Jessie	Stanley	John Baunton
RICHARDS	Walter DALE	WARREN
	d.17.12.1976	
	Timaru, NZ	

5 children   1 adopted son   3 children

Chapter One

Early Worthingtons of Dover–Ancestors of Benjamin Jelly Worthington

Ancestral Worthington family members are known to have been residing in Dover as early as 1594. All, no doubt, emanate from the same stock and can trace their origins back to the Lancashire Worthingtons of Worthington who resided at Worthington Hall, in the parish of Standish, near Wigan. The family was wealthy, very loyal and Catholic, but lost their estates and money during the English Civil War (1642-51) supporting the cause of Charles I and II. Many were forced to flee the country.[1] The origin of the surname Worthington as given in the *Heraldic Journal, 1868*, is Wearth-in-ton, from three Old English words meaning Farm-in-town, a locality surname referring to the place/farm of the family/folk.

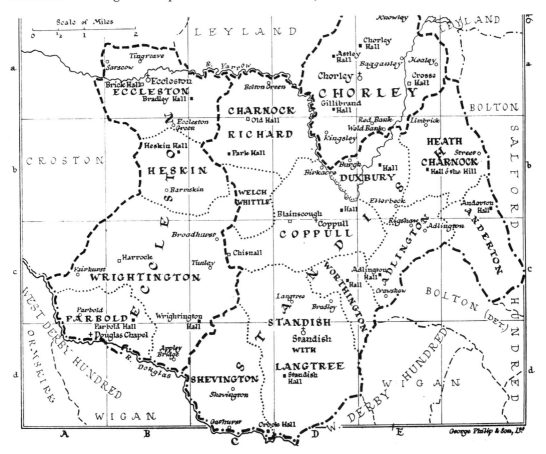

1 Map showing Worthington Hall, Lancashire.

Coat of Arms

All the branches that spring from the Lancashire Worthington de Worthington tend to make use of the same crest, viz: a goat, though with some heraldic variations, described as a goat passant, argent (silver/white) attired, or (gold), in mouth an oak branch, vert (green) fructed (fruited) gold. The Coat of Arms 'Argent three dung-forks sable' (not tridents). The Essex branch bore the same arms with the tincture reversed, i.e. Sable three dung-forks argent. The motto, 'virtute dignus avorum', meaning 'worthy by the virtue of their ancestors' can vary. Descendants of the Worthingtons of Dover have been found to have the motto 'mihi pertinent aequoris undae', meaning 'to me belong the waves of the water (or sea)'. One Dover branch of the family displays the red hand of Ulster with the three dung forks, the same as the arms entered for Sir William Worthington of Springfield, Essex in 1614. There were no male descendants of this Essex Worthington line. The Dover branch of the Worthington family claim the Worthington Coat of Arms as illustrated; however, the College of Arms in London has not verified this claim.

Canterbury Worthingtons

Worthingtons appear in Canterbury records as early as 1396 when Robert Worthington became a Freeman by marriage to Mildred Wormeselle, daughter of John Wormeselle. During an Archidiaconal Visitation of Kent in 1502 Sir Roger Worthington, vicar of Demecherche, now known as Dymchurch, on the coast in the Romney Marsh area, was found to be living there. He is probably the Roger Worthington of Canterbury who made a will on 28 October 1513.[2] He left bequests to Canterbury's parishes and asked to be buried at St Augustine's. Five godsons, namely Roger Sann, Roger Otway, William Pyx, Dyryk Baker and Roger Charnokke, are mentioned as well as a brother, Thomas Worthington. Executors were James Cursam and Richard Squire, parson of All Hallows, Canterbury.

Later records reveal that Avis Wordingtone was baptised on 15 April 1564 at St Alphage, Canterbury, but no parents' names were given.[3] Fortune and Mathew Worthington, both children of Thomas Worthington, were baptised at St Alphage, the former on 16 September 1621 and the latter on 26 October 1633.

The county of Kent has a unique geographical position, being the nearest county to the Continent and one of the closest counties to London. Kentish society was characterised from the Saxon period until the 19th century by a rural middle class consisting in the Middle Ages of a free peasantry among whom villein tenure was almost unknown, and in later times of a numerous, partly-landowning yeomanry of moderate substance. From the Middle Ages it was accompanied by a large group of gentry of small wealth and mostly of native origin. They were fully conscious of their descent, not from medieval villeins, of whom there had been few or none in Kent, but from freemen. In 17th-century Kent the gentry numbered at least eight-hundred and included a few knights. The majority received probably under £500 a year from property scattered over three or four adjoining parishes. Except in the north-west, most gentlemen belonged to families which had been in Kent since the Middle Ages.[4]

Kentish society was led by two or three dozen families of nobility and 'county' gentry, with lands closely connected in one part of the county. In social origin as in territorial influence the titled families and the larger gentry were indistinguishable.

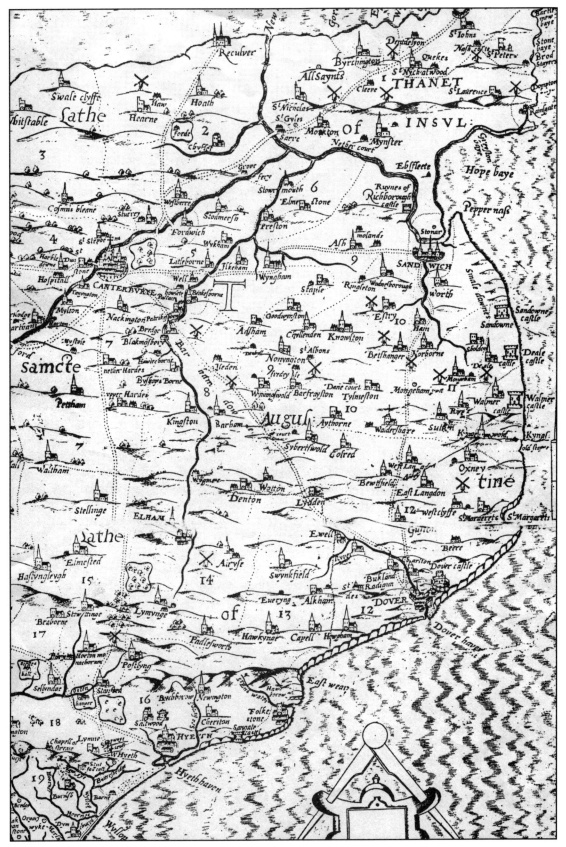

2 Part of Symonson's map of Kent, 1596.

Over half of the twelve or more district noblemen wholly or partly resident in 1700 came from genteel Kentish families which had been ennobled during the previous century.[5]

Dover Worthingtons

In the registers of St James's and St Mary's churches at Dover, the name is written as Wordington up to 1628. There are no further entries of baptisms, burials or marriages in these registers from 1628 until 1671, when the name is written as Worthington. Members of the family continued to reside in Dover until 1906.

Dover annals show the Worthingtons to have been of the upper middle classes, tall, valiant, active, virile, public-spirited, capable men of business and very useful to their town. They were described as true Men of Kent, being born and living on the eastern side of the river Medway. As years rolled on and generation succeeded generation they rose in distinction. Approximately forty-one were Freemen by birth, and some nine are recorded in the town Rolls as coopers possessing great blocks of property in Dover.

Dover Freemen

Dover has one of the oldest established privileges of Freedom dating from before the Norman Conquest with the Rolls dating from 1601. Kent had once been an independent kingdom and there was a great sense of community and general pride in the county. Because the gentry were a community in blood and feeling they were able to act as an independent political force.[6]

The Freemen Rolls recorded the date a Freeman was admitted, by virtue of being born the son of a Freeman. Other methods of admission were by purchase or Order of the Common Council, by marriage, by apprenticeship or servitude and by freehold. No one could be admitted a Freeman until he was 21 years of age. Most claimed admission on or soon after attaining that age as it was a valued distinction.

A Freeman of Dover was a powerful and influential man. Only Freemen had jurisdiction over municipal affairs including the rights to elect Mayors and Members of Parliament, levy taxes, administer justice, and to conduct business or trade within the town walls and port. Dover and Deal owed part of their prosperity to naval defence. The dockyard towns owed their importance to the fact they were near enough to reinforce the vessels in the Downs[7] or to take offensive action against the navy of a Continental power.

Dover District Council has recently revived the tradition of admission to the ancient Freemen Rolls, but only by birthright to proven descendants of Ancient Freemen.[8]

Roger Worthington (*c.*1560-1616)

Roger is the first Worthington ancestor of whom there is any record in Dover. He was born about 1560, and found listed under 'Freemen inhabiting and dwelling in Dover on 15 July 1601'. According to these Rolls he was a cooper.

Roger married widow Elizabeth ffynell/Fynell on 1 January 1581 at Bekesbourne, south-east of Canterbury in the county of Kent.[9] In 1608 he was found to be a

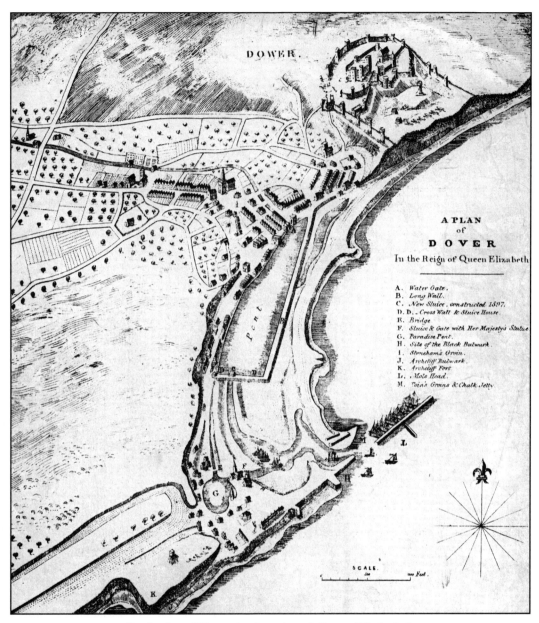

DOWER.

A PLAN
of
DOVER
In the Reign of Queen Elizabeth

A . Water Gate.
B . Long Wall.
C . New Sluice, constructed 1597.
D . D . Cross Wall & Sluice House.
E . Bridge
F . Sluice & Gate with Her Majesty's Statue.
G . Paradise Pent.
H . Site of the Black Bulwark.
I . Stoneham's Groin.
J . Archcliff Bulwark.
K . Archcliff Fort.
L . Mole Head.
M . Tom's Groins & Chalk Jetty.

SCALE.

3   A plan of Dover in the reign of Queen Elizabeth I.

constable of Halvenden and Balles Ward, one of the most ancient offices of the manor, and later of the parish vestry in the early 17th century. The position was an honorary one at this time and required him to report and take action on a great many matters including: felonies committed, escaped prisoners, riots and unlawful assemblies, non-attendance at church, commercial irregularities, licensing of ale houses, compiling Juror's Lists, drunkenness, unauthorised building of additional cottages and dovecotes, vagabonds, intruders, militia Muster Rolls, taking lewd women before the Justice of the Peace and detaining refractory fathers of bastards.[10]

Roger and Elizabeth had at least four children: Alice, who married John More during October 1623 at St Mary's, Dover; Edward, born 1594, whose story follows; John, born 1596, a mariner who married a Miss Somerville and had two children– Marie born 1624 and John born 1626; and Elizabeth born 1598. There was probably another brother named Bartholomew as Kent Protestation Returns for 1641/2[11] show Bartholomew, Edward and John of Dover listed.[12]

Roger died in 1616[13] and Elizabeth in 1600. Both were buried in the churchyard of Old St James's, Dover.

Old St James's Church, Dover

This church stood at the top of St James's Street. The ancient edifice was used as a chapel of ease to the new St James's, the latter being built in 1862 at a cost of £11,000. The old church was restored in 1869 and, until it was bombed during the First World War, was in a good state of preservation. It did not exist at the time of the Norman Conquest in 1066, but it was standing in 1291 during the reign of Edward I (1272-1307). It consisted of a nave and a chancel. In Edward II's reign (1307-27) a stone building with a lofty roof was added on the south side and used as the Courts of the Admiralty and Chancery of the Cinque Ports. In it was preserved the oak chair used by various Lord Wardens, including the Duke of Wellington.

A great deal of business was transacted in the Middle Ages in that old Court House, but little in later years, the last sitting being in 1877. In 1869 at the time of its restoration the church was in a terrible state with broken windows, damp walls and faulty roof. In the churchyard was a tomb of the Collins family, descendants of whom married into the Worthington family, and also of Worthingtons themselves.[14]

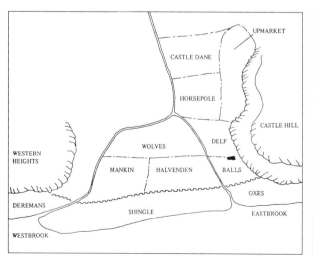

4   Wards in the parish of St James.

5   Old St James's Church, Dover.

6 St James's Street, Dover. Drawn by George Shepherd and engraved by J. Fothergill.

Edward Worthington (1594–pre-1658)

Edward was the eldest son of Roger and was born in Dover in 1594. He was a cooper when he was enrolled with his brother, John, as a Freeman of Dover by birth on 8 October 1621. On 17 September 1617 he was sworn as a constable of Halvenden and Balles ward, four months after his marriage on 12 May 1617 to Susan Elgar at St James's, Dover. He was sworn again on 8 October 1621 in the same ward. They had four children: their eldest son Edward died in 1620, their second son Roger died in 1622, their third son Bartholomew was born in 1624 and married, although no record can be found to date, and their daughter Elizabeth was born in 1628. Edward was deceased by the time his son, Bartholomew, became a Freeman of Dover in 1658.

The Cooper

Between 10 and 15 per cent of the inhabitants of the county were engaged in specialised industries. Most of these worked in textile-manufacturing, building, ship-building or in victualling. Smaller industries such as paper-making employed little labour in comparison. There were only five coopers in central and east Kent between 1640 and 1650.[15]

Until the 20th century coopers wore aprons with bibs, square or pointed, fastened to shirt buttons, and by the 1830s the more fashionable trousers were beginning to replace breeches. Jackets were usual but smocks were occasionally worn and the brewer's cap was very popular.

7 A cooper making a barrel, working in shirt sleeves, bibbed apron, brewer's cap and wearing breeches.

In 1640 a cooper was depicted in doublet, breeches, a slouch hat and a leather apron, which protected him from knife cuts and sparks. (See illustration 7.) R. Holme in 1688 described a cooper at work: 'A cooper in his Waistcote and Cap, Breeches and Hose Ruset: with an Adds lifted up in his right hand and a Driver [a mallet] in his left, trussing up a Barrell with fire out of the top of it'.[16] Trussing up a barrell meant putting it together with heated boards or staves, to make them pliable, within a hoop.

The making of a cask was a notable achievement requiring accuracy, as each curve and bulge had to be tightly fitted together. Many different tools were used including saws, axes, hatchets, knives, chisels, shaves, planes, jointers and other curious tools such as bung ticklers, and bung floggers, a buzz, croze board and iron, a heading swift and iron, a bick iron and a chime maul. When it was made its contents had to meet the exact gauge as to quantity. The admission of apprentices to this trade was done with careful selection.

Working coopers in England also practised a ceremony called 'trussing the young cooper'. This initiation ceremony was performed when the apprentice was turned into a true workman and a full member of the old Trade Guilds.

> A partly made cask (that is without a head) is heated by the fire from the crisset. When it is hot enough (one can be sure his shop mates see to that) it is taken off the fire, the apprentice has to jump inside, and the other workers 'truss him up'. Some of these energetically knock up the willow hoops while others are knocking down, in order that the job may not be finished too soon. The top ends of the staves are rubbed with powdered chalk (to make the hoops stick) the apprentice being also plentifully sprinkled. When considered to be well trussed, the cask is pushed over and rolled with the apprentice inside, to his berth, where he dispenses hospitality and receives from his master his indentures suitably endorsed with a certificate of service.[17]

Many millions of barrels of ale were brewed and drunk each year, partly because of the foulness of much of the water available. Ale was safer to drink unless people lived near a clear natural spring. The barrel was used for many purposes on board ships including storage of food, beverage and gunpowder. In the 17th century large numbers of barrelled herrings were sent overseas through the port of Dover, largely to Flanders and France.

Bartholomew Worthington (1624–pre-1718)

Bartholomew was the eldest surviving son of Edward and Susan Worthington. He married and had two sons, Edward born 1648, whose story follows; and Bartholomew born 1659 whose story also follows, although he is not my ancestor.

Bartholomew became a Freeman by birth in 1658 and both Bartholomews, senior and junior, were councilmen in 1684.

Large families of over five children were rare among 17th-century households. The average was two children and may be attributed to factors such as low fertility, a high death rate and a high infant mortality rate. In the prevailing conditions of Kentish society the craftsman, such as a cooper, was probably able to work independently soon after completing his apprenticeship. His tools cost little, and his first materials such as wood, if not bought with savings, could probably be obtained on credit. On average the tradesman may have married one or two years earlier than a farmer.

The fact that most women married before they were 25 years suggests that the other factors–a high general death rate, or a high infant mortality rate–may have been of greater importance in the small-sized families. While the average expectation of life at birth was about 35 years it was estimated that half of the population died before 16 years[18] and death in childhood was a chief cause of small families. Those who passed the age of 16 years would have had at least an even chance of survival into their fifties and thus only a minority of families would have been cut short by the death of one of the partners in the first ten or fifteen years of marriage.[19]

Of the common diseases, tuberculosis caused by small, badly ventilated rooms rather than malnutrition was the most potent. Plague was one of the worst killers especially in Dover and Deal before the last outbreak took place in 1665-6.[20] Outbreaks of fevers and influenza were far more widespread than those of the plague and most parish registers show signs of the effects of these epidemics. It is unfortunate that burial registers do not usually record the cause of death of each individual.

Bartholomew Worthington (1659-1718)

Bartholomew was a cooper and became a Freeman in 1682. He married 22-year-old Mildred Vibarth in her parish of St Alphage, Canterbury, by licence on 14 January 1683/4[21] and they had four sons.

The eldest son, Bartholomew, was baptised on 12 August 1686 at St Mary's, Dover. He was to have a child by Ann Brooks[22] the same year as he became a Freeman of Dover on 29 September 1710. He married Elizabeth Larkins by licence at St Alphage, Canterbury, on 7 June 1711 although both were of Dover.[23]

8 The *Royal Charles*. The landing of Charles II at Dover, 29 May 1660.

Bartholomew junior was Master Cooper of His Majesty's Victualling Office, Dover. He was also a Justice of the Peace and signed the settlement certificate for William Knott and wife on 9 December 1722. They were moving from the parish of St Mary's, Dover, to St Clement's, Sandwich.[24] Bartholomew was buried on 26 January 1724/5 at St Mary's, Dover. He left a will.[25] His wife Elizabeth was buried in the same place on 17 April 1723.

Their second son Robert was baptised on 19 February 1687/8 at St Mary's, Dover, but nothing further is known of him.

Elias, the third son, baptised on 2 February 1689/90 at St Mary's, Dover, was a cooper and became a Freeman of Dover on 22 November 1720. He owned property, including a freehold house in Limekiln Street occupied by John Rigden.[26] He was buried on 28 December 1773 at St Mary's, Dover, leaving his estate to Robert Worthington and kinsman Elias Worthington.[27] A very eroded headstone, not far from the south disused door of St Mary's Church, records on its front: '... lieth interred the body of Elias Worthington / he departed this life December the 23 or 27 1773 [28 and shipwright in parish register] aged 84 years / Also of Elias Worthington / (? son) ... of the above ... [17 in parish register] Jan 1798 / aged ... years'. An Elias Worthington, born c.1744, was 16 years of age when he was apprenticed on 5 November 1760 with the consent of his uncle Elias Worthington, a cooper of Dover, to Thomas Pascall a shipwright of Dover for seven years.

Edward, fourth son of Bartholomew senior and Mildred, was baptised on 28 November 1691. He became a Freeman of Dover on 29 January 1716 and married Mary/Marie Weston the same year. They had three known children: Elias, Edward and Bartholomew, born between 1717 and 1721. Bartholomew was indentured on 17 May 1736 to Thomas Pascall, boat-builder of Dover, for seven years and received £14. Bartholomew was enrolled on 23 June 1736.[28] Edward was a Master Cooper by 1724 and is mentioned in Dover Apprenticeship Enrolments as an overseer of St Mary's, Dover, in 1732. He died in 1757.[29] Inscribed on the reverse side of the headstone recording the two Elias Worthington deaths is 'Here lieth interred the body of Edward Worthington who departed / this life the (26th ?) of Feb 17-7 [1757 in parish register] aged ... years / Left surviving ... John ... also ... Bartholomew ... / also (Ann ?) wife of ye above / Edward Worthington departed this life the 17 Dec (1759 ?) aged 76 years [widow Worthington buried 21 Dec 1759 according to parish register]. Also ... / son of ye above / Edward Worthington who departed / this life the (5th ?) (July ?) 1760 aged 39 years'.

After Mildred's death in 1692 Bartholomew senior married widow Wilmot/ Wilmett/Willmott Hudson/Hutson on 8 June 1694 at St Mary's, Dover. They had three children: Susan(na) born c.1695 who married Edward Brice who, in turn, was enrolled by marriage as a Freeman of Dover on 30 June 1727;[30] Thomas born 1697 who was buried on 31 July 1698 at St Mary's, Dover, and John born June 1698. (See chart for further information and descendants.)

Bartholomew was buried on 1 October 1718, having written his will on 20 September 1717. He gave £10 to his mother, his real estate at the pier lived in by Nicholas White was left to his wife, Mildred, and after her death to his son John and his wife, Sarah. His will was proved on 6 November 1718.

Edward Worthington (1648-1720)

Edward was born in 1648 and became a Freeman of Dover by birth on 31 January 1672.[31] On 8 April 1672 he married by licence Susan, daughter of Thomas Beard, cordwainer, and Margaret Beard.[32] Although Edward was a bachelor aged 24 years his father gave his consent to the marriage. Susan, described as a spinster and maiden aged 23 years, had the consent of her mother to the marriage. William Beard of Canterbury, watch- and clock-maker, was bondsman[33] which suggests Susan's father was deceased.

William Beard, a clock-maker and Freeman of Canterbury, apprenticed James Ellis a watch-maker on 8 March 1666/7[34] and again when he was aged 28 years on 21 July 1674.[35] Only in the three towns of Canterbury, Greenwich and Tunbridge Wells, serving the needs of an important leisured class, was the more specialised

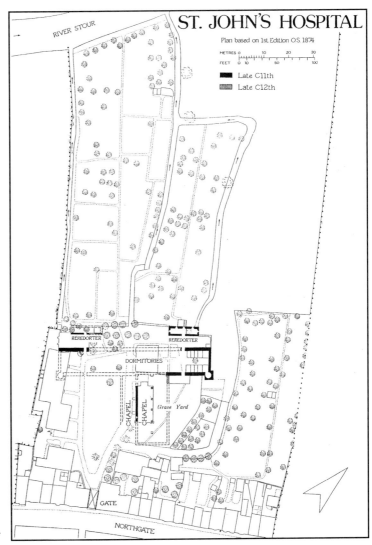

9 Plan of St John's Hospital.

10 West view of St John's Hospital, Canterbury, as it appeared in 1784.

occupation of watch- and clock-maker found. There was little demand for this occupation in smaller towns, dependent for their livelihood on the neighbouring farmers.

The marriage of Edward and Susan took place in the Chapel of St John's Hospital, Canterbury, although Edward was 'of St Mary's in Dover'. Just outside the northern city walls of Canterbury lie the largely forgotten and neglected remains of one of a pair of unique, early almshouses. The Hospital of St John was founded together with the Leper Hospital of St Nicholas at Harbledown by Archbishop Lanfranc in 1084 or early in 1085, and is therefore over nine-hundred years old. Excavation, restoration and conservation work have begun on this site under the administration of the Canterbury Archaeological Trust.

Edward was a cooper like his ancestors before him. In 1705 he became a Freeman of Canterbury by marriage. He and Susan are known to have had four children: Bartholomew, baptised on 2 February 1671/2, who married Elizabeth Holland, became a Freeman of Dover on 19 December 1704 and died in 1723; Edward, baptised at St Mary's, Dover, on 30 August 1674, a cooper of Biggin Street who became a Freeman of Dover on 11 October 1695, married Margaret Baker (died December 1714) on 16 July 1696 at St Mary's, Dover, and died in 1720 leaving a will;[36] John, born between 1676 and 1679, whose story continues; Thomas, baptised on 1 May 1681 at St Mary's, Dover,[37] became a Freeman of Dover by birth on 12 December 1704[38] and married Diana Holland on 10 January 1705/6; and Margaret, also known as Mary, baptised on 4 March 1687/8 at St Mary's, Dover, who married William Jackson on 9 August 1702.

Thomas Worthington was said to be the son of Bartholomew Worthington when he became a Freeman of Dover on 12 December 1704. However there is some difficulty in finding this relationship. Thomas could be the son of Edward Worthington (1648).

Edward White, 'son of Edward White late of Shepy deceased, of his free will and with the consent of his friends', apprenticed himself to 'Edward Worthington the elder of Dover and Susan his wife' on 25 March 1703 for seven years.[39]

Edward Worthington died at Dover and was buried at St Mary's on 20 September 1720. His will, dated 10 October 1719, left his entire estate to his son, Thomas Worthington. His Biggin Street property was already occupied by Thomas when the will was written. No mention is made of Susan, his wife, who was buried at St Mary's on 1 August 1709, or his other children.

John Worthington (*c*.1676-1747)

John was born sometime between 1676 and 1679, the son of Edward and Susan Worthington. On 24 September 1702 he married Ann Fryer at St Mary's, Dover. This was the year in which Queen Anne commenced her reign of England. John was a cooper when he came before John Hollingberry, Mayor of Dover, to be admitted as a Freeman of Dover on 21 November 1703. John was entitled to this 'being the son of Edward Worthington, cooper and ancient freeman of this corporation'.

The Fryers can be traced back to the parishes of Whitfield, Capel le Ferne, Hougham, Hawkinge, Woodnesborough and Alkham. The surname appears predominately in Whitfield where they were described as yeomen. The Whitfield burial register records 'the widow of Thomas Fryre sometime clerk of Whitfield buried 10 March 1635/6 aged 80 years'.[40] Also found were John Fryar of Hawkinge who married Sarah Wanstall of the parish of Whitfield on 30 November 1704;[41] and John Frier of Dover, beerbrewer, who was enrolled as a Freeman on 24 January 1689 'by marriage to Susan Tomesone, one of ye daughters of Richard Tomes'.[42] It is important to note that John and Ann named their first daughter Sarah which was not a known Worthington family first name. She may have been named after her maternal grandmother.

John and Ann Worthington lived at Biggin Street, Dover, and baptised 11 children at St Mary's, eight of whom lived to adulthood. Sarah, baptised on 3 December 1703, married Denis/Dennis Davis, bachelor of Dover St Mary's, at Capel le Ferne on 5 July 1748, by licence dated 1 July 1748; John, baptised on 1 February 1704/5, was buried on 18 February 1704/5; John, baptised on 31 January 1705/6, was buried on 8 May 1716 aged 15 years; Ann, baptised on 30 October 1707, married William Pascall of Dover on 27 December 1729.

11 Freeman declaration for John Worthington of Dover, 1703.

William Pascall of Dover was a barber and periwig-maker. On 5 February 1722 Richard Smitheat, son of Elizabeth Smitheat, widow of Dover, was apprenticed to William for seven years. On 1 January 1727 James Causey, son of Charles Causey late of Dover, pilot, deceased was apprenticed to William for seven years. On 22 October 1731 Tassall Read, son-in-law of Thomas Spratt of Lenham, county of Kent, grocer, was indentured to William Pascall for seven years. John Horne, son of Thomas Horne, carpenter, was indentured to William on 7 October 1736 for seven years.[43]

Mary, John and Ann's fifth child, was baptised on 22 October 1709 and is believed to have married bachelor Joseph Clift by licence at Christ Church Cathedral, Canterbury, on 25 July 1744, both of Dover. Richard, baptised on 23 January 1711, was a cooper and was admitted as a Freeman of Dover by birth on 15 June 1733.[44] He married firstly 22-year-old Susan Twidal of Dover by licence dated 20 July 1734 at Charlton and they had three children: Jane baptised on 20 July 1735, David baptised on 25 April 1737 and Susanna baptised on 10 January 1738. After Susan's death Richard married Hannah Philpott at Canterbury on 27 November 1739.

Andrew, their seventh child, was baptised on 4 April 1714. A cooper, he was admitted as a Freeman of Dover by birth on 30 May 1735.[45] He later became a mariner and drowned at sea in 1749 aged 35 years, unmarried. His will left all his 'worldly goods to his loving sister Sarah Davis of the town and port of Dover'.[46] Not counting fishermen, Kentish shipping employed about 650 seamen in 1629 and 985 in 1701. The increase resulted from the rise of carrying trade in Baltic naval stores and Newcastle coal based on the Thanet seaports. At the end of the 17th century approximately one in thirty of the working male inhabitants of Kent were seamen.[47]

John, baptised on 28 October 1716, married Mary Fryar[48] on 15 October 1749 and was made a Freeman of Dover on 26 October 1749. John and Mary had four children who were baptised at St Mary's, Dover. Their first son, Fryar, was baptised on 26 October 1750, and became a carpenter at Hawkinge. In 1764 he was apprenticed to Robert Court of Acryse, carpenter, for a fee of £10.[49] His will, written on 14 December 1788, was proved on 5 February 1789 leaving property to his uncle Richard Kelcy and his wife Rosamund. He was buried on 13 January 1789 at Hawkinge. John and Mary's second son was baptised John on 12 January 1752, and married Sarah Andrews on 25 October 1781 at St Mary's, Dover. They had three daughters: Mary, baptised on 17 February 1782; Sarah, baptised on 5 October 1783; and Sarah Trevanion, baptised on 4 June 1790, who married Joseph Read on 8 April 1815 at St Mary's, Dover. John and Mary's third son, Benjamin, was baptised on 6 February 1754; Sarah on 26 February 1755; William on 22 September 1758; Edward, baptised on 14 September 1760 at St Mary's, married Sarah Ashman on 24 October 1784 at St James's and lived at 15 Post Lane, near Paradise Pent (Wellington Dock), Dover. Edward and Sarah had three daughters: Mary who died on 14 March 1786 aged eight months; Sarah who died on 12 April 1787 aged four months; and Susannah, baptised on 3 February 1788, who married Benjamin Cornes and had a child. Edward was buried on 14 December, having written a will which was not proved until 21 December 1812.[50] His widow Sarah, née Ashman, of St Mary's was buried on 26 September 1834 at St James's, Dover, aged 84 years. Her will dated 11 September 1833 left household furniture, plate, linen, china, books, real and personal estate to her granddaughter Mary Jell Cornes.[51]

Benjamin, ninth child of John and Ann, was baptised on 18 January 1718/9. He married Ann Dell on 9 April 1751 and his story continues. Mary/Elizabeth was baptised on 15 January 1720/1.

On 29 May 1703 the drummers at Dover were paid six shillings 'for beating and declaring war against France'. On the same date John Worthington (d.1747) was paid eight shillings 'for repairing ye drumm'. He was described as 'ye drummer' when he was paid two shillings for his services on 7 January 1705.[52]

John Spearpoint, son of John Spearpoint of Dover, husbandman, was indentured on 1 December 1704 to John Worthington, cooper and Ann, his wife, for seven years. John Worthington had to provide meat, drink, lodging, washing, aprons and allow him 14 days' work at harvest for his own profit. He was enrolled on 12 July 1711. Also John Worthington of Dover, 'joyner', took apprentice John Campbell for eight years for £10 paid by the 'Hopper Charity'[53] and he was en-

12 Headstone in Old Charlton churchyard of John Worthington who died in 1747.

rolled on 1 March 1724/5. This John Worthington could be a cousin of John the cooper.

Ann Worthington predeceased John who lived to a ripe old age. He was still living on 1 August 1744 'in the eighteenth year of the reign of our Sovereign Lord, George the Second, by the Grace of God of Great Britain, France and Ireland, King, Defender of the Faith ...' when he made his lengthy and informative will.[54] He died on 2 February 1747 and was buried at Charlton on 7 February 1747. His headstone, discovered in about 1987 in Old Charlton churchyard, still stands propped against the fence, as can be seen in the photograph. The round angel face complete with wings must surely be John's image carved in stone.

Benjamin Worthington (1718-83)

Benjamin was born in Dover, the ninth child and sixth son of John and Ann Worthington, née Fryer. He was christened at St Mary's, Dover, on 18 January 1718. Benjamin Worthington was admitted as a Freeman by birth on 26 October 1739.[55] He was a cooper like his ancestors before him and inherited many of his father's tools when he died. He could read and write, and began learning the coopering trade from an early age. William Kitham, son of Robert Kitham hoop-maker of Alkham, was apprenticed to Benjamin on 1 February 1759 and enrolled as an apprentice on 18 February 1759.[56]

13 Maison Dieu, next door to what is believed to be the old Master Victualler's Office and is now the Dover Public Library.

14 Plan of Victualling Stores and Wharves, *c.*1724.

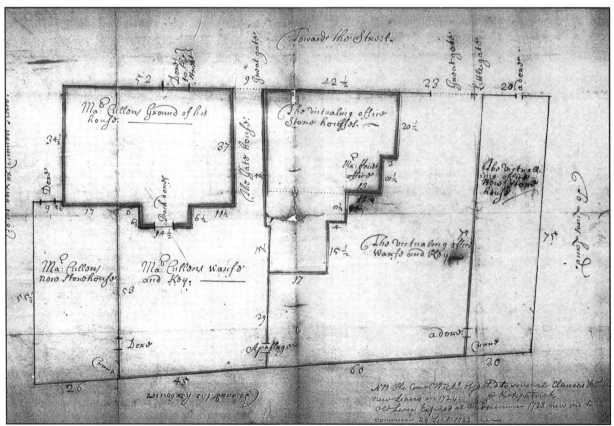

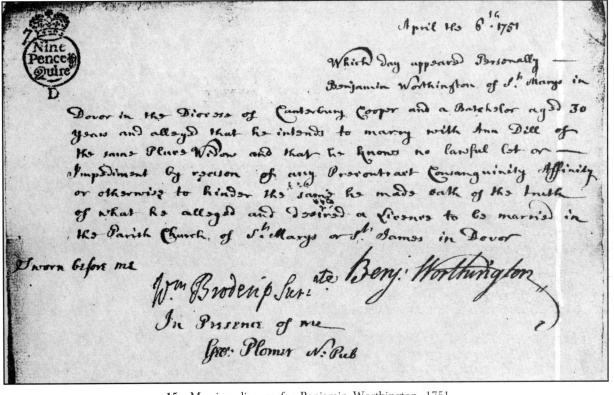

15 Marriage licence for Benjamin Worthington, 1751.

Dover's coopers worked in close co-operation with the Victualling Office. In the reign of Queen Mary the Maison Dieu was converted into a Victualling Office for the Navy and it served this purpose for 300 years. Prior to this conversion for 331 years it had been used as a hospital for pilgrims. Until its closure soon after 1815 the Royal Victualling Department had its headquarters in the Maison Dieu.

The red-brick Jacobean mansion next door to the Maison Dieu was known as Maison Dieu House and was originally built as the residence of the Master Victualler or Head Officer of the Victualling Department after the reign of Elizabeth I. The Victualling Yard was beside the Quay in Strond Street and from here boats were despatched to the fleet in the Downs. In 1834 Maison Dieu House became private property but in 1904 it was purchased by the Corporation for the use of the officials of the Corporation.[57] It is now Dover Library.

In June 1848 the *Dover Express* reported a reduction of the Victualling Office, Dover. Bakers, coopers and apprentices were discharged on account of the peaceful times. Only the four Officers, that is the Agent, Storekeeper, Clerk of Cheques and Master Cooper were to remain, but their salaries were reduced: Agent from £200 to £150, Storekeeper from £50 to £40 (reduced allowance for stationery), Clerk of Peace from £50 to £40, and Master Cooper from £50 to £45.

Benjamin was 33 years of age when he married Ann Dell, a widow. The marriage took place at St Mary's, Dover, on 9 April 1751.[58] Ann Jelly had married Samuel

16 Ann Worthington, née Jelly (1723-1802).

Dell, a churchwarden of St Mary's, Dover, in 1738-40.[59] Samuel and Ann Dell had one known daughter named Affra, whose marriage to John Newport by licence at St Martin in the Fields, London, on 1 June 1771 was witnessed by her stepfather Benjamin Worthington, and her step-uncle Richard Worthington. John Newport is most probably the son of John Newport of St Martin's Lane, St Martin in the Fields, London, widower, who married by licence on 8 January 1750 at St Mary Bredman, Canterbury, Elizabeth Worthington of St Mary Bredman, spinster.

Benjamin and Ann had eight children, but only five lived to adulthood. Henry, named after his grandfather Henry Jelly, was baptised at St Mary's Church on 19 January 1751 and was buried on 25 March 1753. Ann was named after her mother and was baptised on 28 June 1753. She married Thomas Horn(e), owner of the Buckland paper mill,[60] and had several children. Ann Horn was a witness to the marriage at St Mary's of John Andrews to Elizabeth Arthur, a minor, on 30 July 1767. A four-sided tombstone[61] in the Buckland churchyard has the following memorials:

Sacred to the memory of Thomas Horn Esq. late of this parish who died 30th December 1823 aged 70 years leaving a widow and three daughters to lament their irreparable loss, also Ann, widow of the above Thomas Horn Esq. who died the 10th January 1842 aged 88 years.

Also to the Memory of the beloved wife of General Sir I/L/TM Frederick Smith of the Royal Engineers, youngest daughter of Thomas and Ann Horn who departed this life the 2nd April 1867.

Also to the memory of Thomas Horn, Jnr. son of Thomas and Ann Horn of this parish who died 22 March 1807 aged 27 years.

Also of Josias Cocke Esq. who died 19th November 1821 aged 39 years likewise of Maria relict of the above Josias Cocke the wife of William Senfer Esq. of Alkham Rectory of this County and 2nd daughter of Thomas Horn Esq., and Ann of this parish who died 19th July 1831 aged 47 years.

Benjamin and Ann's second daughter, Susanna, was baptised on 16 May 1755 and buried on 6 September 1758 at St Mary's, Dover, aged three years. Elizabeth was baptised on 13 March 1757 at St Mary's, Dover, and married Thomas Gorely on 2 December 1783 at the same church. The Poll for Members of Parliament to represent the City of Canterbury 1790 lists 'Thomas Gorely, Dover, Kent, Hatter' and 'William Gorely, Whitechapel, London, Hatter'. In 1785 Thomas Gorely was elected as a Dover Common Councilman. Several children were born to Thomas and Elizabeth Gorely: Henry who was buried on 25 August 1784, Thomas who was buried on 29 October 1786, and then a second Thomas who was baptised on 10 June 1787 at Dover St Mary's. He survived, became a hatter, married Mary (surname unknown but probably Wood) and had several children including: Thomas Wood Gorley baptised on 20 June 1813 at St Mary's, Dover; Sarah Marsh Gorley baptised on 21 July 1815; Eliza Tumey baptised on 10 December 1791; James baptised on 3 March 1793; John Hope baptised on 10 October 1794 and buried on 19 August 1797; Charles Benjamin baptised on 10 December 1798; and James Spence baptised on 22 February 1801. Thomas Gorely was buried at St Mary's on 9 February 1812. Elizabeth Gorely died on 24 October 1824 at Market Place, Dover, aged 67 years.

Hester Worthington, fifth child and fourth daughter of Benjamin and Ann Worthington, was baptised on 18 February 1759 at St Mary's, Dover. She was a minor aged 20 years, and needed her father's consent when she married William Reynolds by licence on 25 January 1780. Witnesses to this event were George Farbrace and Thomas Horn, her brother-in-law. Hester and William Reynolds had four known children. The first was Elizabeth, who was baptised on 13 November 1780 and married William Leplastrier, bachelor, on 10 July 1802, at St Mary's, Dover. Witnesses were her mother Hester Reynolds/Nye, Thomas Night (?Knight), E. Leplastrier and Thomas Gorely, Elizabeth's uncle and Hester's brother-in-law. Hester and William's second daughter, Hester, was baptised on 17 October 1782, followed by William on 24 July 1785 and Louisa Ann on 30 March 1788. William Reynolds died on 20 February 1791 and Hester married again on 5 April 1798 by licence Edward Nye, a bachelor, at St Mary's, Dover. Witnesses were Edward Bowles and Ann Leggett. One son named Edward was baptised at St Mary's on 29 June 1800. It is not known when Elizabeth Nye died. Her second husband Edward Nye died on 11 March 1838 at Limekiln Street, Dover, aged 73 years. She may have married again as her sister-in-law, Elizabeth Worthington, died at Limekiln Street, witnessed by Elizabeth Smithett.

17 The Dover Council Chamber inside the Maison Dieu showing Chairman's Chair, centre right.

18 & 19 Worthington, Rouse and Jelly altar tomb on the eastern corner of the chancel of St Mary's Church.

Sarah Worthington, Hester's younger sister, was baptised on 20 December 1760. A burial record was found in the registers of St James the Apostle, Dover, for 'Sarah Worthington buried 18th December 1848, of St Mary's aged 85 years'. This could be her death record although she would have been 88 years of age.

Benjamin Jelly Worthington was born on 8 April 1763, followed by Martha who was baptised on 7 September 1766, and buried on 18 September 1769 aged three.

At the Assembly of Dover Councilmen on Thursday 31 August 1775 Henry Jelly Esq. presided as Mayor. It was announced at this meeting that 'Mr Benjamin Worthington, Freeman of this Corporation is by a majority of vote duly elected a Common Councilman in the Room of Mr James Gunman'. Benjamin remained on the Council for the years 1778, 1781 and 1782 along with Messrs. Boynton and Reynolds who were related to him.

On 9 September 1782 when Phineas Stringer Esq. was Mayor, Benjamin Worthington was 'Elected Warden of the Almshouse–Mr Benjamin Worthington for the year'. At the Council meeting held on 31 March 1783 'Mr Benjamin Worthington' was listed as 'sick' and then does not appear in the next list of Councilmen.[62] Benjamin

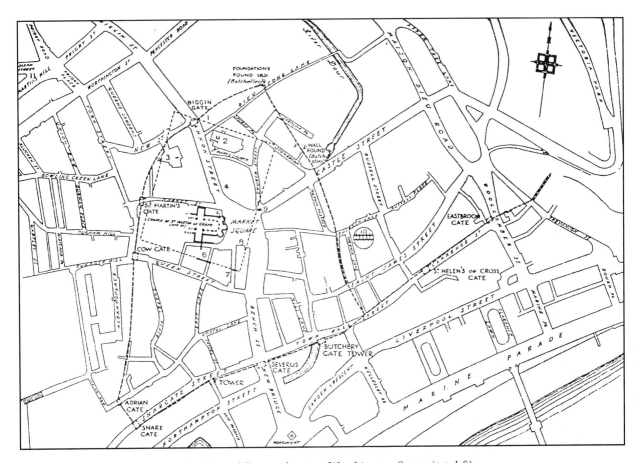

20 Map of Dover showing Worthington Street (*top left*).

died on 25 April 1783 aged 64 years,[63] and was buried on 4 May 1783 in the large altar tomb on the eastern corner of the chancel of St Mary's Church, containing Jelly and Rouse family members.

Benjamin left a will which was proved at London on 14 August 1784 leaving his estate to his wife, Ann Worthington.[64] Ann died on 30 December 1801 aged 78 years and was buried with her husband on 7 January 1802.

Worthington Street

During the 17th century there were about twenty-five small towns of 400 or more inhabitants in Kent, the largest being Canterbury with 6,000 or 7,000 people. Half of these towns consisted of a main street with several little side lanes running into it. Only in a few of the larger towns, such as Canterbury, Sandwich and Dover was there a network of half a dozen or more short streets.

In the corporate towns the streets were roughly paved though probably indifferently maintained. In the non-corporate towns, where the upkeep of the roads was in

21   Seascape off Dover showing Dover Castle.

22   View of Worthington Lane before its widening in 1895, at junction of Priory Place (*left*) and York Street (*right*).

23 Worthington Lane before 1895 widening and re-naming as Worthington Street. Viewed from Pencester Road across Biggin Street.

the hands of a much less vigorous parish vestry or manorial court, paving was more scanty.[65]

Worthington Street is first mentioned historically as Gardiner's Lane. Who Gardiner was is not known but the name has been associated with the lane since the reign of James I (1602-25). The lands on the west side of Biggin Street, when the Priory existed, belonged to that monastery and it is probable that after the suppression, when the land was let to tenants of the Archbishop of Canterbury, this lane was opened as an occupation road from Biggin Street to the Priory fields. Prior to 1783 Gardiner's Lane was the principal outlet from Biggin Street to the Priory, Maxton and Hougham. In Gardiner's time it was probably a mere cart track through a field.

It is very difficult to tell when the first buildings were erected along this track but the four cottages on the north side constructed of red bricks with dormer windows date from about the year 1780.

The name was changed from Gardiner's Lane to Worthington's Lane about the year 1800.[66] According to Bavington Jones–'At one stage one of the Worthington family members who was a wool stapler had warehouses in this lane, and eventually gave it its second name'. No evidence of a Worthington with the occupation of wool stapler has been found during that time period.[67] The warehouses which were built mainly of wood were in later years converted to fodder stores, a slaughter house and stables, much to the detriment of the thoroughfare.

At the upper end of this lane, until 1860, there existed a well-known weighbridge, the property of Joseph Groombridge. In 1860 he removed the weighbridge and sent to the Town Council plans for building on the site. To this the Council objected on the grounds that the proposed building would make the lane too narrow. They insisted that the proposed buildings should be kept back in line with the existing frontages. Mr. Groombridge succeeded in proving that the site of the weighbridge was his to build upon if he chose. The Council admitted his claim, which was settled by 105 feet being surrendered to widen the top of the lane, for payment of £80.

As part of the street improvement scheme in 1895, the lane was again widened.[68] The *Dover Year Book* for 1895 reports in 'Local Government News' that:

> The widening of Biggin Street and Worthington's Lane is now approaching completion. The negotiations for purchasing the property, and compensations have been concluded. Three fine shops have been re-built and occupied. Six more are in the course of re-building and the sites are being cleared for others. Worthington's Lane which would admit only one vehicle, has been widened like Biggin Street, to forty five feet, so that the whole of the centre of the town is furnished with broad thoroughfares ...

In 1896 it was proposed to change the name to Military Avenue but there were strong objections to the old name of Worthington being replaced as was reported in the *Dover Express* on 10 April 1896 under the heading 'The Great Misnomer':

> We hope the Town Council will not persist in the Great Misnomer of calling the widened thoroughfare from Biggin-street to Priory-place, Military Avenue. It is true that near by there is a spot which has for years been called Queen's-gardens, in spite of the fact that there is no queen nor garden connected with the place; but that is no reason why we should dub a place Military when it has nothing to do with the Military, and call it an avenue when it is not an avenue. Worthington's Lane, this thoroughfare has been called for more than a hundred years, and being now widened from 20 feet to 45 feet it certainly would be very appropriate to call it a road instead of a lane, but if the Town Council put up a name plate making any further change they will be calling down upon themselves the curse of the Commination Service which is evoked on those who remove their neighbours's land mark, and sundry other curses also.

Perhaps due to the threat of these curses combined with local pressure, the Council rescinded, as was reported in the *Dover Express* on 1 May 1896:

> Councillor Brown, in accordance with the notice he had given, rose to move the rescinding of the motion of the Managing Committee that Worthington's Lane should be in future known as Military Avenue. He remarked that he was only giving them an opportunity of re-considering an act which had been carried out without any notice having been placed on the agenda paper that it was about to be brought forward. He had himself received representation from people outside, and also from owners of property in the street, that they did not want the name altered. He would be sorry to see the ancient name of Worthington taken away, and he suggested that it should be termed Worthington Street, if Lane was considered too humble. The Worthingtons, he remarked, were an ancient Dover family, closely connected with

the great coaching traffic between Dover and London. They were also merchants and
brewers, and one of them had been an officer in the navy and wrote an interesting
book on the improvement of Dover Harbour a long while ago. He did not think that
as the name Worthington had been allocated by their forefathers, that they should
alter such ancient landmarks.

Councillor Edwin seconded the motion, stating that the name Worthington Street
would be acceptable to the people living in that neighbourhood. The motion was
unanimously carried.

And so the change was confined to the substitution of Lane for Street.[69] A detailed
description of the improvements to Worthington Street was given in the *Dover Express*
later that month on 29 May 1896:[70]

> The whole of the outstanding buildings in this widened thoroughfare, having now
> been removed, we take the opportunity of saying a few words on the improvement
> which has been carried out. This thoroughfare, which was originally called
> Worthington's Lane is very ancient, having been the only outlet from Biggin Street
> in the direction of the Western Heights and the Priory, before Priory Street was
> formed in 1783. As to the origin of the name Worthington's Lane, Miss Horsley, in
> her *Memories of Old Dover* says 'The premises of some wool staplers of this name nearly
> filled the lane at one time, and caused it to be called by the name of Worthington.
> There was also a large family of the Worthingtons living in Dover, one being a wool
> stapler, another the owner of the Ship Inn and Wine Vaults in Snargate Street, and
> another was a Lieutenant in the Royal Navy, who devised plans for improving the
> Harbour, making an elaborate model to show what he thought was needed, and
> writing a book on the subject. There are tombstones of some of the family in St
> Mary's Churchyard.' When the lane was taken in hand by the Corporation as part
> of their improvement scheme, it was a very narrow thoroughfare, in which two
> vehicles could not pass. At the bottom, adjoining Biggin-street was Mr Woods butcher
> shop and slaughter hosue on the South side, and Mr Morris's bakery on the west. The
> remaining portion of the West side was devoted to cottages, and on the South side
> there were two public houses, the Olive Branch and the Forester's Arms, both of
> which have been swept away by the improvement. There was also a Marine Store
> there while at the top was Mr Longley's butcher shop, Mr. Edwin's Priory-place
> premises occupying the opposite corner. The Improvement Scheme has added about
> 25 feet in width to this thoroughfare, the whole of the Southern side having been
> taken down. To effect this Mr Wood's shop and slaughter house, and the premises
> of Mr Paine, Stone Mason, have been demolished, so that the widened thoroughfare
> is out now (although not quite in a direct line) a continuation of Pencester-road and
> there is a clear view from Pencester-road through to the Military-road and to the
> Heights beyond. The rebuilding of the frontages on the widened Worthington's Street
> is not yet completed. At the bottom corner a very handsome rounded frontage has
> been erected, connected with the new frontage of Mr Rubie's Grocery establishment
> and three other shops which have been completed further south in Biggin-street. A
> little further up Worthington's-street, on the lower side of Queen's-gardens, is Mr
> Ezra's Lithographic Establishment. The remainder of that side of the street is not yet
> built upon. The lower sites below Mr Ezra's adjoin Mr Rubies warehouses, and
> probably may be occupied with an extension of those premises. The whole plot lying
> between Queen's-gardens and York-street is for disposal for building sites, and is
> according to the notice board in the hands of Mr A.M. Bradley, Solicitor Market-
> square and Messrs. Cresswell and Newman, Architects, Castle Street.

The Corporation's improvements had no connection with the other side of the street, except at the bottom, where the site of Mr Morris's bakery has been occupied by Mr Wood's butcher's shop, with a slaughter house behind it extending up the street nearly as far as Cave's Court, and the six houses situated in that rather confined place are now in pretty close proximity to that building. Of course, the slaughter house is built on the most approved principles and is in every way well arranged, but at the same time, the Corporation in allowing that structure to be so placed, have not made the best possible arrangement. A considerable portion of the west side of Worthington's-street has been rebuilt. Starting at the top, Mr Edwin has put a handsome finish to the corner. Then come two handsome new shops, the one occupied by Mr Putley, watchmaker (who was removed by the improvement scheme from the bottom of Priory Street). Next door below is another new shop, occupied as the local depot of the Salvation Army. Next below that is another commodious new shop re-built by Mr Edwin which is to let. Then come four old cottages, which for the present retain their primitive state, but which will no doubt, ere long be modernised. Below these are three moderate sized shops which have been re-built, and will shortly be ready for occupation. These three, we believe, are the property of the Mayor (Matthew Pepper Esq.). Two other small houses left as they were, complete the line down to Mr Wood's premises.

In a story on the street names of Dover published in the *Dover Express* during the 1960s, it is written that:

Just around the corner is Worthington Street, earlier known as Worthington Lane. It was here that the family of Worthington owned much land on which was built their mews, stables and farmyard. They kept livestock and hired out horses for riding, and also horses and traps and coaches.

It was probably a very early 'drive yourself' hire firm, though of course there may have been earlier firms who also did this kind of business. Certainly one could go to Mr Worthington, pay a deposit, and drive away a hire trap or coach, though a driver was normally supplied.

Worthington Street still exists today and can be found in the heart of the town of Dover.

Chapter 2

Benjamin Jelly Worthington's Early Life

Benjamin Jelly Worthington was born in Dover on 8 April 1763, the second son and seventh child born to Benjamin, a cooper, and his wife Ann Worthington, formerly Mrs. Dell, née Jelly.[1] Benjamin was born three years after George III became King of England, and he died just two years after the King's death in 1820. The long reign of George III and the life of Benjamin Jelly Worthington witnessed some of the most momentous events in British and world history. There was the American Revolution, the French Revolution, the Napoleonic Wars, the Industrial Revolution, vast tracts of India were being annexed, Australia was being settled, South African Dutch settlers were being brought within British rule, and Canada was being divided up between the English and French.

Benjamin was baptised at 'St Mary's Church of England, Dover'[2] on 1 May 1763 and was the first in the family to be given a first and second name. Until the 19th century it was extremely rare for this to occur and it was a practice only found amongst the upper classes. His second name of Jelly was inherited from his maternal grandfather Henry Jelly who was a prominent citizen of Dover.

24 A 19th-century engraving of St Mary's Church.

Benjamin Goes to Sea

The first American War is better known as 'The War of American Independence'. When a party of colonial patriots disguised in Indian dress boarded three British East India Company ships on 16 December 1773 and dumped their cargo of tea into the harbour in protest against the tea tax and British import restrictions, the port of Boston was closed to commerce by the English government. American discontent with British attempts at taxation had begun in the 1760s, but in these disputes colonists demanded only their 'rights' as Englishmen. Even after the military confrontations at Lexington and Concord (1775), the second Continental Congress which convened at Philadelphia in May disavowed any desire for Independence. However, after continued British provocations in 1775, opinion began to shift. The result was the outbreak of war in April 1775 and the Declaration of Independence on 4 July 1776.

It is not known what a well-educated 16-year-old Dover boy was doing in New York in 1778, however on 10 November of that year Benjamin joined the Navy in New York as a volunteer Able Seaman. His age was recorded in the Muster Book on 'entry to the Ship' as '21 born Dover'. The attitude on most ships to recording ages was casual as men below the rank of officer were only signed on for one voyage at a time and, except in wartime, were afterwards free to join another naval ship, a merchant vessel or stay ashore. Muster Books were used mainly for pay and victuals accounting, and for counting heads at each rank. This was during a period of time when men were being 'prest' by press gangs into the Navy. It is probable that Benjamin reached America as a crewman on another naval vessel. This experience would have enhanced his chance of being accepted by the Captain of the *Unicorn* as an Able Seaman, for the title implied experience and proficiency.

At first there was no official place for Benjamin as one of the complement of 160 men on board the *Unicorn*, a small 20-gun frigate, so he was listed as a supernumerary, or extra man, until 22 January 1779 when he was transferred to the 'Ship's Company' list. The *Unicorn* was one of the ships on which Admiral Sir William Sidney Smith, G.C.B. served, and family legend states that Benjamin served under Sir Sidney Smith. This is not possible as Smith was born on 21 June 1764 and was Benjamin's contemporary. Smith joined the Royal Navy during 1777 and did not become an officer until 1789. They were more likely to have been boyhood friends as Sidney Smith was the son of Captain John Smith of the 3rd Regiment of Guards, who was born in Dover in June 1730. In 1791 John Smith built a curious castellated residence which stood on the shore between Castle Cliff and Castle Jetty known as 'Smith's Folly'. It was here that John Smith died on 23 February 1804.[3]

In late January 1779 the *Unicorn* called at Savannah, Georgia, and again in mid-March. On 3 April Benjamin was promoted to Midshipman. By May the ship had crossed the Atlantic to call at Guernsey dockyard in the Channel Islands before cruising to nearby Jersey. Benjamin was thus present when the *Unicorn*, on 3 May, put three French ships out of action. Further calls were made at Guernsey in July and August, before sailing to Spithead in southern England.[4]

On 24 August 1779 Midshipman Benjamin Jolly [*sic*] Worthington was transferred from the 'Ship's Company' of the *Unicorn* to 'Admiral Pye's Pay List'. This meant he had become part of the retinue of this Admiral and, in practical terms, would normally then have been trained in navigation etc. by an experienced person responsible to the Admiral, who agreed to sponsor the young sailor. It can be assumed, though not proven, that the young man's family knew the Admiral in some way, which would have increased his opportunity for promotion within the ranks. Benjamin's chances were probably destroyed by naval cutbacks following the return of peace after the Declaration of American Independence. Sometimes a man was placed on the same ship as the Admiral, but not always.

Unfortunately defective records for the *Unicorn* leave some doubt regarding subsequent events, but it appears Benjamin did not remain on the *Unicorn*. At the time of Benjamin's transfer to Admiral Pye, Pye had been Commander-in-Chief, Portsmouth, of several vessels. These included the *Arrogant*, on which were 30 of his retinue, while the ship was moored off Spithead. Benjamin was not included, nor was he amongst about one thousand men who came on board, mostly for very short stays, during that period.

The *Brilliant*'s Muster Book 1779-83 indicates that Benjamin had been on board from 25 August 1779, recorded as Midshipman number 114 in the Ship's Company.[5] The *Brilliant* left Portsmouth on about 20 September 1779 for a short voyage, returning to Spithead by the end of the month. Sailing again in mid-October she docked at Lisbon, Portugal, in mid-November. This port then became her regular base for a series of unspecified voyages which appear to have been undertaken in early December 1779, early February, early March, early April, mid-April and early June 1780. Portugal was a friendly state in Britain's continuing war against America and its allies, the French and Spanish.

Some splendid actions were fought by the English Navy, but command of the seas was not consistently maintained. The Americans, under the controversial Scottish sailor Paul Jones, began the fine traditions of the United States Navy. It was the advent of the French fleet on the American side which, for a short time, turned the scale against the British. The war lasted seven years and was brought to an end with

25 The *Dragon* is believed to be the ship with a Commodore's broad pennant in the centre of the picture.

the signing of the three treaties which constituted the Peace of Versailles on 3 September 1783.

The *Brilliant* left Lisbon in August 1780 and reached Spithead in early October. Benjamin was discharged on 30 October to join *Diligente* 'Per Order Sir Thomas Pye'.[6] The *Brilliant*, a 28-gun ship, had been built in 1779, but *Diligente* was a 68-gunner captured from the Spaniards in January 1780. This was a temporary posting for Benjamin and he remained on the ship's muster until 6 December 1780 when he was transferred to the *Dragon*, a 74-gun ship built in 1760.[7]

The *Dragon* was only a transit ship for Benjamin as he was discharged on 31 December 1780 to *La Nymphe*, also known as *Nymphe*, 'Per Order Adml. Pye'.[8] This time he was joining a 36-gun ship captured from the French only four months earlier and now being prepared for sea under Commander John Ford. He had come aboard on 2 January 1781, still described as 'Age 21. Born Dover', working first as an able-bodied seaman until a midshipman vacancy was available. *Nymphe* stayed at Portsmouth until 14 April when she became an escort for a convoy of merchant ships bound for the West Indies. After spending 19-25 April at Cork, Ireland, they sailed westwards, shadowed at first by two Spanish ships until Barbados, a British colony in the West Indies, was safely reached on 20 June 1781.

Having joined the local British fleet, *Nymphe* patrolled the local seas around Barbados and, after sinking a French warship in July, visited other islands of the West Indies: St Lucia, Antigua and Montserrat. On 5 August she captured a French schooner and afterwards made for New York, one of the few American ports still in British

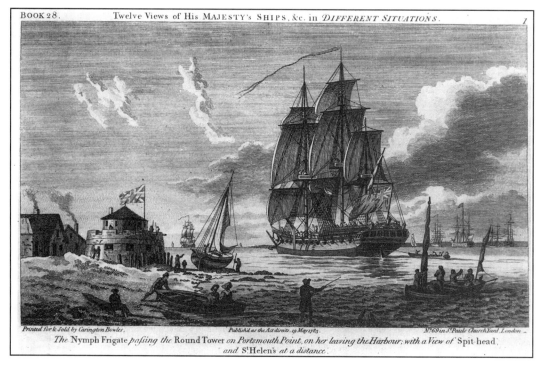

BOOK 28.   Twelve Views of His MAJESTY's SHIPS, &c. in *DIFFERENT SITUATIONS*.

Printed for & Sold by Carington Bowles.   *Publish'd as the Act directs 19 May 1783.*   *N.º 69 in S.t Pauls Church Yard. London.*

The Nymph Frigate *passing the* Round Tower *on* Portsmouth Point, *on her leaving the Harbour; with a View of* Spit-head, *and* S.t Helen's *at a distance.*

26 *La Nymphe*, captured from the French in 1780, passing the Round Tower on Portsmouth Point.

hands, arriving on 28 August. On 1 September *Nymphe* left with a British fleet to patrol the American coastline, blockading enemy ports. She captured an American ship on 21 September, another on 8 October and a third on 12 October.

A brief return to New York preceded a voyage southwards to reach St Kitts, West Indies, in early December and Barbados on Christmas Day 1781. *Nymphe* left Barbados in January 1782 for Antigua where she stayed from 27 January until 11 March. She then patrolled the coasts of Cuba until docking at Port Royal, Jamaica, on 26 May. Her next voyage began on 12 June and took her along the Florida coast to the Bahamas, but by August she was further south at Barbados, St Lucia and Antigua where she stayed until 12 September.

Local patrols preceded calls at Antigua and Barbados, where a long refit took place until 11 January 1783. On this date Benjamin was promoted to master's mate, sharing the navigation of the ship with the master. Their next voyage began with convoy duties but *Nymphe* docked at St Lucia from 7 February until 5 March, leaving only to capture a Spanish ship on 12 March and return the next day. The war was, however, coming to an end and on 12 April she sailed north to Bermuda and crossed the Atlantic to dock at Portsmouth on 25 May. The crew were released on 4 June and Benjamin was paid off in August 1783. This was his last Royal Navy voyage.[9]

Benjamin Returns to Dover

Two important events took place soon after Benjamin returned to Dover. On 20 August 1784 'Benjamin Jelly Worthington, mariner', became a Freeman by birth of the town of Dover, 'son of Mr Benjamin Worthington'.[10] On 30 July 1784 Benjamin and Thomas Chapman were commissioned to serve on the *Tartar* cutter at the port of Dover.[11]

Dover is one of the Cinque Ports which individually and historically have played a prominent part in the defence of the kingdom of England. Cinque Ports were located in originally five, but ultimately 32 towns along the south coast of England. From the 11th to the 17th centuries they enjoyed certain privileges in return for providing the crown with ships and men. England had no Royal Navy at this time. Dover, with its deep sea between sheltering hills, has been a haven for shipping since the Roman occupation, and its general features have changed little since that time.[12] Dover Castle, first built during the Roman occupation, still stands as a fortress on the high bold shores, overlooking continental passenger traffic which from earliest times has passed through this port.

Up until the end of the 17th century, the Dover Customs House hired small vessels called smacks, sometimes helped by the Royal Navy, which were used as a kind of marine police force to watch out for smugglers. In addition 14 Customs sloops, smacks, cutters or cruisers were deployed around the coast. Each of these, the largest about 200 tons, carried a master, a mate and around thirty men. A distinctive identification was flown: 'a jack and red ensign with the seal of office (a castellated portcullis) thereon'. Masters were directed to 'speak with all ships and vessels they shall meet at sea' and, if smuggling was suspected, to 'diligently watch their motions and keep them company until they are clear of the coast'. In times of war these Customs sloops could be taken over by the Royal Navy. Life aboard, whether in peace or war, was hard.

27 Model of *Tartar* Revenue cutter *c.*1784.

The English government maintained a good many cutters as they were able to carry a lot of sail and move very quickly. One English nautical authority, Falconer, described a cutter as having one mast and straight-running bowsprit that could be run inboard on deck.[13] But for this, and the fact that the cutter's sail area was larger and the jib-sheet was differently set as it had no stay, these craft were much the same as sloops. Falconer also stated that a sloop differs from a cutter by having a fixed steeving bowsprit and a jib-stay, so the real difference was that the cutter could run her bowsprit inboard, but the sloop could not.[14] The Judge of Excise Trials, Vol. xxx, 1 July 1795 to 17 December 1795, p.95 in Attorney-General v Julyan quoting expert evidence explained a further difference: 'In a cutter the tack of the jib was hooked to a traveller and there was a thimble fastened to a block which came across the head of the sail. There were two blocks at the mast-head, one on each side. A rope passes through the three blocks by which is drawn up the halliards. The jib of a cutter lets down and draws in a very short time and a cutter usually had channels and mortice-holes to fix legs to prevent oversetting.'[15] After several legal disputes relating to classification of cutters and sloops, the Attorney and Solicitor-General gave a legal distinction in 1822 which also involved the form and build of the hull.[16]

The author Marryat gives the following description of a cutter in *The Three Cutters*.[17] 'She is a cutter,' he writes, 'and you may know that she belongs to the Preventive Service by the number of gigs and galleys which she has hoisted up all round her. She looks like a vessel that was about to sail with a cargo of boats, two on deck, one astern, and one on each side of her. You observe that she is painted black and all her boats are white. She is not such an elegant vessel as the yacht, and she is much more lumbered up … The guns are iron and painted black and her bulwarks are painted red. It is not a very becoming colour but then it lasts a long while and the dockyard is not very generous on the score of paint'.[18]

Uniform was adopted in 1777, when the Masters and Mates took on a naval-type rig (the first set of silver buttons supplied free). Among the General Letters of the Customs Board was one dated 26 June 1804 petitioning the Board for an alteration in the uniform of the commanders of the cruisers and also that of their mates. The Commanders suggested for their own dress:

A silver epaulette, the button-holes worked or bound with silver twist or lace, side-arms, and cocked hats with cockades, and the buttons set on the coat three and three, the breeches and waistcoat as usual:

For the undress, the same as at present.

For the mates, the addition of lappels [sic], the buttons set on two and two, and cocked hats with cockades.[19]

The Board consented to these alterations but epaulettes were not allowed because of the danger of confusion with the officers of the Royal Navy. There was a great deal of jealousy between the Revenue and Navy departments and the reason epaulettes were disallowed may be explained by the fact that epaulettes had officially become part of the Navy's uniform in 1795 although they had been worn by officers since 1780.

The cutters had plenty of fine-looking men all dressed in red flannel shirts and blue trousers. Some of them wore canvas or tarpaulin petticoats, very useful for keeping the body warm in all weathers as they were in the boats night and day. The use of a petticoat as a seaman's article of attire dates back to the time of Chaucer, who wrote:

> A Shipman was ther, woning fer by weste:
> For aught I woot, he was of Dertemouthe.
> He rood up-on a rouncy, as he couthe,
> In a gowne of falding to the knee.[20]

Marryat continued, 'down in the cabin, we shall find the lieutenant who commands her, a master's mate and a midshipman. They have each their tumbler before them, and are drinking gin-toddy, hot, with sugar—capital gin, too, 'bove proof; it is from a small anker standing under the table. It is one that they forgot to return to the Custom House when they made their last seizure.'[21]

Officially Customs vessels were not permitted to enter harbour except for essential repairs or for shelter in really bad weather. A master was paid £1 weekly, a mate 14s., and a crew member 7s. plus an allowance for victuals of 9d. daily 'whereof a notice is to be affixed to the Mast that if good & sufficient provisions are not provided by the Commander, the Mariners may complain'.

An immense amount of smuggling took place along the coast of Britain during the 18th century. The Customs duties on spirits, wine, tobacco and many other commodities were so high that enormous profits could be made by any importers evading duties. In all ports around the coast there were men who went out to sea in swift little schooners or sloops on dark nights, met some French or Dutch boat, shipped their illicit kegs or bales, and then ran for some lonely creek. There were agents in the large towns who regularly received illegal goods and disposed of them in the way of ordinary trade. The

28   Line drawing of an English cutter.

29   Silver cup presented to Henry Jelly, Commander of the *Tartar*, by His Majesty's Customs, 25 December 1784.

smugglers were a brutal and determined class of people. In lonely districts they ill-treated anyone who would not help them. Smuggling was a sordid business which cheated the government of revenue and caused the increase of taxes.

In the 18th century the populace and the smuggling fraternity both shared a dislike of the revenue man on land and sea and made his calling a particularly hazardous one. A mariner on the *Tartar* under Henry Jelly was killed in the line of duty, and it is no less significant that Captain Dubois Smith, commander of the *Lively* cutter and Benjamin Jelly Worthington's colleague of long standing, was wounded three times during his career.[22]

And so, in a climate generally hostile to the efforts of Revenue men, Benjamin's uncle, Henry Jelly, Captain of the *Tartar*, compiled a record of seizures that commands admiration. Between 1763 and 1780 his name is mentioned 188 times in the Register of Seizures.[23] He confiscated during that 17-year period 93,006 quarter-pounds of tea assessed at £20,165 11s., 58,784 quarter-gallons of geneva (gin) together with 2qts, 14pts, and 'several parcels' valued at £12,565 1s. 6d., 17,886 half-gallons of brandy appraised at £4,791 19s. 9d., and 2,043 gallons of rum worth £414 5s. 3d. Added to this haulage he impounded 60 vessels (48 'boats', 2 sloops, 7 galleys and 3 cutters), some of which were claimed for immediate use in the Revenue Service. The aggregate value of the impounded vessels was £1,770 13s. 3d.[24]

By 1784 the Waterguard strength had increased to 44 vessels of various sizes which were manned by a total of over 1,000 personnel. There were 20 more smacks hired from private owners that year, bringing the total running costs for 1784 to £44,355 16s. 11d.[25] The largest of these 44 cruisers was the 210-ton *Repulse* which carried 33 men and was based at Colchester. The second largest was the 194-ton *Tartar* with 31 men, her station being Dover. She was not a hired vessel and was 'on the establishment', meaning the property of the Crown. Of the same tonnage was the *Speedwell* which cruised between Weymouth and Cowes. The 190-ton *Rose* with 30 men was stationed at Southampton. Next in size was the *Diligence*, 174 tons with 32 men, which cruised between Poole and Weymouth. The smallest of all the cruisers was the 41-ton *Nimble* with a crew of 30 men stationed at Deal.[26]

In 1784 Henry Jelly wrote several letters to the Customs Board regarding the state of the vessel which he said was 'leaky in her bottom and wants caulking, cleaning, painting and ballast shifting'.[27] A letter dated 24 December 1784 from Captain Jelly mentions estimates for various articles such as sails, cordage, etc. for the *Tartar*, which

30 Early 19th-century engraving of Western Docks with the Pier District on the right and Granville Dock in the centre. Part of Wellington Dock is seen in the foreground.

probably accounted for some of the £1,304 6s. 2½d. spent on running costs during that year.[28]

The Home Secretary of State, Thomas Townsend, wrote several letters to the Mayor of Deal from Whitehall. On 1 June 1784 he wrote that 'violent outrages have lately been committed by some smugglers at Deal against His Majesty's Officers, particularly in their firing at the Boats of His Majesty's Sloops *Scout* and *Wasp* ... employed in intercepting some Boats which were bringing on shore unaccustomed [illicit] Goods from East India ships .... in the Downs'. He warned the Mayor not to permit a repetition of such 'daring outrages' and berates the local civil authorities for their slackness, hinting at some collusion with the smugglers. The Military, he believed, should have been promptly called in when the trouble threatened to get out of hand. A seaman on board the *Scout* had been dangerously wounded. Later correspondence, dated 18 August 1784, from the Home Secretary to the Mayor of Dover is considerably friendlier than his earlier letters. He was placated by the Mayor's assurances of co-operation with Government and expressions of future zeal in its service. The steps that the Deal civil authorities had taken in an attempt to identify the transgressors had impressed Whitehall. This correspondence provides background to the episode in December 1784 when Prime Minister Pitt despatched troops to burn every Deal lugger drawn up on shore, while naval cutters vigilantly patrolled off shore to ensure that none escaped. The letters reflect the Government's growing impatience with aggressive smuggling activities around Deal and they form a prelude to the strong action taken in December 1784 in which Henry Jelly, Commander of the *Tartar*, earned the gratitude of the Customs Commissioners.[29]

On 30 December 1784 Henry wrote a letter to the Customs Board urging it to continue concerted operations to counter large-scale smuggling off the Kentish coast.[30] These events are probably commemorated on a silver cup, in the possession of a Worthington descendant,[31] which bears the inscription:

> Mr Henry Jelly
> Commander of the TARTAR Cutter
> Presented
> By order of the
> Commissioners of his Majesty's CUSTOMS
> In Testimony
> of their Appreciation of an important Service
> Rendered by him
> to the Revenue under their Management
> on the 25 Dec. 1784

On 24 December 1785 Captain Jelly wrote a letter to the Customs Board giving estimates for various articles such as sails, cordage, etc. needed for the *Tartar*.[32] Letters from 1786 survive regarding Captain Jelly's belated delivery of bills transmitted for work on the *Tartar* and goods. On 21 June 1786 Captain Jelly wrote to the Board wishing to resign from his employment 'on account of his age and ill health'.[33] His story continues in Chapter 4–The Jelly Story.

In 1785 a seizure of contraband black tea was credited to Benjamin Worthington, E. Mowle and E. Columbine. Notice is taken of another seizure by Benjamin Worthington in a letter to the Board dated 14 August 1786,[34] just prior to his promotion to Commander of the *Tartar*.

Chapter 3

Commander Benjamin Jelly Worthington
of the *Tartar* Cutter

On 24 August 1786 the Customs Board received a letter reporting the qualifications of Benjamin and nominating him to replace Henry Jelly as Commander of the *Tartar*. The letter, written by Henry, stated that Benjamin was '24 years of age, he is at present 2nd Mate of the said Cutter in which capacity he has acted two years and is active and capable of performing the duty of the offices to which he is nominated'.[1] Benjamin was formally appointed Commander of the *Tartar* and took up his duties on 2 September 1786. By 10 October he had still not received a set of uniform buttons, an indicator of his rank.[2]

In 1786, by Act 26 Geo. III. c. 40, section 27, it was made lawful for any Commander of any of His Majesty's vessels of war, or any officer by them authorised, to make seizures without a deputation or commission from the Commissioners of Customs. Under the same Act, craft had to be licensed in an effort to prevent smuggling.[3] Quite often the luggers and cutters engaged in the running of goods endeavoured to evade the penalties by possessing foreign colours and ship's papers. Most of these craft and their masters belonged to Deal, Folkestone and other south coast ports of England. For the purpose of evading English law they became burghers of Ostend, despite the fact they could not speak Dutch or French, had very English sounding names and English crew.

In a letter dated 14 October 1786 Benjamin requested two new rowing boats for use on the *Tartar* estimated to cost £32 1s. 6d. In November the same year he reported damage to the cutter received at sea. In March the following year Benjamin described how 'a gale of wind on the 10th instant carried away the *Tartar's* chain plates'. On 20 August 1787 he sought permission for cleaning and painting the *Tartar* 'against the ensuing Winter'.

Benjamin Marries

On 9 January 1787 Benjamin married Elizabeth Collins the daughter of a wealthy brewer, by licence, at St Mary's, Dover. Elizabeth was described as a spinster and a minor and her father, Knight Knight Collins, consented to the marriage. Witnesses at the wedding were the groom's three sisters, Ann Horn, Elizabeth Gorely and Hester Reynolds.[4]

Children of Benjamin Jelly and Elizabeth Worthington

Elizabeth Worthington was a strong, capable woman who raised her family primarily on her own. Her sea-faring husband spent most of their married life at sea in the employ of the Customs Department and enjoyed only brief visits on shore. Benjamin

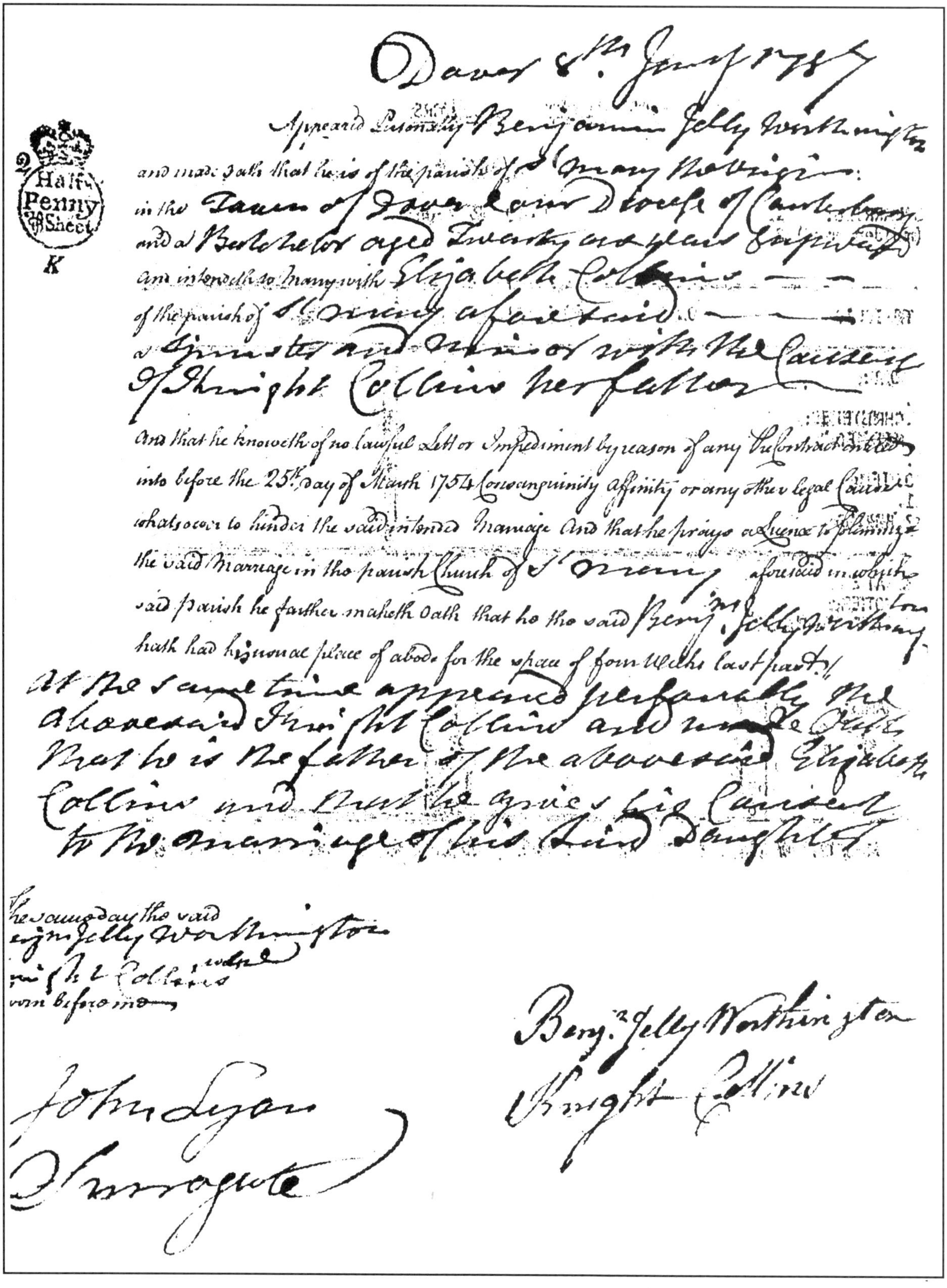

Dover 8th Jan[ry] 1787

Appeared [personally] Benjamin Jelly Worthington
and made oath that he is of the parish of St mary the virgin
in the Town of Dover and Diocese of Canterbury
and a Bachelor aged Twenty one years [upwards]
and intendeth to marry with Elizabeth Collins ————
of the parish of St [mary] aforesaid ——————————
a Spinster and [minor] [or] with the consent
of Knight Collins her father ————————

And that he knoweth of no lawful Lett or Impediment by reason of any Precontract entered
into before the 25th day of March 1754 Consanguinity affinity or any other legal Cause
whatsoever to hinder the said intended Marriage And that he prays a Licence to solemnize
the said Marriage in the parish Church of St [mary] aforesaid in which
said parish he farther maketh Oath that he the said Benj[n] Jelly Worthington
hath had his usual place of abode for the space of four Weeks last past ./

At the same time appeared personally the
abovesaid Knight Collins and made Oath
That he is the father of the abovesaid Elizabeth
Collins and that he gives his Consent
to the marriage of his said daughter

The same day the said
Benj[n] Jelly Worthington
Knight Collins [were]
[sworn] before me

John Lyon
Surrogate

Benj[n] Jelly Worthington
Knight Collins

31 Marriage allegation for Benjamin Jelly Worthington and Elizabeth Collins.

32 Marriage licence for Benjamin Jelly Worthington and Elizabeth Collins.

33 Elizabeth Collins, wife of Commander B.J. Worthington.

and Elizabeth lived in the village of Charlton and had 10 children who were all baptised at St Mary's, Dover: Elizabeth (1788-1828), Benjamin (1790-1852), Mary Ann (1792-1801), Harriot (1794-1861), Charlotte (1796-1861), Hester (1798-1871), William Collins (1800-85), Thomas Knight (1802-56), Henry (1803-66), George (1807-08).

Charlton

Charlton Green was the old centre of Charlton village, which by 1907 had merged into Dover town. It is believed to have extended from Charlton church as far down the riverside as Peter Street and to where the backs of the houses on Salisbury Road and Albert Road mark the limits of the Dover Castle estate. How this green, which was presumably the rectorial manor, became covered with houses and gardens is a problem which might have been solved if the records of the manor were available for that part of the reign of Henry VIII. The piece of riverside land called Charlton Green was separated at an early date from the Castle lands and Maison Dieu lands, and the manors of Charlton and Buckland that surrounded it.[5]

One famous feature of Charlton Green was its pump, which appears to have existed for the supply of spring water ever since pumps came into use. When Dover first became a fashionable seaside resort in about 1817, Charlton Green was regarded as one of the prettiest places in the area. The houses stood back from the road and the gardens between were carefully kept, most of them being occupied by famous tulip beds, which in the summer time were protected by awnings. Other fragrant flowers were cultivated in profusion and rows of beehives showing the busy honey gatherers at work were a great source of interest. The locality continued to maintain these attractions until about 1840 when the green began to lose its rusticity. The Worthington family had moved to other parts of Dover by this time.[6]

During September 1787 Captain Worthington was ordered to the Nore at the mouth of the river Medway, where he was to await instructions from the Collector of Customs at Rochester. The *Tartar* was not in port at the time the order came, and upon her return to Dover, Benjamin related how she had lost her larboard shrouds in stormy conditions at sea, a mishap which obliged him to come into the port of Dover during October to effect the necessary repairs.[7] While in port Benjamin requested a commission be granted to James Ridley, prospective Mate of the *Tartar* in place of Alex Watson who was dismissed.[8]

34   Charlton church in Dover. An engraving by Kershaw and Son, London.

In September 1788 Benjamin submitted two surgeon's bills for payment by the Customs Board for John Newsome and John Graham, two Mariners who were wounded in the course of their duty aboard the *Tartar*.

In January 1789 Benjamin stated he had rented a storehouse at a cost of £4 per annum for the purpose of depositing materials which he considered necessary for the service of the *Tartar* therein, and would like reimbursement of the rent. The Commissioners dealt with the matter of the storehouse hired without their permission from 10 October 1786, by approving the arrangement but informing the Collector that he was 'strictly to enjoin Captain Worthington not to incur any standing expense or any incidental charge exceeding 40 shillings in future without obtaining our previous Orders for that purpose'.[9]

During the early part of 1789 Benjamin had extra leave of six days granted to him by the Board, in addition to leave granted to him by the Collectors of Western Ports.[10]

A letter was sent to Benjamin on the directions of the Commissioners, dated 27 March 1789, with an enclosed copy of 'information received by them respecting certain frauds intended to be committed by a Smuggling Cutter called the *Lyon* belonging to Hastings, Saul Bevil, owner and Master'. They directed Benjamin 'to keep a good look out for and endeavour to prevent and detect the said Frauds. And in case you should capture the said vessel, I am directed to apprise you, in order that you may be upon your guard, that it is understood the crew mean to surrender quietly; but to avail themselves of the first opportunity to seizing on the crew of any

35   The interior of Old Charlton church.

such Revenue Cutter as may take them together with their arms, in order to re-take the vessel and cargo'. The letter was signed 'J.G.'.[11]

By June 1789 Benjamin had informed his employers that the *Tartar* was in a leaky condition and requested permission to carry out caulking, cleaning and painting work upon her.[12]

Benjamin was asked in April 1790 by the Customs Office at Dover to account in writing for certain kinds of unauthor-ised expenditure; his letter was to be sent to the Board.[13] Three months later Ben-jamin expressed the need for a six-oared galley boat and by August declared the *Tartar* again required caulking and paint-ing.[14] By November 1790 Benjamin was seeking reimbursement for the cost of the men he had victualled on board the *Tartar*.[15]

The name of Benjamin Worthington, 'Commander of the Tartar Cutter' and John Andrews, 'Mate of the Tartar Cut-ter' can be found on the list of those who contributed to the Superannuation Fund in the service of the Customs at the Port of Dover, 19 April 1791.[16]

In a letter dated 9 September 1791 Captain Worthington states the necessity of refitting the *Tartar*'s rigging and painting her outsides 'before the ensuing Winter', and warns that the vessel 'is very much in want of a new mainsail, foresail and third jib'.[17]

The Worthington Telescope

George III (1738-1820) was King of England from 1760. Much of his reign was spent in conflict with the Whigs in Parliament who had become entrenched under his father's rule. Ironically he became the American colonists' principal symbol of Eng-lish oppression although in fact Whig policy was responsible for their discontent. When Napoleon threatened England George visited the Kent coast to inspect the arrangements for keeping out any French invasion. He did all he could to encourage the raising of a large army of Cinque Ports volunteers under William Pitt, his Prime Minister.[18] Before the onset of insanity in his later years George III was a well-meaning ruler in a time of great stress abroad and at home.

The *Kentish Gazette* of Friday 11 November 1791 reported that 'Payn's Hotel at Dover is engaged for the Duke and Duchess of York, to be in readiness by the 17 instant'. On the following Tuesday (15 November) it was reported that 'His Royal Highness the Duke of York with his Consort are hourly expected at Dover. Captain

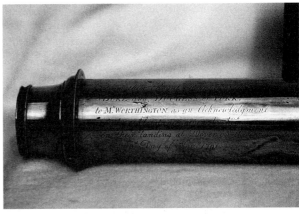

36 Benjamin Knight Worthington, son of Garth John Worthington, holding the telescope, *c.*1984.

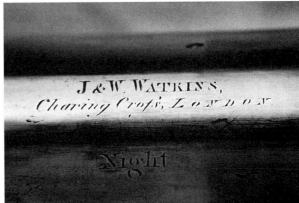

37 The Worthington telescope inscribed 'Presented to Mr Worthington by their Royal Highnesses the Duke and Duchess of York in appreciation of his assistance at their landing at Dover 18th November 1791'. The telescope was made by Jeremiah and Walter Watkins, Mathematical and Philosophical Instrument Makers to His Royal Highness the Duke of Clarence, Charing Cross, London.

Radcliffe, who is now waiting at Calais, brings them over. His Royal Highness on his landing will refresh himself at York House, Dover.'

Frederick, Duke of York, was King George III's second son, and had married Princess Frederica, Princess Royal of Prussia, in Berlin on 29 September 1791. A second marriage service was performed after they arrived in London at The Queen's House (now Buckingham Palace) on 23 November. On Friday 18 November the *Kentish Gazette* had reported under 'London News' that 'the immediate expectation of the Duke and Duchess of York is apparent in the arrival of the six princesses in town. The three youngest very seldom leave Windsor and are now certainly at Buckingham Palace for the purpose of receiving their new sister-in-law. The Duchess of York, who is now for much an object of curiosity has just passed her birthday. She was born on the first of November 1774'.[19]

The Duke of York landed at Dover with his bride, Frederica, on 18 November 1791, and spent the night there before travelling on to London the following day. A day later the newspaper reported that 'yesterday [18th] between eleven and twelve o'clock their Royal Highnesses the Duke and Duchess of York arrived here from Calais after a rough and unpleasant passage of more than seven hours. On their landing they were saluted by the Cannon from the Batteries and received on the beach by the 14th Regiment of Foot, now quartered in the Castle, under the Command of Colonel D'Oylie and conducted amidst a prodigious concourse of people to the York Hotel'.

The *Kentish Gazette* which published the letter continued, 'They came over in the *Minerva* packet, Captain Hammond. Her Royal Highness was so much indisposed with fatigue and fear that she fainted in going upon deck and was put nearly lifeless in a chair into the boat waiting to bring them ashore, it being low water, and from the shore she was carried in the same chair by men to the inn; but receiving some refreshment and going to bed she was happily so far recovered this morning as to be able to pursue her journey towards London.'

Another report to the newspaper, printed on 19 November, stated that, 'Their Royal Highnesses the Duke and Duchess of York were attended by Colonel St. Leger and Sir Sydney Smith. They were received at the York Hotel by the Lord Warden of the Cinque Ports, the Lieutenant Governor of Dover Castle, Lord North, Lady Guilford, Lady Ann, and the Hon. Miss North, H. Banbury Esq.; the officers of the Garrisons and those of the 14th Regiment of Foot.' On Friday 2 December 1791 the *Kentish Gazette* printed a statement: 'We have authority to say, that the report of his Royal Highness the Duke of York's having left a sum of money to be distributed in the garrison at Chatham on his way through Rochester, is untrue, and never customary upon such occasions.' There was obviously a rumour which needed dispelling at the time!

A telescope inscribed as follows: 'Presented to Mr Worthington by their Royal Highnessess the Duke and Duchess of York in appreciation of his assistance at their landing at Dover 18th November 1791' still survives.[20] A brass plaque bearing the Royal Coat of Arms is inserted in the lid of the wooden box in which it is housed.[21]

On 21 November 1791 the baggage belonging to the Duke and Duchess of York was sent by Dover wagon under the seal of the Customs Office to London. The baggage, which had been transported from Calais in the *King George* and *Minerva* passage vessels, landed in Dover on 18 November and consisted of 'five trunks, five boxes, two cafes, two bales, and one bag'.[22]

Sharing the Spoils

Before 1790 there had been a diversity of practice in the method of sharing seized smuggled goods. After the deduction of expenses, profits were shared between the Captain and crew. During November 1791 there was some dispute between the Officers and Mariners of the *Tartar* with their Captain, Benjamin Worthington, over his sharing of the spoils from a large boat called the *Rambler*. Laden with tea and spirits, she had been seized with the help of Captain Dobbins of the *Nimble*.[23] The *Nimble* and the *Tartar* often worked together to intercept smuggling boats from France, with both crews sharing the seizures. On this occasion, Benjamin had not consulted the *Tartar* crew members. In reply to a letter from the Customs Office, however, Benjamin wrote:

> Gentlemen,
> In answer to your letter of the 18 inst, requesting me to deliver to you an account of Sums of money I may have remaining in my Hand of Seizures unclaimed from the time of my commission into the Service with the Circumstances thereof as to the Seizures from Whence they have arisen and to specify the Names and Descriptions of the Persons to whom such Money is due.
> I beg leave to acquaint you that all the Seizures that I have brought to this Port, the Division has been made at the Office and I have received my Part as Commander only. Seizures that have been delivered at other Ports when the Money has become due, I have received the Cutters part and divided the same amongst the Officers and Mariners entitled agreeable to their Honors Order of Sharing therefore I have no money remaining in my Hands whatever.
> I am gentlemen
> B.J. Worthington

During December 1791 the *Tartar* made application to the Customs Commissioners for a new bower anchor, the old one having been lost in the Downs during strong gales.

Benjamin acted as an intelligence officer while at sea, reporting the movement of various ships and their complements of carriage, guns and men.[24] A letter written at sea on 7 February 1792 stated:

> Gentlemen,
> I beg you will inform their honours that I have received authentic intelligence that the *Spider* commonly called the *Morning Rattler*, Kennedy Scout, Master, a lugger carrying about twelve carriage guns with 46 men sailed from Ostend on the 5th instant at eleven at night, wind at s.s.w. having on board a large cargo of spirits and tobacco which it is supposed is meant to be run on the n.w. part of Scotland or Ireland. The same lugger was seen off Gravelin in France about half past two in the afternoon of the following day, proceeding to the westward and from the westerly winds we have had since I think she cannot have got far down channel.
> I am gentlemen
> Your most humble servant
> B.J. Worthington

Unfortunately it is not known whether Benjamin's letter reached its destination in time to intercept this possible smuggling voyage.

A letter from Henry Jelly, late Commander of the *Tartar*, dated 27 March 1792 appeals on behalf of Mr. Thomas Chapman, Mariner, who was never rewarded for his part in the seizure of 58 leards of spirits at Newhaven on 25 September 1785. There is no report of the outcome of this very belated request, which was forwarded to the Newhaven Collector of Customs.

On 30 March 1792 Benjamin replied to a letter received from the Customs Commissioners regarding his responsibilities and the scope of his anti-smuggling operations stating:

> Gentlemen,
> In obedience to their Honours letter to me of the 20th instant I request you will lay before them the following particulars. The station of the *Tartar* Cutter under my command extends from The Gore[25] to Beachy Head, her complement consists of myself, the mate, two deputed, thirteen other mariners and a boy making on the whole eighteen. Her boats are a six oared galley, a six oared boat and a four oared boat which is chiefly used in the Harbour to carry necessaries on board the cutter. Smuggling upon this and the Sussex coast is principally carried on in open Luggers from about eight to eighteen tons burthen. The Cutter being a large object can be seen in the night at a considerable distance, when the smugglers by lowering the sails of the Luggers render them such small objects as not to be concerned and thus they very often escape. From this reason it happens the seizures are generally made by the Cutters boats as we always take care in the daytime to keep the Cutter out of sight of the place to which we mean to send the boat by night to prevent the smugglers suspecting our intentions. When a boat is sent along shore she is manned with an officer and six men from the present complement. The Cutter cannot be kept cruising and is not safe if more than one boat is sent from her at a time. It appears to me that it would considerably increase the chance of making seizures if the complement was sufficient to allow two boats being manned and sent from her at one time and I conceive that four men added to the present complement of the *Tartar* would enable me to send two boats and there would then be seven men and a boy left on board which is sufficient to keep the Cutter cruising, provide for her safety in the case which often happens of sudden bad weather coming on. I am gentlemen, B.J.W.[26]

Concealing the goods

Smuggling vessels had ingeniously contrived hiding places built in, called conceal-ments. It was said there was hardly a craft from barque to dinghy which was not modified to suit the requirements of the trade. Shrimping nets, oars and spars even had hollowed handles to accommodate a long tin can which could contain several pints of spirit. Kegs of spirits could be secreted under the bottom of smacks in a thin contemporary casing. Open boats were also found with double bottoms. Cases of eggs sent from Jersey were fitted with false sides in which silks were smuggled; trawlers engaged in sinking tubs of spirits; a dog kennel which washed ashore was fitted with a false top to hold 30 pounds of tobacco; and clothing such as waistcoats, stays or drawers could be stuffed with tea.[27] These are a few examples of the ingen-ious ways smugglers attempted to evade detection by the Customs Officers.

More letters written by Benjamin to the Commissioners in the early months of 1792 find him applying for a new bowsprit in place of the existing one, which 'is very much sprung' and he volunteered information on the dimensions of the bowsprit. He also requested a new six-oared boat in place of the *Tartar*'s customary one, which was 'upwards of four years (old) and has been continuously employed'. By August 1792, the cutter needed painting, her deck needed caulking, and her rigging needed repair before the onset of winter.[28]

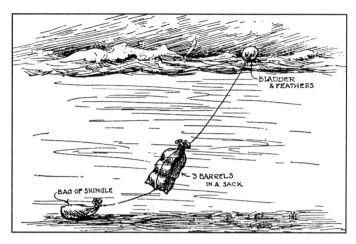

38 The Sandwich device. A smuggling technique in which a bag of shingle acted as sinker, and the bladder kept the sack floating.

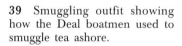

39 Smuggling outfit showing how the Deal boatmen used to smuggle tea ashore.

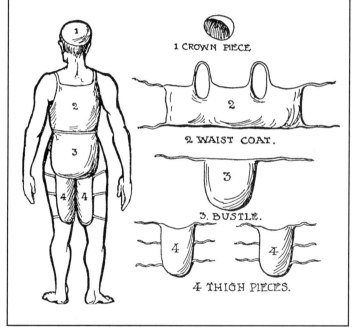

40 Methods employed by smugglers for anchoring tubs thrown overboard.

On 4 September 1792 Benjamin wrote to the Customs Office expressing his concern about why cargo of 240 bags of tobacco and snuff seized from a French lugger, the *Saint Pierre*, on 22 January 1790 by the *Tartar* in conjunction with another cutter, the *Swan*, commanded by Francis Jarman, had remained so long in His Majesty's warehouse that the quality of the goods could deteriorate.[29] Quite often goods seized were deposited in His Majesty's warehouse in Dover where they could languish for a couple of years before being disposed of. As the crew did not benefit from the seizures until they were auctioned or sold, it was in their interest to ensure that goods such as tobacco did not languish in the warehouse for too long.

Wartime conditions

Up until 1793 England had taken no part in the French Revolution as Prime Minister Pitt was a peace-loving man. It was the French, and not Pitt, who actually made the challenge following the execution of their King for treason in January 1793. In the face of royalist insurrection and foreign hostility, France declared war against Britain on 1 February 1793. Captain Worthington was directed to prevent the French privateers from harassing English trading vessels within his cruising station. By February 1793 Benjamin was appealing again for more crew. One of his Mariners, Stephen Matson/Maston, was sick and Benjamin was 'obliged to leave him on shore'. The French privateers carried from 25-40 men and greatly outnumbered the crew of his cutter, so 'in order to put the Cutter in a state of acting both offensively and defensively' he had engaged five more men, 'the whole of the crew now being 22 men and boy which will be a much more equal match to the Privateers which we may probably

41 (*above*) A cutter charging a smuggling boat and striking her on the quarter.

42 (*right*) Combat between smugglers and cutter crews was not uncommon.

have to encounter with. Be assured Gentleman that nothing but the extreme urgency of the occasion could induce me to take such a step without the Honourable Boards order and trust their Honors will not disapprove of the same ...'[30]

By March parts of the 19-year-old *Tartar* were showing signs of wear. The vessel was leaky and in need of extensive repairs to her bottom. Benjamin advised that she be equipped with a new hull.[31] She was given a new deck, four tons of iron ballast, new sails and other materials. On 18 November 1793 he listed necessary supplies for the use of the new *Tartar*: boarding pikes, muskets, pistols and barrels of gunpowder.[32]

A letter from Benjamin dated 27 August 1793 complained to the Board that the high wages given to seamen employed on board the tenders in the service of the Admiralty had meant that he had lost 10 of his mariners to the Navy. He feared that more would leave to seek a better income, and was having trouble replacing those who had left. With a depleted crew he could not use a boat for the *Tartar*'s business, and also faced increased danger when encountering an armed enemy vessel.[33]

Nothing more was heard from Benjamin until 12 April 1794 when he apprehended and subsequently captured a Danish vessel, *Johanna Louisa*, commanded by Peter Jensen Gise, off Folkestone. She was said to be bound for Lisbon in Portugal, but her cargo of wheat was believed to be for France. He had heard that this vessel had taken wheat from Copenhagen to Havre de Grace, Maryland, North America, on her last voyage. The papers of the *Johanna Louisa* were checked and found to be in order.[34]

In order to obtain a Letter of Marque for the *Tartar*, a certificate of description was forwarded following an inspection of the vessel by a John Elwin Tidefurveyn. On 26 May 1794 he stated he had been on board the *Tartar* which was carrying ten two-pound carriage guns. He confirmed that it was a British-built cutter of 100 tons burden or thereabouts, and that Benjamin Worthington was the Commander of a crew of 22 men and one boy, all British subjects. Benjamin obviously overcame his difficulties with obtaining crew and we can assume he was granted a Letter of Marque soon afterwards.

Benjamin Worthington heads the list of Commanders on a chart showing 'An Average Account of Emoluments[35] (arising from the Seizures made at this Port) of each of the Commanders and the Crew of the Vessels in the Service of this Revenue for five Years from 5 January 1794 to 5 January 1799'. He was obviously making a very profitable living, most probably due to his choice of crew which appeared to include family members, and his leadership and business abilities.

Deals from Deal

In February 1795 the *Tartar* was caught on Goodwin Sands and had to be rescued by the people of Deal. The anchor and cable were lost. Compensation of £150 was requested by the people of Deal for their part in this affair and the matter went to arbitration. When anchors were lost in the Downs it was rarely possible to recover them. The men of Deal were renowned for their practice of cutting away an anchor from its cable, only to recover the anchor later and hide it away until they could find an opportunity to dispose of it. The tradesmen's bills for a new anchor and cable amounted to £61 19s. 1d. A letter dated 16 July 1795 was written by the rescuers of Deal:

To the Honorable Commissioners of His Majesty's Customs.

The Humble Petition of John Shewsbury, Longley Barber and William Crisp of Deal, Mariners on behalf of themselves and Everitt Crisp, William Dawes, Wm Middleton, Richard Dawes, Richard Philpott, Richard Robinson, Jno Edwards, Thomas Bailey, Thomas Wilkins, James Barter, Isaac Barber, Leonard Barber, William Durban and Alexander Ollick, Sheweth: That your Petitioners together with the other Persons before setforth are Boatmen at Deal, and on the morning of the 27th day of January last on consequence of hearing guns fired which they supposed to be signals of distress from some vessel on the Goodwin Sands they launched a large boat from Deal Beach in which they all went off and with much difficulty, the wind blowing very hard, a very heavy sea running, and the weather being very thick, reached the Goodwin Sands, when they discovered that the guns had proceeded from the Tartar Cutter in your Honors employ commanded by Captain Worthington, which Cutter was then lying in the Middle of the Sands in a very dangerous situation. That they went alongside her, and by the desire of the Captain put some of their people on board, and when they had got on board and exerted themselves to the utmost of the power and took every measure for the safety of the Cutter, and finding it absolutely necessary cut away the cable by which means they fortunately cleared her off the sands and piloted her the same day in safety into Ramsgate Harbour. That when they had put on board the Cutter such a number of people as was necessary they had the greatest difficulty to clear the sands in the boat, as the weather being very thick they could not discover whether they were at the inner or the outer part of the Sands and several times in going to the Sands and returning, the petitioners and the remainder of their Company were in great danger of losing their lives. That from the situation of the Cutter another badness of the weather at the time your Petitioners reached here they think she was then in great danger and would very probably have been lost had not your Petitioners gone to their assistance. That for the services rendered to the Cutter and the great risk the Petitioners ran of losing their lives they have made a demand of £150 and when it is considered that this sum must be divided into twenty shares they trust your Honors will not think it unreasonable. That most of your Petitioners have large families which they support from their daily earnings and on account of the present high price of provisions they cannot without great difficulty procure them a livelihood and that the sum required by them for their services to the Tartar would now be of great use to them. They therefore humbly pray it is now nearly six months since that circumstance happened that your Honors will take the case into immediate consideration and give an order for their being paid the sum demanded.

And they will ever pray

John Shewsbury, Longley Barber
William Crisp

This matter went before an arbitrator on 27 January 1796 and the Board instructed the Dover Customs House to make a settlement with the Deal boatmen. The Dover House in turn referred the matter to the authority of the Warden of the Cinque Ports, whose representatives judged that the Crown pay the rescuers £140,[36] together with the expenses incidental to the arbitration proceedings, amounting to £151 9s. altogether.[37] It is interesting that William Crisp's name is mentioned in 1801 correspondence in relation to smuggling incidents at Deal.

During the wintry December of 1795 the *Tartar* lost an anchor and part of a cable 'in the late gales'. Benjamin procured another anchor at Portsmouth harbour for £13 16s. 3d. The Board considered the charge to be excessive and the 'Commander is invited to explain it'.[38] Benjamin assured the Board that the charges for the new anchor which he had purchased at Portsmouth dockyard were usual in the circumstances.[39]

The Crew of the *Tartar*, 1795

At Dover on 5 March 1795 Captain Worthington, Commander of the *Tartar*, represented that 14 of his Mariners did not have Protections. These Protections were a documentary form of insurance against impressment, but they were little regarded. During war the Royal Navy resorted to the Press to man its ships. Certain classes of seamen were exempt from the Press, namely seafaring men above 55 years and under 18 years, all who were in their first two years of going to sea, foreigners serving in merchant ships or privateers, and all apprentices for three years.[40] Benjamin wrote, 'We respectfully transmit on the back thereof their names and descriptions and humbly beg your Honors will cause Protections for them to be sent'. When asked why he had not sought Protections for his men sooner, Benjamin replied, 'I have not till this time had a fixed complement and the men were continually changing but there is now a probability of those I have staying with me.'[41] These men were:

> Thomas Read, 42 years, 5 feet 5 and a half inches, fair complexion, short curled hair bald on the forepart, grey eyes with dark eyebrows. Entered 23 May 1794.
>
> John Read, 30 years, 5 feet 5 inches high, dark complexion, dark tied hair, hazel eyes and dark eyebrows. Entered 5 November 1793.
>
> John Walton, 32 years of age, 5 feet 7 inches high, dark complexion marked with the small pox, dark tied hair, hazel eyes with lightish eyebrows. Entered January 1795.
>
> Robert Hopper, 23 years of age, 5 feet 6 and a half inches high, dark complexion, dark tied hair, dark blue eyes and dark eyebrows. Entered December 1793.
>
> Thomas Hatwell, 21 years of age, 5 feet 6 and a half inches high, fair complexion, short brown hair, grey eyes and light eyebrows. Entered 10 October 1794.
>
> James Spearpoint, 21 years of age, 5 feet 5 and a half inches high, dark complexion marked with the small pox, brown hair curled, grey eyes and dark eyebrows. Entered 10 October 1794.
>
> Henry Kemp, 25 years of age, 5 feet 5 inches high, fair complexion, short brown hair curled, blue eyes and lightish eyebrows. Entered 14 December 1794.
>
> James McKever, 28 years of age, 5 feet 5 inches high, dark complexion has a scar on his upper lip, dark tied hair, hazel eyes and light eyebrows. Entered 10 October 1794.
>
> Henry Scoats, 30 years of age, 5 feet 7 and a half inches high, dark complexion, dark tied hair, hazel eyes with dark eyebrows. Entered 5 November 1793.
>
> John Trevanion Wellard, 21 years of age, 5 feet 7 inches high, dark complexion, dark brown hair tied, dark eyes with dark thick eyebrows. Entered 24 September 1794.
>
> James Luckhurst, 19 years of age, 5 feet 4 and a half inches high, light fresh complexion, brown hair curled, hazel eyes with light eyebrows. Entered 21 October 1794.
>
> Thomas Maycock, 23 years of age, 5 feet 7 and a half inches high, fair complexion, light sandy hair curled, blue eyes with light sandy eyebrows. Entered 11 December 1793.
>
> Thomas Harvey, 22 years of age, 5 feet 7 and a half inches high, fair complexion, light sandy hair tied, grey eyes with light eyebrows. Entered 14 December 1794.
>
> Thomas Mummery, 20 years of age, 5 feet 8 inches high, fair complexion, freckled face, short brown hair, grey eyes with brown eyebrows. Entered 10 October 1793.

There were times when the *Tartar* was seconded by the Navy, and temporary cruisers had to be employed by Benjamin and his crew. John Andrews, Chief Mate of the *Tartar*, directed the cruiser during one of these episodes.[42]

43   A Buck print showing Dover town on the right of Granville Dock. St Mary's Church spire can be seen on the right.

The Customs Board kept a tight control over the activities of the Customs vessels and crews. An example of its exactness is illustrated in an extract of a letter dated 2 April 1796 to Captain Benjamin Jelly Worthington: 'They direct you to report on what day you boarded the *Nancy* Cutter of Folkestone and what part of the coast for further consideration and directions. P.S. As well as the day you are to state the time of the day.' The Board appeared very anxious to learn every detail of the *Tartar*'s operation against the *Nancy* on 17 March and also wanted to know whether any goods were on board. The Dover Collector was also instructed to pay Benjamin the sum of £8 3s. 6¼d., the Commander's share of the proceeds of a cutter seized by him on the 16th and carried into Newhaven, as well as the further sum of £8, 'being the rate of 10 shillings for the same'.[43]

Folkestone Fracas

A report by Benjamin dated 7 December 1796 recounts a confrontation at Folkestone between the crews of the *Tartar* and *Lively* Customs cutters, and the Excise cutter *Badger*:

> Gentlemen,
> Being on a cruise in the *Tartar* cutter under my command having reason to suspect that a boat with spirits was expected to run her cargo in the neighbourhood of

Folkstone [sic] in the night of the 4th instant. I agreed with Captain Ridge of the *Badger* Excise Cutter to send our boats along shore to act in conjunction between one and two o'clock the following morning. The boats fell in with a smuggling lugger off Folkstone which they chased on shore at that place and got entire possession of her with her cargo consisting of several hundred half ankers of spirits and soon after they were joined by a boat belonging to the *Lively* Cutter, Captain Smith, they accordingly got an anchor out for the purpose of heaving her off, but there being a swell on the shore the anchor came home. She fell broadside to the beach then immediately a large body of smugglers armed with muskets honed two cannon or trivels commenced a firing on the boats which was returned by them for some time till one of the crew of the *Tartar*'s boat, Henry Baker was wounded by a musket ball in the shoulder when finding that a further attempt to secure the whole of the seizure was ineffectual the number of the smugglers being great the firing kept up by them so much of the luggers cargo as the time and circumstance would admit and which they effected to the number of 173 casks. In the morning about 7 o'clock the officer commanding the *Tartar*'s boat Jno Graham came on board the *Tartar* off Folkstone (he having just come from the westward where she had been the whole of the night cruising in by the Bay) reported the circumstances before stated and that the lugger was then on shore on Folkstone beach that about 8 o'clock Captain Ridge came on board the *Tartar* when we agreed to go on shore and retake possession of the lugger *Endeavour* to launch her and bring her into Dover Harbour. It is necessary here to state that the lugger was never totally out of possession as the boats kept near the spot till the arrival of the cutters to prevent her being got away–on our landing at Folkstone we found that Mr Francis Andrews, Chief Boatman there, had taken possession of the lugger and informed us that he had seized her, that he was present during the whole transaction of the firing and had seized between 50 and 60 casks, part of her cargo. It appears extremely strange that Mr Andrews should not have made himself known to either of the officers commanding the boats till after the firing had ceased that he should be able single and on shore alone, or at most attended by one more boatman to seize so great a number of casks while the seizure could not be maintained by the boat's crews consisting of 23 armed men and more particularly so, as he declares, which is a very strange circumstance that not one of the smugglers were known to him. During the time the smugglers were firing at the boat's crews of the cutters the *Queen* armed tender in H.M. Service was laying close to the shore for the purpose of being hove up at Folkstone beach to be repaired; to her the boat belonging to the *Lively* went to apply for assistance, before they could get alongside a person on board the said cutter hailed them and told them to keep off or they would give them the contents of their guns. The name of the lugger is the *Bee* of Folkstone and is about 40 tons burthen, the officer of the *Badger* being first onboard the lugger, the 173 casks before mentioned have been delivered into the charge of the Excise.

Tartar Cutter, Dover
B.J. Worthington[44]

Subsequent investigations found Benjamin's testimony to be correct. The crewmen were commended for their bravery in repelling the attack. Mr. Andrews was criticised for being aboard the lugger and not making himself known until after the firing had ceased. The inquiry could find no collusion between the smugglers and the Officers. It also failed to find the person on board the *Queen* who threatened to fire on the boat's crew if they did not desist firing upon the people on the shore.

Customs administration

The coast of England and Wales was divided into three districts, each under an Inspecting Commander. Certain stations were also allotted to commanders of the cruisers within each district. Amongst those Revenue cutters stationed at Kent in 1797 was: *Tartar*, crew 23, Tons 100, Guns 10, Commander B.J. Worthington, cruising station–The Gore to Beachy Head.[45]

The Board of Commissioners instructed their Collectors and Controllers 'to observe that one material object of the duty imposed upon the inspecting Commanders is to see that the cruisers are constantly and regularly on their stations, unless prevented by some necessary and unavoidable cause, and with their proper complements of men and boats, and if they are off their station or in port personally to examine into the occasion of their being so, and that they are absent from their station no longer than is essentially requisite'.[46]

The Inspecting Commanders reported to the Board of Customs at the end of every year on the conduct of the Officers within their district, what goods were smuggled, whether smuggling was on the increase or decrease, and where it occurred. Goods which were liable to heavy duties on importation from any country to another were often smuggled. Apart from tobacco, snuff, alcohol and tea, which were smuggled in large quantities, other goods included apparel, wrought brass, copper and iron hardware, cottons, glass, cabinet ware, haberdashery, hats, gold and silver lace, thread, bullion, millinery, stained paper, pottery, manufactured leather, silk manufactures and tin plates. Jno Elwin reported that

> On searching the *Duchess of Cumberland* of Dover, James White Master with passengers, baggage and merchandize from Calais on the 16 March 1792 after the said merchandize was landed I found concealed under the Run the following goods, viz. 3 pieces 52 yards of Lawn, 2 pieces 28 yards of Book Muslin, 6 pair Silk Stockings, 11 silk Handkerchiefs stitched, 3 pair of Silk Shoes, 2 pieces 20 yards of Black Silk, 6 silk waistcoats, 3 remnants of Muslin Embroided and a small parcel of Thread and Laces, 23 pieces of Lawn stitched for Dresses, 16 Lawn Handkerchiefs stitched, 16 Snuff Boxes and a parcel of Drugs, which I seized on account of their being concealed and not being on the manifest nor reported.[47]

In 1820 the preventive work in England was divided into different areas: part was performed by naval cruisers, under command of the Admirals at Plymouth, Portsmouth and Sheerness; part by the Coast Blockade, a force under Admiralty control; part by the Revenue cruisers, originally under the Boards of Customs and Excise, but later placed under the Admiralty; part by preventive boats, formerly under Customs, later placed under the Treasury under the command of the Preventive Controller-General; part by riding-officers still under the Customs and assisted by small bodies of soldiers; and part by a few of the old preventive smacks which still did duty at the mouth of the Thames and at several outports. The last three branches were paid out of the Customs.

Mutiny

Trouble began early in January 1797 when Benjamin was requesting layer guns.[48] In June 1797 he was instructed to prevent vessels from conducting 'mutinous ships' down the Channel. The same year witnessed two naval mutinies: the first took place at the Nore, a sandbank at the mouth of the Thames, and the second was at Spithead, a channel between the Isle of Wight and the mainland forming part of the Portsmouth anchorages. He sent a pilot's bill of £12 12s. for his services from 11 to 16 June. On 16 April 1797 Admiral Bridport's crews, while remaining perfectly quiet and orderly, had refused to set sail. They asked that their pay be raised to 1s. a day and that they get it regularly. The Admiralty granted their requests and promised a free pardon, but there were delays in carrying out the promises. The men grew suspicious, thought they were being cheated, and mutinied again. This time they seized some of the Officers but there was no violence. When they were convinced their grievances were being redressed, they put to sea loyally. The mutiny on the Nore had been a more revolutionary agitation aroused by a man of bad reputation, Richard Parker, who had encouraged insurrection and desertion. He was later hanged from the yardarm of the *Sandwich*.[49]

Later that month Benjamin was requested to give assistance to a Captain Sharp and search 'the passage vessels that ply between this port and Calais in order to detect the importation of forged Bank Notes'. He was extremely displeased by this change of duty and wrote stating 'that at the present moment smuggling is more brisk than it has been for some time past' and that other ports and vessels were involved in this activity besides Dover. It was easy for the Dutch fishing boats which carried turtles to the London markets to import false bank notes, and passengers to conceal them on their bodies, therefore making detection very difficult. He also stated that his

44 Cutters at the Quay, Dover. An 1839 engraving by artist George Shepherd.

crew would suffer from loss of revenue, as there was no reward to be made by seizures of bank notes.

He was probably not compelled to carry out his new duties under Captain Sharp as the *Kentish Gazette*, 4 September 1798, reported that 'Another lugger with upwards of 800 half ankers is likewise sent into this port by Captain Benjamin Worthington of the *Tartar* Custom-house Cutter, which he captured after a chase of twenty-four hours'.[50]

In October 1798 the *Tartar* was refitted at Deptford. Benjamin took sufficient paint and oil to paint the cutter's new mast, hull and stern lockers. A new four-oared boat (22-feet long, breadth 5 feet 6 inches) was required as the old one built by Simon Walker three years earlier for £12 18s. had been worn out by service and decay.

Benjamin was very active in public affairs and the Dover Corporation Accounts for 1798-9 record, 'In this year the accounts were first officially called the accounts of the Chamberlains'. James Lamb and Benjamin Jelly Worthington were the Chamberlains and William King, a shipbuilder, was the Mayor.

A letter dated 26 October 1797 endorsed an application by the Mate and three Mariners to receive their due share of the seizure made by the *Tartar* in their absence, saying that 'they were sent onshore by me being incapable of duty'. John Graham reports that Captain Worthington was on board the cutter at the time he made a seizure of spirits on the 16th of last month and that Michael Marden, John Wellard and Richard Cloke had complained of being sick before being sent ashore.[51]

During 1798 the *Tartar* was refitted again at a cost of £140 6s. 7d. and a new half cable of 60 fathoms was acquired for £31 15s. In answer to a petitioner, Benjamin declared he had every reason to believe that a chest of arms was thrown overboard from the *Ann* and, being convinced that the *Ann* had been 'continually employed in the smuggling line', he was induced to seize her.[52]

The *Tartar*'s Victualling

Benjamin regularly had trouble obtaining reimbursement for the costly victualling of his vessel, and appears to have patiently and politely persisted in reminding the Board, by correspondence, of their duty until they obliged.

He was permitted to give an account to the Board of his losses sustained in victualling the crew of the *Tartar* from 5 July 1796, but could not produce all the evidence, as 'a great part' of his records had been lost at sea. He was unable to show vouchers to match expenditure, 'but it has always been the custom of this Port to allow the crew of the Cutter a stated quota of provisions, the same in the Harbour as at sea'. Benjamin added that the *Tartar* was victualled for five weeks when she sailed from England on 2 November last. He therefore made an account up to December.

In September 1799 Benjamin wrote to the Customs Commissioners reporting

> that this part of the coast between the South Foreland and Dungeness is continually infested with French privateers, treble the number within the last month or two that has been during the war, the destruction to our trade has been very considerable. The *Tartar* is 101 tons, her complement of men twenty-two and a boy, which number I find is not sufficient for a vessel of the size to act properly against those of the enemy which have on board from thirty to sixty men as when our great guns are manned with a sufficient number there is not more than three or four left to the small arms to attend the sheets. It is often the case that one man or two is left sick on shore.

45 Account showing the prices and quantities of provisions expended on board the *Tartar*, 1795.

46 The *Ship Inn* at Rye, Sussex, showing under the sign a list of Revenue cutters including the *Tartar.*

Benjamin went on to beg the Board for four more crew, making the total complement 26 men and a boy, 'which will be but an equal establishment to those cutters nearly her size, and will be the means of defeating the enemy more effectually in case of falling in with them.

In a letter dated 14 September 1799 Benjamin asked that the contraband of 240 bags of tobacco and snuff bound for Kentish shores, which the *Tartar* and *Swan* cutters had seized from a French lugsail boat in January 1790, be condemned. Cutter crews could not receive their commission for smuggled goods until their auction or destruction. Benjamin knew the 1790 capture had not been condemned already as the French Ambassador had submitted a claim for the goods. As England was at war with France in 1799 he doubted the French application would be renewed and urged the Board therefore to condemn the cargo for the benefit of the *Tartar* and *Swan* crews. He hoped the Board would agree that the French claim was fraudulent and made 'open at the instigation of the British smuggler whose property no doubt the goods were'.[53]

Also in September 1799 Benjamin certified that 'John Knocker of Dover took charge and piloted the *Tartar* Cutter under my command from The Downs to the Texel on the late Expedition against Holland and back to The Downs where he left her in safety on the 7th instant, for which service he is to receive the sum of £21 as per agreement'.[54]

Loss of the *Tartar*

Between 2 November 1799 and early 1800 the *Tartar* was part of an expedition to Holland when she tragically disappeared at sea with the loss of all hands. On 25 November 1799 the Controller wrote to the Board stating 'we are extremely sorry in having to report to your Honors the apprehensions that are entertained for the safety of the *Tartar* Cutter in the service of the revenue at this Port–she sailed on the 2nd instant from hence for the Helder under the command of the Mate but had not arrived there on the 19th nor has she been heard of since her departure ... from the very heavy gales of wind she must have had to encounter with, there are many reasons to fear she is lost'.[55]

Several weeks later Commander Worthington gave an account of his fears and operational difficulties:

> A great deal of time has now elapsed since the sailing of the *Tartar* Cutter, it being upwards of ten weeks and not the least information of her whatever has been received gives me the greatest reason to believe she most certainly must be unfortunately lost.
>
> I beg you will be pleased to state to their Honors that at this season of the year the present temporary Cutter which was ordered during the absence of the *Tartar* on the late expedition to Holland is utterly unfit, being an open vessel of only 33 tons which renders her unequal to encounter the gales now prevailing, or to afford that shelter to the crew to enable them to keep to sea. Smuggling is now carried on chiefly on this part of the coast in luggers from 40 to 60 tons having on board 12 to 16 men'. He explained that these vessels in general were armed, which 'renders the present vehicle unequal to cope with them.

He asked for a temporary cruiser, possibly one that had already been seized and condemned, to be made available in her stead.[56]

Benjamin received permission to proceed with the *Tartar*'s temporary cruiser to St Ives, Cornwall, to take possession of the *Providence*, a seized cutter, and bring both vessels back to Deptford. He claimed however that his temporary cruiser was quite inadequate for this task. It was very small, and had no deck to protect himself and his crew of eight men from the weather, as westerly winds were strong and prevalent at this time of the year. Benjamin suggested that as there were several vessels bound for Plymouth with the King's stores, the men could board one of these and disembark at Plymouth. They could then be conveyed to Falmouth by the Plymouth Revenue cutter, where they would be only a short distance from St Ives– a few hours walk in fact. Benjamin himself wished to travel overland 'to obtain as many men as their Honors should think fit for getting ready for navigating the lugger to Deptford against the arrival of the other men from Dover'.[57]

Applications were made by relations of the *Tartar*'s crew for the payment of wages due to the seamen. The Treasury made a lump sum payment of £8,081 to be distributed amongst the Commanders and crews of the cutters who had taken part in the expedition to Holland. Benjamin disputed his share of the payment, especially as the *Tartar* had been lost and some of his crew had lost their lives.

List of Officers, Mariners and other Persons on board the *Tartar* when she sailed for the Texel (Netherlands) 2 November 1799:[58]

James Norris, Mate, married, widow pd 5 May 1800 (Amy)
John Graham, Deputed Mariner
Nicholas Marden, married, widow pd 26 May 1900 (Mary)
John Wellard, married, widow pd 24 May 1800 (Susan)
Henry Baker, father pd 20 March 1800 (Henry)
Edward Witnall, brother pd 30 January 1800 (John)
William Witnall, married, widow pd 3 April 1800 (Dorcas)
Thomas Petts, father pd 8 March 1800 (John)
John Courins
Richard Cloke, married, widow pd 14 March 1800 (Sarah)
John Dawson, married, widow pd 23 May 1800 (Ann)
Thomas Hutton, brother pd 13 May 1800 (John)
John Spearpoint, father pd 29 March 1800 (Jno)
Edward Nash, mother pd 24 April 1800 (Eliz Long)
James Epps, father pd 7 March 1800 (Richard)
Thomas Wilden, married, widow pd 24 May 1800 (Sarah)
William Reynolds, mother pd 6 May 1800 (Hester Nye)[59]
James Marsh, father pd 13 October 1800 (Jas Marsh)
John Knight, mother pd 23 May 1800 (Mary Knight)
James Keefe, mother pd 20 June 1800 (Ann Keefe)
Geo Saunders, extra man shipped 16 Oct 1799 in room of Thomas Chapman, sick, father pd 17 July 1800 (George Saunders)
A deputy was requested for Thomas Chapman, a regular *Tartar* crew member, when he became incapacitated by a paralytic stroke.[60]
George Wickes, Pilot, married.

James Norris, Mate of the vessel, was one of those who died. His wife, Amy Norris, was reportedly left in the greatest distress, a widow with a five-year-old son who had no means of support. She wrote petitioning for a pension from the Board and requested compensation for the loss of her husband's belongings which were on board:

Feather bed, bolster & pillow, blanket & quilt	5.10.0
Two coats & one surtout coat	4. 0.0
Three waistcoats.	1.10.0
Five pair of breeches	1.15.0
Two great jackets	2. 0.0
Two short jackets	1. 0.0
One pair of boots	1. 1.0
Three pair of shoes	0.12.0
Two hats	0.14.0
Eight cotton shirts	2.12.0
Three white shirts	1.11.6
Eleven handkerchiefs	1.13.0
Twelve pair of stockings	2. 0.0

A silver watch 4. 4.0
A book of charts 1.11.6
Cash for vessels use as the Commander was ill and unable to go 15.15.0

Total £47. 9.0

It is interesting to find what the Mate of a cutter had in his wardrobe in 1800. Benjamin was lucky not to have taken part in this expedition which ended so badly. Six widows of *Tartar* crew members: Mary Marden, Ann Dawson, Sarah Wilden, Dorcas Witnall, Susan Wellard and Sarah Cloke petitioned the Treasury for pensions. They recapitulated the well-known events leading to the *Tartar*'s tragic disappearance. The cutter 'last sailed from Dover bound to the Helder and has since never been heard of and it is supposed foundered at Sea in the heavy Gales of wind which came on soon after she sailed and that every soul on board perished'. The widows were reduced to extreme poverty and distress.[61] Benjamin confirmed their story to the Board. The Board wished to know why Amy Norris did not join with the other widows in petitioning the Lords of the Treasury for pensions. Apparently Mrs. Norris was not aware of the petition and was advised by her father, John Andrews, ex-Chief Mate of the *Tartar* and now Commander of the *Nimble* to apply to the Board 'rather than pursue the former mode for relief'.[62] A later application for a pension was received from the widow of George Wickes, a Pilot lost in the *Tartar*.[63] It would be three years before the mother of Mariner James Keefe, Ann Keefe, petitioned for a pension and compensation for certain articles valued at £13 6s. in her son's possession on board the *Tartar* when it was lost at sea. Benjamin confirmed that Keefe was on board and that the articles named by her were those usually taken to sea by Mariners.[64]

For the information of the Board, a certificate of the baptism of Thomas Ratcliffe was produced in connection with his nomination as the Mate of the *Tartar* in place of James Norris, deceased. He was 64 years of age, an active Mariner by profession. At the same time the office records indicate he was under prosecution for smuggling in 1774, which would have disqualified him for the position.[65] James Ireland, baseborn son of Jane Ireland, was then nominated as Mate of the *Tartar* and proof of his baptism was sent to the Board. A Mariner by profession, he had been Mate of a cutter in the service of the Admiralty during the whole of the war. He had never been suspected of smuggling operations.[66]

In March 1800 the Captains of the *Tartar* and the *Lively* were asked to recommend a crew member to serve on board vessels named *The Duke* and *Valiant* at Sandgate Creek. The Commander of the *Lively* had no one suitable, but Benjamin 'recommends Jonathan Bayley as a proper man who is willing to serve on board either *The Duke* or *Valiant*; he has been a Mariner under my command in the *Tartar* Cutter and temporary cruiser ever since 1797 and has always conducted himself well'.[67]

The new *Tartar*

A new *Tartar* had to be constructed and prepared for service under the command of Benjamin. He submitted a bill to the Board for a new boat and materials; two boat sails, storm jib and mainstay as well as for refitting and painting as ordered.[68] This letter describes the beginning of the fledgling vessel's career: 'Gentlemen, Mr Brown our Surveyor for Sloops having by his Memorial of the 4th instant stated that the *Tartar* Cutter building at Cowes[69] for the Service ... will be ready for launching on or about the 28th instant, and that it will be necessary for the Commander and Crew to be there ... We direct you to order Captain Worthington to unrig the temporary cruiser now employed by him and enter his full complement of Mariners, and also direct Captain Smith of the *Lively* Cutter to take them on board, likewise their provisions and stores, and conduct them to Cowes. And after he has landed them, to cruise with the *Lively* until the *Tartar* shall be ready to proceed for London and then to convoy her to the Nore.'[70]

Richard Vinall, a boatman from Eastware, was employed during 1800 as Mate on the temporary cruiser under the command of Captain Worthington. There was some question by the Board as to whether Benjamin went constantly to sea in the temporary lugger or whether she was navigated by Vinall.[71] On 18 September 1800 Vinall reported the particulars of a seizure made by him two days earlier. Vinall stated he proceeded on orders from Captain Worthington who had received information that a cutter's boat was planning to run a cargo of contraband goods into Eastware Bay. Benjamin later recommended that Richard Vinall be positioned as a deputed Mariner on board the *Tartar* in place of John Graham who had perished with the previous *Tartar*.[72]

War with Napoleon

Although the Revenue cruisers were employed primarily for the purpose of protecting the Revenue, from time to time they were mobilised for coastal defence. Benjamin was involved for a short time between October 1801 and March 1802 with special work in connection with what was known as the 'Alien Service', helping the Royal Navy in the war at sea against Napoleon. For some time he was employed between Dover and North Foreland 'preventing improper communication between this Country and France'. The Royal Navy was under the command of Admiral Sir Hyde Parker, with Horatio Nelson as second in command at this time. A letter from Lord Pelham, one of His Majesty's Prinicipal Secretaries of State, to the Board commends Benjamin for 'they [the Board] have much pleasure in receiving such a satisfactory account of your good conduct in the Service from which you are now removed'.[73]

Benjamin quickly returned to the more mundane tasks of keeping the *Tartar* seaworthy in the service of the Revenue. The Commissioners received a letter from Benjamin saying that the *Tartar* is in need of caulking and painting and they replied, 'the Season of the year is too far advanced for doing these works and therefore you are to direct him (Worthington) to apply in the Spring of the next year to do the needful'.[74]

Deal Smugglers

Deal had the worst reputation as a smuggling town, and raids were often made on the houses and luggers drawn up on the beach. Smugglers' boats were destroyed by military force but actions like this failed to deter the Deal traders.

Smuggling continued regardless, carried on by such large gangs of men that the government believed there was no hope of checking it but by the constant and most

47 Revenue cruiser chasing smuggler by night on the Kentish coast.

48 H.M. cutter *Wickham.* An early 19th-century King's cutter.

active vigilance of strong military patrols. Militia were stationed within the town of Deal and the surrounding area to help control the situation and offer land-based support to the Customs Service. Often the militia arrived too late to retrieve the situation, the goods and mob having vanished. When, as was often the case, regular forces were otherwise engaged in wars, the militia units were often called upon to bear the brunt of anti-smuggling operations. The militia was a body of men conscripted by ballot ostensibly for home defence. They were not taken very seriously and were often suspected of helping rather than hindering the smugglers.[75]

On 17 November 1801, Benjamin sent William Ireland, the Mate of the *Tartar* along the coast in the six-oared boat, believing that goods might be landed at Deal as there had been a great deal of 'flashing and blazing several nights before'. At seven o'clock the boat crew sighted a lugger, the *Ned* of Deal, off Walmer and followed her to the north end of Deal where she anchored so the shore boats could take out her cargo. The *Tartar* crew boarded the lugger *Betsy* without resistance and before the cargo could be taken out, on account of the fresh winds. Immediately one of the *Tartar*'s men cut the rope that was fast on the shore but before they could set the sails a crowd of about one hundred and fifty longshoremen in a murderous mood came onto the scene and attacked them. A pistol was seized from one of the *Tartar*'s men by one of the Deal men who presented it, 'but it fortunately flashed in the pan'. The Revenue men were forced to quit their prize otherwise, the Mate reported, some of them would surely have been killed. There was no opportunity to examine the illicit cargo, but the Revenue men were certain that the lugger had plenty of spirits and other articles on board.[76]

A few days later on 22 December 1801 a similar incident occurred. Captain B.J. Worthington and Captain Dubois Smith,[77] Commanders of the *Tartar* and the *Lively* respectively, related a violent incident in which the *Tartar* and *Lively* crews boarded and seized a smuggling lugger but later had to relinquish her to the smugglers. The Revenue men initially drove off the vessel's crew of 22 men, but when the lugger ran on to the beach and an unsuccessful attempt was made to float her off, some goods were unloaded and transferred into the *Tartar*. At length 'a great number of people armed with Musquets' attacked the Revenue men, who defended the beached lugger for half an hour but finally retreated before a continual hail of musket shot. Two boatmen were wounded, one of them critically. The 65-ton lugger, the *Ned* of Deal, was registered in the name of William Crisp, one of the seamen awarded compensation for assisting the *Tartar* when it had run aground in 1796. The *Ned* originally had a cargo of 1,200 parcels of goods, of which 854 parcels of crepes, cambricks, starch, spirits, tobacco and cards were secured by the Revenue men. It was later discovered that all materials, muskets, swivels, etc. had been removed from the lugger which had been crippled and was no longer seaworthy.[78]

The Commissioners, after reading the reports of the incident, directed Captains Worthington and Smith to 'take every possible method of discovering and apprehending the Offenders concerned in the obstruction and outrage and give immediate notice thereof confidentially to the Secretary'. They also directed 'the most accurate description you can give of the lugger in question be transmitted to him forthwith'.[79] In conjunction with the above instructions, the Commissioners issued a directive for an advertisement to be placed in the provincial newspapers seeking information from the public and offering a reward of £100.[80] By 19 August 1802 there was still no public response.[81]

Following a directive from a Mr. Hume, Benjamin reported from the Customs House Dover on 5 November 1801 on the present state of the Waterguard for the prevention of smuggling:

> The Tartar cutter with a complement of 23 men including the Commander and Mate. The Tartar is a new vessel built within the present year, her Commander and Mate are both young men, she is well manned and filled and in every respect equipped for her proper duty. Two tidesurveyors and 12 boatmen, a Galley and a Harbour boat. There is a vacancy in the office of one of the Tidesurveyors but a person is nominated to it, and is now under instructions. The other Tidesurveyor is active and fully capable for his employment. There are also vacancies in the Boatmen which it would be very desirable should be filled up as from the prospect of an open communication with France, there will be a very considerable deal of Duty to be done, by this class of officers here, and as the pay of extra men employed during vacancies is only 2/- a piece no persons have been hitherto found, who would accept of the temporary appointments. Of the boatmen here only six can be said to be fully capable of the active duty required of them, their names we respectfully subjoin in the margin [Henry Jones, Chas Toucher, Richard Cole, Jno Mathartt, Reynold Mowle, Jas Kingford]—on the other four we beg leave particularly to speak
> —Stephen Somes is 75 years of age and tho still a hearty man is not sufficiently active for the employment of a boatman, but as his faculties are perfectly entire we submitted to your Honors in our Letter of the 14 May 1800 No 178 that he might be employed as a Tidewaiter in the guarding of ships
> —Robert Clements has been in a state of idiotism from the effect of a paralytic complaint and has done no duty for a considerable time past, we informed your Honors of the state which this man was in, on our said Letter of the 14 May 1800 and of there being no probability of his recovery in our Letter of the 16 April last No 149 [page missing][82]

Two days later Benjamin was appealing for more mariners as John Graham was lost in the original *Tartar* and Thomas Chapman had been ill for some time. He requested commissions for John White and Stephen Smith, 'two active young men now on board the *Tartar* Cutter'. His need was especially urgent because he expected smuggling in the vicinity of the *Tartar* to increase in scale, and wanted to be able to send two boats from the cutter instead of his present one.[83]

On 23 December 1801 Benjamin was foreman of the court, for a trial held at the Court Hall, Dover,[84] and Thomas Pattenden, who resided at 1 Townwall Street, and had a charmingly picturesque flower garden running down to the river,[85] was on the grand jury.

On a later occasion Benjamin made an oath before Jonathan Osborn, Justice of the Peace for Dover,[86] that having been reimbursed by the Board for personal losses sustained in victualling the *Tartar* crew up to 5 January 1801, he was in arrears again for the year from 6 January 1801 to 5 January 1802, and requested the outstanding sum of £184 0s. 5¾d. be paid to him, calculated at the rate of five pence three farthings for each man. The Collector of Customs confirmed that his figures were correct.[87]

Between 1802 and 1803 Benjamin again had problems getting reimbursement for his personal expenditure in victualling the *Tartar*. He had been out of pocket to the tune of £157 8s. 1½d. On 7 May 1803 he wrote giving the reasons why his expenditure had exceeded the stipulated allowance, and although he had been unable to produce vouchers for the money spent he had furnished proof of the expenditure.

After the *Tartar*'s deputed Mariner, John White, resigned in June 1802 Benjamin was anxious to engage Stephen Smith as a replacement. The 24-year-old had sailed with him 'a considerable time'. Two weeks later John White was required to testify that the *Chance* lugsail was seized about one and a half miles from the shore of Dover, within the port limits.[88] In September the same year Benjamin sought directions for the disposal of a lugger and sundry other boats seized by him, presuming 'they have all been condemned', and requested his share of the value of the *Fox* lugger seized by him and taken into the service of the Customs.[89] Benjamin and the Commander of the *Lively* cutter petitioned three months later for a share of the fines recovered on the licence bonds of the *George* and *Dolphin* luggers.[90]

Yet another new foresail and mainsail were required by the *Tartar* in 1802 at an estimated cost of £75 17s. 3d., showing they were expensive even in those times. A new galley and cable cost £99 5s. in 1803. The old galley had become unserviceable after three and a half years continuous use.[91]

War against France

From 1803 to 1805 England was engaged in war against France and her allies. Napoleon was carrying on his great designs for the invasion of England or Ireland. The serviceable arms on the *Tartar* in January 1803 were 10 carriage guns, six pounders, nine muskets, eight pairs of tomahawks and 12 boarding pikes.[92] Benjamin requested musketoons saying that 'particularly in the summer, two six oared boats with 14 persons are sent along the shore and each man is given a cutlass and a pistol, but a musketoon would be very serviceable for a part of the boat's crew—viz two to each boat—in lieu of muskets by reason of their being short and handy and would do more execution if required.'[93] In May the Board requested Benjamin to give a description of the four guns required by the *Tartar* in lieu of the number 'which from tempestuous weather were obliged to be thrown overboard'. The *Tartar*'s mast and bowsprit were sprung in the same storm.[94]

In a letter dated 7 January 1805 Benjamin requested the reimbursement of charges for pilotage and for victualling Pilots and Officers on board the *Tartar* while she was under the orders of the Admiralty. These charges amounted to a total of £19. Thomas Dowers, Pilot, had been sent on board by Admiral Thornborough for 29 days between 2 and 30 April 1803 when two trips were made between Gravesend and Deptford. Lieutenant Jones was on board for eight days from 21 to 28 June, and Lieutenant Cameron on board for 17 days between 24 and 30 September, both by order of Admiral Montague. The pilot of H.M.S. *Panmortalitic* was on board for eight days by order of Captain Bligh, on a survey of the coast of Holland from 21 to 30 September 1804. Lieutenant Gill was sent on board from 17 May to 29 June 1804 by Admiral Bowley. Thomas Hanew, Pilot, was also ordered on board by Bowley between 20 May and 25 August, during which time the *Tartar* made two voyages to the Baltic.[95]

On 30 December 1803 Benjamin submitted a bill to the Board for the rent of a storehouse used for the *Tartar*. In February 1804 the *Tartar* was at anchor in the Downs when she was driven into by the brig *Betsy* of London during a storm. As a result of the collision the *Tartar*'s bowsprit and spreadyard was carried away. A bill of £84 1s. 4d. was transmitted for repairs. At the same time the vessel was caulked and painted over a period of two days with ten caulkers and one shipwright working on her. The Board invited Benjamin to explain the types of canvas he purchased in repairing the jib mainsail, gaft topsail and waistcloths and to account for what, in the official view, was excessive and unauthorised expenditure.[96]

Dirty work at Dungeness

In a letter dated 21 March 1805 Benjamin related an incident off Dungeness in which the *Tartar* and the *Lively* Excise cutter had chased a lugger into Dungeness Bay on 25 February. Anticipating an attempt to run goods, he despatched his Chief Mate, William Ireland, and a party of men, including five from the *Lively* to keep watch from the west side while boats from the *Tartar* and *Lively* took up their stations opposite. When a large lugger appeared, she was immediately boarded by William Ireland, who duly seized a substantial cargo of spirits, tobacco and tea.[97] After an hour, armed men from Lydd and Dungeness mustered and attempted a rescue. They ferociously attacked the Revenue men, and firing began on both sides. The Lancashire militia from No. 3 Battery nearby were requested to assist with securing the seizure. A party of men was sent to lend assistance, whereupon the smugglers fled, leaving behind one of their number who had been killed. The smugglers could not be identified but it was established that the dimensions of the captured lugger corresponded with those of the lugger *Diana* of Folkestone.[98] In November 1805 the Board was petitioned for payment of the *Tartar* crew's share of the *Diana*, which had since been taken over for the service of the Navy.[99] A bill 'for the cure of a wound on the head of Henry Tilden and one on the knee of Richard Harris, mariners belonging to the *Tartar* Cutter received by accident on board while in the execution of their duty' was probably related to this incident.[100] Nine years later two men, Jeremiah Maxtell and Thomas Gilbert, were arrested, taken to London, and charged at the Old Bailey as participators in the attempted rescue. The case against them was remarkably defective and it is a matter of wonder that they were arrested at all on such flimsy evidence. The verdict was in favour for the defendants.[101]

The Crew of the *Tartar*, 1805

A list of the crew of the *Tartar* who had no Protections was recorded on 26 June 1805. The personal details of the 18 crew members form the major part of this communication:

Henry Bayley, aged 22, dark complexion, 5 feet 8 and a half inches high, dark short hair, dark eyes and scar on his forehead

John McLean, aged 24, swarthy complexion, dark brown hair and tied, 5 feet 6 inches high, dark eyes

William Bervish,[102] aged 20, dark complexion, short brown hair, 5 feet 5 inches, grey eyes, lost his forefinger of right hand

John Nuckel,[103] aged 27, dark complexion, short dark brown hair, blue eyes, 5 feet 6 and a half inches high, has a scar on his left breast

Bennet Paul, aged 19, swarthy complexion, light hair tied, 5 feet 2 and a half inches high, hazle eyes

John Finn,[104] aged 21, light complexion, short brown hair, 5 feet 5 and a half inches high, dark eyes

Edward McCordial,[105] aged 20, fair complexion, short light brown hair, 5 feet 5 and a half inches high, dark eyes

Thomas Allen, aged 21, dark complexion, short dark brown hair, 5 feet 5 and a half inches high, dark eyes

Duncan Cook, aged 38, dark complexion, short dark brown hair, 5 feet 7 and half inches high, grey eyes

James Greenstreet,[106] aged 26, fair complexion, short light brown hair, 5 feet 5 and half inches high, grey eyes

Joseph Howett, aged 38, fair complexion, short light hair, grey eyes

Isaac Jennings,[107] aged 26, dark complexion, short dark hair, 5 feet 6 inches high, dark eyes

Richard Andrew,[108] aged 20, fair complexion, light hair tied, 5 feet 8 inches high, grey eyes, has a wound on the upper part of the right thigh

Skinnen Norton, aged 24, dark complexion, dark curled hair tied, 5 feet 3 and half inches high, light grey eyes

George Gambriel,[109] aged 25, light complexion, short dark hair, 5 feet 4 and half inches high, grey eyes, impediment in his speech

John Hammond, aged 22, light complexion, short brown hair, 5 feet 6 inches high, neake [?] eyes, scar on his left arm

Edward Norwood,[110] aged 21, fair complexion, red hair, 5 feet 9 inches high, light grey eyes

George Gladman,[111] aged 21, brown complexion, short brown hair, 5 feet 6 inches high, dark eyes[112]

In response to Benjamin's request for a commission for William Scarlett, the Board in turn asked a series of questions. Why is the man whom Scarlett is intended to replace absent in the first instance? What is the present state of his health and will he ever return to duty? Has his commission been deposited with the Collector? When was he last paid his salary? How many seizures have been made by the *Tartar*?[113] Unfortunately the answers were not recorded in papers that survive.

In 1806 the *Tartar* required outfitting and painting at a sum of £161 4s. Permission was requested to proceed to Deptford for refitting and repair work to the *Tartar*'s copper bottom. Cordage used in repair of the cutter was paid by weight, as related by Benjamin: 'Myself or the Mate attend the weighing of the same and at all times when cordage is making of any magnitude, such as standing rigging or cables, I always attend the making of the same.'[114]

In answer to the Board's enquiry, Captain Worthington gave an assurance that no member of the *Tartar* crew was able to discover the identity of any of the *Greyhound*'s crew, seized by the *Tartar*, who had escaped on being delivered to the Dover Magistrates.[115]

Benjamin was still pursuing the matter of the French lugsail boat he had seized in 1790. Once again he expressed the hope that proceedings against the boat and goods would be resumed now that the war with France was over, 'as the goods are now in a very perishing state'. He was finding the shortage of manpower a growing problem and applied for another Officer, not least because he anticipated more smuggling than ever in the winter of 1806.[116]

A further report was forwarded to the Board on the health of mariner Thomas Chapman, whose complete incapacity was reiterated and for whom a replacement had already been hired. In March 1807, four months later, the Controller reported Thomas's condition had remained the same for several years and he was 'in tolerable bodily health but incapable of moving except on crutches from the effects of a paralytic stroke'.[117]

The Customs House, Dover

Primary records reference Cust. 54 at the Public Record Office, Kew, consists essentially of letters and various communications from the Collector to the Commissioners of the Customs (Board) sitting in London. The Collector was responsible for all the Customs business at the port of Dover, amongst other things. He was accountable to the Board for a wide variety of matters, ranging from responsibilities for monies paid for Customs to making sure that Revenue vessels were properly manned and officered and efficient instruments of government policy. The correspondence that passed between the local Collector and the London based Board of Customs was by the standards of the day voluminous. In 1792, for example, no fewer than 746 letters went out from the Dover Customs House to the Commissioners in London.[118]

An 1805 request for printed forms from the Dover Customs House gives an idea of the extent of the paperwork which had to be completed by the Customs officials in the course of their work:

6	Quire[119] of sheets of the seizure and disposal of goods except teas
3	books (bound) and 3 quire each of the above
12	Certificate Books for procuring Excise Permits
48	Parchment Certificates for British Plantation Registry (of ships)
2	Quire of Surveyors Certificates of admeasurement
3	Riding Officers Journal Books
12	Quire of Riding Officers Journal sheets
6	Quire of Riding Officers Quarterly Abstracts of Seizures
1	Quire of Quarterly Superannuation account Sheets
½	Quire of Yearly Superannuation account Sheets
6	Quire of Coal Warrants
1	Quire of Monthly Account Current Sheets
6	Quire of Boarding Bills[120]

Benjamin Suffers a Severe Illness

Benjamin and his family were living in Snargate Street, Dover,[121] when after many hard working years at sea Benjamin's health began to deteriorate. He was 47 years of age when the effects of cold sea water began to affect his joints. Evidence of this appears in a letter written by him at Dover on 16 March 1807:

> Gentlemen,
>
> I beg leave to inform you that in consequence of an attack of the rheumatic gout which proceeded from a severe cold, obliged me to leave the cutter in charge of the mate off Dover the 14 January last, which soon after came on so violent as to confine me to my bedroom and at times to my bed for several days together. I am now in the recovery but am still confined to my room and unable to walk. I have therefore to request you will represent the same to the Harbour Board praying that T.H. will be pleased to allow me to share in a seizure of a lugger and her cargo made by the officers of *Tartar*, in conjunction with the *Lively* Excise cutter in the night of the 7th inst off Folkstone [*sic*] and enclosed I beg to transmit a certificate as the state of my complaint from my doctor.
>
> I am etc. B.J. Worthington

Things haven't changed much as far as getting time off work is concerned!

F. Thatcher, M.D., wrote 'I the undersigned do certify that Capt. Worthington has been attended by me for a rheumatic gouty affection from the 28 January to this present 18 day of March. The greater part of the time he has been altogether confined to his bed, and is at the present period incapable of leaving his room.'

Further Customs Office communication confirmed the certificate 'was signed by a Physician of real respectability'. It was found that Benjamin's illness happened while he was at sea and, apart from a period of indisposition from 25 June to 16 July 1806, Benjamin had actively performed his duty at sea with the *Tartar* for long stretches of that year as follows: 5-26 May, 29 May-21 June, 25 June-13 August, 21-22 August, 25 August-27 September, 8-27 October, 1-10 November, 17-27 November, 8-26 December 1806, 13-20 February, 21-23 February, 3-14 March, 12 April until present date when he is now at sea (15 April 1807).[122]

According to the same letter Benjamin was on board the *Tartar* when the following seizures were made. These were:

20 May 1806 – Lugsail boat and material with 266 casks of spirits delivered at Dover.
18 July 1806 – *Nancy*, *Venus*, *Hope* and *Po* Luggers seized by order of the Harbour Board on Deal Beach in conjuction with the *Stag*, *Lively* and *Nimble* Cutters.
29 July 1806 – *June* Lugger seized as above in conjuction with the *Nimble* Cutter.
13 October 1806 – Lugsail boat and materials with 458 casks of spirits in conjuction [*sic*] with the *Swan* and *Lively* Cutters.
19 November 1806 – Lugsail boat and materials with 496 casks spirits.[123]

The Collector of Customs in his letter of 15 April 1807 concluded by saying that 'Captain Worthington is gradually recovering and can now leave his house, although he is not yet fit for duty'.

Escape of the *Betsy* Smugglers

During Benjamin's illness the Collector reported on the seizure of the *Betsy* of Folke-stone. The *Betsy* had been chased and boarded by Revenue Officers from the *Tartar* and the *Lively* who captured 14 smugglers, assigning seven to each vessel. The smug-glers brought on board the *Tartar* were ordered below by the Mate, William Ireland, who was in charge of the vessel. They were not put in irons, had no guards placed over them, and were allowed on deck, one or two at a time, 'to do their necessary occasions'. The ship anchored in Dover about 2 a.m. in the morning of 8 March, when Ireland retired to his cabin to sleep, having put deputed Mariner Robert Scarlett, the only Officer besides himself on board, in charge. While Scarlett was supervising the clearance of a wreck from across the cutter's bow, the smugglers made off in the *Tartar*'s boat and there was no boat available for any pursuit to be attempted. Ireland was not informed of the incident until sometime afterwards when he came up on deck. The *Tartar*'s crew, most of whom were asleep at the time of the escape, could not say who the escapees were.

As a result, charges were brought against Ireland and Scarlett for allowing the seven smugglers, who were believed to have fired upon the Revenue vessels, to escape from the *Tartar*. The Collector at Dover was asked at the hearing to ascertain who the Master of the *Betsy* was and whether she was licensed by the Admiralty. He replied he could only rely upon rumour that the Master was Thomas Godden, one of the two people rescued in the first instance by the mob. However, no evidence of this was likely to be forthcoming and the *Betsy* was not licensed by the Admiralty. The Board requested the provincial press assist in the search for the smugglers who had escaped from the *Tartar*.[124]

Following this incident Robert Scarlett was discharged on 9 April 1807 and Wil-liam Richardson, Mariner, was nominated for a deputation to replace him, 'being very steady and active'.[125]

The following year William Lilbourne, Commander of the *Lively*, queried the propriety of rewarding the crew of the *Tartar* for the apprehension of four smugglers found on board the *Betsy*. Of the seven men on board the *Lively* who were brought ashore at Dover, three were rescued by a mob while the remaining four were sent to Newgate Gaol in London. They were acquitted but fined £100, later reduced to £50. Captain Lilbourne claimed the whole reward for his crew, although he did concede that Stephen Smith and six other members of the *Tartar* were not implicated in the escape of the seven smugglers from the latter vessel.

The Comptroller at Dover bestowed high praise upon Stephen Smith but heavily criticised Lilbourne's Officers and crew, 'whose prevaricating testimony' had resulted in the bill against the four smugglers being thrown out by the Grand Jury at the Old Bailey. Benjamin testified on behalf of Stephen Smith, alleging that Smith and his men assisted by the soldiery, apprehended the smugglers although the *Tartar* crew's share of the reward was contested by James Galloway.[126]

In a letter dated 21 September 1807 Captain Worthington and Smith were ad-vised by the Board to watch for four suspicious vessels which had left Lydd and were expected to return with cargoes of spirits on board.[127] By the summer of 1807 smug-gling in England and Wales had increased to what the Commissioners of Customs called an 'alarming extent'. An Act was therefore passed to ensure more effectual prevention and once again the Revenue Officers were exhorted to perform their duty to its fullest extent. They were threatened with punishment in case of any dereliction of duty while rewards were held out as an inducement to zealous action. Under this new Act Army, Navy, Marines and militia had to work together to prevent further smuggling and to seize smuggled goods.

Between Dover and Rye a considerable amount of tobacco, snuff, spirits and tea was smuggled into the country. The government knew that towns on the coast of Sussex and Kent, in particular Hastings, Folkestone, Hythe and Deal were heavily involved. Large gangs of men went to daring lengths, and even when they had been captured and impressed they frequently escaped and returned to their previous life of smuggling.

In a request dated 8 August 1808, for a new light six-oared galley boat Benjamin remarked that in the summer of the previous year smugglers from Deal to the North Foreland had used fast rowing galleys. They had either come across from the continent directly or had unloaded goods from vessels far out at sea in light, calm weather so as to run them into the shore. He anticipated that this practice would continue in the present summer of 1808. His own six-oared galley boat, equipped for hugging the shore in winter, was too heavy and too broad to challenge these lighter and faster galleys.[128]

Pensions

A system was instituted in the year 1808 by which the widows of supervisors and surveyors of Riding Officers and Commanders of cruisers were allowed £30 per annum, with an additional allowance of £5 per annum for each child until he or she reached the age of fifteen. The widows of Riding Officers, Mates of cutters and Sitters of boats specially stationed for the prevention of smuggling, were allowed £25 per annum and £5 for each child under fifteen years. In the case of widows of Mariners they were to have £15 a year and £2 10s for each child till the age of fifteen. Amongst those thus rewarded were Ann Sarmon and her three children. She was a widow of the Commander of the *Swan* cutter stationed at Cowes. The other recipients were one child of the Mate of the *Tartar*, and the widow and children of the Commander of the cutter *Hunter* of Yarmouth.[129]

The *Tartar* was in need of further attention during 1808, requiring new sails, caulking, painting and an examination of her copper bottom. The bill for a new six-oared galley was transmitted, and Benjamin explained how the *Tartar* had lost her bowsprit and spreadyard in a gale while at anchor in the Downs. He asked for replacements from Deptford.[130]

On 30 May 1808 the *Tartar* seized the *Nancy* lugsail boat belonging to Sandgate with a cargo of 320 casks of spirits, and Benjamin requested a share of the seizure as the vessel was licensed.[131] On 2 March 1809 Benjamin claimed the reward offered for two smugglers on board a lugger seized by the *Tartar*.[132]

During August 1809, Benjamin was absent from the station for some days, 'guarding a fleet of East India-Men to the River Thames and knowing there were several long galleys over from this part of the Coast before I left the Station, I informed Mr Ireland I should go on shore to collect what information I could and also to get ready some necessaries for the Cutter we were then in want of, directing him either to anchor or take the chance of cruising the night'.[133]

During the wintry January of 1810 gales forced Benjamin to cut the *Tartar*'s anchor cable with the anchor still attached while anchored in the Downs. It was later retrieved by a Dover boat and the usual sum of £29 12s. paid for its salvage.[134]

A letter of 28 May 1810 reported that Benjamin had problems when his Mariners refused to leave their families in Kent in order to serve as boatmen on a lengthy trip to Chester.[135] It is not known why this trip was necessary.

During the early part of 1810 Benjamin submitted bills of £12 for pilotage from Dover to Yarmouth, £241 for a new cable and hawser and a refit of the *Tartar*, and £25 17s. for a new six-oared boat.[136]

'Capt. B.J. Worthington' is found listed in an 1811 Directory for Dover and 'Mrs Elizabeth Worthington' can be found at 'Charlton' in 1832/33. Benjamin also appears on the Voters List for Mayor of Dover 1813.

Victualling costs 1814

After 10 October 1814 the allowance for victualling the crews of the Revenue cruisers was increased as follows: for victualling Commander and Mate, 3 shillings a day and 1s. 6d. per lunar month for fire and candle. For Mariners the allowance was 1s. 10d. a day each. The daily rations supplied to each Mariner on board the cruisers consisted of 1½ lbs. of bread and two quarts of beer. If flour or vegetables were issued the quantity of bread was reduced, and if cheese was supplied the amount was reduced in proportion to the value and not the quantity of the item. In order to obtain uniformity, a table of the rations as outlined above was fixed against the fore side of the mast under the deck of the cruiser, and also in some conspicuous place in the Customs House.[137]

A Cutter's First Aid Chest

Elaborate instructions were also issued regarding the use of the tourniquet, which 'is to stop a violent bleeding from a wounded artery in the limbs till it can be properly secured and tied by a surgeon'. The medicine chest of these cruisers contained the following articles: vomiting powders, purging powders, sweating powders, fever powders, calomel pills, laudanum, cough drops, stomach tincture, bark, scurvy drops, hartshorn, peppermint, lotion, Friar's balsam, Turner cerate, basilcon (for healing 'sluggish ulcers'), mercurial ointment, blistering ointment, sticking plaster and lint.[138]

The Customs Board certainly did their best to make the floating branch of its Preventive Service (see p. 52) as tempting and efficient as it could possibly be. With its fleet of cruisers well-armed and well-manned, with good wages, the offer of high rewards and pensions, and privileges second only to those obtainable in the Royal Navy, the administration of these cutters could not be blamed for the poor numbers of smugglers captured.

Yarmouth Port Establishment

In a letter dated 28 August 1817 the Board wrote to the Collector at Dover advising him of a report from the Collector and Comptroller at Yarmouth, dated 18 August

1817, 'with reference to an application made by Mr B.J. Worthington, late Commander of the *Tartar* stationed at the Port of Yarmouth, who is placed on the list of Superannuated Officers at an allowance of £180 per annum praying for the reasons wherein stated that he may be paid such allowance at Your Port in future ... We direct you to pay Mr Worthington the allowance in question by quarterly payments and the Collector is to take credit for the same from time to time in his account ... referring to the date of this order, and annexing proper Receipts as Vouchers, observing that where Mr Worthington does not personally attend to receive the same a Certificate be produced under the hands of the officiating Clergyman or Churchwardens of the Parish ... he is living.'[139]

The above reference makes it clear that Captain Worthington had retired from the Revenue Service at Yarmouth, not Dover, and by August 1817 had returned to his native town in order to spend his remaining years there. The question which arises is when did he leave Dover with the *Tartar*, and for how many years was he operating out of Yarmouth? The answer is unclear in the records. The last mention of him with the *Tartar* in the Dover Port Records before 1817 is a letter dated 25 February 1813[140] in which he claimed his rightful share of a seizure made as far back as 1808. There is in fact no evidence from that letter that Captain Worthington and the *Tartar* were currently on the Dover Port Establishment in 1813. The last definite mention of Captain Worthington and the *Tartar* operating out of Dover port in the Dover Records is in a letter dated 28 November 1810[141] where a bill is transmitted for the *Tartar*'s new six-oared boat.

We do know, however, that Captain Worthington belonged to the Yarmouth Port Establishment as early as 7 April 1812.[142] So it seems probable he was transferred to the Yarmouth Port Establishment at some period after 28 November 1810 and before 7 April 1812. The Yarmouth Port Records only begin on 31 March 1812.

Protections were issued to the Mariners belonging to the *Tartar* under the command of Benjamin at the port of Yarmouth. The Mariners were D. Day, William Robinson, Gordon Lamb, Gill Ladd, Abraham Bott, Jno Williams, William Springet, Robert Brightman and M. Baldry.[143] A month later a Protection was issued as requested for Henry High.[144]

During 1812 Benjamin was asked to explain why he employed a Mariner, William Witheat, who had been dismissed from the cutter *Repulse* in 1809. Benjamin's reasons were not accepted, and he was ordered to discharge Witheat and 'to take special care not in future to employ any Person who has been dismissed from the Service of this Revenue'.[145]

In a letter dated 12 May 1812 Benjamin requested he be allowed to exchange the *Tartar* for the *Beagle* cutter which was lying in the port of Yarmouth. As the exchange appeared to be beneficial to the Revenue Service the proposal was accepted. Benjamin was ordered to proceed to Deptford to effect the exchange, the necessary orders having been given to their Surveyor. The names of the cutters had to be changed to correspond with the Officers' commissions.[146]

By March 1814 we find Benjamin unable to carry out his duties at Yarmouth. He was evidently suffering from a recurrence of the same complaint that incapacitated him in 1808. On this occasion, however, the Mate of the *Tartar* was also sick and this led to a problem for which a local solution was found. A Mr. Brown, second Mate of the *Ranger* inspecting cutter, who was qualified to take charge of the *Tartar*, was directed to cruise upon the adjacent coast for 10 to 14 days until one of the Officers belonging to the *Tartar* had sufficiently recovered to resume his duty.[147]

By June Captain Worthington had returned to duty. A report by Captain Sayers, Inspecting Commander of the Northern Ports District, stated that the *Tartar* was in need of repair. Benjamin was directed to proceed with the *Tartar* to Deptford along with the *Ranger* and 'to acquaint Mr Seppings, Our Surveyor of Sloops, of his arrival to whom we have given the necessary directions for causing the said Vessel to be repaired'.[148]

By March 1815 the *Tartar* was in need of a six-oared boat but the first estimate for the same was considered extravagant. Other estimates were requested 'on reasonable terms', and 'to report if the Wash Snakes are intended to go all round the Boat'.[149] By May of that year the Commissioners had ordered the boat, which was to be provided at the port of Deale.

A couple of months later, at Benjamin's request, a refitting of the *Tartar* was ordered.[150] Shortly afterwards he reported the loss of the *Tartar*'s spread yard which was 'carried away by the *Big Hind of Aberdeen*'. Application had been made to the owner to pay the bill for the new yard.[151] A commission for Mr. Samuel Clarke to be a Mariner on board the *Tartar* cutter was transmitted.[152]

Retirement

A letter from Mr. Lushington dated 13 June 1816 authorised Mr. B. Worthington to be placed on the list of Superannuated Officers at an allowance of £180. This marked Captain Worthington's official retirement, although the letter suggested that he had ceased to be an active Commander some while previously.[153] The *Tartar* cutter, however, was still operational in August 1816, as the following references indicate. On 23 August 1816, commissions on board the *Tartar* were granted to James Ireland and Thomas Franklin (second Mate), and on 27 August 1816 the *Tartar* was one of several vessels about which the question arose as to what should be done with their unserviceable stores at Yarmouth Port.[154]

49   Buckland church, Dover.

There is a suggestion that the *Tartar* was sold or was intended for sale in 1817 as a petition 'of Edward Tanner on behalf of Jonathan Blacker praying that a British Register may be granted to a vessel called the *Tartar*' was issued in that year. Vessels with a British Register, or those which were entitled to one, fetched a correspondingly higher price at any subsequent sale. The rule certainly applied to vessels seized by Customs Officers which were later offered for sale on the general market under the Revenue laws.[155]

The *Tartar* continued as a Revenue cruiser and Lieutenant Woolnough was in command when he claimed a share of the contraband thrown overboard from a

50 Memorials to Benjamin Jelly and Elizabeth Worthington, and their son Thomas Knight Worthington, in part of Buckland church earlier known as the Worthington chapel.

smuggling galley chased by his boats and later picked up by the *Pioneer* schooner, the *Asp* tender, the *Badger* and the *Lively*.[156]

Up to 1821 the Revenue cruisers were the most important of all the means employed for suppressing smuggling. When the Commissioners of Inquiry compiled a report concerning the Revenue Service they concluded that the efficacy of the vessels employed in protecting the Revenue was not proportionate to the expense incurred in their maintenance. They advised that their numbers be reduced and whereas in 1816 they were under the care of the Admiralty, they should now be restored to the control of the Customs. The Officers and crew of these cruisers were still to be selected by the Admiralty.

It was a Treasury Minute of 15 February 1822 which directed that the whole of the force employed for the prevention of smuggling 'on the coast of this kingdom' was to be consolidated and transferred to the direction of the Customs Board.

The number of cruisers was reduced considerably. From 47 Revenue craft employed in England in 1821 there were only 32 two years later: *Mermaid, Stag, Badger, Ranger, Sylvia, Scout, Fox, Lively, Hawk, Cameleon, Hound, Rose, Scourge, Repulse, Eagle, Tartar, Adder, Lion, Dove, Lapwing, Greyhound, Swallow, Active, Harpy, Royal George, Fancy, Cheerful, Newcharter, Fly, Seaflower, Nimble, Sprightly* and *Dolphin*.

After his retirement Benjamin would have been able to continue to participate in local affairs as he had done when he was at home during his working life. On 23 December 1801 Benjamin was the foreman at the Court Hall when a case was being tried by grand jury. He and Elizabeth were no doubt able to spend more time together and attend local functions and events. A small theatre had been built in Snargate Street, Dover, in 1790.[157] The *Kentish Gazette* regularly advertised plays and on Friday 4 March 1796 an advertisement appeared for:

> Theatre Canterbury
> by Mrs Baker's Company
> by desire
> for the benefit of............
> and
> for the benefit of Mr Worthington
> on Tuesday 8th March
> The Tragedy of Alexander the Great or The Rival Queens
> with chevy-chace and other entertainments
> Tickets to be had of Mr Worthington
> at Mr Homan's, Westgate

and on 8 April 1796:

> Theatre Canterbury
> On Saturday April 9 by particular desire
> for the benefit of Mrs Worthington
> The comedy of
> The Rivals
> with High Life Below Stairs
> and other entertainments

Benjamin Jelly Worthington died on 27 October 1822 aged 59 years. The Customs House, Dover, advised the Commissioners on 28 October 1822, 'We respectfully inform Your Honours that Mr Benjamin Jelly Worthington, a Superannuated Commander of a Cutter at this Port died yesterday'.[158]

He was buried in the family vault at Buckland church which is situated about a mile and a half inland from Dover town centre.[159] A marble wall memorial inside the Buckland church in the Worthington chapel reads:

> Sacred to the memory of
> Benjamin Jelly Worthington
> who died 27th October 1822
> aged 59 years
> also of
> Elizabeth relict of the above
> who died 30th June 1845
> aged 76 years.

In his will, dated 15 January 1822, Benjamin left his freehold house and contents situated in the parish of Charlton to his wife, Elizabeth. His monies in public stocks and securities he left to his wife and brother-in-law, William Collins of Dover.[160]

Various publications have stated that Benjamin Jelly Worthington resided at Maxton Manor. This is doubtful as his will clearly states that he left a freehold house in the

parish of Charlton. Maxton Manor lies in
the parish of Hougham and his son, Henry
Worthington, later owned it.

Elizabeth Worthington died of 'spasms'
on 30 June 1845 in the parish of St James.
Elizabeth Smithett of Limekiln Street was
present at her death. She left a will.[161]

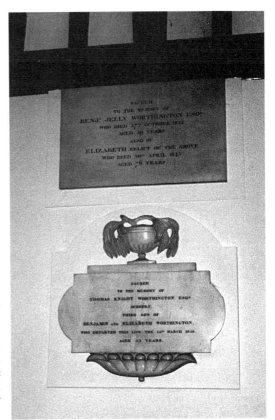

51 Worthington family monument in Buckland
church.

52 A 19th-century engraving of a drawing by J.E.
Youden dated 1822. The original watercolour hung
for many years in the Town Council Chambers,
Maison Dieu, Dover. It shows Dover Market Square
on market day with a stage coach rounding the
corner from King and Bench Streets on the way to
London. Interesting features include the old *Fountain
Inn* to the left of the Guildhall and the old prison
to the right of the Guildhall, next door to the baker
and hairdresser.

Sketches of Dover No 3
The arrival of the Steam Boats

No sooner does a distant line of smoke
Proclaim the Bologne steamer to be near
Than fly and donkey-chaise are straight bespoke,
To carry gaping idlers to the Pier.

Mark, how they stand in crowds along the Quay
Straining - with outstretched neck and eager glance -
What think you now that they are come to see?
Some grand ambassador direct from France?
No - half a dozen wretches sick from sea!

She nears the side; the wheels are stopped; the stream
Is whizzing all its wondrous strength away;
And 'Dumbie's' eyes intelligently beam
The signal that his lips refuse to say.

The rope is thrown him - head and stern are fast;
And now the ladder's lowered on the deck,
While at its foot young M—e stands to check
Illicit goods that might be smuggled past.

The pale faced pasengers now, one by one,
With tottering knee, ascend the slipp'ry stair:
While 'Ship Inn, Union, York Hotel, sir, Gun,
The London, Dover Castle, Shakespeare, - Where
Is it you please to go?' ring through the air.
Good Lord! defend me from those horrid touters,
For as a nuisance, they are out-and-outers.

But now the crowd has seen this packet clear,
Away they go, in one long struggling string,
Across the drawbridge, to the other pier
To see what more the Calais boat may bring. A.W'

page 8, 13 June 1835

Sketches of Dover. No 4
Arrival of the steam boats continued

'Heu! quibus insidiis, qua me circumdedit arte.'

But while the Calais boat is drawing near
I'll take a stroll upon the Southern Pier,
For there I'm sure to find some curious wretches,
And very proper subjects for my Sketches.

There is an old man-who in storm and calm,
Summer and Winter, paceth up and down
Those ancient planks. He beareth 'neath his arm
A spyglass, rather worn. He may be known
By many tokens, but his face I ween
Can never be forgotten when once seen.
It is a bronze of an unusual kind,
A mixture as it were, of many a hue;
Brown from the sun, and scarlet from the wind,
And here and there, a little dash of blue'
Doubtless from cold, while over all is thrown
A tint of brass, peculiarly his own.

I've marked this man, and when the pier was full,
I've seen his features lighted up with pleasure:
His little eyes, at other times so dull,
Would twinkle then like misers o'er their treasure.
I've marked him pause, and take a quick survey
Of all around-then, fixing upon one
Advance and all at once abruptly say-
'Fine vessel that there, underneath the sun,
'East Ingyman, sir, fourteen hundred ton-
'May be, your honour's sight is somewhat nigh;
'Here, take my glass, it's very good you'll find;
'Altho' mayhap, it has a queerish rind.'
Nor pauses the old fox, for a reply;
But leaves his glass, and says, 'I'll come by and bye.'
The stranger peeps, when back comes B—s again,
And thus pours forth his lamentable strain:
'Hard times, sir, these, nothing at all in view-
'More hands for work, than work for hands to do;
'Interest's all-for no one looks at worth;
'It's quite un-possible to find a birth.
'Upon my davy, as I'm standing here
'This blessed morn, I haven't tasted beer;
'And as for backy, lord! this many a day
'I've had a mind to throw my pouch away.

'None but a few great folk have got the wealth:
'But please your honour - like to drink your health.'

Few from this pressing speech can e'er refrain;
And thus one glass, doth many glasses gain. A.W'

Published in the *Dover Telegraph*, 18 July 1835

Sketches of Dover No.4
The Arrival of the Steam Boats. Concluded

'Nee gens ulla tuos aeque celebrabit honores.'
I'm one of that old fashioned set who glory
In all the ancient customs of the nation-
In short, to speak the truth-I am a Tory-
And dread the present spread of innovation.
I love old customs - and I love to see
Due honour paid to the nobility;
And well it pleases me to mark the state
With which this ancient place receives the great.

No sooner is it buzzed about the town,
That some great personage is coming o'er,
Than half the population hurry down,
And visitors and townsfolk line the shore.
Then, every one that's got a spy glass-spies,
And every one that has not got one - tries
To do his best without - and strains his eyes.
At length, the packet comes - and on her bow
A little flag is flutt'ring to and fro:
This little flag is not put up to show
(As some may think) which way the breezes blow,
But is a well-known signal that the boat
Bears on her deck some personage of note.
Between the piers, at length, she swiftly glides,
And in two minutes at her anchor rides.

A tall spare man is standing on the deck,
His eyes deep sunk - his features worn with care -
And wrapp'd in sables to the very neck,
As though he feared the lightest breath of air.
But though bowed down by sickness - still, I ween,
There is something in his noble mien
That tells the courtier. Now, with hat in hand,
Old – goes up, and begs his guest to land.
He bows, and followed by a scanty suite,
Ascends the rocking stair with doubtful foot.
And now he places foot on England's shore,
A signal's given - and, with mighty roar,
The cannon peal their welcome. Earth and sky,
And sea - in one long mingled sound reply;
While every staff displays its gayest flag,
From England's standard to the humblest rag.
Now from the throng an officer steps forth,
Whose breast is covered o'er with decorations,
(Yet not these orders - but his native worth,
Has gained for him the people's admiration) -
And he, with courteous phrase, rehearsed before,
Conducts the Envoy to his carriage door.
Bang go the steps - the carriage whirls along,
And scatters, right and left - the mighty throng.
At length it draws up at the Ship Inn door,
While there the crowd is thicker than before.
On either side the guards of honour stand
With arms presented - while their well trained band
Welcomes the envoy to his native land.
Quick as a light - see W—n approach,
And smiling - hand his Lordship from the coach;
And with a grace to be excell'd by none,
Ushers his noble guest to Number One.
And here, at length, the noble disappears,
Mid clanging bugles, and the people's cheers.

Draw near - ye democrats, and mark this scene,
Ye that would lay all ceremonies by -
Ye that would sweep away whate'er has been
Endeared to us from our infancy -
Ye that would tread the ermine in the mire,
And rob the mitre of a brilliant gem -
Ye that, by deep laid tactics, would conspire
To pick to pieces, even the diadem.
Draw near, and see, that though you have forgot
The honours due to rank - this town has not. A.W.'

Published in the *Dover Telegraph*, 3 October 1835.

Chapter 4

Children of Benjamin Jelly Worthington and Elizabeth Worthington (née Collins)

Elizabeth Worthington (1788-1828)

The first child of Benjamin Jelly and Elizabeth Worthington, Elizabeth was born 2 April 1788 and baptised 20 April 1788. Twenty-two years later on 24 July 1810, she married Henry Fairthorne of St John's, Shrivenham, Berkshire, bachelor, by licence at St Mary's Dover. Witnesses at the wedding were their relatives Charles Fairthorne, Charlotte Fairthorne and Harriot Worthington. Thomas Fairthorne of Wiltshire was the Bondsman.[1]

Elizabeth and Henry Fairthorne had nine children. The eldest Benjamin Edmund Fairthorne married firstly Miss A. Roberts of Slade End, a hamlet in the parish of Brightwell near Wallingford, Berkshire and secondly a Miss Trollope. Little is known about Henry, their second child. The eldest daughter Augusta remained unmarried. Hester Sophia married Mr. Carpenter and had one son. Their third daughter Mary Anne married Thomas Greenwood of Eastingford Manor, near Wallingford. Charlotte married W. Roberts at Slade End. Little is known about Elizabeth and Edward or about Harriet, who was baptised 4 November 1818 at St Mary's, Dover. Their fifth daughter remained unmarried. Elizabeth Fairthorne died 3 April 1828.[2] In 1845 the family were living at Brightwell, near Wallingford, county Berkshire.

Lieutenant Benjamin Worthington, R.N. (1790-1852)

Benjamin was born between the end of March and the beginning of April 1790 at Dover, the first son of Benjamin Jelly Worthington and Elizabeth Worthington, née Collins. He was baptised on 16 May 1790 at St Mary the Virgin Church, Dover by John Lyon, Minister.[3]

53 Lieutenant Benjamin Worthington (1790-1852).

54   One of Benjamin Jelly Worthington's daughters.

Benjamin grew up beside the sea and entered the Royal Navy as a 14-year-old midshipman on 18 January 1804. His first ship was the *Utrecht* 64 (guns), under Captains John Wentworth Loring and Fras. Pickmore, stationed in the Downs.

Midshipmen were originally senior petty officers and some were 'young gentlemen' aspiring to become Lieutenants. From 1794 newly rated midshipmen were regarded as future commissioned officers although the position never attained the dignity of a commssion. From 18 April 1805 until 20 March 1806 Benjamin was employed on the *Trusty* 50 (guns), Captain George Argles; from 21 March 1806 until 11 April 1806 as a supernumerary on the *Puissant* 74, Captain John Irwin; from 12 April 1806 to 22 August 1807 as midshipman on the *Latona* 38, Captain James Athol Wood, when he deserted. He was reinstated on 17 April 1808 and served again on board the *Puissant* until 30 December 1808. From 31 December 1808 he was employed as a midshipman on *Dromedary* store ship, Master-Commander Samuel P. Pritchard and by 31 August 1810 had served a total of four years, seven months, three weeks and four days.[4]

Benjamin was on board the 1,100-ton store ship HMS *Dromedary* when she departed from Portsmouth, England on 22 May 1809 and sailed into Sydney Harbour on 28 December 1809. On board were 592 people consisting of 10 officers, 406 men and 97 women and children. The *Sydney Gazette* for Sunday, 31 December 1809, reporting the following: 'On Thursday arrives from England, after a passage of eight months, His Majesty's Ships Dromedary of 40, Captain Pascoe [*sic*], and Hindostan of 50 guns, Captain Pritchin [*sic*], having on board the 1st Battalion of the 73rd Regiment of Foot.'

Also on board was the governor elect for the colony of New South Wales, Lachlan Macquarie, his wife Elizabeth and their children. Governor Macquarie wrote, 'We go out in two very fine ships–large and commodious–named the *Hindostan* and the *Dromedary*–both being troop ships. ... Mrs Macquarie and I embarked on the *Dromedary*, as being by far the finest ship of the two.'[5]

The 73rd Regiment of Foot embarked on board the *Dromedary* at Yarmouth before the ship proceeded to Spithead where it waited a fortnight to collect Governor Macquarie. He was attended by Colonel O'Connell, Captain Pasco and Mr. Ellis Bent, Judge Advocate General. The voyage of seven months and six days was via Rio de Janeiro, where Lieutenant Crane and Ensign McLain went ashore in kilts to the amazement and admiration of the Portuguese. On 23 August they departed for Table Bay and Cape Town which they reached on 23 September, before continuing southwards around the Cape of Good Hope two days later. The journey was long and made more tedious by Commander Pritchard and Captain Pasco who were chasing foreign vessels as prizes.[6] A Swedish vessel worth £45,000 was captured in the Bay of Biscay. There was a lot of illness on board the *Hindostan* and by 2 November there were only 150 tons of water left, causing some concern for the 51 children on board. King Island in Bass Strait was a welcome sight early in December.[7]

As far as Midshipman Benjamin Worthington was concerned the voyage was not without incident. Benjamin arrived in Sydney harbour confined in irons. It was intended that he be court martialled; however, he was reduced in rank and transferred from the *Dromedary* to the *Hindostan* to serve before the mast.[8] Benjamin was joined in this affair by another midshipman and the acting second master. On Christmas Day 1809, Charles Cleveland, second master, was insulted by an army officer who struck him. He returned the blow which gave the adjutant a black eye. Commander Pritchard described their behaviour as 'Scandalous, Mutinous and violent Conduct' and accused all three of getting drunk.[9]

By 28 February 1810 the two midshipmen had been reinstated to their former positions by Captain Pasco. He had received several applications from the master of the *Dromedary* and from Governor Macquarie begging him to relent 'as their Conduct, previous to the affair complained of, had been good, and that in this affair they had been led on by the Acting Master …'.[10]

More drama associated with the *Dromedary* appeared in the *Sydney Gazette* on Saturday, 10 March 1810 which read as follows:

> On Wednesday last, a very serious accident the cause of which is still unknown occurred in Sydney Cove, which had nearly occasioned the loss of His Majesty's store-ship *Dromedary*, a very fine vessel, formerly a 38 gun frigate. About five o'clock p.m. she was discovered to be on fire in the lower tier, and notwithstanding every exertion which could be possibly made, it was not finally extinguished till near 12 o'clock. The fire must have continued for a considerable time before it was observed, as the smoke issued suddenly from her stern in thick clouds, and the lower deck was so warm as nearly to prevent the sailors from standing on it. Eight feet and a half deep of water was introduced into her hold by scuttles cut in her side, pumps buckets etc. before they dared venture to open the hatches on the next deck, lest the influx of air should have accelerated the progress of the flames, and the ascending smoke have suffocated everyone near to it. Fortunately the gun-powder had been deposited in the Government Magazine on her arrival here, otherwise she must have exploded. When access was at length had to the seat of the fire, the spirits (of which there was a large quantity) were found so heated as to be nearly boiling, and some of the casks so much burned that a Gentleman pushed his finger with the slightest touch through one of them into the spirits; of course they must have been in imminent danger of catching the flame; and had this taken place the ship must have been inevitably destroyed.
>
> The alarm was early communicated to Government House, where a numerous party of Naval and Military Officers and other Gentlemen were sitting at dinner. Ceremony, on such an occasion, was easily dispensed with, and every person ran to render what assistance he could on an occasion threatening not only destruction to the ship herself, but to the various other ships lying close by her. Capt. Pascoe [sic] of H.M.S. *Hindustan*,

Capt. Porteous of the Porpoise, and Mr. Pritchard, Master Commanding the Dromedary, all went on board with the utmost dispatch, and by their unremitting exertions finally stopped the progress of this destructive element. Col. O'Connel, [sic] Commodore Bligh, & Col. Foveaux stood on the beach along which the Dromedary had been towed, giving such commands as the occasion required, and rendering very essential service by their judicious directions. Reports were reguarly made at short intervals to His Excellency the Governor, who with his Lady, beheld the whole scene from the viranda [sic] of Government House, full of anxiety not only for the fate of the ship herself, but that of the other shipping, and the numerous lives that must have been lost in case of her destruction. Mr. Pritchard, who is rather inclining to corpulency, was seen exerting himself with all the activity of youth itself, giving his commands in every quarter of the ship, most ably assisted by Captains Pascoe and Porteous, and the other Officers of H.M. ships, to whom it is much owing that this fine vessel was rescued from the destruction which so closely threatened her.

Midshipman Benjamin Worthington sailed from Australia with the controversial ex-governor and naval officer William Bligh, Colonel Paterson and members of the New South Wales Corps. The *Sydney Gazette*, 12 May 1810, reported:

Monday morning last a salute of 19 guns was fired from the battery at Dawes Point on His Majesty's ship *Hindostan*, bearing Commander Bligh's broad pennant getting underway to drop down to the Heads, from whence this day she sailed to England with the *Porpoise* and the *Dromedary*.

On 13 January 1811 Sir Roger Curtis, Baronet, Admiral of the Red, and Commander-in-Chief of His Majesty's Ships and vessels at Spithead and in Portsmouth Harbour, wrote a letter on board the *Royal William* in response to Benjamin's letter to him regarding the loss of his certificates during the fire on board the *Dromedary* in Sydney Cove 'and requested that the same may be dispensed with when he is examined touching his Qualifications to serve as a Lieutenant in the Royal Navy ...'.[11] Letters of testimony were forthcoming from W. Patterson, Captain and of HMS *Puissant* and Commander Pritchard who said:

These are to certify the Honourable Principal Officers and Commissioners of His Majesty's Navy that Mr Benjamin Worthington has Served as Midshipman on board His Majesty's Ship the Dromedary, under my Command, from the 31 Day of December 1808 to the 12 December 1810, during which time he behaved with Diligence and Sobriety, and was always obedient to Command; he had the Charge of a Watch to New South Wales and home again, which he performed to my Satisfaction, and I beg to Recommend him for Promotion.

Given under my Hand this 12th Day of December 1810

S.P. Pritchard Master Commanding.[12]

After being discharged from the *Dromedary* in England on 31 August 1810, Benjamin served on the *Puissant*, Captain W. Pattison; *Roebuck* 44, Captain Richard Curry; *Briseis* and *Leveret* sloops under Captains Charles Thulow Smith and George Wickens Willes, and *Hibernia* 120, flag ship of Sir William Sydney Smith on the Home, West India and Mediterranean stations.

The rank of lieutenant was the most junior of the ancient commissioned ranks and his first commission marked the real beginning of a man's career as a quarter-deck officer with prospects of command. Lieutenants were considered to be gentlemen whatever their actual social origins.[13] Benjamin applied to become a lieutenant on 6 March 1811 and acted as a junior lieutenant in the *Briseis* that same year. Between 15 May 1811 and 30 July 1811 he deserted but returned to the same ship as an able seaman until he was reinstated as acting lieutenant on 3 August 1811. His rank varied between able seaman, master's mate and midshipman on four different ships between 30 September 1811 and 2 February 1813.[14]

On 2 February 1813, the date of his commission, Benjamin was appointed to the *Swiftsure* 74 under Captain Edward Stirling Dickson from which ship he removed in the following month to the *Ajax* 74 as 5th lieutenant with 590 men under Captains Sir Robert Laurie, Robert Waller Otway and George Mundy. In her he co-operated in the seizure of St Sebastian and assisted at the capture on 17 March 1814 off Scilly of *L'Alcyon*, a corvette of 16 guns[15] and 120 men. He also escorted from Bordeaux to Quebec a squadron of transports, having on board 5,000 troops, destined to reinforce the English army in Canada. He became semi-retired from the Navy at the age of 25 years on 23 November 1814 and received half pay.[16] Although he missed the Battle of Trafalgar he served on ships involved in that episode and he was present when his ship bombarded San Sebastian in Spain during Wellington's Peninsula War.

Benjamin and Mary

Three years after his retirement from the Royal Navy Benjamin married Priscilla Belford by licence on 27 November 1817 at Gorleston with Southtown, Suffolk, England. Witnesses to the marriage were Charlotte and Anne Belford, two members of the Gordon family and William Collins Worthington. Little is known about the Belford family and Charlotte Louisa Belford who married John Barnard Turner at Lowestoft, Suffolk on 27 May 1824 could have been Priscilla's sister. It is not known

55 Oil painting, measuring approx. 6 x 4ft, of Lieutenant Benjamin and Mary Worthington, *c.*1834 by either William Salter or Sir John Watson Gordon. In possession of Jean Hankey, Aberystwyth.

56   *Grand Hotel* and sea front mansions where Benjamin Worthington lived, photographed pre-1892.

whether Benjamin and Priscilla had any children or what became of Priscilla as her burial has not been found. During Benjamin's address to the Dover Humane Society in 1836 he referred to 'his residence on the coast of Norfolk' and this may be where he spent that little known part of his life between 1819-1831.

Benjamin became a Freeman of Dover by birth on 12 June 1818. The yearly register of Dover Freemen records his address as Charlton Road, Dover between November 1832 and November 1833 and Strond Street, Dover 1834-1835. Mr. B. Worthington and Mr. H.N. Watson were received as members of the Dover Corporation at an inauguration dinner according to the *Dover Telegraph*, 16 November 1833.[17] During this time period Benjamin subscribed to a *Topographical Dictionary of England* by Samuel Lewis in which his name was listed when it was first published in London during 1837.

Benjamin was 44 years old when he married, secondly, Mary Lee on 12 August 1834 at St Martins in the Fields, London. Mary was born *c.*1810 at Sandwich, Kent and was 20 years younger than her husband. An expertly executed oil painting of Benjamin and Mary Worthington hangs in his great-granddaughter's living room in Aberystwyth. Benjamin is in naval uniform and wearing the Naval General Service Medal with bars for San Sebastian and Curacao. The artist is believed to be either William Salter or Sir John Watson Gordon.

In December 1835 a subscription list 'for the relief of Suffering Protestant Clergy in Ireland' published in the *Dover Telegraph* lists Mr. B. Worthington £1 and Mrs. B. Worthington £1. Benjamin and Mary bought a house at 1 Marine Parade, Dover and lived there for several years.[18] In 1838-9 this house was valued at £40 with an annual assessment or rate of 13s. 4d. Benjamin also owned a house at Eastbrook Place valued in 1838-9 at £80 with an annual assessment of £1 6s. 8d.

Seven children are known to have been born to Benjamin and Mary Worthington and baptised in Dover. They were: Alfred Worthington (1835-1925), Benjamin Worthington (1837-74), Mary Ann Worthington (1838-65), William Worthington (1839-41), Elizabeth Worthington (1841-1908), Edward Worthington (1843-1924), Priscilla Worthington (1844-8).

Their youngest child, Priscilla Worthington died of a lumber abcess on 11 October 1848 at Strond Street aged four years and was buried at St James the Apostle Church on 19 October 1848. The 1851 census records the family at 25 Strond Street, a terrace of houses in the parish of St Mary's. Fourteen-year-old Benjamin was a scholar and still living at home. Mary Worthington employed two house servants, Caroline Taylor, aged 29 years, a native of Dover, and Madelina Tucker, who was the same age and born in Margate.

Benjamin's Efforts to Improve the Harbour

Benjamin was a fearless and expert sailor. He would sail in very rough seas for mere pleasure and in weather far too rough for the ordinary seaman. The townspeople would gather on the beach front to watch the clever manoeuvring of his small yacht on leaving the harbour with no one on board but himself. This was a difficult undertaking at most times and especially so in bad weather.[19]

On 8 October 1836 he wrote a letter to the *Dover Telegraph* on life saving. He also occupied his leisure time and spent some of the best years of his life and a great deal of money on projecting schemes for the improvement of Dover Harbour. It is believed that one such improvement scheme was shown to Her Majesty Queen Victoria, who with her mother frequently stopped at Worthington's *Ship Hotel* when going to and from the Continent. The *Ship Hotel* was owned by Benjamin who together with his brother Henry had bought the famous establishment from the previous owner, Mr. Charles Wright in February 1834. Benjamin was described 'as a fine, tall, gentlemanly man, superior to the ordinary run of hotel landlords of that day—more refined'. He was also very wealthy and 'was regarded as a £30,000 man'.[20]

It was not until Benjamin was summoned to give evidence during 1836 before a Select Committee of the House of Commons enquiring into the state of the Dover Harbour, that he began to devise any concrete plans for improving the harbour. His recollections of the harbour encompassed a period of over thirty years and he stated that

> I do not know of a single work that has been carried on that I can really say has improved the harbour. We are as subject to a bar now as ever we were, and I consider the natural qualities of the harbour to have been quite destroyed. It was formerly known, even to a proverb, that Dover Harbour as a dry harbour when once entered, was the safest harbour in England; but its qualities are now entirely superseded, from its being surrounded by perpendicular walls; and formerly the original state of the harbour in the south-west side formed a bight, a sort of bay, which was surrounded by the beach, and this beach caused the swell to be subdued in the harbour; it was placed for it to fall into and become exhausted; not only that, but it was a very convenient and safe place for vessels taking refuge to moor in; and it has also rendered the harbour dangerous for vessels to enter by thus being contracted.

He added that no one would now willingly moor his vessel in the outer harbour, but these difficulties could to some extent be overcome by the provision of a beaching place where ships could safely ground if unmanageable in stormy weather. It would also have the effect of diminishing the swell. Such a place had formerly existed in what was called the Green Fields, the south-west side of the harbour just mentioned, occupied in 1980 by the wet and dry docks.[21]

His public spirited attitude and his endeavours to make Dover a safe harbour were greatly influenced by an ever increasing number of shipwrecks. In 1836 a Select Committee of the House of Commons was appointed to enquire into the causes of so many wrecks. Britain then had 24,500 ships which employed 250,000 men. Statistics indicated that for every 16 sailors who died of diseases, 11 died from drowning. Between 1833-5, 1,573 vessels were wrecked and 129 were either lost or missing. Entire crews of 81 vessels were drowned and 1,714 persons perished. Benjamin produced a map delineating the alterations he had in mind. The Committee was impressed by his presentation and he was recalled after half an hour and asked to put his views in writing by the following morning.

Members of the Committee appointed to enquire into the state of Dover Harbour were Mr. Fector, Sir Edward Knatchbull, Mr. Majoribanks, Mr. Thomas Baring, Mr. Hume, Sir Charles Adam, Mr. Herries, Mr. Robert Steuart, Mr. Plumptre, Mr. Ingham, Sir John Rae Reid, Lord Viscount Mahon, Mr. Bernal, Mr. Elphinstone and Mr. Robinson.[22] The inquiry examined many witnesses including John Hawkins, Clerk of Works; John Shipdem, Register; John Iron, Harbour Master; John Benjamin Post, Cinque Ports Pilot; Daniel Peake, Cinque Ports Pilot; Philip Hardwicke, Receiver of Harbour Rents; James Walker, Harbour Engineer; William Prescott, Chairman of Meeting of Inhabitants; Richard Wardle, Engineer's Assistant; Robert Hammond, Warden of the Pilots; Philip Going, shipowner; Captain Boxer, R.N.; Isaac Pattison, Harbour Pilot; Humphrey Humphrey, Chairman of the Common Hall; Captains

57   Mid-1800s engraving of Dover Harbour showing Wellington Dock in the foreground with exit to tidal inner harbour on the left and Granville Dock on the right.

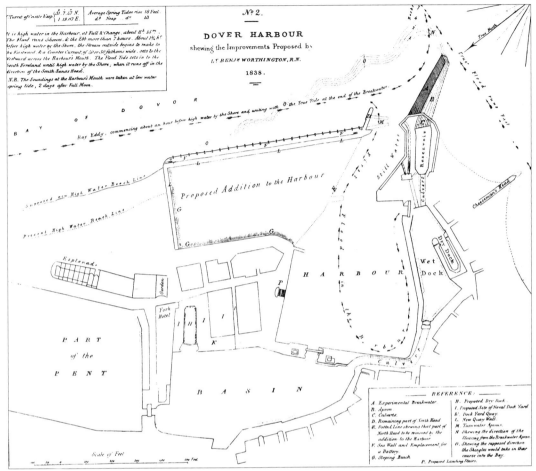

58 Map of Dover Harbour showing the improvements proposed by Lieutenant Benjamin Worthington, R.N., 1838.

H.D. Jones, R.E., Elliott, R.N. and William Cubitt, C.E. government witnesses and Lieutenant B. Worthington, R.N. The evidence given was remarkably varied. There was a great weight of evidence to the effect that the works carried out during the last 20 years had made the harbour worse. The harbour officials strongly approved the new sluicing scheme then under construction but the witnesses sent down to examine the harbour on behalf of the Government disapproved of the form and situation of the pier-heads, and several experienced witnesses were strongly in favour of the proposals of Perry, Smeaton, Rennie and Walker for getting rid of the shingle by extending the South Pier.[23]

During October 1836 the Board of Honourable Commissioners of Dover Harbour sent for Benjamin, and his models and plans were handed to the harbour engineer. He had thought out a scheme for the general improvement and enlargement of the harbour and had spent some £400 on the project to demonstrate its advantages. As a result he received many flattering testimonials and these gave him encouragement to persevere in his endeavours.

In devising his plan, Benjamin endeavoured to strike at the root of three great evils, viz: the bar, the heavy swell at the mouth of the Harbour and the swell within the Harbour. Benjamin believed that it was the duty of every man to contribute something, however trifling, to the sum of human happiness.

During 1838 Benjamin wrote *The Proposed Plan for Improving Dover Harbour with Practical Observations and Illustrations*, printed and published by W. Batcheller, Dover 1838. This reference book was written by a man who stated that early in life he had been 'educated in the school of usefulness rather than where literary blandishments were studied and his one desire was to benefit his town'. His 174-page technical publication is now occasionally found in antiquarian rare book lists and when a copy is found it is often minus the seven plates of maps and illustrations.

In the introduction Benjamin states that his motives in coming forward with his scheme 'are entirely uninfluenced by the most remove views of personal advantage, for under any circumstances I should decline the acceptance of profit or emolument of any kind, supposing my plans should be adopted'. Later in the book he says,

> The first impulse was given by my being called upon to give evidence before a Committee of the House of Commons appointed to enquire into the state of Dover Harbour; I never sought nor expected to be called upon to give an opinion on the subject, having considered that my opinion would not have been thought of the least value in so high a quarter. The time, however, that elapsed between the receiving of the summons and of being called upon to attend, gave me some opportunity to direct my attention to a plan of improvement, and, by the time I was directed to appear, I had partially developed the one which I have since had modelled in an improved form, and which I have submitted to the inspection of many scientific gentlemen, Naval and Military officers, engineers, etc, many of whom have voluntarily sent me their testimonials in its favour.

Benjamin includes in his Treatise the 51 testimonials he received in favour of his scheme thanking him for his efforts, many very lengthy, but all very appreciative. An example of those received are as follows: Commanders of H.M. Mail Packets, four signatures; Members of the Fellowship of Trinity Pilots, nine signatures; Harbour Pilots and boatmen of Dover, 50 signatures; Commanders and Managers of vessels in the Passage Service, giving names of the steam vessels, seven signatures; Second Masters of H.M. steam packets, three signatures; Pilots belonging to the Admiralty Packets, five signatures. Many testimonials were received from naval and military men as well as private individuals and personal friends.

Some 67 persons inspected the plans and models and these included the Duke of Wellington, Lord George Lennox, M.P., Lord Graves, Lord Grimston, M.P., the Duke of Sutherland, Francis Baring, M.P., Sir John Rennie, Lord Loftus, Lord Fitzroy Somerset, Lord Southampton and Earl St Vincent.

On being examined before the Select Committee, Benjamin says he felt he ought not to find fault with what was being done, without suggesting some alternative plan. The works he advocated were of two kinds, the object of one being to improve the harbour and the other to enlarge it. He proposed to prevent shingle from lodging in the harbour mouth and to lessen the troublesome agitation in the tidal basin by constructing a timber breakwater. Secondly he advocated building a tidal dock outside the harbour, at the back of the North Pier.

Mr. James Walker, a civil engineer who had been in practice 25-30 years, was first consulted respecting the harbour in November 1834 when he received a letter from the prime warden, the Duke of Wellington, asking him to report on the condition of the harbour. He also gave evidence before the House of Commons in 1836.

Benjamin's scheme was ultimately rejected because of the expense, which in his evidence he had said he was unable to estimate. The decision was also not surprising as the harbour engineer, James Walker, who was asked to consider Benjamin's proposal, had already had his plans and works criticised and condemned by Benjamin on earlier occasions. He received the following notification following a Session of the Honourable Warden and Assistants of Dover Harbour held on 27 October 1837:

> The Board considered Mr Worthington's Plan of Improvement of Dover Harbour and heard Mr Walker's opinion thereon. Considering all circumstances, the Board felt that they cannot carry Mr Worthington's plan into execution, and ordered that the Plans and seven Plates be returned to him with the thanks of the Board for the interest he has taken in the Harbour.
>
> Extracted from the Minutes.
> John Shipdem Register.

At the time there were other political schemes afoot of which Benjamin knew nothing. The final outcome saw the Commissioners enlarge the inside of the harbour in a modified and mutilated form. In 1848 the Admiralty Pier was commenced and it achieved the same purpose as Benjamin's breakwater would have done.[24] The book which Benjamin wrote contains a wonderful collection of plans and opinions, ancient and modern, and it is still a valuable work of reference today.

Benjamin was described as a 'thoughtful native of Dover'[25] and a 'man of great foresight and sound judgement and one who was enthusiastically inclined to work for the benefit of the Port of Dover without any other reward than the satisfaction of having done something for the advancement of Dover'.[26]

During November 1836 Benjamin addressed the Dover Humane Society meeting on the subject of life-boats and life-buoys. He had originally published his

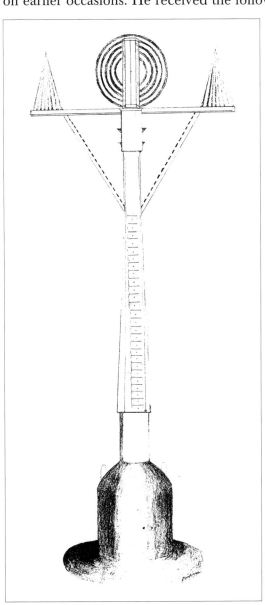

59 Line drawing of a proposed warning and safety beacon 'Projected by Lieutenant B. Worthington, R.N., F.R.S.'

ideas along with those of others, as a means of preserving life at the entrance to the port of Dover, by a letter in the *Dover Telegraph* recommending the establishment of life-buoys and proposed a subscription for that purpose. He was doubtful whether life-boats alone were sufficient. Most of the accidents happened before the harbour's mouth in a strong current and heavy surf. When men were immersed in broken water they were soon exhausted and quickly became the prey of the elements. During a residence on the coast of Norfolk, he had witnessed the practical use of the life-boat upon Captain Manby's principle, and also that of his mortar for throwing ropes to stranded vessels. He went on to say that there the coast is flat and the sort of life-boat used there would be totally inapplicable to the Port of Dover. Benjamin avoided any further discussion as to what would be appropriate as a resolution had been passed to solicit the aid of the Duke of Wellington and the Harbour Commissioners. He was one of several speakers who gave their views.[27]

Light Ships

It is family folklore that Benjamin invented the first light ship, named *Mornewick*, for service in the Channel to protect ships running on to the Goodwin Sands. No authentic record of this can be found in records pertaining to the Admiralty, Lloyds, Corporation of Trinity House or the Dover Harbour Board. There is some evidence that Benjamin built a light ship and the Dover Museum did have a model of such a ship in 1928. Two paintings in the museum dated 1843 depict a light ship in a storm and in the other as being in a calm. The description at the foot of the pictures is as follows: 'A drawing representing the warning and Life-boat Beacon by day and a light by night in a storm and in a calm, projected and respectively dedicated to the Royal Navy and Commercial Navy of England by their obedient servant, Lt Benjamin Worthington, R.N.'.

There is nothing to prove that the Lieutenant got any further than giving his project to the naval world and supplementing this by a model. It is not likely he would have gone to the considerable expense of fitting out a light ship and manning

60 'A Drawing representing the Warning and Life-Boat Beacon in a Calm. Projected and respectively dedicated to the Royal and Commercial Navy of England by their obedient servant, Lieutenant Benjamin Worthington, R.N.'

61 'A Drawing representing the warning and Life-Boat Beacon by day and a light by night in a storm. Projected and respectively dedicated to the Royal and Commercial Navy of England by their obedient servant, Lieutenant Benjamin Worthington, R.N.'

it unless he was assured that he would be refunded by the Admiralty or the Dover Harbour Board.

Culverins

When Mr. Bottle's chemist shop was built in Dover during 1838 two pieces of ordinance, called culverins, were found buried in an old wall. Lieutenant Benjamin had these cleaned and mounted and presented them to the Museum of the Naval and Military Institution, London.

A culverin is one of the earlier forms of obsolete large cannon, of great length, generally an 18-pounder and weighting 50 hundredweight. During 1928 a letter was written by a family historian to the above institution to ask if the culverins were in a position that would allow a photograph to be taken of them. A reply was received from the curator of the 'Royal United Service Institution' stating that in 1893 'when the Museum was moved from Whitehall Yard into the Banqueting Hall, Whitehall, many of the exhibits appear to have been transferred to the Royal Artillery Institution, Woolwich'. The secretary of this institution responded to a letter of inquiry regarding their whereabouts stating, 'There are five culverins in the Rotunda Museum but there is nothing to show that they were presented by Lt Benjamin Worthington, R.N. and unless you can give me details, such as inscriptions or mottoes, it would be impossible to identify them'.

It is possible they may be in one of the other London museums. They are not likely to have been dismounted, and if two mounted culverins could be found they might well be claimed to be those presented by the lieutenant.

Land acquisition in New Zealand

According to a New Zealand Land-Order dated 1 October 1840, Benjamin Worthington of 1 Marine Place, Dover, Kent, Lieutenant R.N. purchased five sections of town land in New Plymouth, New Zealand, each consisting of one quarter of an acre, from the Plymouth Company of New Zealand. The town plans record that Benjamin bought section number 1598 bounded by Lemon Street, section number 936 bounded by Courtenay Street, adjoining sections 659 bounded by Devon Street and 672 bounded by Powderham Street, and one other, details unknown. These purchases were entered on record 27 March 1856 by Andrew Sinclair, Colonial Secretary and Registrar.[28] It is not known whether they were developed by members of the family who were entitled as heirs and assigns to the land after his death. Lieutenant Benjamin's eldest son Benjamin sailed to New Zealand and settled there about 1856 and could have had an interest in them. Unpaid rates amounting to 5s. were due in 1855.[29] The land was probably sold by his heirs sometime after 1856.

Benjamin and his brother Henry Worthington were business partners, their activities being discussed further in the chapter on Henry.

Indenture 1845

Following the death of Elizabeth Worthington, widow of Benjamin Jelly Worthington, on 30 April 1845 an Indenture was made on 21 August 1845. This interesting and informative agreement was drawn up between

Benjamin Worthington of Dover in the county of Kent, Lieutenant in Her Majestys Navy, and Benjamin Fairthorne of Shrivenham near Farringdon in the County of Berkshire and Harriet [sic] his wife (late Harriet [sic] Worthington spinster), Charlotte Worthington of Dover aforesaid spinster, George Finch Jennings, Dover aforesaid Esquire and Hester his wife (late Hester Worthington spinster) together with Robert Potter of Lydden in the county of Kent Esquire and Henry Worthington of Dover aforesaid Esquire

and other family members indemnifying themselves against all future 'actions, suits, accounts and claims' etc. as executors under the terms of Benjamin Jelly Worthington's will.[30] Following Elizabeth's death Benjamin Jelly Worthington's estate was finally settled.

Worthington Property 1848

After living in Marine Parade it appears that Benjamin moved to Eastbrook Place where he lived for some time before finally dying in Strond Street. His sister Hester Jennings and brother Thomas Worthington were neighbours.

The contents of Benjamin's property, Eastbrook House at Eastbrook Place, were advertised for sale by public auction in the *Dover Telegraph* on Saturday, 13 May 1848 and described by Messrs G. Flashman & Co. as an 'extensive sale of valuable modern household furniture and effects, china, glass, etc. etc. by order of the proprietor Benjamin Worthington, Esquire'. Another advertisement a week later gave more detail of the forthcoming auction which was to take place on the premises of Eastbrook House on 24 and 25 May. The contents were to be sold without reserve and comprised

> several mahogany pillar four post bedsteads and furniture with mahogany cornices; twelve very superior goose-feathered beds, bolsters and pillow and thick-bordered horse-hair mattresses and paliasses; large Witney blankets and counterpanes; excellent mahogany circular and straight front chest of drawers; mahogany and painted dressing tables and appendages; large mahogany box-frame and tray dressing glasses; painted bedroom chairs and towel horses; mahogany bidets and commodes; set of Spanish mahogany Trafalgar chairs (with carved backs depicting Trafalgar war ships); handsome Mahogany couch in hair seating; large Turkey, Brussels and Kidderminster carpets; Turkey and other hearth rugs; bronzed fenders and steel fire-irons; set of mahogany dining tables; valuable mahogany bookcase, handsome mahogany loo table on carved pillar stand; large and excellent painted bookcase; painted wardrobe; mahogany Pembroke and other tables; painted floor-cloths, stair carpets and rods; a set of antique hall furniture, embracing hall chains, tripod flower stands, side table, umbrella stand, hall lamps, etc. etc. Excellent dinner and dessert services with a large variety of useful kitchen and culinary utensils. Also a number of valuable old prints in oak frames.

Benjamin also advertised a store to let in the *Dover Telegraph* on 27 May, 3 June and 10 June 1848.

Benjamin died at 25 Strond Street on 13 February 1852, aged 61 years, of congestive heart disease. Strond Street was a terrace of houses which stood on the site now occupied by the harbour station. He was buried 21 February 1852 in the family tomb in the crypt of St James the Apostle, Dover. His wife Mary lived at Effingham Crescent in 1858[31] and died in London on 1 August 1864 aged 54 years. She was buried in the family vault at Buckland churchyard, Dover.

62   Worthington hillside vaults in Buckland, St Andrew's churchyard, Dover.

Probate of Benjamin's relatively short will was granted on 4 April 1852 to Mary Worthington, widow, John Boyton and William Collins Worthington. Thomas Knight Worthington, the fourth executor, renounced the probate and execution of the said will, codicil and Letters of Administration. Benjamin left his printed books, household goods, furniture, plate, linen, china, glass, earthenware, prints, pictures to his wife with three calendar months to select which items she preferred to keep for herself and the children. John Boyton was bequeathed £100 provided he carry out his duties as executor. All lands, messuages, tenements and real estate were left to Mary Worthington, John Boyton, William Collins Worthington and Thomas Knight Worthington their heirs, executors, administrators and assigns.

Mary Ann Worthington (1792-1801)

The third child of Benjamin Jelly and Elizabeth Worthington, Mary Ann was born 17 March 1792 and baptised 15 April 1792 at St Marys, Dover. Mary Ann died 15 October 1801 and is interred in a vault beneath St James Church, Dover with her youngest brother George.[32]

Harriot Worthington (1794-1861)

Harriot, sometimes spelt Harriott, was born 7 June 1794 and baptised 6 July 1794 at St Mary's, Dover, the fourth child of Benjamin Jelly and Elizabeth Worthington. Between 1810 and 1841 she married Benjamin Fairthorne a farmer and native of Bishopstone, Wiltshire. In 1845 they were living at Shrivenham, near Faringdon, Berkshire.[33] They had no children. Harriot died on 25 September 1861 at Shrivenham of cancer of the bowel aged 67 years. Benjamin Fairthorne was still living at the time of her death and was described as a gentleman.

Charlotte Worthington (1796-1861)

Charlotte was baptised 21 February 1796 at St Mary's, Dover, the fourth daughter and fifth child of Benjamin Jelly and Elizabeth Worthington. She remained unmarried and lived at 5 Eastbrook Place,[34] Dover, close to her sister, Hester Jennings and brother-in-law, George Finch Jennings. Charlotte had her own private income[35] and owned a house in Folkestone Road occupied by a Mr. Williams between 8 January- 14 April 1853. She died on 8 January 1861 aged 64 years and is buried in a family vault in St Andrew's, Buckland Churchyard, Dover.[36] A marble memorial plaque records her passing. She left all her property to her niece Elizabeth Harriot, the fourth daughter and ninth child of Henry Worthington, whom she had previously adopted.

Hester Worthington (1798-1871)

Hester was born 3 January 1798 and baptised 29 January 1798. On 29 September 1831 she married George Finch Jennings, brother of her sister-in-law, Mary Worthington. On the marriage licence Hester is described as a spinster aged 31 years and George, a bachelor aged 29 years. They had no children.

George Finch Jennings was a landed proprietor[37] and woolstapler[38] as well as being an artist. He and Hester lived at Eastbrook Cottage, 109 Eastbrook Place where they were cared for by two servants, Esther Post and Elizabeth Friend.[39] The Rating List for Dover 1838-39 gives the house and garden a value of £100 and a rate payment of 13s. 4d. was due. Hester was a fundholder[40] and George held the position of Pavement Board Commissioner,[41] Dover Councillor,[42] and in 1847 was an Alderman in the Dover Corporation[43]. A memorial in the Buckland Churchyard reads: 'Sacred to the Memory of GEORGE FINCH JENNINGS Esq. Justice of the Peace of the Town of Dover who died April 24th 1866 aged 64 years. Unto thine hand I commit my spirit. Thou hast redeemed me O Lord God of truth. Also of HESTER wife of the above who died at Dover February 16 1871 aged 76 years.'

William Collins Worthington (1800-1885), M.D., M.R.C.S., F.R.A.S., L.S.A.

Also born in Dover, home to his family for seven generations, William Collins Worthington was the seventh child and second son of Benjamin Jelly and Elizabeth. Born on 27 February 1800, he was baptised at St Mary's Church and named after his maternal grandfather and an uncle.

With his father so often working away from home, following orders to cruise off the East Coast, it was thought best the children were sent to school. William was sent to Mr. Nicol's school at Yarmouth until 1815, when at the age of 14 years he was placed in the care of a Mr. Hardy, house surgeon at the Norfolk and Norwich Hospital.

As a resident house pupil for the next three years under Doctors Rigby and Phillip Martineau, William gathered a thorough insight into medicine and surgery, in particular lithotomy, the incision of a duct or organ for removal of calculi. Through his studies William developed a great love for surgery, in which he was later to excel. During his pupilage he also became a member of the Norwich Physiological Society.

63 Dr. William Collins Worthington.

After completing his internship, William entered the Middlesex Hospital and worked under Sir Charles Bell, a Scottish physiologist who discovered the distinction between nerves of motion and sensation. William also studied anatomy at Joshua Brook's School. In 1818 he went to London in order to refine his hospital skills and lodged with a Mr. Acret's family, a surgeon who lived in Bedford Square. After passing an examination on 5 November 1819 William became a member of the Royal College of Surgeons and remained at the college until 1821. In 1820 he passed another important exam and became a member of the Apothecaries' Hall which entitled him to the nominals L.S.A. Candidates for licences from the Apothecaries' Company served a five-year apprenticeship before their exam.

By August 1821 William had moved to Lowestoft, Suffolk, a market town seaport and fashionable bathing place on the most easterly point of England, overlooking what was then called the German Ocean. Situated 115 miles from London, the streets of Lowestoft were well paved and lit. The houses, chiefly of brick, were

neat and modern, and the inhabitants are well supplied with water from springs; the air is considered highly salubrious, especially to invalids ... There is a good theatre, in which performances take place every alternate year; also a spacious and elegant assembly room, where balls are held at Christmas, and concerts twice a week during the bathing season, and a subscription reading room and library.[44]

The cliffs surrounding Lowestoft were said to 'abound with organic remains, such as the bones and teeth of the mammoth, the horns and bones of the elk ... and shells and fossils of various kinds'.[45]

Among William's first achievements in Lowestoft was the establishment in 1822 of the Cottage Hospital, which grew rapidly in size until it contained 30 beds. In April 1822 William entered into a planned 10-year partnership with Mr. Ball, a surgeon, after agreeing to pay him the sum of £500. In the same year William was also appointed surgeon to the new Mutford and Lothingland General Dispensary or Infirmary, established and supported by public subscription and contribution through the joint efforts of a Dr. Barry and himself.[46] A more 'commodious' building was erected in 1839-40 in order to cope with the 400 to 500 patients treated annually and the 700 to 800 patients 'in-doors'.

Sometime before 1868 a Museum of Pathological Anatomy adjoining the infirmary was donated to the Infirmary by William Collins Worthington.[47] For half a century William was active in an extensive practice, a continual contributor to medical literature and a keen pathologist who lost no opportunity of making a post-mortem examination.[48]

Some of William's publications included: *Vaccination*; *On Stricture of the Trachea*; *Fissions Communicating between the Bladder and Ileum, simulating stone*; *Sacculated Oesophagus*; *Aneurism* and in *The Lancet*, 'Paracentesis'. He was a member of the Medico-Chirurgical Society of London and was admitted as a Fellow to the Royal College of Surgeons on 26 August 1844 (F.R.A.S. Hon.). He continued to be listed in the annually published *Medical Directory* until 1867.[49]

On 1 August 1826 William married Sarah Scott, eldest daughter of Samuel Scott a solicitor of Bungay, Suffolk, at St Mary's Church in Bungay.[50] In July 1827 William and Sarah purchased the house they already lived in from Mr Miller, a solicitor, for the sum of £1,500. The couple had 13 children, all born in Lowestoft:

64 Sarah Worthington, née Scott, as a young woman.

Ann Charlotte Worthington (1827-35)
Elizabeth Harriette Worthington (1828-66)
William Scott Worthington (1830-70)
Samuel Francis Worthington (1831-4)
Charlotte Emily Worthington (1832-1903)
Hester Sarah Worthington (1834-1922)
Francis Samuel Worthington (1836-1912)
John Scott Worthington (1837-83)
Marion Worthington (1838-1932)
Edward Scott Worthington (1840-)
James Copland Worthington (1841-1906)
Ann Scott Worthington (1843)
Caroline Crosse Worthington (1846-83).

William kept a diary and in it were recorded events such as the death of his uncle and namesake, William Collins, in July 1831 aged 68 years, following a short illness of 'gout in the stomach'.[51] His uncle was buried on 8 August in St James Churchyard, Dover. In August 1831 William wrote that his partnership with Mr. Bell had been dissolved by mutual consent, three months short of the 10 years originally agreed upon.

Other diary entries from this era include mention that his brother Tom (Thomas Knight Worthington) from Upton Woodside had stayed with the family and that his sister Hester had married Mr. George Jennings on 29 September 1831, 'both of whom I meet in London'.

That William was a very earnest and religious man was evident from the daily jottings and self examinations in his diary and also from his lengthy will. After

65 Sarah Worthington (1802-55).

attending two church services at St Peter's every Sunday, it was his habit to make notes on the sermons and apply the teachings to himself, and he wrote many earnest prayers for grace and enlightenment. He was most anxious and careful about his wife's and children's religious training and family Bible readings and prayers were a daily occurrence. Today his religious views would perhaps be considered calvinistic and narrow, for he also believed in the incapacity for true faith and repentence of the natural man, efficacious grace and final perseverance.[52]

In 1832, due to Sarah's continual ill-health, William considered leaving Lowestoft for a milder climate and starting a new practice elsewhere. He beseeched the guidance of the Almighty in fervent words; Sarah's health improved and his patients increased in number so they decided to stay in Lowestoft.

At about this time a cholera epidemic was raging throughout parts of Europe, depopulating whole districts. William noted, 'Every thinking and serious person cannot but regard the present time as most awful. May it please God to awake my poor sinful soul to a deep sense of the importance of watchfulness and prayer and of the necessity of being found ready to meet this visitation.'

He continued, 'In March 1832 cholera is raging in England and a Fast and a Day of Intercession is ordered by the King, William IV. In Paris 7000 persons are attacked in 15 days, including the Prime Minister, some 40 a day.' A few months later cholera again broke out in London, attacking all classes. It was also prevalent in Yarmouth, Norwich and Lowestoft, the United States of America and Canada. By 1833 the epidemic was almost over and amidst great national rejoicing an April Day of Thanksgiving was ordered by the King.

In the previous year there was a note in William's diary to the effect that the House of Lords had rejected the Reform Bill, causing great consternation and misgivings throughout the country. The first Reform Bill was introduced in Parliament in 1831 and Parliament was dissolved. The Bill was later reintroduced and passed the Commons, before being rejected by the Lords. King William IV, however, by Commission, gave his consent in 1832 to the passing of the Reform Bill which had two main objectives, the redistribution of parliamentary representation and extending the qualifications for voting so that more citizens could vote. It effectively destroyed the monopoly of political power held by the landed gentry.

In October 1833 William accepted the post of Honorary Secretary to the Lowestoft branch of the Bible Society. He considered the position a great privilege, but also a serious responsibility. In May 1834 he was 'grateful' that he was able to establish a prayer meeting in his own house on Saturday evenings and thanked God, asking that it be blessed.

For a busy and hard working doctor whose duties did not cease with the setting of the sun, his great interest in religious matters shows his sincerity for the spiritual welfare of those around him. His life was not without tragedy. William wrote of his own and Sarah's great sorrow at losing their son Samuel Francis at the age of five years from scarlet fever. Nearly four months later their eldest child Ann Charlotte died of the same disease, aged seven years. William outlived his nine siblings, his wife and at least seven of his 13 children.

In the 1851 census William's family were listed as living at 194 High Street, Lowestoft, Suffolk.[53] Those present at the time were: William and Sarah; their children Elizabeth, William, Charlotte, Hester, Mary Anne [sic] and Caroline who were listed as 'scholars at home'; George (Finch Jennings) Worthington, nephew 17 years, born Dover, Kent, medical student; Frank Workman, pupil 17 years, born Berkshire, Reading; a housemaid, Mary Adecible, 19 years; cook, Phoebe Cole, 26 years; nursemaid Elizabeth Yallop, 16 years and Samuel Yallop, 14 years, the servant and errand boy.

Sarah Worthington died in 1855 aged 53 years and in the 1861 census William was found at 37 London Road with his 22-year-old daughter Marion, a five-year-old grandson Henry (Scott) Till son of Elizabeth and Lawrence Till, and a cook, housemaid and footman. His youngest child Caroline Crosse Worthington was boarding at a small private school in Lowestoft at the time, as her siblings before her had done at various schools in Lowestoft and London.

In an 1868 commercial directory William was listed at 41 London Road; daughter Hester Norton and family were listed at 115 High Street; his son Francis Samuel and family were at 37 London Road and son James Copland and family were living on Marine Parade, all in Lowestoft. 'Worthington & Sons, surgeons, 37 London Rd' was listed in the same directory under 'Trades and Professions', as both sons previously mentioned became doctors and Francis Samuel had also become a surgeon.[54]

What was termed the 'old town' of Lowestoft in 1868 consisted of one street running north to south, parallel with the shore, about one mile in length. Many of the houses had extensive views of the North Sea. The 'new town' on the south side of the harbour, known as South Lowestoft, was 'second to none in the kingdom as a marine residence for families'.[55]

Lowestoft was regularly visited by the nobility and gentry who favoured the dry climate and beach composed of firm hard sand intermixed with shingle. It was a thriving town in terms of industry and culture and boasted a mortality rate of 17 to 18 people per thousand less that of London. In 1861 the population of Lowestoft was

9,534 but such was its rapid growth that by 1871 the population was approximately 13,620, situated over 1,485 acres of land.[56]

The church William attended twice each Sunday, the Gothic-styled St Peter's, was erected in 1832-3 as a 'chapel of ease' in consequence of the distance from the town of the parish church, at a sum of £3,400. The Church Building Society contributed £600, the sale of pews raised £900 and the remainder was obtained by public subscription. St Peter's was closed to worship in 1972 and demolished in 1975. A feature of the town, which in 1975 was said to have remained unchanged since Cromwell first ordered it in the 17th century, was the nightly 8 p.m. curfew rung on the town hall bell.[57]

William retired from his practice in 1872, leaving it to his son Francis. He remained living in his house at 41 London Road with two servants, Elizabeth Long, aged 61 years, the cook Sarah Ann Scarff, aged 46 years, and a nurse Hannah P. Reeve, aged 53 years, to care for him. His narrow and severe views of life did not mellow with age. His enthusiasm for temperance apparently led him to empty the entire contents of his cellar into the gutter and he was much opposed to his son Francis's latitudinarianism in going for walks on Sundays and for allowing his young daughters to wear silver bangles. These bracelets were possibly part of the Egyptian silver jewellery collection mentioned in the will of Francis's wife, Helen Felicite Worthington.

William was known to suffer fits of depression from time to time, principally over money matters, when he would speak of himself as ruined. Considering his very large family this is understandable; however, he was a wealthy man. At the same time he enjoyed giving pleasure and once a year held a strawberry feast in his garden for all the old almhouse women of Lowestoft. His grandchildren were invited to entertain them, not always with satisfactory results as running races and playing active games after a feast had its dangers.

After his retirement William lived a very simple and abstemious life which he considered to be the explanation for his longevity. His mental faculties were unimpaired to the last. He was greatly respected and esteemed by all classes of the community amongst whom his long, useful and most honourable life had been passed.

William died of pneumonia on 31 January 1885 at 41 London Road, Lowestoft aged 84 years and was buried in the family tomb in the churchyard of St Margaret's parish church, Lowestoft. This altar tomb was demolished in 1984 when part of the churchyard was made over to Waveney District Council as 'open space'.[58]

A detailed 15-page will written by William included specific instructions for his funeral:

> I desire and direct that my funeral may be a walking one and conducted very quietly, that my Grave be not bricked that the bearers may all be members either of the Church of England Temperance Society or the Blue Ribbon Army and that no mourning be given to any of my family friends or servants.

William appointed his son Francis and his sister Elizabeth's son, Edward Fairthorne of Brightwell in the County of Berkshire as 'Gentlemen Executors and Trustees of this my Will', which was dated 12 July 1883. In the first of two codicils, dated 14 October 1884, William appointed his friend Alexander Fraser of Wisbech Saint Peter in the County of Cambridge to be an additional executor and trustee. The second codicil, dated 8 January 1885, related to the estate of his deceased son, John Scott Worthington, and his descendants. At the time of his death William's personal estate was valued at £27,223 17s. 6d. and resworn in June 1886 at £27,397 17s. 9d., a very considerable fortune at the time.

In his will William left instructions for the establishment of generous trusts to ensure his children and grandchildren were well provided for. He also left the following bequests:

> to the trustees or trustee for the time being of this my Will the sum of fifty pounds … which I direct them to invest … and to apply the dividends or interest arising therefrom in the purchase of Tracts or Religious Books exclusively from the Religious Tract Society for the use of both the out and indoor patients of the Suffolk Hospital …

> I also bequeath … the sum of two hundred pounds to be … invested … and to pay the dividends or interest arising therefrom into and equally between my Daughter Charlotte Emily Leman and my Daughter in law Helen Felicite Worthington during their joint lives and after the death of either of them then the whole to the survivor of them during her life to be distributed entirely at their and her own discretion amongst the Poor of Lowestoft aforesaid—and on the decease of such survivor I bequeath the sum of one hundred pounds to the Trustees … of 'The Lowestoft Hospital' … and the remaining one hundred pounds to the Trustees … of 'The Lowestoft Convalescent Home' …

> I also bequeath all my share, right and interest in the Leasehold, dwelling house buildings and hereditaments known as 'The Cocoa Tree Tavern' with the appurtenances situate in the High Street

66 Tomb of Dr. William Collins Worthington, his wife and some of his children in St Margaret's churchyard, Lowestoft. This tomb was demolished in 1984 when part of the churchyard was made over to Waveney District Council as 'open space'.

> in Lowestoft aforesaid to the said Francis Samuel Worthington and my son James Copland Worthington their heirs, executors, administrators and assigns in equal share absolutely.

> I bequeath to the London Temperance Hospital the sum of Twenty Five Pounds and to the Church Missionary Society, the British and Foreign Bible Society, the London Society for promoting Christianity amongst the Jews and the London City Mission the sum of twenty pounds each and to the Royal Medical Benevolent College Epsom and The British and Medical Benevolent Fund the sum of Ten Pounds each to be applied in furtherance of the same temperance Hospital and Societies …

> I bequeath to William Symonds, formerly residing with me as surgery messenger the Legacy of Twenty Pounds … I also bequeath the following Legacies to Alexander Fraser of Wisbech and my Godson Cecil Herbert Fraser the sum of ten pounds each. To Elizabeth Long the sum of ten pounds and Sarah Scarf the sum of one hundred pounds, if respectively in my service at my decease. To Hannah Peninnah Reeve the sum of ten pounds. To my servant Henry Franklin Mitchell and his wife or the survivor of them the sum of five pounds. To Henry Lambert & his wife and their daughter Mary

Lambert, being the mother, father and sister of my late servant Emma Lambert or the survivors or survivor of them the sum of twenty five pounds ... To my daughter Hester Sarah Norton the sum of five hundred pounds. To each of my Grandchildren: Henry Scott Till, Herbert Jennings Till, Wilfred Worthington Till, Richard Goodwyn Till, Helena Felice Slade, and Florence Edith Till the sum of five hundred pounds and to Daniel Meadows of Great Yarmouth, Surgeon, the sum of two hundred pounds as a mark of esteem and regard.

I bequeath to the said Francis Samuel Worthington the service of plate presented to me by the Governors of the old Lowestoft Infirmary. To the said James Copland Worthington my Silver Tea Kettle and Silver Bread Baskett presented to me by Miss Mihill. To my son Edward Worthington my Gold Watch & chain, my Silver Fish Knife and Fork, my Silver Drinking Cup and large Tankard and also my Snuff box presented to me by Mr Glasspoole, my small Silver Waiter and my small Silver candle stick.

To my daughter Charlotte Emily Leman, two sets of theological works to be selected by her and the Cabinets in the Drawing room presented to me by Solomon King Fuller. To the said Hester Sarah Norton my Piano Forte. To my Daughter Marion Wetton the screen worked by Miss Kate Ray. To the said Charlotte Emily Leman, Hester Sarah Norton and Marion Wetton, all my household goods and furniture, glass, china, plate and plated articles, linen and wearing apparel (not otherwise disposed of by this my Will) to be equally divided between them share and share alike.

To the Baroness Berners 'The life of Saint Paul' presented to me by the Reverend William Nottidge Ripley in two volumes. To the said Francis Samuel Worthington and James Copland Worthington equally all my Medical Books and anatomical prints and Drawings and portraits of Medical men and to the said Francis Samuel Worthington, Edward Worthington, James Copland Worthington, Charlotte Emily Leman, Hester Sarah Norton and Marion Wetton all the remainder of my books portraits and paintings.

I give and devise unto the said Francis Samuel Worthington all the Real Estate (if any) to which I shall be entitled at the time of my decease To hold the same unto the said Francis Samuel Worthington his heirs and assigns for ever. I bequeath all my securities for money and the rest residue and remainder of my personal Estate and Effects whatsoever and wheresoever to the said ... (executors), their executors and administrators ...

William stated it was his wish that his friend James Edward Fraser and partners, William James Wright and Alexander Fraser, solicitors of Lowestoft and Wisbech handle his legal affairs after his death. William left his eldest surviving son, Francis a reading that was 'not to be used until you return from my funeral, and then in the presence of your brothers and sisters'. Written on 24 February 1880 it read:

Exhortation of a dying father to his children. Pray to God for the help of His Holy Spirit to enable you through life's journey, firstly, to honour Him in your own persons; secondly to honour Him in your families; thirdly, to honour Him in your legitimate calling of life and duty; fourthly, to honour Him in your intercourse with your fellow creatures.

Remember God's own words, 'Them that honour Me I will honour, and them that despise Me shall be lightly esteemed.' I Samuel II,30.

Seek first the Kingdom of God and His righteousness and all things needful shall be added unto you. Matt VI,33.

May God the Holy Spirit bless these words to you daily by imprinting them on your memories and implanting them in all your hearts, is the earnest prayer of a loving father through Jesus Christ. W.C. Worthington.

Thomas Knight Worthington, M.D., M.R.C.S. (1802-1856)

Thomas was baptised on 29 August 1802 at St Mary's, Dover, the eighth child of Benjamin Jelly and Elizabeth Worthington. He was made a Freeman of Dover by birth on 23 July 1830 and voted in the 1841 election for two barons to serve the town and port of Dover in Parliament. Like his brothers Henry Worthington of Strond Street and Benjamin Worthington of Marine Place, Thomas voted for Sir John Rae Reid, Bart. and Mr. John Halcombe, 'Serjeant-at-Law'.[59]

Thomas became a Licentiate of the Society of Apothecaries in 1827. He was a member of the Royal College of Surgeons from 2 June 1829, when he was listed as being at Swan River, Western Australia. From 1833 his address was given as Dover and he was last listed as a member of the college in 1858, two years after his death, although he had ceased to practise when the census was taken in 1851. He remained unmarried and lived in Eastbrook Place near his two sisters, Charlotte and Hester.

A marble plaque on the wall of Buckland Church, Dover has the following memorial: 'Sacred to the Memory of Thomas Knight Worthington Esq. Surgeon third son of Benjamin and Elizabeth Worthington who departed this life 14 March 1856 aged 53 years'.

The day after his death the *Dover Telegraph* reported under 'Deaths' that 'Thomas Knight Worthington, Esq.' had died 'after severe and protracted sufferings, endured with exemplary patience'. The *Dover Telegraph* 3 May 1856 reported that

> The late Thomas Knight Worthington, Esq., has bequeathed £50 to The Hope Charity Institution which has just completed its 30th year of usefulness to the sick poor. This Institution was established in 1826 when nine persons, tradesmen and pilots of Dover agreed to subscribe one shilling per month each for the purpose of aiding any poor neighbour in affliction, and from that small beginning a charity has grown up, which is now an important auxiliary to the Hospital and Dispensary ...

Henry Worthington (1803-1866)

Born in Dover on 2 October 1803, Henry was the ninth child and youngest surviving son of Benjamin Jelly and Elizabeth Worthington. He was christened on 18 December 1803 at St Mary the Virgin Church in Dover as his siblings before him had been.

Henry was firstly a farmer and later a very active and enterprising businessman in partnership with his oldest brother, Benjamin. At the time of Henry's birth, Benjamin was about to enter the Royal Navy as a midshipman. Benjamin retired from a distinguished career in the Navy in November 1814 and a few years later he and Henry became business partners.

Henry was 23 years of age and living at Charlton in Dover when he married Mary Jennings of 'The Shrubbery', Buckland, eldest daughter of George and Mary Jennings at St Mary's, Dover on 21 September 1827. They had been granted a marriage licence at Canterbury on 3 September 1827.[60]

Henry was enrolled in the Dover Register of Freemen on 5 September 1828. His occupation was given as 'wine merchant'. It is interesting to wonder what his teetotalling brother, William Collins Worthington, thought of Henry making and selling alcohol!

Henry and Mary had 10 children, nine of whom were born in Dover. They were: Benjamin Worthington (1829-60), Henry Worthington (1831-54), George Finch Jennings Worthington (1833-98), Charlotte Mary Worthington (1835-1918), Thomas

67   Henry Worthington (1803-66).

68   Mary Worthington, née Jennings.

Knight Worthington (1836-96), Sophia Worthington (1838-83), Maria Henrietta Adelaide Worthington (1840-post 1895), Daines Balderston Worthington (1842-65), Elizabeth Harriot Worthington (1843-99), Robert Worthington (1845-1916).

The children were raised at Maggot Farm, Alkham, four miles from Dover, until the family moved to Maxton. Nestling in a valley of hills, Alkham is one of the places where wild orchids grow. Today the very narrow Megget Lane, originally called Maggott Lane, winds up to Megget (Maggot) Farm which lies almost along the ridge of hills. Outbuildings and a modern bungalow now surround a square farmyard and the old farmhouse made of flint which is covered with greenery and ivy. Although the farm's name was probably changed due to the modern connotations of the noun 'maggot', the *Shorter Oxford Dictionary* gives the meaning of the word as 'small'. The farm house and farm buildings were made of flint as were many of the buildings in the area at this time. Flint is found wherever chalk is found. Apparently there was a large walnut tree in the garden and resident children enjoyed listening for nuts falling on the slate roof.

In the Earl of Radnor's 1839 Manorial Roll Book of his Country Manors, Henry Worthington was listed as owning no.13 Wolverton Manor, free land, rent 1s. 9d.

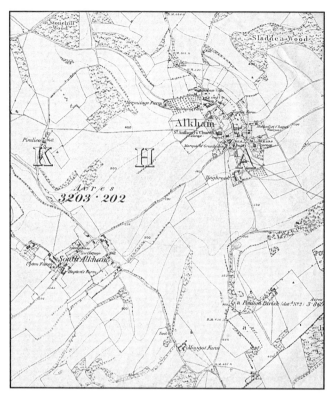

69 Survey map showing Alkham and Maggot Farm, 1872-3, published 1877, 6" to 1 mile.

70 Aerial view of Megget Farm, South Alkham, *c.*1970.

This was a block of land and not a manor house. In the 1840 Earl of Radnor's Manorial Roll Book of his Country Manors, Benjamin and Henry Worthington own nos.21 and 21B Manor at Halton, free land for which they pay 4s. 7d. and 1s.; four acres of land called Long Close and 12 acres of other land. He also owned seven acres of land at Whitfield Sole near South Alkham.

No Worthingtons were recorded in the Alkham church registers but the family is listed in the 1841 Census. At 'Whitfield Sole', Alkham, the enumerator recorded Henry Worthington's occupation as farmer. Both he and Mary were aged 30 years. Benjamin, their eldest son was aged 11 years, Henry was nine years old, George seven, Charlotte five, Knight (christened Thomas Knight) three, Elizabeth (christened Sophia) two and Amy (christened Maria Henrietta Adelaide) aged one year. Also present were two female servants, Elizabeth Bishop and Ann Banks, both aged 40 years.[61]

The land owned and occupied by Henry, known as Maggot Farm, was listed on the Alkham tithe map 1842 as:

No.368	Maggot Farm	homestead	1 rood 28 perches
No.369	Barn Meadow	meadow	3 roods 37 perches
No.370	Pond Meadow	meadow	2 acres 1 rood 0 perches
No.371	Long Meadow	pasture	2 acres
No.372	Footpath Meadow	meadow	2 acres 1 rood 16 perches

Payable to the vicar £1-1-10
Payable to the appropriator £0-0-0.[62]

71   Megget Farm house, *c.*1930s.

The Worthington family moved from Alkham in 1846 and in the 1851 and 1861 census George Gates farmed land which Henry still owned. George Gates was probably Henry's farm manager. By 1857 the Kent Poll Book records that Henry was living at Hougham but still owned freehold land in Alkham.

A notice advertising the sale of Maggot Farm was placed in the *Dover Telegraph* on 5 December 1857. It stated: 'A compact fertile farm (with dwelling house and suitable farm buildings) called "The Meggot" in the parishes of Alkham and Poulton, containing 18 acres of arable land, ten of which are tithe free. For particulars ... apply to Mr James Worsfold, Estate Agent, Dover.'

At the time of the 1871 census, George Gates was living at Maggot Farm aged 79 years, which suggests he either bought it from Henry or was managing it for the new owner. The farm at this time had grown considerably to comprise 120 acres, with two labourers employed, one of whom was Stephen Gibsy who lived at Maggot Cottage. Also accounted for at Maggot Farm on this census were members of Gate's extended family, James Tomsett, a nephew aged 47 years; Mary A. Tomsett, niece aged 45 years and Annie and George Tomsett, aged 18 and 12 years respectively.

Worthington's Safety Coaches

The final overthrow of the French dictator Napoleon in 1815 saw the resumption of communication with the Continent, but the foreign mail service had a very poor reputation for efficiency. Slower than the inland mail, it was described in a report to the Post Office in 1827 as being 'worked in an abominable manner'.

Although the vehicle which carried the letters was actually a privately owned stage-coach, it was run under the direction of the Post Office and known as the 'Paris Mail', carrying the post for the mainland of Europe on Tuesdays and Fridays, between London and Dover. Mail coaches worked to very strict rules and timetables. Highwaymen were common and if the coach broke down the guard, who was armed, had to leave the passengers and go ahead with the mail.

The proprietor did his best but it was not an easy schedule to maintain with any regularity. The tidal nature of the service meant that mails from abroad came in at all hours of the day and night.[63] Providing the foreign mail landed in England before 10 a.m., there was no difficulty and letters were transported routinely from the *Ship Inn* by the 'Paris' coach to London. It was late deliveries from abroad, or the unexpected arrival of Government despatches which were a problem and to enable these to reach their destination in a reasonable time they were conveyed by the 'Inland' coach. The mail coach had right of way on the roads and the guard used a horn to warn travellers of his approach, and tollgate keepers to open their gates, the mail coach being exempt from charges.

Quayside at Dover the routine was for the captain of the incoming boat to hand the mail over to the packet agent. He in turn took them to the packet office where the letters for Dover were taken out. The remaining post was given to the guard of the mail coach who secured them in a pouch on the roof. At Canterbury the coach stopped for 15 minutes while the guard bundled up the mail destined for London.

As well as the mail coaches, which could only carry a limited number of passsengers, there were other stage lines which ran between London and the southeast coast. All of them took much the same amount of time on the road, travelling at an average speed of seven to eight miles an hour. The service they provided was extremely well conducted. In 1820 there were 12 daily return coaches to London running from the various inns and hotels at Dover.

There were some serious accidents in the early years of the coach service when so called 'flying coaches', containing four passengers pulled by six horses and travelling at great speeds, overturned, with occasional fatal results. Safety therefore became an issue and the word was often incorporated into the names of many of the coaches, or the companies which ran them.[64]

The flying coach era lasted only a few years and was replaced in 1786 by regular Dover-London mail coach services which carried a few passengers as well as the mail. A single fare cost 30s. for inside travel and 16s. if you sat outside. Besides being exposed to the elements, outside passengers often had to walk up the bigger hills and help push the coach if it stuck in mud pools which were a common feature of the roads. Henry and Benjamin Worthington ran the Worthington Safety Coaches from the *Ship* and *Paris* hotels and from the general coach office. In *Pigot's Directory* of 1839 Henry is listed as a coach proprietor and he and his brother Benjamin own a livery stable. The breed of horse often used for pulling the coaches was the Cleveland Bay. The Worthington-owned coach 'Telegraph' left the *Ship Hotel* at 07.30 for Charing Cross and Holborn followed by the 'Express' at 10.00 which also stopped at Piccadilly and Cheapside. The 'Tally Ho' left at 13.00 for the same destinations and the 'Defiance' at 18.00 for Charing Cross and Cheapside, where it arrived early the next morning.[65]

A timetable published under 'advertisements' in the 1841 *Batcheller Guidebook* for 'Worthington's mail and general coach office', at the *Ship Hotel* in Dover informed:

London and Dover Royal Day and Night Mails, mornings at ¼ past 8, in 7 ½ hours!!! without change of Coach or Coachman. Evenings at ¼ past 9, in 8 hours.

N.B. Mr W. begs to inform the Public that his is the only Office in Dover where places can be secured for the Royal Mails.

Coaches to London - The Express or Eagle every morning at ¼ before ten, in 9 hours! without changing Coach or Coachman. The Tally-Ho every day (Sundays excepted) at 1 o'clock.

The Defiance, every Friday at ¼ past 6.

To Herne Bay - The Red Rover, superior patent safety four-horse coach, every morning at 7 o'clock, (Sundays excepted, then at 9) in time for the Steam Packets to London.

To Hastings, Brighton and Tunbridge Wells - The Reliance, every Tuesday, Thursday and Saturday mornings at ½ past 10.

Worthington's Safety Coaches were one of the four major companies making passenger-only runs to London, breaking the journey into five stages like the mail coaches.[66] The total distance travelled by these coaches varied between 72 and 73 miles, depending on where passengers were picked up or set down. With breaks for meals it took the coaches all day to reach their destination. These trips, which usually took nine hours, left Dover on the London road for the first 15 miles, passing the Maison Dieu on the right and the Priory on the left, before proceeding via Charlton, Buckland, Ewell, Lydden and Barham Downs and eventually arriving at Canterbury for refreshments.[67]

The journey's second stage consisted of 16 miles, running through Harbledown, Boughton Hill, Ospringe and Bapchild and so on to Sittingbourne for further refresh-

72   Dover to London mail coach.

ment. The third stage to Rochester was 11 miles and the fourth to Dartford lay acrosss the river Medway, via Gad's Hill, Gravel Hill and Dartford. The final 15-mile stage went through Crayford, Bexley Heath, Welling, Shooter's Hill, Blackheath, London Bridge, the City and West End. Here the horses were changed at the great inns and fresh teams stood by for the return journey home.[68]

In addition to the long-distance coaches there were also local services from Dover. These went to places such as Ashford, Deal, Hythe, Hastings, Herne Bay, Ramsgate and Margate.

In 1838 William Cubitt, the engineer of the South East Railway, estimated that 33,000 people travelled from London to Dover by coach per annum, a further 26,000 travelled between Canterbury and Dover, and 18,000 journeyed between the gateway to the continent and Herne Bay.

The 1838-39 Rating List for Strond Street, St Mary's Parish, Dover ('Pier Ward') lists: Worthington B. and H. annual value of a yard - £48, and the assessment of 16s.

Security posed certain problems and thefts did occur. In one instance, John Matthews, a coach porter at the *Ship Hotel* office was remanded on suspicion of stealing a parcel of 400 sovereigns, and found not guilty.[69] It appears the newly founded Dover police force were on the case however, because in August 1836 stolen property–the missing sovereigns, were recovered from John Matthew's garden where they had been buried.[70] It appears from the minutes of the Dover Watch Committee on 15 and 18 August that a grateful Henry rewarded the officer responsible for recovering his missing money. Rewarding an officer for doing his duty was considered not appropriate by the Watch Committee, but tripped by the vagaries of terminology the Committee conceded that: 'It appearing that the sum received by Sergeant Obree from Mr Henry Worthington was a free gift from the latter, the Committee consider it is not a case for their interference'.

On another occasion the *Dover Telegraph* of 24 July 1841 reported that David Banks, a horsekeeper at Lydden, 'was yesterday afternoon fully committed for trial at the next assizes at Maidstone by J.M. Fector Esq., charged with stealing at Lydden seven bushels of corn, the property of Mr Henry Worthington'.

On the 31st day of that month David Banks, 37 years of age, was

indicted for stealing seven bushels of corn and oatmeal, the property of Henry Worthington, at Lydden. It appeared that the prosecutor, who is a large coach proprietor at Dover, was in the habit of sending, every day, several sacks of corn to Lydden, where the coaches change horses. On the 20th instant, six sacks of corn were sent there, one of which was given to the prisoner, who was one of the horse-keepers, which he took into his stable. The quantity was sufficient to supply the horses for twenty-four hours, but it was all gone in about two hours after it was received. On inquiry being made respecting the corn, he said that he had given six or seven sieves to another horse keeper, named Stanley, from whom he had borrowed some a few days before. Such, however, was proved not to be the case, and the prisoner absconded next morning, but was taken into custody on the following day. Guilty. Two years' hard labour.

About 1841 Henry and Benjamin paid taxes for stables on the north side of the *Bell Hotel* at Lydden. The coaching house for the main road was a little further along the road at the *Half Way House Inn.* Horses were usually taken to the coaching house for a few days at a time in case they were needed, and some would have been from Worthington stables.[71]

The arrival of the Railway

The era of the coaches peaked about 1830 when there were as many as 4,000 carriages operating in Britain, employing about 150,000 horses and 35,000 coachmen, guards and other employees. However by 1850 the railways had almost replaced them.

On 21 June 1836 the Royal Assent was given to an Act of Parliament authorising the London and South Eastern Railway to build a line from London via Croydon, Oxford, Tonbridge, Ashford and Dover. Many years and route changes later the first section of railway line was opened between London Bridge and Tonbridge on 26 May 1842. Three months later on 31 August the next section of line between Tonbridge and Headcorn was opened and Henry arranged for coaches to leave the offfice of the *Ship Hotel* in Strond Street, Dover at 9.15 a.m. and 11.00 a.m. each weekday to enable travellers to catch the London train and to convey those returning home. As an added inducement they were also taken up and set down at their respective residences in Dover without charge.[72]

After the South Eastern Line from Ashford to a temporary terminus at Folkestone was officially opened on 28 June 1843, the south-east coast was linked by rail with London. Trains were already running to Dover Harbour station, situated immediately behind the *Ship Hotel,* when Benjamin Worthington placed the following advertisement in the *Dover Telegraph* on 11 March 1843:

Increase of trains on & after Tuesday the 14th of March, 1843.

B.WORTHINGTON begs to inform the Public, that he has made arrangements with the South Eastern Railway Company for a NIGHT TRAIN, at Seven o'Clock, from the SHIP HOTEL OFFICE, DOVER, for the conveyance of Passengers, Parcels, and Light

Goods - returning from London at eight in the Evening. Places can be secured and Parcels booked at the following Offices in London - Griffin's Green Man and Still, Oxford Street; Golden Cross, Charing Cross; Spread Eagle, Regent Circus; George and Blue Boar, Holborn; Bolt in Tun, Fleet Street; Cross Keys, Wood Street; Swan with Two Necks, Lad Lane; and Spread Eagle, Gracechurch Street.

Although the brothers continued to operate Worthington's safety coaches for some years, the carriage of passengers became a steadily decreasing aspect of their business operations. The train station at Dover Harbour was immediately behind the Worthington *Ship Hotel*, which must have been both convenient for guests and beneficial to the Worthington's business.

The *Ship Hotel*

An advertisement in the *Kentish Gazette* on 29 July 1796 announced that the *Ship Inn* had been taken over by T. Wright, late of *Kings Head*, from Mr. Harvey 'who had had had the *Ship* for many years'. Another early reference to the *Ship Hotel* was recently found in a recipe book: 'It is related of the Duke of Wellington—I believe by Lord Ellesmere— that when he landed at Dover in 1814 after six years absence from England, the first order he gave at the Ship Inn was for an unlimited supply of buttered toast!'.[73]

Mr. Charles Wright was the proprietor some time between 1823-26, until the hotel was severely damaged by fire in 1832. In February 1834 Henry and Benjamin Worthington bought the *Ship Hotel* after Mr. Wright had been declared bankrupt.[74]

On Saturday 1 March 1834 there appeared a small notice in the *Dover Telegraph,* a local newspaper published every Saturday:

73   *Worthington Ship Hotel,* Worthington Safety Coach and Worthington Packet Steamer.

74 19th-century engraving of *Worthington Ship Hotel* with Western Heights in the background. The Customs House and annex to the hotel survived long after a warehouse was built on the hotel site.

THE SHIP HOTEL, DOVER,
(late Wright's)

B. & H. WORTHINGTON respectfully announce, they have taken the SHIP HOTEL, DOVER. As every arrangement that can conduce the comfort of their Patrons will receive their most zealous personal attention; & as superior accommodation will henceforth blend with reasonable charges, they venture to hope for a continuance of that pre-eminent patronage so long accorded to this establishment by the nobility and public. J.BIRMINGHAM will continue to superintend the Custom-house department.'

The custom-house adjoined the *Ship Hotel*. In photographs it appears on the right of the hotel.

Wright's bankruptcy notice appeared in the *Dover Telegraph* on 22 March 1834. Also in the paper that day was a small notice placed by the Worthington's regarding:

THE SHIP HOTEL, DOVER

From the numerous enquiries that have been made on the subject, B. & H. Worthington beg respectfully to state that

THE LONDON ROYAL MAIL

continues to leave their Office every Evening at a Quarter before Ten O'clock. Superior Posting. Coaches to London 4 times a Day. Conveyances to Margate, Ramsgate, Hastings, Brighton &c.

The hotel stood with its front facing the harbour and its rear entrance in Strond Street. There are paintings, drawings and engravings of the *Ship Hotel*, Worthington packet steamer and Worthington coaches executed during the Worthington era. An 1844 Burgess engraving depicting the view of Dover Harbour from the windows of the *Ship Hotel* is held in the Dover library picture collection.[75]

Benjamin and Henry had business cards printed picturing their new hotel on one side and the following message on the other:

B & H Worthington, in announcing they have taken the Ship Hotel, respectfully solicit a continuance of that pre-eminent patronage it has so long enjoyed from the Nobility and the Public. A constant personal attention to the comfort of their patrons, Superior accomodation & economical charges embolden them to hope for general support ...

It seems they were indeed supported, for the following list of guests at the *Ship Hotel* was printed in the *Dover Telegraph* on 22 March 1834:

The Prince De Laval Montmorency, Col. Sir E. Miles, Capt Heneage, Mrs & Miss Boyle, Fras. Baring Esq. MP & his lady & suite, H. Stuart Esq., Hon. Mr Phipps, Capt Davidson-Cornewall Esq., Mr Provost, Brother, his lady etc., Col. Proctor & son, the Baron & Baroness de Kessel, Mr Klein & suite, Major Norcliffe-Weston Esq., Mr Rondeau de Courcy, Mr P. Fletcher, etc from France. The Earl Carrington & suite, Capt Wetenhall, Le Baron de Conteuiz, Mr & Mrs Hinde & suite, Capt Ellice RN., Hon. Capt Pellew RN, Le Chevalier de Mattos; Miss Hamer, Major Bethune, Sir W.C. Anstruther Bart., Sir James & Lady Fitzgerald & suite, Lord Leveson & the Hon. Mr Pitt, for the Continent.

Obviously the change of ownership of the *Ship Hotel* was not allowed to pass without celebration. On 26 April 1834 the following advertisement appeared in the *Dover Telegraph*:

DOVER.

THE MAYOR and CORPORATION intend DINING at the SHIP HOTEL on Thursday, the 1st day of May next, to celebrate the taking of that establishment by MESSRS. WORTHINGTON: when the Mayor and Corporation will be happy to meet any of their fellow Townsmen and other Gentlemen on that occasion. ** Tickets to be had at the Bar of the Hotel, one pound, one shilling; to include Dinner, Wine, and Waiters. 14th April, 1834.

The following report of the evening was written up in the *Dover Telegraph* on Saturday, 3 May 1834:

75   Engraving of the emblem used by the *Ship Hotel* on hotel stationery, etc.

A most numerous and repectable party of gentlemen dined on Thursday at the Ship Hotel, at the invitation of the Mayor (J.W. Pilcher Esq.) and Corporation, to celebrate the Messrs. Worthington's taking this extensive establishment. His Worship presided and was assisted by M. Kennett Esq. The company consisted of most of the Corporation–J.M. Fector Esq., H. Latham Esq., J. Ward Esq. and many gentlemen correspondents of the hotel from most parts of England.

The dinner and dessert consisted of every delicacy in season; and the choice and costly wines of Messrs. Worthington fully sustained the high reputation of the Ship Hotel.

'Non nobis Domine' was given in excellent sytle by four professional gentlemen; after which the King, Queen and Royal family were drank with tremendous cheer. His Grace the Duke of Wellington's health (whose birthday it happened to be) was received with deafening applause, and every sincere wish for many happy returns. The health of Mr. Fector being proposed, and drunk with every mark of respect and the loudest testimonies of approbation, that gentlemen returned an appropriate acknowledgment of the honour conferred on him. The healths of the worthy hosts having been most heartily received and duly honoured, Mr B. Worthington returned thanks, in a very neat speech for the favour conferred on his brother and himself. The evening was constantly enlivened by the gentlemen alluded to; and such was the hilarity that prevailed, that the grey streak of dawn was visible before the company wholly separated.

A notice in the *Dover Telegraph* on 28 June 1834 informed:

B & H Worthington respectfully announce, (in consequence of the pressing request of many Gentlemen and Friends) that the Foreign Mail will henceforth start from their office, Ship Hotel, Dover, every Monday and Friday, at a quarter before Twelve o'Clock, and perform the journey to town in Eight hours and a half, without change of Coach or Coachman. The great convenience to the public will be instantly apparent, when it is recollected the Tally-Ho does not leave Canterbury on Mondays. Ship Coach Office, 20th June 1834.

Further news gleaned from the *Dover Telegraph* include the following, printed on Saturday, 20 September 1834:

Departures from Worthington's: Mr Gower, Marquis and Marchioness of Salisbury, Mr & Mrs Poulteney, Mr & Miss Sturge, Lady Congreve, Mr H. Herbert, Madame Vannett, Lord Lyndhurst, Mr & Mrs Rubini, Mr Sykes, Hon. Capt Ashburnham, Mr Alexandre, Madame Belgrain, Misses Archer & Robberds, Lady Charlotte Hamilton, Mr Weston & family, M. de Grenier, Mr C. Burnsby, Mr & Mrs Blount, Mr Berthelot, General Bradshaw, Mr & Mrs Easthope, Mr Elliot, Mr H. Pearce, Baron Rothschild, Mr Vansittart, Lord Brudenell, Mr & Lady Sarah Wandesford & family.

And this from the *Dover Telegraph* on Saturday, 4 October 1834:

HIS EXCELLENCY BARON OMPEDA, the Hanovian Ambassador, accompanied by the Baroness & suite, landed on Monday from H.M. Packet, 'Ferret', Capt Hamilton, & proceeded to Worthington's Hotel where they received the devoirs of the civil & military authorities; & afterwards proceeded to town under a salute from the battery at the Heights.

His Excellency the Count de Mille Flores, the Spanish Ambassador, arrived at Worthington's Hotel on Wednesday evening & embarked next morning, on board the Brittania, for Boulogne, under the usual salute of artillery. The Marquis of Landsdowne also arrived at the same Hotel on Thursday and embarked yesterday for the Continent.

Headed 'Local Intelligence' in the *Dover Telegraph* on 15 November 1834 we discover:

The DUKE OF WELLINGTON – During his prolonged sojourn at Walmer Castle, the Lord Warden frequently partook of the sports of the field with East Kent Harriers, which besides the regular meetings, were occasionally thrown off at the special request of the noble duke. His Grace, having left the Castle on Tuesday for the metropolis, changed horses at the Ship Hotel in this town, and proceeded through Hythe and Ashford, for the purpose of paying a passing visit to the Earl of Winchelsea, at Eastwell Park.

Departures from 'Worthington's Hotel' on 22 November 1834 included:

Mr Saunders, The Marquis of Ailse, Lord & Lady Augustus Fitzclarence, Gen. Swayne, Mrs Welldale Knollys, Mr Eyre, Countess Rendlesham, Rev. Dr Baggs, Mr John Grant, Mr Vavonsour, Mr Phillips, Mr Vanhoffer, Col. Irvine, Col. Peel, Mrs

Desborough, Mr Henage, Mr Shafto Adair, Mr Hay, Mr Wordsworth, Lady Selina Bridgeman, Mr Atkinson, Mons. Hassalet, Mr Jaqueson, Mr Butler Thornton, Mr Sturgeneger, Mr Perring and Mr Lake.[76]

In the *Dover Telegraph* on 13 December 1834 we learn of the:

Landing of SIR ROBERT PEEL. - The arrival of the Right Honourable Baronet at a late hour on Monday night, and his almost immediate departure for the metropolis caused considerable disappointment to hundreds of the inhabitants and visitors, who had anticipated the opportunity of expressing their respect for the new minister, by giving him a most cordial reception. Each arrival of the packets, for the three previous days, had been looked at with evident anxiety; and on Saturday, in particular, when one of the vessels form Boulogne bore a distinguishing flag at her mast head, though not the signal arranged to denote the presence of Sir Robert. The assemblage on the piers was the most numerous and respectable that has beenwitnessed there for some time. Lady Peel and Miss Peel remained at Worthington's Hotel till next morning, when they were visited by Sir Robert Wilson, Mr H. Baring &c. At ten o'clock, the family carriages having been landed from his Majesty's packet Ferret, Capt. Hamilton, who had the honour of bringing Sir Robert to England, her ladyship & suite left the hotel, amidst hearty cheers, for London.

'Local intelligence' in the *Dover Telegraph* on 27 December 1834 reported the arrival of:

The Landgravine of Hesse-Homburg - Her Royal Highness the Princess Elizabeth, sister to his Majesty, and Landgravine of Hesse-Homburg... landed here yesterday morning, from H.M. packet *Fire-fly*, Captain Sherlock. The Princess, attended by Lord Adolphus Fitzclarence, Capt Freemantle R.N. and two of the King's pages, proceeded under a Royal salute of 21 guns to Worthington's Hotel, where she was received by Col. Arnold commanding the garrison, and a guard of honor of the 88th Regiment ... Her Royal Highness's intention of proceeding by the Coast Road to St Leonard's and Brighton having beeen made known, one of the Messrs. Worthington immediately started express to provide the requisite relays of horses on the line to Hastings, and soon afterwards the Princess and suite left the hotel amidst the cheers of the public; and under a second royal salute from the Heights. A royal cortege posting along the coast is not an every day affair, and we fear the relays that could be provided must have proved very inferior to the turn out from Worthington's, which was excellent in every respect, and, with the postillions in purple and crimson caps and jackets, presented an imposing appearance.
   Her Royal Highness, who we are happy to say looked extremely well, was pleased to express her gratification ... at the style of arrangement and the comfort which she had experienced at the hotel.

'Local intelligence' on Saturday 17 January 1835 revealed that:

GENERAL ALAVA, the Spanish Envoy Extraordinary, arrived here on Tuesday by His Majesty's Packet, 'Crusader', Capt. Lyne. His Excellency & suite proceeded to Worthington's Hotel and after taking refreshments, departed for London under the customary salute from the guns at the Redoubt.[77]

Dover Telegraph, Saturday 21 February 1835:

On Monday, His Majesty's packet 'Crusader', Capt. Lyne, & the French Government packet *L'Estafette*, arrived from Calais; the former having on board H.E. PRINCE

ESTERHAZY, the Austrian Ambassador, who proceeded to the York Hotel, and soon afterwards started for London. General Count Sebastiani, the new French Ambassador who with his Lady & Suite arrived by the *L'Estafette*, remained for the night at Worthington's Ship Hotel from whence his Excellency & company proceeded early next morning, under a salute of fifteen guns, for the metropolis.

Dover Telegraph, 28 March 1835:

Local Intelligence. Dover Harbour - His Grace the DUKE OF WELLINGTON, accompanied by the Lieutenant Governor of the Castle, and other members of the Harbour Commission, had an interview with SIR ROBERT PEEL, on business relating to the further improvement of the port on Wednesday. Today being the anniversary of the birth of our esteemed representative, J.M. Fector, Esq. and a dies-non in the House of Commons, he avails himself of the opportunity to pay a short visit to his constituents; and has invited the members of his committee to dine at the Ship Hotel this evening. So indefatigable is the honourable member in his Parliamentary duties, that, although solicited to attend the annual ball in honor of his birthday, he leaves early on Monday, to attend the call of the house in the evening. On Tuesday night, about ten o'clock, Lord Cowley, His Majesty's Ambassador to the Court of the King of French, arrived at Worthington's Ship Hotel, from London. At Sunrise next morning, a guard of honor from the 88th Regiment, attended by their brass band, was paraded in front of the hotel, and saluted his Excellency on his embarkation on board His Majesty's Packet Ferret, which left the harbour under the usual salute of Artillery.

ADVERTISEMENTS.

BY SPECIAL APPOINTMENT.

SHIP HOTEL,

Strond Street, and on the Quay.

WORTHINGTON & BIRMINGHAM.

THIS Hotel, so long held in deserved estimation, is most desirably situate, close to the Custom House, the Packet Station for Calais, Ostend, and Boulogne, and within two minutes' walk of the Railroad Terminus.

It commands most beautiful views of the Castle, the Channel, and from its windows the Coast of France may be distinctly traced from Calais to Boulogne; offering to the Continental and Home Tourist advantages seldom possessed by any similar establishment.

The vast Cellars of the Hotel are stored with the choicest Vintages, while its *Cuisine* will be found to possess every varied delicacy of the season.

76 Advertisement for the *Ship Hotel* in *Batcheller's New Dover Guide*, 1845.

Guests of the *Ship Hotel* were not always glamorous, however, as the following suggests:

The Turkish Ambassador, whose arrival we shortly noticed in our late impression last week, was received in the state apartments at the Ship Hotel; from whence after enjoying the luxury of the charbouc, his Excellency and suite set off for the metropolis. It being after sun-set, the customary honours and salute were dispensed with. The Effendi is a fine looking personage; and when made up for his diplomatic character, may no doubt appear highly imposing. But there was an air of meanness about the travelling habiliments of the Embassy in general that bespoke any thing but eastern grandeur. The carriages,

three in number, were also of an inferior description; and from the length of their
journey, so much out of repair that the mandate for moving was for some time disobeyed;
until the assistance of the coachmaker provided the means of expedition.

The following report of the 'Splendid entertainment' given by John Minet Fector
Esq. M.P. to the 'Numerous Members of His Election Committee' as previously
mentioned was reported in the *Dover Telegraph* on 4 April 1835:

Mr. Fector arrived at Kersney Abbey on Saturday last, as we then stated, for the
purpose of meeting his Committee. In the evening he repaired to Worthingtons' Ship
Hotel, where at seven o'clock, the honourable member sat down with his friends to one
of the most sumptuous entertainments ever given in that eminent establishment. The
dinner, to use a common but applicable expression, comprised every delicacy in season
… This was followed by numerous toasts and speeches. Amongst the toasts proposed
was that for Mr H. Worthington & Mr E. Rutley, the vice presidents of the Committee,
for the estimation in which the Chairman held their kind services. Mr H. Worthington,
in returning thanks, regretted the absence of his colleague, but who, he had no doubt,
entertained the same wishes with himself in support of their good cause, to promote
which he would be ready at all times to repeat his past exertions, and trusted he should
never be found wanting in the interest of their honourable member. The dinner speeches
continued around the repeal of the malt tax and the effect of the repeal of the corn laws
on the agriculturist. Toasts were drunk to Sir Robert Peel and his Majesty's Ministers.
Songs were sung between each of the speeches by a choir. Mr B. Worthington proposed
the healths of Mr. Coleman and Mr. Harrison; two gentlemen who greatly contributed
towards the success of the honourable member among the out-dwellers.

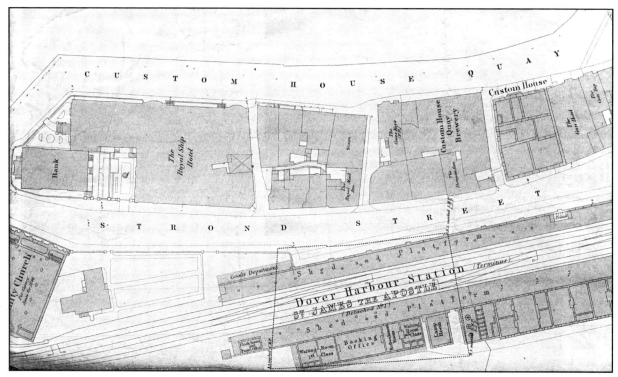

77   Map survey 1858 showing the *Royal Ship Hotel* between Custom House Quay and Strond Street.

The dinner continued until eleven o'clock when Mr Fector arose and begged his leave and suggested 'that some other gentleman do now take his chair.' This being complied with by Mr Pilcher, the worthy member said, that after spending one of the most happy and agreeable evenings of his life, it was with unfeigned regret he now found himself compelled to wish so many friends, good night ...

'Local intelligence' in the *Dover Telegraph*, 9 May 1835:

Arrival of the DUCHESS OF CAMBRIDGE. His Majesty's packet *Crusader*, Capt. Lyne with the Royal Standard flying at the main, arrived here at four o'clock on Monday afternoon, having her Royal Highness, with the two young princesses and suite on board. Her Royal Highness was received from the packet by Colonel Arnold, commandant of the garrison, and a guard of honour from the 88th Regiment. The Royal Standard being immediately hoisted on the Grand Redoubt, a double royal salute was alternately fired from thence, and from H.M. Sloop *Camelion*, at anchor in the roads. The Duchess proceeded to Worthington's Ship Hotel, and was followed by the officers of the Garrison, the band of the 88th and the guard of honour to receive Prince George, whose arrival from London at 5 o'clock was announced by a second salute of Artillery. The intention of her Royal Highness to remain during the night at the Hotel having been signified due preparation was made for the occasion. The dinner party in the evening consisted, besides the Royal Duchess, Prince George and the Princesss Augusta, of the Baroness Ahlefeldt, Colonel Sir James Reynett, Captain Hay, and the Rev. Mr Wood, tutor to the Prince. The departure of their Royal Highnesses at nine next morning, was attended with a repetition of the same ceremonies and salute that marked their arrival. The royal party and household occupied four carriages; and the uniform appearance of the postilions, with their horses turned out in that superior style by which the Ship establishment is distinguished, gave due effect to the Royal Cortege ... The Marchionesses of Wellesley, Conyngham and Anglesey and the Ladies Paget, with their respective suites, have arrived at Worthington's Ship Hotel, this week, from the Continent.

The following occasion was a very important one for Dover. The original report in the *Dover Telegraph* on 10 October 1835 took up several columns:

DEPARTURE OF THE KING AND QUEEN OF THE BELGIANS - VISIT OF THEIR ROYAL HIGHNESSES THE DUCHESS OF KENT AND THE PRINCESS VICTORIA

On Wednesday evening the Messrs. Worthington, of the Ship Hotel, received intimation that the Royal Party would arrive at the Ship Hotel to breakfast next morning. They were also directed to forward the requisite post relays to Eastry, for the purpose of bringing the Royal carriages on by the Waldershare Road from Ramsgate; and accordingly four pairs and a set, comprising twenty-two horses, were dispatched before daylight on Thursday. At nine o'clock a double royal salute of the Artillery announced the arrival of the Royal Cortege. The town, the piers, the ships in the harbour, and all the public establishments were gaily decorated with flags and banners. The Royal Standard was also hoisted at the Grand Redoubt, but a thick fog overhung the Castle and Heights till a short time after the Royal arrivals. As soon as the mist had dispersed, the Standard was perceived and saluted by His Majesty's Steam Ship *Lightning*, at anchor in the bay. The Belgian flag also was hoisted at the Bank of Messrs. Latham.

At the entrance of the Ship Hotel, the Royal Party were received by Colonel Arnold (of the Royal Engineers, Commandant of the Garrison,) Colonel Cockburn of the

Artillery, Lord Charles Wellesley and a guard of honor with the band of the 5th Regiment of Foot, and by the Mayor and Corporation of Dover in their robes, and the insignia of office. Shortly after the King and Queen of the Belgians, the Duchess of Kent and the Princess Victoria had entered the breakfast room … (following breakfast) … it was intimated to their Majesties , and to the Duchess and Princess, that the Corporation were desirous of presenting addresses …

They were received in a private room and the addresses followed a welcome to the Port of Dover and thanks for the honor conferred on 'our ancient and loyal town … ' Her Royal Highness read the following reply: 'Gentlemen, I was unprepared for this mark of your attention, but am sensible that your loyalty to the King has led you to seize this occasion to evince it, by thus receiving the Princess, and myself, on our arrival here. We are exceedingly gratified by the reception we have met with and such demonstrations of regard must always lead us to act, so as to merit the attachment of the country. As we come here to attend the embarkation of two very dear and illustrious relatives, our feelings on the termination of their visit, forbid us remaining to see what is interesting in this port; but I hope to bring the Princess on some future occasion, to Dover.

An address to the King and Queen of the Belgians followed. During the repast:

His Majesty, addressing himself to Lord Charles Wellesley, expressed his gratification at the great changes effected in Dover within a few years, and his admiration of the fashion and elegance he beheld on every side. After the Corporation had been severally presented, the members retired; when the Officers of the Garrison had the honor of being presented to the Royal Personages. A little before 10 o'clock, Captain Hamilton of His Majesty's Packet Ferret entered to announce that the flood had made sufficient for the vessel to sail. The hall and passages being lined with the corporation and many persons of note, the Royal Party passed through the state appartments, and proceeded on foot, by Strond street to the packet at the New Quay, opposite the Council-house. The procession was preceded by Messrs. Worthington, uncovered. The Queen and the Duchess walked in front, accompanied by the Duke of Wellington; the King and Princes followed, accompanied by Col. Cockburn, Col. Arnold, John Minet Fector Esq. M.P., S. Latham Esq., the Belgian Vice-consul, Sir John Conroy, Sir Robert Gardiner, M. Van de Weyer and other members of the Royal Households, the Mayor and Corporation and other official characters.

The guard of honor was paraded on the Quay, opposite the packet, and the immense concourse of spectators completely covered the piers, the quays, and every situation where even a distant view could be obtained of the embarkation. The windows and parapets of the houses were also lined with spectators who, waving their handkerchiefs and hats, joined in the hearty cheers by which all were saluted. The pressure of so large a multitude was unavoidable; the Royal Party were, nevertheless, embarked with the greatest facility, and not an incident of any kind occurred. The King and Queen then took their leave of the Duchess of Kent and Princess Victoria, and also the Duke of Wellington. As the Mayor was leaving the vessel, the Queen extended her hand to him, and begged him to assure the corporation and the inhabitants generally, how much pleased she felt at the reception she had met with from all classes, which was echoed by the King. As the packet was cast off, the guard gave a general salute; the national anthem was struck up and the vessel stood to sea under a second discharge of the artillery on the heights, which was returned from His Majesty's ship *Lightning*, on the Ferret's clearing the harbour with the Royal Standard flying. Immediately on the departure of their Majesties, the Duchess of Kent and Princess Victoria ascended their carriage amidst the cordial cheers of all who could get near them …

A very large and solid mahogany royal bedstead, complete with royal crown and Coat of Arms, was reputedly slept in by Princess Victoria. This bed apparently still remains in the possession of a Worthington family descendant.

Further reports of guests regularly appeared in the *Dover Telegraph* such as the following on 24 October 1835:

> The Duke and Duchess of Sutherland and family with a retinue of twenty persons and five carriages arrived at Worthington's Hotel on Monday evening. Next morning they embarked for the continent. His Grace has taken a house in Paris for three months … Lady Stanhope visited Dover on Monday. After a few hours stay at Worthington's, Her Ladyship, who travels in the good old English baronial style, returned to Walmer … Orders have been received at the Ship Hotel to prepare for the reception of the Duke of Devonshire, on his way to the Continent … The Earl of Thanet left the Ship Hotel on Monday for the Continent.

The following news appeared in the *Dover Telegraph* on Saturday 7 November 1835:

> A ridiculous and apparently a mischievous paragraph has been inserted in some of the London journals this week, stating that Viscount Burghersh had fallen through a trap-hatch at Worthington's Ship Hotel in this town. His Lordship has not been in Dover for some years and moreover there is not a trap-hatch in any part of Messrs. Worthington's establishment.

Further unusual news headed 'The Siamese Twins' appeared in the *Dover Telegraph* on 28 November 1835:

> The arrival of these interesting brothers from America on Sunday last, created no small degree of interest among the visitors and inhabitants of the town; and our annual fair commencing on the following day, a general expectation prevailed that the public curiosity would be gratified. The young gentlemen however, it appears, are already in circumstances which place them above itinerant exhibition; and consequently no offers could induce them to delay longer than was necessary, their journey to fulfil an engagement in Paris. The Countess of Warwick, The Earl of Scarborough, and a few other persons of distinction were favoured with an interview, through the introduction of Dr Harris, the friend and companion of the brothers. On the boat which brought them from the ship Resolution, entering the harbour, the tide was low and they had in consequence to ascend one of the iron ladders at the Cross Wall. These ladders are merely bars of iron not exceeding twenty inches in length, grooved into the perpendicular face of the quay; yet the twins ascended together with all the agility of practised seamen. Their language, manners and appearance are decidedly English; and the style in which they lived at Worthington's Hotel, fully supported the national character which they have adopted. On Tuesday they embarked on board HM packet *Firefly* for Calais, displaying the same liveliness of disposition and activity that marked their landing and has appeared throughout their short sojourn at Dover.

The news on Saturday 23 January 1836 was:

> The Duke and Duchess of Bedford are expected at their residence in Waterloo Crescent on Monday. The Duchess arrived at Worthington's Hotel on Tuesday evening, for the purpose of inspecting the preparations made for their reception. Her Grace also made the requisite arrangements of the houses engaged for the Marquis and Marchioness of Abercorn and the numerous suites of both the noble families … The Earl of Roden has arrived at the Ship Hotel.[78]

A few years later in November 1842, when the young Queen Victoria drove with her Consort through the streets of Dover, she may have pointed out the *Ship Hotel* where she had stayed as a young princess with her mother the Duchess of Kent. The Prince Consort could in turn have directed the Queen's attention to the *York Hotel*, where he had stayed the night in 1840 after arriving in England for his marriage.[79]

From October 1837 until September 1838 extensive building took place at the *Ship Hotel* as a new wing was added at a cost of £779 14s. 4d. The annual value of the *Ship Hotel* as listed on the 1839 St Mary's Parish Rating List under Pier Ward, Customs House Quay was, 'Worthington H & B, value £561, annual assessment £9 7 shillings'.

Found at the *Ship Hotel*, Strond Street, Dover at the time of the 1841 census was Benjamin Worthington aged 45 years, along with 14 servants who were nearly all born in Kent. They were Sarah Nethersole, 40 years; William Silk, 35; Caroline Caresvill, 25; Amy Andrews, 20; Maria Pay, 20; Eliza Pratt, 25; Elizabeth Garlinge, 15; John Blythen, 35; Jemima Lee, 20; Jane Wood, 40; Ellen Stacey, 15; Ann Wright, 20; Elizabeth Watkins, 20; and Mary Charlton, 15 years. Three merchants, William Jones, 70 years, Edward Jones, 60 and Edward Thomas, 30 were staying at the hotel along with eight other guests, John and Ann Pointer, both 50 years, Podgy Rawlings, 40 and his manservant John Evans, 30, Maria Fromont, 60, Susan Child, 70, Mary Child, 60, Isabella Child, 35 and Knox Child, 30 Clerk in Orders.

Confirming the *Ship Hotel* was a most fashionable and stylish place to stay in Dover, as well as being very large, the following arrivals and departures were listed in the *Dover Telegraph* on 31 July 1841:

> Apartments have been ordered at Worthington's Ship Hotel for the following:- Lady Bruce & suite, who are expected to arrive this evening; Sir Sandford & Lady Graham & suite expected on Monday next, and Mrs Fanny S. Puxley ... The Duchess of Hamilton & suite, the Marquis of Douglas, Lord & Lady Carrington, Le Comte de Hitty, the Hon. James Knox, Hon. Capt. Campbell & suite, Mr Justice Bosanquet, Cols. Wallace, Wade & Toone & families, Capt Hancock & family, Mr & Mrs Arcedeckne & suite, Mr & Mrs Hopegood, Mr & Miss Mitchell, Mr & Mrs Palmer, Mdme de L. Aigle & family, Master Wellesley, Mrs Joliffe & family, Mr & Mrs Heathcote & suite, Mr & Mrs Martineau & family, Doctor & Mrs Turner, Rev. Mr Hamilton ... (etc. etc.) are among the departures from the 23rd to the 30th instant., to the Continent, from Worthington's Ship Hotel.

On 4 May 1844 the *Dover Telegraph* reported the following arrivals and departures from the establishment:

> the Prince Zarlo, Prince Sangri, Baron Therin, Baroness Rothschild & son, Lord Graves, Lady Jane Hamilton, Archdeacon Law & family, Col. & Mrs Carbonnel, Capt Loftus, Madame Wulf, Rev. J. Bateman, Mr & Miss Houlden, Mr & Mrs Roper, Mr & Mrs Holland ...

On 18 March 1845 an advertisement appeared in the *Dover Telegraph* announcing the 'Important sale of freehold estates'. The sale was to take place at the *Ship Hotel* on 28 May and included

> that well frequented hotel, known by the name of the Ship Hotel, at Dover, together with house adjacent thereto, and the stables and coachhouses now occupied therewith

by Messrs. Worthington and Birmingham. The situation, intrinsic value and susceptibility of improvement of this very beautiful property entitle it to more than the ordinary attention to capitalise.

The 1851 census reveals the *Ship Hotel* belonged to John Birmingham aged 51 years who was present with his wife Mary aged 45 years, son John J. aged 24 years, daughter Sophia aged three years and 14 servants. John Birmingham was most likely the same J. Birmingham who was the superintendent of the Customs House Department of the *Ship Hotel* when the Worthingtons took it over. He became the proprietor of the *Ship Hotel* about 1844.[80]

Under 'Local Affairs' in the *Dover Telegraph,* June 1853, guests arriving at Birmingham's *Royal Ship Hotel* still included royalty and titled aristocracy. On 9 February 1861 the *Ship Hotel* was sold to Mr. Rowland Rees who formed a company to carry it on, Mr. Birmingham having given it up to take over the *Lord Warden Hotel.* The directors of Mr. Rees' company were directors of the London, Chatham and Dover Railway. The property eventually passed to them and the office of cross-channel steamers was established in the western part of the premises, the eastern part at that time being the site of Bradley's Stores.

In the *Dover Express* on 23 April 1864 it was stated that a club was proposed to be established in the part known as Cambridge House. Apartments were also to be made available for a school of art according to the paper on 21 April 1870.

Two announcements of particular interest in the *Dover Express,* 18 May 1877 indicate a change of role and the end of an era for the *Ship Hotel*:

THE CONVALESCENT HOMES - Owing to the removal of the Convalescent Homes from the Old Ship Hotel, Mrs Rusher has purchased the Granville Chambers, and Mrs Marshall's Home will remove to Brighton.

BUSINESS ENTERPRISE - We hear that the Old Ship Hotel, and now used as a Convalescent Home, has been purchased by Messrs. Bradley & Co. who intend to erect another substantial warehouse similar to the one they have already. The plans will be carried out by Mr Stiff. The new building will have a frontage to the quay of at least 93 feet. The conductors of the Convalescent Home have had notice to leave at the end of the present month.

Messrs. Bradley and Son purchased the convalescent home on 18 May 1877 and sadly demolished most of the former *Ship Hotel* in February 1878 to provide a site for Bradley's corn store.[81] The rest of the hotel was apparently sold in January 1899 for £1,500. Part was then used as the Railway Marine Offices until the new railway terminus at South Pier opened in 1914. This part of the old building was demolished about 1947. The annexe was at one time Admiral House, the Dover Naval Headquarters, and may have survived until the 1960s. An establishment in Strond Street was allowed to use the 'Ship Hotel' name and sign from 1872.[82]

Maxton House

When Henry and Mary's children were of school age and Henry became more involved in his business interests, the family moved closer to Dover. The Manor House at Maxton on the outskirts of Dover then became home to the Worthingtons. The *Dover Telegraph* for Saturday 11 April 1835 contains an advertisement which fits the description of Maxton Manor:

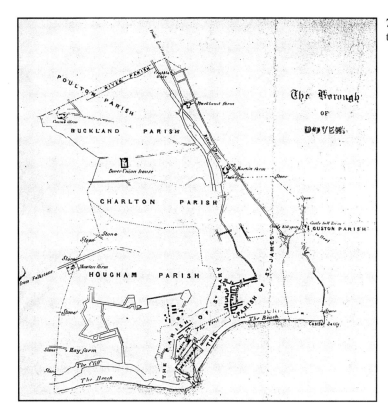

78   Map showing parishes in the Borough of Dover.

DOVER

To LET, with immediate possession, on very reasonable terms, a very excellent and convenient

FAMILY RESIDENCE

With Couch-house and Stable, extensive Garden, Lawns, &c.&c. situate at Maxton, near Dover and adjoining the Turnpike-road leading to Snargate, Hythe &c. The above premises are in excellent repair and fit for immediate reception of a large family. The furniture, which is exceedingly neat and good may be taken at a valuation if required. For particular enquiries enquire of Mr Lamb, Estate Dover, April 3, 1835.

Henry rented the property from Mrs. Fector, who lived there prior to the Worthingtons. In 1846 Henry was paying rent of £72 per annum and rates of £54, rated at 2d. in the pound, for the Mansion House, coach house and garden at Maxton. John Minet Fector of Dover changed his surname by Royal Licence dated 12 February 1848 to Laurie and moved to Maxwelton House, Dumfries. In 1849 Henry bought the house from Mrs Fector and:

> all that the Manor or Lordship of Maxton in the Parish at Hougham ... all that messuage[83] or Manor called Maxton. Home field 17 acres 1 rod 3 perches; Heights bottom 19a 0r 17p; Little Stepping Down 4a 0r 38p; Meadow 4a 2r 23p; and stepping down 17a 1r 16p ... and also all that messuage or dwellinghouse called Maxton with the Brewery brick chimney shafts and other erections and buildings ... and also all that ... 'Hare and Hounds', Maxton.[84]

Besides land, through this purchase Henry acquired a cottage, barn, stable, pig stye, lodges and other land adjoining Maxton.[85]

A historical overview of Maxton Court, within the Parish of Hougham, reads:

> Maxton Court was one of the ancient Manors of Hougham. The ownership of the Maxton Manor can be traced from the time of Henry III when it was held by Sir Stephen Manekyn, for Knight's service in the defence of Dover Castle. Manekyn's daughter Alice alienated it to William Archer who at that time was the chief of the twenty-one Dover master mariners, who provided the twenty-one ships for the King's service, and for working the monopoly of the passage between Dover and Calais. His son William passed the estate to John Alkham, of Alkham, whose descendants held it until the close of the reign of Edward IV, when it passed to Roger Appleton; and after his day it was held in succession by the Hobday's, the Harmans, the Hales, and ultimately went to the Andrews family, one of which was Mayor in the reign of Elizabeth. The Andrews sold it to the Peppers, who held it till the reign of James I and then sold it to Sir Thomas Wilfred of Ilden. In the reign of Charles I it passed to the Richards of Dover, and it was carried by his daughter Mary in marriage to Mr Thomas Fogge of Dover. The Fogges in due course sold it and in 1783 it was owned by Mr Thomas Bigg, Inland Revenue Officer of Dover who resided there and improved the mansion. In the early part of the 19th Century it was the residence of the Worthingtons of Dover, and it is still known as the Manor House, and situate on the main road just beyond the tram terminus.[86]

The manor, an agricultural estate, was historically the unit of local government. Its head was the lord of the manor, or landlord, who held the estate from the king either directly or through one or more mesne, or intermediary lords. During the 19th century the holding of manor courts, the organ of manorial administration, gradually came to an end. However it is known from the following notice published in the *Dover Telegraph* on 2 August 1851 that Henry held at least one such meeting of his estate's tenants:

Manor of Maxton

> The Court Baron of Henry Worthington, Esq., Lord of the above named Manor, is appointed to be held at the Manor House, called Maxton House … on Tuesday the 5th day of August instant, at eleven o'clock in the forenoon precisely, when and where all persons who owe suit and service in the said Court, are to make their appearance to do the same, and such of the tenants of the said Manor as have hitherto neglected to make entries of their Estates on the Court Rolls of the said Manor as they ought to have done, are required to attend with the particulars of their respective Estates, to make such Entries and to pay their reliefs according to the Custom of the said Manor, or otherwise they will be proceeded against as the Law directs. Kennett and Son, Stewards.

The courts traditionally met at intervals laid down by the custom of the manor, usually anything between six weeks and six months. From the 16th century the court baron administered the agriculture of the manor, the lord's and tenant's rights and duties, changes of occupancy, and disputes between tenants. Custom governed everything and checked the rights and duties of both the lord and the tenants. The principle was, 'Justice shall be done by the lord's court, not by the lord'. A steward convened the court and usually presided over it. All tenants were bound to attend and follow the traditional agenda of the occasion or would find themselves fined.

Henry mortgaged the property to his brother Benjamin Worthington in 1851, and 12a 1r 33p adjacent to Maxton House was sold in 1852. All the bricks, tiles and: 'all soil and compositions erections and machinery of all kinds connected with the making of bricks and tiles', and the facility to dig for brick earth were used as collateral, but no mention is made of brewing.

Resident at Maxton House on the night of the 1851 census was Henry Worthington aged 47 years, brewer and head of the household. He and wife Mary, aged 45 years, had four children at home: Henry aged 19 years, brewer; Charlotte aged 16 years, unmarried scholar; Maria aged 10 years, scholar and Robert aged six years, scholar. Two female servants and one male servant were also accounted for.

Further down Folkestone Road at number 17, the census revealed the residence of a schoolmaster and his wife, a governess, three servants and 11 scholars from all over England. Included amongst these boys were Danns (Daines) Worthington, aged seven years, born in Dover and Edward Worthington, aged eight years and born in Dover.

By 1 July 1853 a brewhouse is included as part of the Worthington estate at Maxton and by 22 April 1856 the property owned by Henry is described as 'House and Garden, three cottages, brewhouse, engine house and brickfield at Maxton'. The number of cottages was increased to seven on 30 April 1857.[87] Over the years, tenants of the cottages Henry owned are occasionally named in the record books. For example, on 5 February 1858 William Brazier occupied a house, buildings and land owned by Henry Worthington.[88] William Brazier and George Chamen occupied Maxton House at the time it was sold to John James Allen of Maxton Brewery, Dover in 1885.

On 8 September 1858 George Worthington, Henry's third son, was the occupier of Maxton House, as he was at the time of the 1861 census. According to this census George was the 26-year-old unmarried head of the household. His occupation is given as Master Brewer but the following year George decided to study medicine and went on to become an eminent surgeon. Henry was 57 years of age in 1861 and his occupation was given as landed proprietor. Mary was 55 and only two children remained at home, Maria aged 20 years, unmarried and her brother Robert aged 16 years.

One of Dr. George F.J. Worthington's sons, Dr. Oscar Clayton Worthington, lived at Maxton House with his wife Elizabeth early this century.[89] Unfortunately this old manor fell into disrepair and has now disappeared entirely. Like many of the large homes in England it became too costly to maintain.

The Diamond Brewery

The Diamond brewery was the building closest to Maxton Manor on the Folkestone Road and it is believed to have been built by Henry after he bought the property from John Minet Fector, Esq. in 1849.

At various times of his life, such as the christening of his seventh child Maria Henrietta Adelaide on 2 December 1840, Henry gave his occupation as that of wine merchant[90] or brewer. The yearly registers of Dover Freemen regularly record Henry as a wine merchant–at Snargate Street in 1832/3, at Strond Street in 1834/5 and as an innkeeper in 1836. A notice in the *Dover Telegraph* on 6 September 1834 reports that J. Poulter had taken over Henry Worthington's (wine, spirit and porter merchant) business at 157 Snargate Street, Dover. Mr. Poulter was perhaps only managing the

79 Map showing Maxton Manor House, Diamond Brewery and *Hare and Hounds*.

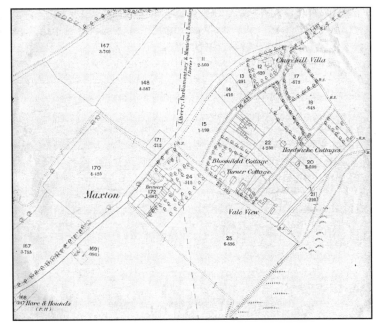

business because the following information was placed in the *Dover Telegraph* on 29 April 1843 by Henry: 'extensive offices and warehouses, no.157 Snargate Street, where places can be secured for the several trains and parcels, goods and luggage booked and forwarded to any part of the kingdom with the utmost regularity and dispatch'.

Caves situated in the limestone cliffs of Finnis Hill, Dover, a very good storage place for wine because of the even temperature and humidity, were listed beside Henry's name in the rating book for St Mary's Parish, Dover ('Pier Ward') 1838-9. Valued at £7 10s. with an assessment of 2s. 6d., these caves are still used for storage. Another entry attributed to Henry in the same rating book was for a lodge with a valuation of £15, and an annual assessment of 5s.

The name Worthington appears as owner of 'wine vaults near Snargate Street' on 19 February 1841 when George Gray was the occupier.[91] A Worthington may have owned these vaults prior to this date. However the church record books for the 1830s do not name the owner of a property, only the occupier. George Gray occupied the property here as far back as 1818 but it is described as a house on Western Heights. It is not described as wine vaults until 3 November 1840. Perhaps this was the date when the Worthingtons purchased them. George Gray ceases to occupy them by 10 November 1843 and 'Worthington' occupied the wine vaults from 16 February 1844-16 August 1844. B. and H. Worthington occupied the vaults from 16 February 1846 until 20 November 1846 and David Barnard occupied them from 16 July 1847-27 April 1850 although B. and H. Worthington still owned them.

An article in the *Dover Express* and *East Kent News* on Friday, 26 December 1941 queried the 'much discussed origin' of the Snargate Street caves. The journalist refers to a book called *Ireland's History of Kent* (published 1829) which said:

We are informed by Mr Batchellor that Mr Hight, in constructing the wine vaults for Mr Worthington, in Snargate Street, when excavating the ground for a poaded vault, at about ten feet from their entrance discovered in the fissures of the rock the beach that had been washed in by the force of the waves; and, at a few feet farther from the entrance, masses of beach were clearly discernible; affording convincing proof that the sea formerly washed against the base of the cliffs in question.

The article went on to say that although the date Mr. Hight built the vaults had not been found, a Mr. Hight, builder, lived at 7 St James' Terrace, Dover in 1837. The caves belonged at some stage to the once well-known firm of wine merchants Messrs. Court & Co, who were in business in Snargate Street prior to 1837 and it is possible that the vaults constructed for the Worthingtons may have been an addition to the network of caves already in use by Mr. Court. A plan of this firm's use of the caves was printed in an *Official Illustrated Guide to the South-Eastern Railway*, issued in 1863.

In *Kelly's 1855 Directory*, Henry Worthington is described as a farmer and brewer of Folkestone Road in the Parish of Hougham. Henry alone is listed as owner of the Snargate Steet wine vaults from 17 October 1855 until 8 January 1863, with D. Barnard the occupier. The Crown appears as owner in October 1863 and Barnard and Co. own and occupy them from January 1864.[92]

Two of Henry's sons were known to be brewers. The last record of a brewer in the family relates to his youngest son Robert. The 1870 *Kent Post Office Directory* includes under brewers: Robert Worthington, Maxton, Hougham, Dover.

The brewery premises, along with all his estate in Maxton, were left in Henry's will dated 16 December 1865, to his brothers-in-law, the Rev. Peter Harnett Jennings of Longfield Rectory, Gravesend and Robert Finnis Jennings of River, Esquire. These properties were left in trust, to pay yearly rent equally to his daughters Sophia and Maria Henrietta while they remained single. Upon their marriage or deaths the properties were to be sold at auction. After Sophia's death in Rome in 1883 and

80   Maxton Manor House and Diamond Brewery from newspaper visitors supplement, *c.*1895.

Maria's 1885 marriage in Rome the estate was auctioned on 30 July 1885 in accordance with the terms of the will. John James Allen was the successful bidder for ' ... All the Manor or Lordship of Maxton in the Parish of Hougham otherwise Huffam ... And also all the messuage of dwellinghouse called Maxton with the Brewery brick chimney shafts and other erections and buildings.' Allen payed £1,500 for the house and grounds and £350 for the brewery. His purchase also included: 'all that messuage or tenement beer house and premises known by the name or sign of the "Hare and Hounds" and the appurtenances thereto belonging situated at Maxton'. It appears from the property's sale indenture that Robert Worthington was the lessee of the brewery and beer house which were situated within a mile of each other.

The brewery was sold again in 1889 to Stanley Single; in 1891 to Edwin Dawes and in 1898 to Thos. Phillips and Co. Ltd., brewers of West Malling, Kent and Dover against whom a winding up order was made in December 1907. On 14 April 1908 the first meeting of creditors was heard in London and the deficiency of funds was estimated at £55,000.[93] The company and its assets were sold off and Alfred Leney & Co. of Phoenix Brewery, Castle Street, Dover, purchased the Diamond Brewery and other properties. It was then run as an Off Licence with parts sold gradually over the years.[94]

Mary Worthington, née Jennings (1806-1865)

On 16 May 1840, Mary and either her mother or sister-in-law Mrs. Jennings, had a narrow escape from what could have been a serious accident. Both women appear to have remained calm and less excited than the *Dover Telegraph* journalist who reported the:

> Providential Escape - On Friday sennight, about half past seven in the evening, an accident occured to Mr Matthew Kennett, solicitor, of Dover, which might have been attended with fatal consequences. As that Gentleman was driving his phaeton with two horses through the lane leading from Shepardswell into the Turnpike Road, between Canterbury and Dover, having on the box with him his man servant and two daughters in the carriage, the front axletree suddenly broke on the off side, and precipitated Mr K. into the hedge. At the same moment the splinter bar and step on the off side broke, and falling on the heel of the off hind leg of the off side horse, tore away the shoe. Bates, the man servant, recovered the reins and endeavoured to pull the horses up: however, in trying to do so, he was thrown out. The horses then continued up the lane, the near side horse alone pulling the carriage; and turned the corner into the turnpike road, mending their speed, and proceeding towards Lydden Hill; before descending which, one of the young ladies jumped out, and escaped without injury; the other was shortly after thrown out and received a serious concussion, but is doing well; the horses went down Lydden Hill at a fearful pace, although the front part of the vehicle on the off side was dragging on the ground. They were ultimately stopped going up the hill out of Lydden, and it is believed from the appearance of the phaeton, that neither of the horses kicked the whole way. Mrs Jennings and Mrs H. Worthington had a most providential escape. They had taken a drive to Shepardswell, and were on the point of entering the cariage to return, when Mrs W. said she should like to take a walk around the flower garden, during which time Mr Kennett's carriage passed. Had they started, as proposed, the consequences must have been fatal, as the carriage would have been in a narrow part of the lane, where it would have been an impossibility to have passed. On discovering the accident, Mrs H. Worthington kindly offered the use of her carriage,

in which Mr Kennett and his daughters were conveyed home. Rickman, the driver of the Express coach; and Overy, the York express post boy, very kindly lent every assistance in their power. Neither Mr Kennett nor his servant received any serious injury.

The Mr Kennett involved in the above incident was probably part of the family who were Kennett & Son, solicitors, the stewards of the Court Baron at Maxton House.

An impression is given that Mary was a benevolent woman in a statement made by a charwoman, Sarah Prescott, 44 years of age, who was charged with stealing some carpet, five pieces of drugget, a canvas bag, pair of tongs and a dish, the property of Henry Worthington., Esq. The court reporter of the *Dover Telegraph* stated in that paper on 17 April 1852 that:

> Police-constable Geddes and Sergeant Burridge deposed to finding the property stated … at the prisoner's house, Chapel Hill, Buckland. Sarah Chapman, servant of prosecutor, identified the property as belonging to her master. The things were thrown aside in the laundry as of no use. Cross-examined by Prisoner–I did not give permission to Prescott to take any of the articles produced.
>
> The Recorder stopped the case at this stage, and the jury, by his direction, returned a verdict of not guilty. The wording of the verdict on the second count attracted some attention–'Not guilty, because Mrs Worthington is not here.' In discharging the prisoner the Recorder adverted to a common custom with charwomen of considering themselves at liberty to appropriate to their own use certain articles seen by them at the house in which they were employed, and which they chose to designate as of no value.

Although very successful in his endeavours, Henry appears to have been a quiet and unassuming man. He had a high sense of civil duty as he was a member of the Dover Coucil and of the Election Committee for the M.P. Mr. John Fector, Esq, who has been mentioned many times in this chapter. The Paving Commissioners Minutes for 1831 also list a Henry Worthington.

Henry and Mary lived in very comfortable circumstances. Perhaps their children needed fresh pastures and new challenges because towards the end of the 19th century all the family had left Dover and moved to either another county or country. Mary Worthington died at the age of 59 years on 28 August 1865 at Chandfontaine, near Liège in Belgium. She was buried on 1 September 1865 at St James', Dover. Death notices for both Mary and her son Daines Balderston Worthington appeared in the *Dover Express* on 9 September 1865. Mary's stated her death was 'deeply regretted by her family and a large circle of friends'.

Henry died of enteric fever and odema of the lungs four months later on 4 January 1866 at Eldon Cottage in Worthing and his body was brought from Broadwater, Sussex, to be buried on 10 January 1866 in a vault at St James' Church. The church was bombed during the Second World War and only the ruins remain.

Henry's son George Finch Jennings Worthington was a doctor at Worthing and would have tended his sick father. It is interesting to note that on the night of 2 January 1866, two days before Henry died, Worthing was flooded by an extremely high tide and as the *Brighton Gazette* reported: '… the water soon reached the summit of the Esplanade and poured over into the road, flowing thence into South Street as far as the Post Office and even inundating part of Montague Street. The encroachment of the tide filled the minds of the people of Worthing with considerable alarm.'

Montague Street runs parallel to the seafront for about half a mile, with South Street at its eastern end and Eldon Cottage where Henry died at the western end, about 150 yards from the sea. Apart from the real possibility of flooded homes, George probably had to wade back and forth in flood waters and torrential rain carried by a howling south-easterly gale, with giant waves crashing over the Esplanade only 150 yards away, to tend Henry. It is therefore no wonder that Dr. George did not register his father's death until 9 January.[95]

Probate of Mary Worthington's will was granted on 6 March 1866, under certain limitations to her brothers Robert Finnis Jennings Esq. of River House in the Parish of River, and the Rev. Peter Harnett Jennings of Lilley, Hertford. Henry's will was proved the day after Mary's with probate again granted to Mary's brothers. Their effects were valued at under £800. It appears the couple had been living in Belgium for some time before their deaths.

As previously mentioned, Henry left his estate to be divided equally between his two unmarried daughters, Sophia and Maria Henrietta Worthington. After their death or marriage of his daughters the estate at Maxton was to be sold and all his children would benefit from the sale.

In Mary's will, written in 1861, she requested that all the property over which she had power of disposal under the will of her late father was to go to her husband, and after his decease was to remain in trust for her sons, Daines Balderston Worthington and Thomas Knight Worthington equally. Daines however died in New Zealand five months before his mother.

George Worthington (1807-1808)

George was born 31 December 1807 at Dover and baptised 19 February 1808 at St Mary's, Dover, the 10th child of Benjamin Jelly and Elizabeth Worthington. He died and was buried with his sister Mary Ann on 2 March 1808 in the family vault at St James', Dover.

81 Back left to right: Ethel M. Worthington, Alfred Worthington, Reginald F.P. Worthington; front left to right: David H. Worthington, Ernest Worthington, Anne Worthington holding baby Alfred R. Worthington at Aberystwyth.

Chapter 5

Grandchildren
of Benjamin Jelly Worthington and Elizabeth Worthington

The Children of Lieutenant Benjamin (1790-1852) and Mary Worthington

Alfred Worthington (1835-1925)

The birth of Alfred, the first child of Lieutenant Benjamin and Mary Worthington, on 14 September 1835, was announced in the *Dover Telegraph*. On 21 October 1835 he was baptised in St Mary the Virgin Church, Dover.

Alfred was a man of fine physique and over six feet in height, features which characterise most male descendants of Benjamin Jelly Worthington down to the present day. Alfred had independent means due to his father's wealth and his mother's large annual income. Like his father he was always interested in open air sport and travel. He spent some time visiting France and Belgium for sporting activities. At the time he visited France he could go anywhere provided he did no damage, but in Belgium a sportsman had to show sporting rights over 150 acres before he was granted a gun licence. His uncle, Henry Worthington, who was living in Belgium at the time, provided him with the necessary qualifications.

Alfred also took a two-month voyage to Canada by sailing ship where he stayed for four to five years indulging his love of hunting and fishing in the Canadian backwoods. His snowshoes are in the possession of his great-grandson, Richard Hankey.

On his return to Dover he married on 11 February 1862 at the Trinity Church Dover, by licence, 19-year-old Elizabeth Ashtell Godden, daughter of John Ashtell Godden, a Cinque Ports pilot. Witnesses to this event were J.A. and Jane Hall Godden.

Cinque Port pilots formed an important section of the community for over four hundred years, often with powerful positions in local government. From the early 16th century they were engaged in piloting

82 Alfred Worthington (1835-1925).

83 Ernest and Amy Worthington.   **84** Elizabeth A. Worthington, née Godden.

ships through the dangerous seas of the Dover Straits, across the Channel to north-western Europe, the mouth of the river Thames, and to ports along the east coast of England. A very select group of men, they built themselves a small gallery at the west end of St Mary's Church in Dover, which can still be seen today. Accessed by a ladder from the entrance lobby of the church, the pilots could come and go as needed during church services without disturbing the congregation.

Alfred and Elizabeth's first two children were born in Dover and the next three children were born in the small village and parish of Guston, two miles north east of Dover. They were: Alfred Benjamin Worthington (1863-99), Ernest Worthington (1864-?), Amy Beatrice Worthington (1865-post 1925), Alice Maud Worthington (1867-1951), Edward Walter Worthington (1868-9).

Amy Beatrice's birth was announced in the *Dover Express* on 4 November 1865. During 1869 there was a serious outbreak of plague in the district which affected cattle, causing them either to die or be killed. Edward Walter died as a result of this disease and Alfred became very ill, most probably from drinking the milk of infected cows. A neighbour lost several children. Sir Morrel Mackenzie,[1] whom Alfred consulted, advised him to go to Aberystwyth for the bracing air of the Welsh coast. The family and one female servant, Sarah Ann Lott, who was born in Guston,[2] packed

85 Alfred Worthington's children.

up their belongings and moved, most probably by sea, to Aberystwyth where Alfred soon recovered his health. He bought 5 Queens Road and the first recorded mention of his presence in Aberystwyth was in the *Aberystwyth Observer* on 7 May 1870 when he made a donation to a fund established to send a local visually handicapped girl to a special school.

The 1871 census records Alfred's occupation as artist, painter and photographer. Alfred was also an accomplished violin player. Shortly after his arrival he took over an abandoned photographic studio at 35 Marine Terrace where he worked for a few years. By September 1872 the family had moved to premises in Terrace Road which had previously been a public house named *The Bull and Mouth*. It is now the site of Boots, the chemist. He retained the publican's licence for a short time to maintain the property's value but did not run the premises as a public house. He appears to have rebuilt the site and incorporated a photographic studio in the new building. Most of the *carte de visite* photographs taken by him carry his Terrace Road address where his obituary said he lived for 12 years.

There are conflicting accounts of the number of children born to Alfred and Elizabeth Worthington, ranging from 10 to 15 in number. I have found 14 children in total, nine more children having been born in Aberystwyth. These were: Edwin

86 Alfred B. and Ernest Worthington.

87 Amy B. and Alice M. Worthington.

Arthur Worthington (1869-post 1925), Elizabeth Florence Worthington (1872), Reginald Frank Patrick Worthington (1873-1936), Frederick Augustus Worthington (1874-1958), Archibald Godden Worthington (1876-7), John Llewellyn Worthington (1877-90), Charles Lee Worthington (1881-1906), unnamed stillborn (1878), Ethel Mary Worthington (1883-post 1925).

Alfred and Elizabeth's eldest child, Alfred Benjamin, was 32 years of age when he married 19-year-old Hannah Neale on 12 June 1894 in the parish church of Llanbadarn Fawr. Hannah was the daughter of Joseph Neale, a decorator. They are known to have had one son, Edward, who died as an infant in 1896, before Hannah was widowed after five years of marriage. Reginald Frank Patrick Worthington was 22 years of age when he married 18-year-old Anne Roberts of 19 Prospect Street, Aberystwyth, the daughter of Henry Roberts, a plate layer. This event took place on 30 July 1895 in the parish church of Aberystwyth. Frederick Augustus Worthington aged 21 years of 14 Vulcan Street married Gertrude Parkin aged 19 years of 14 Prospect Street on 1 November 1897. Gertrude was the daughter of John Parkin, agent. Ethel Mary Worthington married Septimus Coulton during 1923 and they had two daughters, Alfreda who died aged five years and Jane Elizabeth, known as Jean, born 6 April 1928 who married Ken Hankey and is living in Aberystwyth.

88 Left to right: Reginald F.P., Edwin A. and
Frederick A. Worthington.

89 Ernest Worthington (1898-1917), Welsh
Regiment. Killed in action at Flanders.

90 Reginald F.P. Worthington (standing) with two of his brothers (seated).

By August 1882 the family had moved to Cambrian Place and this was the address given by Alfred's son, Edward, when he appeared in court charged with the heinous crime of playing cricket in the street in 1883. He was fined one shilling.[3] The move to Cambrian Place may have been prompted by Alfred's increasing involvement in decorating slate at one of the slate enamelling works. His decorated fireplaces, often featuring local views, are still sought after and one can be found in the Ceredigion Museum. Slate enamelling was a local speciality at this time with five firms involved. Alfred worked primarily for Messrs. Morris and Jones.

Alfred purchased a couple of trawlers and his sons became expert fishermen. During September 1885 Alfred and his eldest son Alfred were together on board their fishing boat *Providence* when they had an accident trying to negotiate the harbour entrance.[4] Considerable damage was done to the boat and nets. Alfred junior died of a heart attack trying to save his boat which had begun to drag its anchors in a gale. He was buried on 30 May 1899 in Aberystwyth Cemetery. At the time of his death Alfred and Hannah lived at 2 Crynfryn Buildings. Charlie drowned at the age of 25 years while yachting in the bay with Captain Bill of Aberdovey and he was buried in Aberystwyth Cemetery on 20 June 1906. His yacht was found drifting with no one on board and it is believed that one fell overboard and the other

91   David H. (seated) and Alfred R. Worthington.

92   *The Herring Fleet*, oil painting by Alfred Worthington.

93   *Champion*, oil painting by Alfred Worthington.

attempted to rescue him—both were presumed drowned. Ernest, Alfred's second son, was drowned in Hamburg one Christmas Eve.[5] Having lost so many members of his family to the ocean, it is not surprising Alfred was a member of the Aberystwyth Lifeboat crew.[6]

Alfred depended entirely on his art and creative talents for a living and to keep his large family. When young he received art lessons from an artist until this study was interrupted by the artist's death. Alfred was remarkably industrious with his brush and hundreds of paintings were executed by him and can be found in many homes in the west of Wales. He painted local scenes of Aberystwyth in the artisan tradition and these have always been in great demand. A raffle of 10 of his paintings put on display in a shop in Eastgate Street raised enough money to make good the damage done to their boat *Providence* after the accident in 1885. The *Cambrian News* of the day commented rather ambiguously that 'some of the paintings are of real merit'.[7] At the time of his death in 1925 one large painting of the Marine Promenade from Constitution Hill to Pen Dinas hung in the Town Hall and one of Llyn Llygad Rheidol in Plynlymon was hung in a prominent position in the corridor of the public library. Alfred's favourite scenes included landscapes, ships, Llanbadarn Fawr Church, which he painted depicting each of the four seasons, and Aberystwyth Harbour. Animals and birds also featured in many of his paintings; the *Gogerddan Hunt* of 1875 is one notable example.[8] Some of Alfred's paintings were included in an exhibition of Welsh artists at the National Library of Wales in 1993. Thanks to the interest of the curator, Michael Freeman, Ceredigion Museum has an extensive collection of over sixty examples of his finest works of art displayed on the stairway.

After one of his trips to the east, Ernest brought home a monkey named Ginnie. She became very fond of Alfred but did not like Ethel. When Alfred received his daily mug of beer, the monkey drank the beer and then threw the mug at Ethel.

By 1891 Alfred was living with his family at 4 Vulcan Place and his occupation was given as artist in painting. He lived at that address until at least 17 December 1903 when his wife Elizabeth was buried in the Aberystwyth Cemetery at the age of 58 years. By 1920 he was living with his daughter, Ethel at 17 Rheidol Place. Alfred has been described as a genial bohemian who, so long as he could have his pipe and just enough to eat and drink, cared very little for household comforts or his attire. According to living family members some of the family had a liking for alcohol. In July 1924 he was granted Letters of Administration for all his unmarried brother Edward's estate but he died before he or any of his family could benefit from the large sum of money he would have been entitled to.

Despite his earlier illness, Alfred was fit and healthy for the remainder of his 89 years and could be seen in his latter years walking about the town with a firm tread. Alfred died on 1 February 1925 at his daughter's home and was buried on 5 February 1925 in Aberystwyth Cemetery by the Rev. R.A. Roberts, M.A. of St Michael's. Six children were still living, Messrs. Edward and Reginald Worthington of Aberystwyth, Frederick Worthington of Oldham, and daughters Mrs. James Jones of Penmaesglas Road, Mrs. J. Coulton of Rheidol Place and Mrs. William Jones of Port Talbot. Family members present at the funeral included Harry, Reggie, Doris and Lizzie Worthington, Messrs. Alfred Worthington Jones of Swansea, Richard Jones, Nurse Gwladys Jones and Misses Lizzie and Olwen Jones (grandchildren).[9] Alfred's will was drawn up on 4 January 1904 and left 'all that I possess to my youngest daughter Ethel

94 Paintings by Alfred Worthington.

Mary Worthington'. On 13 July 1925 his estate was valued at £60 3s. and probate of his will was granted to Ethel Mary Coulton.

Benjamin Worthington (1837-1874)

Benjamin was born on 23 January 1837 and baptised 30 March 1837 at St James the Apostle Church, Dover the second son of Lieutenant Benjamin and Mary Worthington.

Little is known about his early life except that, like his brother Alfred, he developed a love of boats and the sea. On 1 July 1858 Benjamin married his first cousin Charlotte Mary Worthington. Charlotte, aged 23 and of the parish of Hougham, appeared personally before the Rev. John Puckle, Clerk Surrogate, on 29 June 1858 to obtain a licence to marry Benjamin of the parish of St Mary's, aged 21 years. The marriage in the parish church of Hougham was witnessed by George Finch Jennings Worthington, brother of Charlotte, and Mary Worthington, one of the mothers of the bride or groom.

Not long after they married Benjamin and Charlotte departed from London on the 419-ton *Lady Alice* and arrived in Nelson, New Zealand on 15 January 1859.[10] Captain Smith was Master during the sea voyage of between 80-100 days from England to Nelson when a 'chief' cabin fare would have cost 50 guineas and upwards, a second cabin fare 28 guineas and upwards and a third cabin intermediate enclosed berths 22 guineas.

Benjamin and Charlotte rented a house during their first year in New Zealand. Assessment for the rates of Block G in the town of Nelson in November 1859 revealed: 'No 89. Worthington, owner Just. Taylor. Cottage, wood, three rooms, built 1858, value £60, value to sell of whole property £250'.

All houses were built of wood or raupo, as some of the houses which were built of brick were found to be unstable when earthquakes occurred. A tolerable house would have cost £10. The costs of groceries at Parnell, near Auckland, during July 1859 was halfpenny for a four pound loaf of bread; butter two shillings and threepence per pound; eggs three shillings a dozen; milk sixpence a quart; soap sevenpence per pound; meat sevenpence to eightpence for beef or mutton; soda threepence per pound; honey one shilling per pound; tea and coffee cheap and sugar five shillings and twopence (moist).

It is not known why this couple left the relative comfort of Dover, Kent, England for Nelson, South Island, New Zealand. There was nothing happening in New Zealand

> that would warrant the expectation of any greatly increased prosperity; the gold diggings, though steadily worked, exhibited no wonderful results; and the dullness of trade prevailing in this and the neighbouring province, through the want of a market for exports owing to the low prices of grain then ruling, did not improve the state of affairs.[11]

The electoral roll for 24 July 1866 found that Benjamin and Charlotte had moved from Nelson around the Tasman Bay to Motueka where they lived 'upon Bishop's land, section 28'. The 1861 population in Nelson of 9,952 had increased to 23,814 in 1867 due in part to the Taranaki War which took place in the early 1860s, when the wives and children of settlers in Taranaki were removed to Nelson. After the war ended many took up the offer of a free passage to return to Taranaki but many stayed behind in Nelson. The population more than doubled due to the goldrush on the

95   Benjamin Worthington, January 1872.

West Coast. Thousands of ounces of gold were regularly brought to Nelson and thousands of men were scattered over the countryside looking for fresh deposits of the precious metal. Nelson profited greatly. A market was established for all the farming produce of the district. By April 1866 it was calculated that Nelson was receiving revenue at the rate of £40,000 a year from the West Coast.

There were other signs of progress within the city of Nelson. The maritime facilities at the port were steadily growing and a lighthouse beamed on the waters of the bay. Streets sprung up with large and tasteful buildings; there were spacious halls; a system of education for every child was implemented; the people were well fed and many possessed properties; a system of waterworks for the city was ready to be laid; several of the more dangerous rivers had been bridged and the citizens were justly proud of their progress.[12]

Benjamin and Charlotte remained at Motueka until 1873 when they disappeared from the electoral rolls and went to live in Queen Street, Thames, a town in the North Island. Benjamin was able to indulge his love of sailing in the Firth of Thames and Hauraki Gulf. Riding, boating, cricket and bush excursions were the chief outdoor amusements of the colonists. The Thames goldfield was opened by proclamation on 31 July 1867 and 'Auckland entered upon the golden age which is now before her'. It was suggested in the *Colonial Handbook* of that time that 'Persons not accustomed to labour should be possessed of some capital. Gentlemen without a profession or capital are the most unsuitable.'[13]

Benjamin and William Hastie were joint owners of a yacht called *Columbo* which was sometimes referred to as *Colombia*. Both men drowned when their vessel sank on 7 February 1874 during a storm on Auckland Harbour. William Hastie was 45 years old and engaged to be married. He was formerly landlord of the *Separation Hotel,* Wade, the old name for Silverdale.

The storm that took Benjamin Worthington's life was reported in the Auckland *Weekly News* of 9 February 1874:

'gale broke over Auckland Harbour on Saturday evening 7th February. There was not much notice of the storms arrival. Barometer had not indicated such a violent and sudden change–called a tornado. Serious damage was done around the Harbour and partial or complete ruin to many ship owners. Loss of two lives indicated. One yacht lost while on passage to Waiheke Island ...

The yacht was found in shallow water off the breakwater and efforts were made to raise her the following Tuesday afternoon 'as she is a staunch little craft, well found and is believed to be only slightly injured by the gale'.[14] Her two owners were heard to remark that they intended to make themselves snug for the night. Screams were heard by the bath-keeper during the gale coming from the direction of the yacht. The next morning when the vessel was found sunk there was no sign of the two men. It was therefore believed that they went down with the yacht. When the vessel was recovered there was still no trace of Benjamin and William although the bodies of two dogs were discovered on board. Clothes, a small amount of money, a gold and silver watch, diamond ring, a gun and other property were found on board and taken in charge by the police. One of these watches had stopped at ten minutes to three and the other at one o'clock. The latter was found in a box and the former was found tucked in a sail that had been rolled up. The yacht received some damage to her bottom and the dingy was found broken up on the breakwater the morning after the gale. It

96 Charlotte Mary Worthington, née Worthington.

is doubtful whether the men attempted to swim ashore, or endeavoured to effect a landing by means of the dingy or were drowned in the yacht and their bodies washed out of her.

At the coroner's inquest into Benjamin's death, the deceased was described as 'thirty-seven years of age, his usual place of abode lately was at Thames. He was a married man, and leaves a widow without children'. A more detailed account of this event was given as follows:

26/2/1874, Coroner, Auckland. Benjamin Worthington at the dwelling-house of Hudson Fernandez known by the name of The Railway Terminus Hotel in the Province of Auckland in the Colony above mentioned on Friday 13th February 1874 before Thomas Moore Philson M.D. one of the Coroners.... Joseph Holland being sworn saith that I am a Boatman belonging to the Pilot Station; I live at the North Shore. Yesterday Thursday February 12th about 8.30 a.m. I put Captain Burgess the Harbourmaster on board the Ship *Allahabad*, and on leaving in the Pilot boat I happened to see an object floating in the water about midway between the North Head and Bean Rock lighthouse with a seagull perched on it. I went to see what it was and found that it was the dead body of a man. I reported the circumstance to Capt. Burgess who directed me to take it in tow and report to the special constable stationed at the North Shore which I did. Constable Bond came with me and took charge of the body. I was unable to identify the body, it was advanced in decomposition and had several days in the water. It was clothed with a Crimean shirt, serge coat, a black painted oilskin outer coat, cloth trousers with leather waist belt, and circular brass clasp, with the device of snake in it. The feet were naked–in the breast pocket of the serge coat I found a small calico bag which was empty. About 4 o'clock p.m. Sergt. Baker removed the body from the North Shore to the dead house in Official Bay. While at the North Shore I saw Constable Bond remove from the left little finger of the left hand a gold ring (produced). I have seen the body this day.

Signed Joseph Holland.

The next person to give evidence was

Thomas Knight Worthington being sworn saith; I am a Farmer residing at Ngaruawahia, Waikato. I have seen a dead body lying in the dead house Official Bay this day and identify it as the body of my first cousin Benjamin Worthington who was proprietor of the Cutter *Colombo* lately wrecked in the port of Auckland, and has been missing since Saturday last February 7th. I identify the deceased by his personal appearance and stature; and also by his clothing; more particuary by the leather waist belt; the buckle and clasp which is peculiar–deceased has worn that buckle upwards of 20 years. Deceased usually wore a gold ring on his little finger of his left hand–the one shown me resembles that worn by deceased. Deceased had one of his front teeth much worn down. This mark also corresponds with the teeth of the body. Deceased's height was 5 feet 11 inches. His age was 37 years. His occupation was that of a gentleman. He resided at Shortland. He was married and has left a widow who is at Onehunga. He has left no children. I don't know whether deceased made a will or not.

Signed T.K. Worthington.

Sergeant James Baker being sworn then continued with his statement and duly signed his name. The jury returned the verdict of 'Found Drowned'.[15]

Benjamin is buried in the old Auckland cemetery, under and next to Grafton Bridge–just near the grave of Governor Hobson. Charlotte was living at Onehunga and Benjamin was living at Shortland at the time his death took place. Five months later Charlotte married again and more of her life is recorded in her biography.

Mary Ann Worthington (1838-1865)

Mary Ann was born 30 April 1838 and baptised 2 June 1938 at St James the Apostle Church, Dover, the eldest daughter of Lieutenant Benjamin and Mary Worthington. She did not marry and died at Worthing, Sussex on 30 November 1865 at the age of 27 years. Her body was taken back to Dover where she was buried with her mother in Buckland Churchyard B Vault on 5 December 1865.[16] Her death was reported in the *Dover Express* on 9 December 1865. Letters of Administration were granted on 20 March 1866 at the Principal Registry to her brother Alfred Worthington of the parish of Guston near Dover, gentleman. Her effects were valued at under £300.

William Worthington (1839-1841)

William was baptised 7 October 1839 at St James the Apostle Church and was buried there on 10 April 1841.

Elizabeth Worthington (1841-1908)

Elizabeth was born on 31 March 1841 at Dover and baptised 3 May 1841 at St James the Apostle Church, the second daughter of Lieutenant Benjamin and Mary

97   Elizabeth Worthington, née Worthington (1841-1908).

Worthington. She was 23 years of age when she married her first cousin George Finch Jennings Worthington by banns at St Stephen's Church, Westbourne Park, parish of Paddington in the county of Middlesex on 18 April 1865. George was a surgeon residing at Broadwater in the county of Sussex and Elizabeth was living at 2 Talbot Road Villas, London. Her sister Mary Ann Worthington and John Boyton were witnesses to the marriage. George and Elizabeth Worthington had three sons and three daughters: Harry Edward Worthington (1867-1936), Oscar Clayton Worthington (1869-1958), Elizabeth Mary Worthington (1871-1955), Alice Frances Worthington (1872-1930), George Benjamin Worthington (1875-post 1930), Charlotte Wilhelmina Worthington (1879-1930).

The story of her life can be found in more detail in George Finch Jennings Worthington's biography. After the death of George in 1898 Elizabeth went to live at 'Kent Lodge', in the village of Twyford, Berkshire. Elizabeth died on 6 January 1908 and her body was taken back to Dover for burial in the Buckland Cemetery vault on 11 January 1908. Administration of her estate valued at £411 5s. 4d. was granted in London to her son, Harry Edward Worthington.

Edward Worthington (1843-1924)

Edward was born 2 January 1843 and baptised at St James the Apostle, Dover, on 25 April 1843, the youngest child of Lieutenant Benjamin and Mary Worthington.

He was considered 'one of the kindest and best of men and greatly loved by those who knew him'. He never married and held a secretarial appointment at the Seamen's Hospital, Greenwich for over 40 years. In 1881 he was lodging with John Fletcher, a Customs House Officer, his wife and adopted daughter at 6 Huddington Terrace, Greenwich.

Although usually resident in his later years at 'Percy Villa', 42 Drewstead Road, Streatham, Surrey, Edward died at his sister Elizabeth Worthington's home, 'Kent Lodge', Twyford, Berkshire on 31 January 1924 at the age of 82 years. He was taken back to Dover for burial in the Buckland Churchyard vault. Administration of his estate which was valued at £110 6s. 3d. was granted in London on 22 April 1925 to his niece Elizabeth Mary Worthington, spinster. A former grant had been made in July 1924 to his brother Alfred Worthington when the estate was valued at £182 11s. 8d. but Alfred died on 1 February 1925 before settlement of the estate was finalised. Knight, Knight & Rutley of 20 Hanover Square, London produced a catalogue for their auction on Thursday, 10 July 1924. The following lots were listed 'by order of Executors of the late Edward Worthington, Esq' and of particular interest was the antique oak cabinet which was made for Lord Nelson on the *Victory*. I wonder who owns it now?

98 Edward Worthington (1843-1924).

The Children of William Collins (1800-1885) and Sarah Worthington

Anne Charlotte Worthington (1827-1835)

The first child of William and Sarah, Ann was born in Lowestoft on 13 August 1827 and her baptism was recorded two days later in the Lowestoft parish register. Ann died of scarlet fever at the age of seven years on 24 March 1835, causing her parents great sorrow.

Elizabeth Harriette Worthington (1828-1866)

Born in Lowestoft, a record of Elizabeth's baptism can be found in the Lowestoft parish register on 19 November 1828. Elizabeth married the Rev. Lawrence William Till on 16 June 1853. Lawrence was the son of Richard Till, a Lowestoft gentleman. They had seven children before Elizabeth's death in 1866. Those mentioned as beneficiaries of £500 each in their grandfather's 1884 will were: Henry Scott Till, Herbert Jennings Till, Wilfred Worthington Till, Richard Goodwyn Till, Helena Felice Slade and Florence Edith Till.

William Scott Worthington (1830-1870)

William was born in Lowestoft and baptised in Lowestoft parish church on 17 February 1830. At the age of 21 years he married Selina Ann Clay on 6 May 1851 at All Souls' Church, Marylebone, Middlesex. The daughter of Matthew Clay, a Sergeant Major of the Fusilier Guards, Selina was born at Langham Place, London.

The young couple set sail for Melbourne, Australia on 10 May 1851, four days after their wedding. Upon reaching Adelaide, South Australia, some five months later, William posted a long letter to his father-in-law:

> Ship Asia
> August 20th 1851
> Lat.35 Long.135.15

My dear Mr Clay,

I have no doubt you have for some time been anxiously looking out for news from me or dear Selina for some time and your anxiety has doubtless been much increased at not receiving one before but contrary to our expectations we have fallen in with no vessels by which we could forward any letters we have at the same time being so near 5 or 6 vessels as to be able with the trumpet to speak with them and they have promised to report the Asia as safe and all on board well. Thank God we have had altogether a most prosperous and beautiful voyage and to day for the first time we just saw land though very indistinctly, we have now been on the wide ocean for 16 weeks and have not seen an outline or speck of terra firma until this morning when we came in sight of Kangaroo Island, tomorrow we hope to anchor in Holfast Bay and on Monday to get into the Port of Adelaide, there unexpectedly we have to stop 3 or 4 weeks after that we have to go on to Port Phillip in the Asia which as you know is the place of our destination. I trust that if we find things as we anticipate we shall not stop on board the vessel while she is in port and then being able to be absent for a few hours only on shore—but I anticipate going up 30 miles trip into the country, to Mount Barker a most beautiful and picturesque village and stay for three weeks or so up there, this place is recommended to us by the Captain as being a very cheap and beautiful place–but I shall let you know more about this when I am at Adelaide, as I hope there I shall find a homeward bound vessel to take my letters on–I shall not give you in this letter any detail of our voyage as you will receive with this letter a log giving a detailed account of our voyage. I will merely state that we had about 160 passengers on board some respected the others the contrary, we find Captain Roskill and his wife most kind and attentive to our comforts, and the Asia though an old is a first rate sea ship but rather slow, for I can say if we had been in 9 vessels out of 10 we should have been under water during some of the rough weather we have encountered–the provisions on board have been very good and abundant–plenty of water–and by making friends with the Captain's steward I have generally been able to get dear Selina a tit bit daily–it is a curious fact but before Selina came on board she never touched malt liquor but owing to the salt meat and certain routine of diet, I found it necessary for her to take a little ale or porter daily which I am sure has during the tedious voyage given a tone to her stomach and kept her appetite going– Selina was at first for the first 2 or three weeks very sea sick but she got over it and on the whole has been in good health and I think I may say has not lost flesh though at times she has suffered from faintness and headache especially during the hot weather and the last week, her eyes being naturally rather weak, she has had two very painful little pustules form on the eyelids but I am thankful to say they are now better, we experienced the weather very hot under the line and for some days we felt it severely– though thank providence we were not becalmed under the line though we fell in with one vessel, which had been becalmed 21 days on that equator–with all the children and people we have had very little sickness, one poor lady and her little baby died, they occupied the cabin next ours Mrs Henry that was her name was very sea sick and she made I fear no effort whatever to overcome it, consequently she became weaker and weaker by degrees and finally died of exhaustion and her little baby soon followed I never thought much of death on shore being perhaps so much accustomed to it, but certainly a death and burial at sea is very sober, a solemnity, that one however strong minded the person may be, can not overcome–seeing a fellow creature launched from the Gangway into the sea and the weeping Husband and children being present and many of the passengers in tears–with these two exceptions we have been fortunate as regards the state of health, but the diet on board, is so well regulated, and the ship so well ventilated between decks–I could not describe to you the happy days I have passed with my darling Selina–our cabin is very comfortable though small, we are hardly ever absent from each other except when I take my pipe–Selina makes many nice little things which adds much to the slight comforts by way of food on board though in a day or two we shall have an unlimited supply of fresh Beef and Mutton, different kinds of vegetables & of bread, the enjoyment of which no one can appreciate so much as those who have been deprived of them for several weeks Mrs Cooke became rather indifferent to Selina's society after she had been a few days on board, and she became very intimate with a young person by the name of Lynch, whose society Selina neither took much delight in, so consequently we have kept very much to ourselves, but nethertheless we have one or two very nice, and very respectable families on board and whose society have proved very respectable to Selina.

I have met also with a Engineer husband to the poor lady who died on board, a particularly nice man and most willing to afford any information he can, he has several relatives in Australia besides property in the interior of the country, and nothing can exceed the high views and anticipations of a man's succession in Australia if he goes to work in a proper manner. Mr Henry also says that it is also impossible for a man not only to live confortably but to lay by much more money than he could in England and I have not the slightest idea but that my highest anticipations will be realized, he has also put me up to many little useful hints. Mr Henry says that I shall not find the least difficulty to getting up with a Settler for a year or so to get experience, and there will be many persons looking out for overseers and will be glad enough to receive me and at the end of the time when you leave he gives you for his services 30 or 40 pounds worth of cattle to commence stocking your run or farm.

If I can find time I intend writing to Mr Ashton and Mr Orpwood as I think they will very much like to hear from us, and I shall always have reason to remember them after their great kindness to me–Selina will enclose letters with mine–we often now that the evenings are cold sit in our cabin and talk over our homes and we love to think and talk over these little matters, and often do we talk of you at Bedford and when we shall see you all again, but we are so happy together in our own society and all our endeavours are to make each other comfortable and happy.

We have had some very rough weather as you will see by the log I send you but we have gone through it all our crockery wear has slightly diminished, and you must excuse it if you find my writing not quite so legible and straight, as you must remember we are not so steady on board a ship as you are on land but on the whole we have been very comfortable and time has passed almost imperceptibly, so quietly it has flown, it often appears to me nothing more than a dream since I left Southampton.

Monday is the first of September. I shall probably go with my friend Henry for a day's shooting, but not partridge shooting as I was want to do. If I can I intend sending you home from Australia a few bird's skins as they are already preserved and if stuffed will make a beautiful ornament for your room as the parrots and parraquets in Australia are very beautiful and fly about in myriads, but curious enough there are no singing birds out there.

Dear Selina is now very busy knitting which she seems very fond of and has helped to pass many hours away while I am either reading or writing, and she has made several very useful things; when the weather was warm we used to sit out nearly all day long under the awning on the poop but since the weather has been rough and cold we have sat in our cabins in the evening and I dare say Mrs Clay has often pictured to herself Selina and myself in it high busy, as the day she came to look over our cabin she seated herself in the armchair with tears in her eyes, but remember we are so happy and comfortable and love binds us together stronger and stronger every day and I trust there are many years of happiness and prosperity in store for us and that ere many years have passed we shall all meet again to enjoy the comforts of a family circle.

We have been able to have washing done on board, though our boxes have to be brought up from below and we have generally on taking clean linen out put back our dirty ones–though there are some things I have not seen since I left Southampton, I rather fear for my beautiful gun but I trust it is all safe as well as the rest of our goods.

Every Sunday service is performed by the Revd D Packard in the morning, and in the afternoon by the Revd Townend in the fine weather service is performed on board, using the Capstan which is covered with the Union Jack as a reading desk. The bell is tolled, the Captain, his wife and all the officers, Midshipman, passengers, and sailors are present and it really is a very imposing sight all decked out in clean linen and the sailors so clean and neat, it is indeed a beautiful sight the Captain is very strict as regards the observation of religious duties on board his vessel, when the weather is cold or wet service is performed between decks.

October 11th. You will see my dear Sir that more than a month has elapsed since I began this letter and only one opportunity that I am aware of has been afforded of sending letters on and that I did not know until it was too late. After we had brought to an anchor in the Bay which is about 15 miles from the Port we were obliged to lay there for a week waiting for the high tides, as we could not get over the Bar at the entrance of the River before then; then we had to sail down a most beautiful river for about 6 miles and indeed you cannot form any idea of the contrast between the sea and the beautiful trees after so long a voyage,–after we had got moored securely in the Port one and all set out to get some fresh bread, butter, etc–and indeed dear Selina and myself did most thoroughly enjoy these fresh provisions–The Port is 7 miles from the town of Adelaide, never was there known such a wet winter as this has been, the roads have been impassable and consequently things are high but now that fine weather is setting in the prices are coming down–After looking about us for a few days and going up to the Town I fixed upon lodgings for dear Selina and myself and here as circumstances have turned out shall we be for the next 3 or 4 months certainly–and perhaps locate ourselves here entirely, but we must wait for Mr Edd Pearl's coming out.

I have before in this letter spoken of Mr Henry–a Civil Engineer–he has been very kind to me indeed–he and his family have been stopping in Adelaide, this gentleman happened to hit upon a plan for a bridge to go over the river Torrens; the river which separates North from South Adelaide; he sent the same plan to the Governor of Adelaide, and he together with the Council are so pleased with it they have given him orders to build the bridge. I am appointed his head overseer and Mr Cooke his head engineer–so for the present as I am in no particular hurry, it is a very good opening for me–it will keep us well–which is better than spending the money we shall want for other purposes–and we shall be enabled to look about us in the mean time Mr Henry is gone on to Port Phillip to place his children safely in the hands of some of his relations and then he returns to Adelaide–I expect to see him back in 10 days.

Dear Selina has been so well since we have got ashore and are snug and comfortable in our lodgings, the person who keeps them is a very kind and amiable woman and the house well situated we look on to the most superb and grand range of thickly wooded hills you can imagine, we have been a few miles up in a cart into the country. There is a very good road out between the mountains and you ride between immense lofty mountains and the effect is very grand–I took my gun with me and shot some very beautiful birds, plenty of most beautiful parrots–Laughing Jack asses and various other beautifully plumaged birds but no singing birds.

The Port of Adelaide is a very dirty insignificant little place but still full of business– and I have no doubt in a few years will be quite an altered place they are building in every direction. The town of Adelaide is really a well built town, with good wide streets, omnibuses–coaches etc.–and has a great air of comfort and wealth; the shops are very good indeed you can get anything you want and only 15 years ago it was nothing but a vast plain–overgrown with trees, shrubs etc–and it is a large, well built town with Churches–Exchange–Banks, Local court, Supreme courts, Prison–and people are making a good deal of money–with diligence and perseverance but I never intend to settle in the Town–my idea is the country for nothing can exceed the magnificence of the country. Port Phillip as you know was my intended destination and after the Bridge is built I shall go on there I think unless any thing unforseen turns up. I shall be able to write to you constantly now. I only grieve you have not had a letter before this. The vessel we came over in is gone on to Melbourne she has been lying in Port about a month but it will not take her more than 4 or 5 days to get to Melbourne it is only 500 miles from Adelaide.

I assure you my dear Mr and Mrs Clay though I have been now more than half round the world and been on the water nearly five months it appears merely as a dream, but I am as happy with dear Selina we try to make everything as comfortable for each other as we can–we are seldom away from each other, and I never was happier in my life. Selina will enclose a letter with mine–write as often as you can and send us all the news–also some papers–God bless you all and with kindest love to Mrs Clay and all your family.

Believe me ever
your most affectionate son
W.S.Worthington

October 12 1851

P.S. The account of my voyage I have not had an opportunity of finishing, but I will endeavour to do so and forward it with my next letter which will not be long after the arrival of this one.

　　When you write, do not send the letters by overland as they may be many weeks in India before a vessel may start from there to Australia, but send them by a vessel bound direct to Australia and direct William S. Worthington

General Post office
King William St
South Adelaide
South Australia

and also put the name of the vessel by which the letter is sent.

　　Selina is now triming afresh the bonnet Mrs Clay gave her the day we left London which was May 10th 1851

Wednesday evening. 7pm
By the Overland Mail from Singapore
By the vessel Balleguith
Mr Clay
　Tavistock St.
　　Bedford
　　　Bedfordshire
　　　　England'[17]

William and Selina had settled in Melbourne, Victoria by the time their first child, Amelia Scott was born on 16 June 1852 and baptised 25 August the same year by the Rev. Brickwood at St Andrew's Church of England, Brighton. About October 1853 William's cousins Henry Worthington and his brother George Finch Jennings Worthington were in Victoria, probably staying with their cousin and his family at Brighton. George had studied medicine with his uncle, William Collins Worthington, before travelling to Australia. Henry died of fever at Brighton, Victoria aged 22 years, six months later on 18 April 1854.

　　William and Selina were living at Brighton when their second daughter, Charlotte Elizabeth was born on 13 September 1854 and baptised on 9 May 1855. William's occupation on his daughter's birth certificate was given as 'Superintendent of Station'. Two more daughters were born in Melbourne; Marion Esther, 1 January 1857 at Cheltenham (she died in 1858 áged one year), and Caroline Hester, born 5 May 1859 at Argo Street, Prahran. William was listed as a bushman on his third daughter's birth certificate.

　　The Worthingtons had returned to Middlesex by the time of William's death at home on 12 December 1870. Administration of the personal estate of William Scott Worthington, Commercial Clerk, late of 7 New Street, Brompton was not granted until 1 October 1885, possibly because his father managed the estate until his own death. Valued at £175 0s. 3d., administration of his Estate was granted to his widow Selina, of 25 Christchurch-terrace, Battersea in the County of Surrey.

William Collins Worthington instructed the trustees of his will to: 'pay the dividends, interest and income' of £2,000 to Selina Worthington, until she either died or remarried. In the trusts he set up for his grandchildren, money became available to them after their parents' deaths; when they married or turned 21 or 24 years, whichever was stipulated; or three years after their grandfather's death, whichever happened last.

Amelia Scott Worthington of 17 Harpur Green, Bedford married Walter Hurman, a cabinet maker of 22 Wellington Street, Bedford and son of Ferdinand Hurman, a tailor deceased, on 2 June 1878 at the Register Office, Bedford. Witnesses were C. Desborough and Emma Augusta Richards.

Charlotte Elizabeth Worthington of 100 Powerscroft Road, Hackney was married to Harry Relph, an accountant residing at Taunton, son of Isiah Hill Relph, gentleman. The marriage took place on 14 October 1878 at the parish church, Hackney, Middlesex and was witnessed by I.N. and Eliza Bateman. It is not known what became of Selina and her daughter Caroline Hester Worthington. The 1881 census for St Mary's, Bedford revealed a Selina Worthington living in that parish who was head of the household, born in London, aged 45 years.[18] There may also have been other children born to William Scott and Selina Worthington after they left Australia and returned to England.

Samuel Francis Worthington (1831-1834)

Born in Lowestoft during June 1831, Samuel Francis, was baptised at Lowestoft Parish Church on 14 February 1832. He died of scarlet fever on 30 November 1834 at the age of three years and his name was engraved on the side of his parent's tomb in St Margaret's churchyard, Lowestoft.

Charlotte Emily Worthington (1832-1903)

Born in Lowestoft on 17 November 1832, Charlotte was baptised at Lowestoft Parish Church on 17 June 1836. Charlotte married Henry Leman who in 1881 was a Bank Manager in Lowestoft and is mentioned in her father's 1883 will:

> And whereas Henry Leman, the present husband of my said daughter Charlotte Emily Leman some time since borrowed of my said son Francis Samuel Worthington a sum of money on promisory note of which the sum of three thousand pounds still remains owing at interest. Now in case the said Henry Leman shall not either in my lifetime or within ... calender months after my death pay the whole of the said money ... I authorize and direct the said Trustees and Trustee at the expiration of twelve months after my decease to pay the then unpaid portion thereof with all interest due thereon out of the said sum of two thousand five hundred pounds bequeathed to them.

Charlotte and Henry Leman had three known children. They were Catherine, born about 1856 at Yarmouth, Norfolk; Albert J., born about 1862 at Yarmouth, who became a bank clerk and Leonard W., born at Lowestoft.

In the 1875 edition of the *Cambridge, Norfolk and Suffolk Directory* Henry Leman is listed at 62 High Street, Lowestoft. In the 1881 census Henry and family were still at 62 High Street Lowestoft. Those present were Henry, aged 61 years, Charlotte E., aged 48 years, Catherine, aged 25 years, Albert J., aged 19 years and Leonard W., aged six years. They employed a cook and a housemaid at that time. Charlotte died in a mental hospital in 1903.

Hester Sarah Worthington (1834-1922)

Born in Lowestoft on 26 November 1834, Hester's baptism can be found in Lowestoft parish records on 17 June 1836. Sometime between July and September 1860 Hester married Edmund Palmer Norton, a gentleman, who six years previously had been Gentleman Steward of the Manor of Lowestoft. Edmund was probably related to her brother John Scott Worthington's wife, Mary Elizabeth Susannah Norton. In the 1868 issue of *Morris & Co's Commercial Directory*, there is an Edward Palmer Norton, Esquire at 115 High Street in Lowestoft.[19]

Hester and Edmund Norton had five children. Hester died in her nineties on 15 June 1922 in Norfolk. Probate was granted to her nephew William Scott Till Worthington, gentleman, son-in-law Arthur Llewellyn Vaughan, medical practitioner, and her daughter, Gertrude Mary Goodwin (wife of Arthur Charles Goodwin M.D.) on 6 December 1922 at Norwich. Her estate was valued at £10,810 1s. 6d.

Hester's daughter, Hester Ethel Mann was left a set of pictures known as 'The Hours' and her other two daughters, Louise Emily Vaughan and Gertrude Mary Goodwin, were left pictures of equal value. The remainder of her personal estate was left to her three daughters apart from the sum of £400 which was left to the four daughters of her late son Edmund Scott Norton and £200 to Hester Wood Norton and Henry Wood Norton, the children of her son Henry Edward Norton.

99 Francis Samuel Worthington, aged 20 years. (Photo by Delany & Co., Lowestoft.)

Francis Samuel Worthington, M.D., F.R.C.S., L.S.A. (1836-1912)

Born in Lowestoft on 1 May 1836, the baptism of Francis was recorded in the local parish register on 17 June 1836. Francis followed in his father's footsteps by becoming a registered doctor on 13 May 1859. His listing on page 616 of the *London and Provincial Medical Directory* 1869 reads: 'L.R.C.P. 1862 London, M.R.C.S. England 1859, L.S.A. 1860 (Middlesex) Surgeon Lowestoft Infirmary. Late House Surgeon Middlesex Hospital.'

At the time of the 1861 census, Francis was living at 147 High Street alone, aged 25 years. He joined his father in the family medical practice at Lowestoft early in 1862. On 2 October of the same year,

100   Dr. Francis Samuel Worthington.

Francis marrried Helen Felicite Till, only daughter of Mr Richard Till of Clapham and Lowestoft. Helen was the sister of his brother-in-law, Lawrence William Till. Francis and Helen had five children: Helen Frances Worthington (1863-1920), Janet Marion Worthington (1870-1952), William Scott Till Worthington (1872-1955), Richard Till Worthington (1875-1936), Beatrice Worthington (1879-1961).

In 1880 Francis was elected President of the East Anglian Branch of the British Medical Association and he was for many years surgeon to the Lowestoft Hospital and Convalescent Home.

The 1881 census for the county of Suffolk lists four of Francis and Helen's five children. Their third child and eldest son, William Scott Till Worthington, was at boarding school at this time. The children found living at 37 London Road were: Helen Frances, scholar, aged 16 years; Janet Marion, scholar, aged 10 years; Richard Till, scholar, aged five years; and Beatrice, aged one year. The children had an unmarried Dutch governess, Frederika L. Lessor, aged 35 years, who was born in Copenhagen. The family also enjoyed the assistance of six unmarried servants: 64-year-old Elizabeth Thurton who was cook and domestic servant; Sara A. Bacon, 38 years, a nurse and domestic servant; Ann E. Doyley, aged 34 years and Selina R. Ennis, aged 27 years, both housemaids; Edna S. Richardson, aged 18 years, undernurse and domestic servant; and George Mobbs, 15 years old, errand boy and domestic servant–all born in East Anglia.

Francis was very interested in natural science and in his latter days spent time in microscopical studies, becoming an authority on Rotiferae (minute aquatic animals).

In the 1893 *Medical Register* Francis Samuel's address is given as: 'The Beeches, Lowestoft, Suffolk'. Their home was sometimes listed as being in 'Stowmarket, Suffolk', as it was in the probate entry which followed Francis's death at the age of 75 years on 23 April 1912.

Francis was buried in St Margaret's cemetery at Lowestoft and probate of his will was granted to Helen and his sons, William Scott Till Worthington, colonial broker, and Richard Till Worthington, surgeon. The estate was valued at £30,984 12s. Helen was left everything except a silver claret jug given to Francis by the Honourable Mrs. Berkely (late Lady Fitz Harding) and the gold watch, chain and appendages which he usually wore which were bequeathed to his son William. His microscopical instruments and appliances were left to his son Richard.

Francis also stipulated it was his express wish that his wife would provide so that at her decease their unmarried daughters would be bequeathed with 'sufficient furniture to furnish a house of residence'. Helen Frances was to receive £50 a year and

101   Dr. Francis Samuel Worthington.

102   Helen Felicite Worthington, née Till. (Photographed by John F. Worthington at Lowestoft, 1922.)

Janet Marion and Beatrice £250 a year so long as they remained unmarried. If one married she would receive £200 annually and the other remaining unmarried £300 annually.

Helen Felicite Worthington died on 18 September 1922 and was buried in the Lowestoft Cemetery with her husband. In her will, written 3 December 1919, she appointed her two sons as trustees of her estate and left most of the household contents to her then remaining single daughter Beatrice, who lived with her at 9 Corton Road, Lowestoft. This was in accordance with her late husband's will. The possessions she originally bequeathed to Beatrice included:

My Gate Table, my Oak Wagon, Two red leather covered Oak Armchairs, my Mahogany Dower Chest, the Oak Book Case, the Dining Room Carpet and Velvet Curtains, any four Framed Engravings which she may choose, the Fender Coal scuttle and Guard, Two Bronze jugs, the Clock, Two Candelabras and the Round Dumbwaiter (all of which except the gate table were in my dining room at 116 Thorpe Road Norwich). All the contents of my drawing room … including the piano, carpet, curtains, Egyptian screen, looking glass, all blue ornamental china and any four framed watercolour drawings (except that by Whichelo hereinafter mentioned) … All the contents of the large bedroom … facing South West and opposite my room and also the sofa covered rose colour the carpet and blue screen and all the pictures out of my bedroom at 116 Thorpe Road aforesaid. All the contents of the dressing room adjoining the large bedroom aforesaid and eighteen Chinese pictures and any twelve of the unframed engravings in Portfolio which she may choose … Two iron bedsteads with bedding and sufficient furniture for rooms for two maids and all the contents of the spare room … also all the contents of the attic bedroom … which was occupied by the said Beatrice Worthington. And also all my household linen and as many of the necessary articles for the pantry kitchen and garden as she may require and choose.

I also give her the following articles of plate namely twelve large and twelve small forks, twelve large table spoons, twelve desert spoons and twelve tea spoons, one gravy spoon, one soup ladle, one salad spoon and fork, two silver salt cellars and spoons, twelve desert knives and forks in case, the small plated kettle and stand, two silver sauce boats, the silver tea caddy, two plated round vegetable dishes with silver rims, two plated hot water dishes given to my husband by Sir Thomas Lucas, the silver coffee and its tray formerly belonging to my mother … one pair of silver candlesticks, the brass tea tray used by me and twelve steel table knives, the silver square tea pot and its tray, the silver muffineer used by my husband, the silver box engraved given by Mr Birkbeck, the silver tea service given to my husband by Mrs Fowler, the silver embossed milk jug, one pair of diamond earings, one diamond horse shoe broach [sic], one pair of Gold Egyptian bracelets, my gold watch and chain and my cameo bracelet set in gold, also such of my books as she may wish for and choose.

Helen added two codicils to her will; the second was written on 18 April 1922 after Beatrice married Francis Alfred Worship Cobbold, a solicitor. In this codicil Helen wrote that although Beatrice was now married and therefore it was no longer necessary to carry out her late husband's wish, she still wanted her youngest daughter with whom she had lived so long 'to have a larger share of my furniture and other household goods than my other surviving children'.

She did revoke a few family heirlooms such as the two plated hot water dishes, the Rosa Bonheur and Landseer pictures plus her bedroom furniture which she gave to William Scott Till Worthington; the silver engraved box and one brass bedstead which matched the one already given to William's daughter Mary went to Richard Till Worthington; and the gold set cameo bracelet was rebequeathed to Janet Marion Jervase Hatt.

Helen left her eldest son, William Scott Till Worthington, the watercolour by Whichelo; to her son Richard she left her *Encyclopaedia Britannica*, glass and silver claret jug, and the silver tea pot, two milk jugs, coffee pot, sugar basin and tongs given as a presentation to his grandfather W.C.Worthington. To William's wife Mabel Helen left a carriage clock marked 'Money Lowestoft' and Richard's wife received her widest silver Egyptian bracelet and two framed sepia drawings. Her grandson John Francis Worthington was left a small silver box engraved 'F.S.Worthington' and her granddaughter Mary Worthington a gold link chain given to Helen by a Mr. Prince, a silver and mother of pearl pocket fruit knife and fork, an enamelled cameo bracelet given to Helen by a Miss Norris and her onyx brooch and earings. Granddaughter Helen Olivia Worthington received another silver pocket fruit knife and gold engraved bracelet.

Helen left her eldest daughter Helen Frances Wilson her two half hoop diamond rings, diamond bar brooch, and the set of silver tea pot, milk jug, sugar basin and tongs formerly lent to her brother Richard. Daughter Janet Marion received a diamond cross, gold Egyptian necklace, one pair of silver candlesticks and 'the silver cigarette box anonymously given to my husband'. Daughter Janet and Beatrice also received the Egyptian curios and mounted and unmounted photographs. The rest of her plate, plated goods, china, glass, pictures, prints, books and all other articles of household or domestic use and all wine and consumable stores and outdoor effects were left to all five children, to be divided among them. Helen's other assets included a share in her father's residuary estate–which she directed be divided among her five children.

Seven months later on 2 July 1920 Helen added another codicil bequeathing daughter Helen Frances Wilson an additional £50; however Helen Wilson died three weeks later. It was also written in this codicil that William was to receive a grand-father clock with a picture of a ship which moved with the pendulum; and Beatrice the other grandfather clock. Helen Felicite's address at this time was 14 Gordon Road, Lowestoft.

John Scott Worthington (1837-1883)

John was the eighth child and fourth son of William Collins and Sarah Worthington, born 23 September and baptised 5 November 1837 in Lowestoft. He emigrated to New Zealand in 1861 where he married 17-year-old Mary Elizabeth Susannah Norton, daughter of Henry Dawson Norton and Sarah Elizabeth Ann Norton, nèe Scales of Great Yarmouth, Norfolk, on 18 May 1861 at St Paul's Cathedral in Dunedin, Otago. Sarah had been in Dunedin for eight months and John for three weeks at the time of their marriage so they must have known each other in England. Sarah's father Henry, a builder, gave his consent and was a witness to the marriage.

The family lived in Queenstown where John and Mary had 14 children before John died on 12 June 1883: William John Worthington (1862-1952), Ethel Scott Worthington (1864-1956), Alice Charlotte Douglas Worthington (1865-1951), Percy James Worthington (1866-1938), Maria Edith Worthington (1868-1915), Jessy Mihill Worthington (1869-1907), George Vigers Worthington (1870), Sydney George Woolley Worthington (1871-2), Laura Fraser Worthington (1872-1968), Francis Worthington (1873-5), Gipsie Sara Worthington (1874-1940), Alfred Ernest Worthington (1876), Harold Fairthorne Worthington (1877-1938), Charles Woolley Worthington (1879-1945).

John Scott Worthington worked as a clerk, landholder and gold receiver. A news-paper report from page four of the *Otago Witness*, 17 January 1863, states that: 'The first report from Mr Worthington, the newly appointed Commissioner of the Wakatipu Gold Field was received in Dunedin yesterday ...'. The position included calculating populations of the transient mining townships which sprang up wherever gold was found, granting prospecting claims and informing the Government of what minerals were found where and in what quantities. John Scott's report continued,

> Miners have been rushing principally to the westward, and are in a very unsettled state. I should estimate that one half of the population are doing nothing but searching for new ground, or following up successful prospectors. The population during the past week have been steadily migrating westward, on the track of a man who goes by the name of 'Moonlight'.

Like his niece, Francis Samuel's daughter Helen Frances, John Scott may have had an interest in astronomy. It was reported in the *Otago Witness* on 17 June 1871 under 'News of the Week' that an observatory was established in Queenstown under his charge.

John owned 24 acres of land worth £110 at Lake County and land in Queenstown worth £500 at the time of his death at the age of 45 years from cancer of the tongue on 12 June 1883 in Queenstown.[20] He was buried in the Queenstown cemetery where three of his infant children were also buried. Executors of his will [21] were his wife, James Douglas of Frankton, a surgeon, Richmond Beetham, resident Magistrate of Christchurch and Wesley Furton, a Queenstown solicitor. The estate was basically set up to ensure the support, maintenance, education and bringing up of his children to the age of 21 years and/or until his daughters were married. His wife would have most control over the children, 'so long as she continue my widow' and brought up the children 'to the satisfaction of the said Trustees'. The death or remarriage of his wife appeared one and the same to John but with so many children to care for it is hardly surprising that Mary married William Branson, accountant and commission agent, the following year. Two children were born at Blenheim to Mary and William Branson, William on 3 April 1888 and Margaret on 3 April 1889.

It is interesting to note that, in a codicil to John Scott's will, written two months before he died, he declares:

> should any of my children enter any Roman Catholic Convent Nunnery or other institution belonging to or in any shape or form connected with the Roman Catholic persuasion then and in such case any such child or children of mine ... shall absolutely forfeit all real or personal property money or moneys and all benefit advantage and interest to which such child or children would be entitled to ...

An obituary published in a Queenstown newspaper after his death states:

> We extract the following from the *Cromwell Argus* which, we have no doubt, will be interesting, although painful, to many of our readers, from the high reputation of the family in our midst:-

> 'The life of the late Mr. John Scott Worthington, which came to a close on Tuesday last, at Queenstown, was a busy one from early manhood to almost death's closing scene, etat 45 years. He was present at the Crimean campaign, being an attache of the medical department. He came of a medical family, whose name is also a very old one in the County of Suffolk. His father, who survives him, and his two brothers, are physicians in that county. Lowestoft is their chief domicile and at that place the deceased was born. After the Crimean War was over, the spirit of activity possessed him, and a hum-drum life at home having no charms for him he chose to follow the more adventurous career of a colonist. He came to this colony in 1858. The deceased gentleman became possessed of a sheep run, near Messrs. Cargill and Anderson's at Mount Benger. At that date pastoral pursuits were surrounded with difficulties, and it was not an easy thing to clear and stock a piece of country. The late Mr. Worthington was then but a young man and possessed of little colonial experience. He fought, however, bravely against obstacles, but the battle did not end in his favour. He then entered the Civil Service of the Province of Otago, in the year 1861, being appointed a clerk, we believe, in the Sheriff's department. His great aptitude for figures, quickness of conception of facts, and the celerity and ease with which he worked, recommended him for a higher appointment. He became clerk to the R.M. and Warden's Courts, and clerk to the District Court, which position he held to the period of his decease, dying actually in harness. He had a facile way of getting through his multifarious duties, and yet found ample time to engage in a number of other matters. Though not one of the originators of the first Acclimatisation Society, he soon began to take an

active part in the experiment of stocking our mountain streams with trout and other fish. The care and skilfulness displayed by him were simply invaluable, and the success of his efforts are manifest in that he hatched over a million trout in three years and superintended their distribution throughout this (Vincent) Lake and Southland Counties. The great success that rewarded these efforts are known to all. In any local and social affair connected with Queenstown, and often in other places, he took an active interest. He was a keen sportsman, and ardent cricketer–though but an indifferent bat a capital fielder–and was at one time Captain of the Volunteers. He was remarkably fond of botanising, of mineralogy, of tree planting and gardening. Evidences of this are apparent around his residence, in the Queenstown acclimatisation grounds etc. He was secretary to the Wakatipu Hospital for many years, and his previous surgical experience, and that acquired at the hospital enabled him to be of service to Dr. Douglas and other surgeons in many cases of difficult operations. Chiefly known as Clerk of Courts, he was in that capacity ever courteous and obliging. He did not spare himself if he saw he could do some good. "After office hours" was seldom the excuse received from him. Some of the legal gentlemen harldy liked that assistance he rendered, and the answers he gave to miners and others. He considered it his duty to afford all information in his power about things under his control, but abstained from volunteering advice. During the last six months the deceased suffered frightfully, but bore the torture stoically to the end. He hardly, or it may be perhaps said never, complained of his state. He was possessed of immense moral courage, and his constitution must have been a grand one. He was sensible to the last. He wrote down to his son Willie, 'I want light, it is so dark,' and a little later he appealed to Mrs. Worthington to bring in some lights. The room was lit up at the time, and the eyes of the deceased were open. Immediately he returned his head to the pillow, he slept that sleep from which there is no awakening here. An active brain, an energetic system, a warm, kind heart had ceased to exist. He was surrounded by members of his family, who witnessed how a good man can die peacefully.'

Marion Worthington (1838-1932)

Born in Lowestoft on 13 December 1838 and baptised at the local parish church on 7 July 1839, Marion was the ninth child of William Collins and Sarah Worthington. Marion married Henry Wetton sometime after 1853 and had two children. Henry died on 14 June 1900 and his widow along with Harold Wetton and Henry John Sidwell, gentleman, were granted probate of his will and an estate worth £27,227 11s. 1d. on 7 September 1900. Henry's address at the time of his death was Abbey-House, Chertsey, Surrey.

Marion was living at 7 Rydal Road, Streatham, Surrey when she died on 11 March 1932 and her estate was left to her son Harold Wetton and his wife, Jessie Sarah Mabel Wetton and valued at £803 2s. 11d.

Edward Scott Worthington (1840-?)

Edward was born on 4 March 1840 in Lowestoft and baptised 6 September 1840, his parents' 10th child. He emigrated to Canada where it is believed he married and lived for the most part of his life. He had five children, the youngest of whom, also named Edward Scott, is written up in the next section of this chapter.

James Copland Worthington, M.D., L.R.C.P., L.S.A., M.R.C.S., L.F.P.S., L.M. (1841-1906)

Born 28 November 1841 and baptised on 6 February 1842 at Lowestoft, James followed in his father's and older brother's footsteps and became a Doctor of Medicine at Edinburgh on 17 February 1870.

The 1901 *Medical Directory* has the following entry concerning James:

L.R.C.P. Edin. 1877; M.R.C.S. Eng and L.S.A. 1865; (Middlx & St Bart.); prize in Clinical Medicine and Surgery, Middlesex 1865; Consulting Surgeon Lowestoft Hospital; late medical advocate Lowestoft Convalescent home and House Surgeon Middlesex Hospital. Contributor 'Instrument for fascilitating operation of tracheotomy and laryngotomy' published in the *Medical Times Gazette* 1866; and 'Treatment of Fractures by elastic extension' published in the *British Medical Journal* 1867.

His other qualifications included L.F.P.S. Glasgow and L.M. Dublin. James practised at Brinnington, Stockport for a time before he joined his brother Francis as a partner in the Lowestoft practice.

A very handsome man, James married Harriett Myatt Vigers, daughter of Francis Vigers a surveyor of Hersham, on 10 July 1867 at Hersham Church in Surrey. The hamlet of Hersham lay midway between Esher and Walton-on-Thames. Harriett's father Francis worked for a firm called Davis & Vigers, land surveyors and auctioneers, based at 3 Frederick's Place, Old Jewry, London.[22]

103 Dr. James Copland Worthington.

James and Harriett had nine children: Laura Scott Worthington (1869-post 1906), George Vigers Worthington (1870-1942), Frank Vigers Worthington (1871), John Vigers Worthington (1872-1951), Dorothy Maude Worthington (1873-1898), Frank Vigers Worthington (1874-1964), Rubie Elisabeth Worthington (1877-1963), Phyllis Mary Worthington (1880-post 1909), Dulcibella Mary Gooch Worthington (1885-1976).

At the time of the 1881 census of England and Wales the family were living at 28 and 29 Marine Parade with Anna Jollye a 34-year-old governess, Charlotte Monkman, a 26-year-old cook, Catherine Rushman, a 25-year-old parlour maid, Frances M. Bullock, 30 years and Phoebe Hutle, 18 years, both nurses, and Elizabeth M. Smith a 19-year-old house maid.

They were still at this address when the 1891 census was taken; however, they had a boarder and their domestic staff consisted of three housemaids, a cook and footman. Their boarder, Elizabeth Seniech from Hanover in Germany was a school governess.

The 1893 *Medical Register* lists James' qualifications as: 'Member Royal College of Surgeons, England 1865; Lic. Soc. Apoth. London, 1965; Lic. Roy. Coll. Phys. Edin., 1877.'

After his retirement James lived at Belcombe Brook, Bradford-on-Avon. At the time of his death on 4 June 1906 he was living at 4 Victoria Mansions, Kirkley, Lowestoft and his estate was valued at £32,513 2s. 8d. Probate was granted to his friends the Rev. Lancelot William Hale Andrews of Lowestoft, clerk in Holy Orders and his son John Vigers Worthington, company manager.

James asked that his funeral be as plain as possible; that his wife and Frank Vigers receive a legacy of £300 each, that Harriett receive all pictures, prints, books, plate, plated articles, linen, china, wines, liquors, provisions, household goods, furniture, horses, carriages, chattels and effects and be given £700 for purchasing furniture if she were not living in a house furnished with James' furniture at the time of his decease. Harriett was also to receive an income of £800 per annum for the maintenance of herself and her two youngest children Dulcibella and Phyllis.

His eldest daughter Laura Scott, who lived in the Convent de la Visitation Mont Sant Amand Les Gand in Belgium where she was known as Soeur Marie Teresa Joseph, was left an annuity of £10 per annum.

James stipulated that,'my trustees shall not invest any part of the said trust premises upon any stocks funds or securities guaranteed by the Government of India or upon the stocks, funds or securities of any Railway in India whether guaranteed or not'. Trusts were established to benefit equally all his children and/or grandchildren and the executors of the estate were given £105 each for their trouble.

Ann Scott Worthington (1843-1843)

Baptised in December 1843 in Lowestoft, Ann lived only three months and was buried at Lowestoft on 28 December 1843. Her name appeared on the side of her parents' tomb under those of her brother Samuel Francis and sister Ann Charlotte.

Caroline Crosse Worthington (1846-1883)

The youngest child of William and Sarah was born in Lowestoft on 6 September 1846. She married Henry J. Powell between July and September 1866 and died in London on 14 February 1883. Caroline and Henry Powell had seven children.

Children of Henry (1803-1866) and Mary Worthington

Benjamin Worthington (1829-1860)

Benjamin was the first child born to Henry and Mary Worthington on 29 November 1829. His baptism took place on 23 January 1830 at St Mary's, Dover.

Benjamin and his younger brothers and sisters were born into a large, well respected and wealthy family. His early days were spent on Maggott Farm at South Alkham, between Dover and Folkestone, situated in the chalk and wooded Alkham valley. Amongst the rolling hills of eastern Kent he could ride horses, swim in the ponds and climb walnut trees. When he was older he could sail in Dover Harbour.

All the children were well educated. The elder children may have gone to a local school as boarders; certainly the younger children did. Daines and his cousin Edward are known to have attended a small, local boarding school.

Benjamin was a brewer working in his father's business when he was made a Freeman of Dover (by birth) on 28 June 1854. However the call of the sea was stronger than the family business and in 1854 he was a seaman on board the *Roxburgh Castle*. Benjamin was 3rd mate on board the 560-ton *Emma Colvin* when it sailed for New Zealand on 23 February 1856 under Captain Nicholson and arrived in Nelson on 3 June 1856 with immigrant passengers. He became certified as a second mate, ticket no.17768 at London on 24 November 1857.[23] Benjamin was a bachelor and 3rd officer on the Peninsular and Steam Oriental Steam Navigation Company's S.S. *Malabar* anchored at Bombay in the East Indies when he died of a liver abscess on 27 April 1860 aged 30 years. He was buried the following day at Back Bay, Bombay.[24] Benjamin was 4th mate on board the S.S. *Malabar* during an earlier trip to Gibraltar. The S.S. *Malabar* was lost at sea on 25 May 1860 a month after Benjamin's death. His estate was left unadministered by his father after a former grant in August 1860 and on 24 May 1866 Letters of Administration were granted to his uncle, Robert Finnis Jennings Esquire of River House in the parish of River, Kent, he being one of the executors of the will of Henry Worthington. His effects were valued at under £200.

Henry Worthington (1831-1854)

The second son of Henry and Mary Worthington was baptised at St Mary's, Dover on 9 November 1831. He was raised with his brothers and sisters at Maggot Farm at Alkham. He had no apparent career as he was described as a gentleman and unmarried when he died aged 23 years on 18 April 1854 in Melbourne, Victoria, Australia. His brother George Finch Jennings Worthington, who had studied medicine in Suffolk with his uncle William Collins Worthington was the informant, and according to his death certificate they had been living in Victoria for six months. Also living at Brighton at the time was William Scott Worthington, son of William Collins Worthington, and family.

Henry was probably the paying passenger 'Henry Worthington' on board the 923-ton ship *Otilla* which arrived in Melbourne on 15 October 1852 or the paying passenger 'Henry Worthington' on board the 1,106-ton ship *Constance* which arrived in Melbourne on 27 December 1852. Both ships had departed from Liverpool in England and Henry may have been exploring the world prior to his sudden death. During his illness Henry was under the care of Thomas Michell, surgeon but died at

Brighton of a fever which he had for five weeks. He was buried by Rev. Samuel Taylor on 19 April 1854 in the church grounds of St Andrew's Church of England, one of the oldest burial grounds in Melbourne and still beautifully kept. No head-stone can be found.

Brighton has always been one of the better suburbs of Melbourne and, at the time Henry was there, it was both an agricultural district and a residential one where many of Melbourne's merchants settled with their families.

Letters of Administration of Henry's estate were granted to his uncle Robert Finnis Jennings of River House on 24 May 1866. His effects were valued at under £200.

George Finch Jennings Worthington, M.D., M.R.C.S., L.F.P.S. (1833-1898)

George was baptised on 4 December 1833 at St Mary's, Dover, the third son of Henry and Mary Worthington and was named after his uncle, George Finch Jennings, Mary's brother.

As a medical student he went to live with his uncle, Dr. William Collins Worthington, at Lowestoft and was residing there in April 1851 when the census was taken. The following year he was exploring the world like his brother and cousin. 'George Worthington' was a paying passenger on board the 789-ton barque *Mary Harrison* which arrived in Melbourne from Adelaide 13 August 1852. He was living in Melbourne when his brother Henry died there in April 1854 as was his first cousin, William Scott Worthington and his family.

104   Dr. George Finch Jennings Worthington.

George worked for a time in the family business at the Diamond Brewery as a brewer. His occupation was given as brewer when he was made a Freeman of Dover (by birth) on 29 June 1859. He continued his medical training at Middlesex and St Thomas' Hospitals and obtained his M.R.C.S. (Member of the Royal College of Surgeons) England in 1863, L.F.P.S. (Lic. Fac. Phys. Surg.) Glasgow in 1864 and became a registered doctor on 23 March 1867.[25]

On 18 April 1965 he married his first cousin, Elizabeth Worthington, daughter of Lieutenant Benjamin and Mary Worthington, at St Stephen's Church, Westbourne Park, London. Their marriage notice appears in the *Dover Express*, 29 April 1865, 'Elizabeth Worthington second daughter of the late Lieutenant Benjamin Worthington, R.N. of Dover to George Finch Jennings Worthington Esq. of Worthing, Surgeon'. More information can be found about Elizabeth in her biography. George and Elizabeth had six children: Harry Edward Worthington (1867-1936), Oscar Clayton Worthington (1869-1958), Elizabeth Mary Worthington (1871-1955), Alice Frances Worthington (1872-1930), George Benjamin Worthington (1875-1957, Charlotte Wilhelmina Worthington (1879-1930).

George was living at Broadwater in Sussex at the time of his marriage after which he and Elizabeth lived at 1 Heene Terrace 1869-71. They moved to 7 Heene Parade, West Worthing with their growing family in 1871[26] and remained there until 1875. Between 1875 and 1878 George travelled as Surgeon Superintendent of H.M. Emigration Service and was on the medical staff of the South Australian Government. His address in 1877 and 1878 was 156 Collins Street, East Melbourne and Stone Hall, Wallingford, Berkshire.[27] Dr. George made two trips to South Australia as Surgeon Superintendent, the first on board the 1,137-ton ship *Alumbagh* which sailed from London on 20 November 1876 under Master E.W. Pratt and arrived in Adelaide on Friday, 16 March 1877.[28] He described the voyage with 353 government immigrants in steerage '… as most pleasurable. Concerts were held, temperance meetings organized, and as a last resource the spelling bee was introduced as a measure where-with to kill time and make things pass agreeably.' Three hundred and fifty-five immigrants embarked at Plymouth and on the passage three births and five deaths occurred. No serious illnesses were reported. His second trip was on board the *Hydrabad* which departed from Plymouth on 25 November 1877 and arrived in Adelaide on 25 February 1878.

After his career as a surgeon in the Mercantile Marine, George practised at Sidcup, Kent from 1879 until 1892 and was instrumental in founding Chislehurst, Sidcup and Cray Valley Cottage Hospital, 'an institution replete with every comfort for the relief of the sick and suffering'. Dr. Poole and others wanted the hospital built in Sidcup but George and many other doctors in the district wanted it built at St Mary Cray and their opinion prevailed. In 1890 at the Cottage Hospital George performed a remarkable amputation of the leg, remarkable because the patient was in his 74th year. The operation took only 18 minutes from the time the man arrived at the hospital to his bed. The patient afterwards married his second wife and lived for many years.

105   Dr. G.F.J. Worthington's calling card.

106   Thorncliffe, Poole Road, Bournemouth.

George was the author of the following pamphlets: *Bathing, its Uses and Advantages*, published London, Worthington 1868, *Hygiene*, also *The Incubation of Disease, especially in relation to Measles and Chicken pox*.[29] He was made a Member of the Royal College of Physicians, Ireland 1880 following an exam there in 1868. He was also made a Fellow of the Obstetric Society in London and a Founder Fellow of the British Gynaecological Society.[30]

The family were living at 'Bath Villa', Foots Cray in 1881 and 'Highden', Sidcup by 1891 with three servants.[31] In June 1892 Dr. George and his family went to live at 'Thorncliffe', Poole Road, Bournemouth west. The local Sidcup newspaper reported that

An interesting ceremony took place at the residence of Dr Worthington, Highden, Sidcup on Saturday evening last. A valuable carved oak English chime clock, with carved oak bracket to match, together with a set of entree dishes were presented to him. The inscription engraved on the silver shield was as follows:- 'Presented to Dr Worthington by several of his patients as a tribute of their great esteem and regard on his leaving Sidcup, June 1892' ... Dr Worthington who spoke under great emotion thanked those both present and absent for the very valuable present in token of the esteem and regard which had just been presented to him and also for the many kind words which had been spoken in testimony of the appreciation of his professional services, and regret at his leaving Sidcup. He could assure them that the chimes of the beautiful clock would ever be a reminder of that evening's events, and would be a lasting memento of the kind and warm hearted friends he had left behind him.

George kept in close contact with his cousins in New Zealand as a letter written by him about his daughter Alice's wedding on 19 December 1895, originally accompanied by a newspaper cutting of this grand, much talked about event, was known to be in the possession of Edith Watson, née Worthington.[32] George died at Bournemouth on 20 March 1898 aged 64 years and was taken back to Dover where he was buried in the family vault in Buckland Churchyard on 24 March. His very brief will dated 1 April 1897 left his entire estate, valued at £486 18s., to his wife, Elizabeth, the sole executrix. Witnessess were Geraldine Eleanor Pole of Shute House, Devon and Clara Annie Fogg, Little Thurrock Hall, Essex. Letters of Administration were granted in London on 1 June 1908 to Harry Edward Worthington, surgeon, the effects being valued at £132 0s. 7d.

Charlotte Mary Worthington (1835-1918)

Charlotte was the fourth child born to Henry and Mary Worthington, on 29 January 1835. Her first marriage took place at Dover on 1 July 1858 in the parish church of Hougham when she married her first cousin, Benjamin Worthington. The marriage was by licence which Charlotte had obtained and more can be found out about her life with Benjamin in his biography in this chapter.

Charlotte and Benjamin sailed to Nelson, New Zealand on board the *Lady Nelson*, arriving in January 1859. What attracted them to the shores of New Zealand where only the 'sober and industrious will succeed'? Charlotte's brother, Thomas, had been an apprentice on board the *Cressy* in 1850 which had brought many immigrants to Nelson. He obviously was impressed with what he saw as he eventually returned to live in Nelson. Perhaps it was an advertisement like this one placed in the *Dover Express* on 10 July 1841 which attracted them:

107   Charlotte Mary Worthington.

NEW ZEALAND
PRELIMINARY LANDS

NELSON SETTLEMENT.- Allotments each consisting of 1 Acre of Town, 50 Acres of Suburban, and 150 Acres of Rural Land are now selling at the price of 300 pounds. Deposit, 30-150,000 pounds are to be expended in emigration in this particular settlement …

EMIGRATION

A free passage is offered by the New Zealand Company to their Settlements (including Provisions and Medical Attendance during the voyage) to Agricultural Labourers, Shepherds, Miners, Gardeners, Brickmakers, Mechanics, Handicraftsmen, and Domestic Servants, being married, and not exceeding 40 years of age, to Single

Females under the age of near Relatives, and to Single Men, accompanied by one or more Adult Sisters, not exceeding in either case the age of 30 years. Strict enquiries will be made as to qualifications and character. In these Settlements there are neither CONVICTS nor SLAVES, and the RIGHTS of the NATIVES are protected. Apply personally, or by letter to …

The colony of Nelson was established in 1841 when members of the New Zealand Land Company first set foot on the open plains south of Bank's Peninsula.

The New Zealand Company was primarily a business concern formed for the purposes of capital in colonisation and was viewed with some suspicion by the Home Government. The company's activities were questionable for they sold 100,000 acres of land in Nelson before they possessed the title to a single foot.

Captain Wakefield bought the site of Nelson and the whole of the surrounding districts including the Waimeas and Motueka for £443 8s. 10½d. Wakefield was involved in similar land schemes in South Australia.

The first settlers arrived in Nelson in 1842 after long voyages from England. They found that they had bought land which had not even been surveyed. When the New Zealand Company ceased to exist in 1844 the settlers nearly starved. There were no supplies of food and the men had very little prospect of earning money to buy what little there was.[33]

Over the next ten years conditions improved and by 1859 Nelson was described as 'one of the most pleasant places of sojourn in New Zealand'.[34]

Charlotte and Benjamin lived in Nelson for some years before moving to Auckland where Benjamin was drowned during a storm on Auckland Harbour on 12 February 1874. On 21 July 1874 Charlotte married William Morris in the Office of the Registrar Of Marriages, Auckland, witnessed by Edward Bennett, Barrister at Law and C.F. Griffiths an articles clerk. William was described as a bachelor and a builder and carrier when he married Charlotte. He was a native of Berkshire, England and the son of William Morris, a builder. He was also the licensee of the *Kurapaponga Hotel* at one time. Older members of the family always felt that 'she had made a bad mistake marrying Mr Morris'.

William Morris died of chronic bronchitis at Warren Street, Hastings on 25 May 1909 aged 69 years. He was buried in the Hastings Cemetery on Thursday, 27 May 1909. His obituary published Tuesday, 25 May 1909 by *The Hawke's Bay Herald-Tribune Limited* said:

108 Charlotte Mary Morris, née Worthington.

109   William Morris.

An old and respected resident of Hastings passed away at his home in Warren Street early this morning in the person of Mr William Morris. Deceased was a native of Berkshire, England and arrived in New Zealand in 1860, landing at Auckland. Mr Morris and his wife, resided in that town for 25 years after which period they moved to Hawke's Bay, residing in Napier for about ten years. They then came to live in Hastings. Deceased carried on a wood and coal business for some time and afterwards entered the employment of Mr E. Newbiggin for whom he worked for about eight years. He was one of the first members of the Hastings Borough Council, which position he occupied for some years. He was licensee of the Kurapaponga Hotel some years back. He leaves a widow to mourn his loss. The interment takes place at 2.pm. on Thursday.

Charlotte Mary Morris died on 23 June 1918 at Hastings aged 84 years. Her burial was a private interment, alongside her second husband. An obituary appeared in the *Hawke's Bay Herald-Tribune Limited* on Tuesday, 25 June 1918.

> Mrs Charlotte Mary Morris, relict of Mr William Morris, who passed away at Hastings on Sunday, in her 85th year, was a well known and highly respected citizen. Deceased landed in Nelson from England sixty years ago. She resided for some time in Auckland, Napier, finally settling in Hastings, where she resided for the past thirty-five years, mostly with Mr & Mrs T. Donovan. Deceased was twice married, but had no family. Her husband, the late Mr William Morris was one of the first Borough Councillors in Hastings, having been elected in 1886.

Charlotte wrote her will while living in Napier on 13 September 1913. Appointed as Executors were Edward Heathcote Williams of Hastings, Provincial District Solicitor and Alfred Williamson Parkinson of Hastings, Law Clerk. Charlotte directed that all her rings she may be wearing at the time of her death should be buried with her. She gave and bequeathed to her niece Katherine Worthington of Brecon Road, Stratford, spinster, her gold bar brooch set with diamonds. She bequeathed to her niece Adelaide Worthington of Brecon Road, spinster, her gold watch and chain and pendants and amethyst ring. She gave Rebecca Donovan, wife of Timothy Donovan of Hastings, carter, her gold buckle brooch, her bedroom furniture and bedding not including any trunks or boxes in her bedroom. She bequeathed to her nephew Henry Benjamin Worthington of Punewhaka, Taranaki, sheep farmer her 'large photographic albums and family portraits with names affixing hanging in my room'. Charlotte bequeathed the sum of £25 to the person who nursed her in her last illness to be divided equally if more than one person. All personal estate including life assurance policies, real estate and leasehold estate were to be sold and the money used to pay funeral and testamentary expenses and debts. Herbert James Clifton, Commercial Traveller of Ponsonby also benefited from the residue of her Trust Fund.

The Worthington family photograph album was in the possession of Annie Hill, daughter of Henry Benjamin Worthington. The family portraits are hanging in the hallway of Mrs. A.G.H. Horsfield's home in Fielding, New Zealand. Marie Horsfield is the daughter of Annie Hill and she is the current custodian of the photograph album.

Thomas Knight Worthington (1836-1896)

Thomas was born on 31 October 1836 at Dover, the third son of Henry and Mary Worthington. He was christened on 27 January 1837 at St Mary's Church, Dover.

The only information passed down through the generations about Thomas's early life is that he was a 'Dunbar Cadet'. By some miracle his indenture of apprenticeship to Duncan Dunbar survives. His four-year apprenticeship began on 28 August 1850 when Thomas was 13 years of age for the sum of one shilling. The document is signed by his father, Henry Worthington.[35] For a man to say that he had been a 'Dunbar Cadet' would indicate that his training had been in ships where the highest standards prevailed.

Duncan Dunbar & Sons, wine merchants and ship owners, gave their address as 95 Fore Street, Limehouse in 1852. Duncan Dunbar was an ex-director of the East & West India Dock Company. He was also on the Committee of Management of Lloyd's Register of British and Foreign Shipping. He is well known in Australia as the owner of the 1,321-ton sailing vessel *Dunbar* which sank off South Head, Sydney on 20 August 1857 with loss of 121 lives. There was one survivor who managed to swim ashore. Dunbar was the first to introduce clippers on the Australian run in 1850. The 'Blackwall Frigates' was the term applied to the magnificent class of ships of which he owned a number.

Thomas appears in the Register of Seamen's Tickets 1845-54, at the Public Record Office, Kew, no.503553 (also found with no.503555). It states that Thomas Knight Worthington was born at Dover, Kent, 31 October 1836. His capacity is 'apprentice', height 'growing', no details of hair, complexion, eye colour were given; he first went to sea as an apprentice and had never been in the Royal Navy or been involved in foreign service. No address is given where it is requested. This certificate was issued at London 29 August 1850.[36]

His first voyage as an apprentice was with Eugene Winston who was apprenticed at the same time as Thomas, and a fellow apprentice, 17-year-old London-born Thomas Clibborn Montano, ticket no.393144, who later married his sister, Elizabeth Harriot Barbour, née Worthington. Thomas joined the *Cressey* at London on 30 August 1850 and left it on 29 December 1851 at London. They departed from Plymouth, England on 3 September for Lyttleton, Canterbury, New Zealand.[37] A total of 782 emigrants were on board four ships, the 730-ton *Charlotte Jane* captained by Alexander Lawrence; 761-ton *Randolph* under Captain Dale; 634-ton barque *Cressey* (built Sunderland 1843, Class 11 A1) under Master Joseph Dennison Bell and 850-ton *Sir*

110 Indenture between Thomas Knight Worthington and Duncan Dunbar, 1850.

George Seymour. Their passsages were arranged by the Canterbury Association, New Zealand. Each ship carried a chaplain and schoolmaster; and among the cargo was a printing press, a library of 2,000 books presented by Oxford University, a church organ and several prefabricated 'frame houses' in sections. The *Cressey* sprang her fore-topmast south of the Cape of Good Hope and did not reach Lyttleton until 27 December 1850, some eight days behind the rest of the fleet.[38] This was Thomas Knight Worthington's first visit to New Zealand, at the age of 13 years. The *Cressey* sailed from Port Lyttleton on 22 May 1851 and arrived in Galle, Colombo 10 June 1851, Madras 16 June 1851, before returning home.

On 17 June 1854 Thomas is listed as an apprentice on board the *Phoebe Dunbar* after it had returned to the Port of London. This 630-ton ship, Class 13 A1, was built at Sunderland and owned by Duncan Dunbar. Her master was Forbes Michie on the voyage which commenced 5 May 1853 from London to Dublin for the conveyance of prisoners to Swan River, Western Australia.[39] The ship's log records that 102 prisoners with their 21 wives and 42 children and 295 male convicts embarked on 31 May for the 89-day voyage which arrived in Western Australia on 30 August

1853.[40] Some of the crew took their discharge in Freemantle on 17 October 1853 and the ship reached its final destination of Kingston on 17 June 1854.

On Wednesday, 25 October 1854 Thomas was one of the crew which left London on board the *Nile* of London, a 763-ton, Class 13 A1 ship built at Sunderland in 1849 and owned by Duncan Dunbar.[41] The voyage from London on 30 October sailed via Plymouth, where 306 government-assisted immigrants consisting of married couples and their families embarked on 11 November for Australia via the East Indies. The ship under Master Sinclair arrived at Port Adelaide, South Australia on Tuesday, 6 March 1855. The ship's log reports that Thomas Worthington, 3rd mate and Frank Hankey, 4th mate were absent all day from the ship without permission. By Thursday, 8 March they were considered to have deserted.[42] Thomas remained in Adelaide for at least two months and was described as a labourer when he was admitted to Adelaide Hospital by 'Authority of the Destitute Board' on 14 May 1855 for 'syphilitic warts'. He was discharged from hospital on 5 July 1855[43] and from the crew of the *Nile* at Adelaide on 24 July 1855.[44]

At age 18 years Thomas is listed as being on the 1,835-ton *Sea Park*[45] which had carried convicts to Freemantle, Western Australia on its previous voyage. The *Sea Park* left London for Adelaide and Calcutta on 5 March 1855 under Master Thomas.[46] Thomas joined the *Sea Park* on 24 July 1855 at Adelaide as an able seaman and was discharged 9 April 1856 at London. He is recorded on the 'Index to the Entries relating to the Crew and Report of Character' where his ability in seamanship is described as 'Good' and his conduct 'Very Good'. On 16 October 1855 at Calcutta he is recorded in the ship's log as being 'obliged to leave off work on account of warts on his yard'.[47] On 19 October he 'went to hospital and was discharged on the 6th November and went to his work'.[48]

On 7 April 1855, between the two *Sea Park* voyages, Thomas departed London on the *John Pink*, a 283-ton ship built in London during 1830. The master's name was Jones and the owner Carter & Company. The voyage was London to Australia and London to West Indies, Class 12 AE. Research in shipping records for Thomas Knight Worthington clearly showed that there were two Thomas Worthington apprentices, sailing on a ship called the *John Pink* of London at this time.

The last ship Thomas was known to have sailed on was the *Charlotte Montrose*. She was in fact the *Charlotte* of Montrose, a 211-ton ship built at Montrose 1851. Her master was Alex Buick and her owner D. Walter.[49] Thomas's previous ship is listed as the *Sea Park* of London from which he was discharged on 9 April 1856 in Lon-

111   Thomas Knight Worthington as a young man.

don. He joined the *Charlotte* as an able seaman on 6 August 1856 at London and was discharged 10 October 1856 at London after a foreign voyage. He was 19 years of age.

According to his death certificate, Thomas Knight Worthington was about 22 years of age when he arrived in New Zealand in about 1858. Shortly after his arrival Thomas was joined by his sister Charlotte and her husband, their first cousin Benjamin Worthington. Later the same year Daines Balderston Worthington, one of Thomas's younger brothers, joined the growing family group.

Charlotte and Benjamin moved to Motueka, about ten nautical miles from Nelson and about twenty miles by land. Thomas moved to Moutere in the same geographic area and was recorded in 'Moutere Rolls' from 23 June 1868 until 1872-3 when the entry was crossed out. The entry read: 'Nos 346/472/523/558. Worthington, Thomas Knight, Motueka, Leasehold, Moutere sections 3,4,5,6, & 7.'

This Moutere Roll entry for 1868 is the first positive evidence of Thomas Knight Worthington's presence in the South Island. He had saved sufficient funds to lease some land 10 years after his estimated time of arrival in New Zealand.

Thomas met his future wife Mary Ann Tucker when she was living in Nelson with her family. Mary Tucker was born in London, England on 6 September 1842, the daughter of Elijah and Marianna Tucker. She emigrated with her family when she was sixteen. This family group comprised her parents, elder sister Frances and younger brothers, Henry, Charles and Arthur. They left England in January 1856 and arrived in New Plymouth on the *Chatham* on 18 May 1856.[50] A few months after their arrival in New Plymouth the family moved to Nelson because of the outbreak of war between the Maoris and settlers.

Elijah Tucker was a printer in London at the time he decided to come to New Zealand. He was in business with his brother-in-law John Russell Smith, at Perry's Place, Oxford Street, London.[51] On arrival in Nelson Elijah took up a variety of work as a schoolmaster, compositor and journalist. He was editor of the *Colonist* for some time and in his day the Nelson *Colonist* was considered the most powerful newspaper in the colony. He moved frequently and at various times worked in Canterbury, on the *Marlborough Press*, started one of the Wanganui papers, and was at Westport and Charleston on the South Island West Coast.[52]

The following is a letter Thomas wrote to Mary Ann when he went to Kaikoura to work, prior to their marriage in 1870:

Kaikoura
July 1st

Dear Mary,

I received yours date of the 3rd about three weeks after date, the rivers have been up which delayed the postman.

I think you managed very well in wasting paper, & do you expect me to follow your example by answering all those questions. Considering that I am giving you three to one you ought to think yourself flattered. I wrote my first letter on the 5th the day after arrival. I forget what I told you of the journey, but as you want to know all about it you must take the chance of repetition question no.1. We made Nelson the first day nothing particular to note except that the foal nearly got drowned in the Moutere river, & we had great difficulty in getting the mare to cross, we managed by blindfolding her. We ate nothing man or beast until we arrived in town, there we went to the Royal & saw the pretty Miss Maloney we met on the landing as I was shown to my room—she had been doing a nap. I agree with Arthur (Mary Ann's

112 Thomas Knight Worthington.

113 Mary Ann Worthington, née Tucker, photographed in Auckland.

brother) and think her good looking & that is all to it. Mutton chops & sausages, beef steaks & a good bed costs 8/-, 2 day started about 10. Mare looking none the worse arrived at Coopers just before dark. I bought 2lbs biscuit in town & they gave us a bit of cheese at the Royal which served for dinner. Coopers gave us a very fair square feed man & horse for 7/6 each–bed was better than expected. 3 day. Mare & foal rather stiff at starting but went better after getting warm–about ten miles of road through the Kaituha very muddy bathed at Loom's, pigshead & jam tart which was very good–damages 2/6 each. Travelled on crossed the Wairau about 4 o'clock & made a long days journey & camped at Palmers arrived about six made supper off cold beef and onions which Arthur liked. I should have preferred something hot went to bed at eight but not to sleep, very bad accomodation, bad beds, no sitting room & everything bad about it. Only about half inch of candle left so must cut this short. Journey to be continued. We have had a week at the bush & consider it will pay. We have other work to do, that is getting fencing, we have 400 posts & rails to get now– expect to make 10/- per day. Dont I wish I was within a cove of you then.

Kisses & love to all

Good night

Ever yours

Tom.

Pangatotara to Nelson 35 miles		Flaxbourne	$\frac{97}{35}$
Coopers	27 "	Clarence	33
Palmers	35 "	Kaikoura	$\underline{30}$
	97		195

An analysis of Thomas's handwriting by a graphologist reveals a romantic futuristic thinker who was intuitive, deliberate in actions and an observer of small detail. He could be self-destructive and held on to secrets well. He was a wise instigator of actions and new ideas and had a great love of life when in a very positive frame of mind. He had a well mannered and diplomatic front and a gracious manner. Determined and not easily discouraged, he was held in high esteem by those who knew him. Prior to writing the above letter he had made an important and correct decision. He had a strong faith, was smart, creative and talented.

Thomas and Mary Ann's marriage in 1870 was not without incident. They were actually married twice as a letter written by the Rev. Charles O. Mules explains:

> Explanation of Circumstances surrounding the forwarding two different certificates to the Registrar General in the case of Marriage of Mr T.K. Worthington and Miss Mary Ann Tucker.
>
> The parties obtained the usual certificates from the Registrar who is referred to in Mr Pickett's letter on the other side of the page—the death of Mr W. Bell prevented the Marriage from taking place at Appleby, for which place the certificate was issued, and Mr Worthington forwarded under his own hand a request to Mr Picketts the Registrar for an amended certificate, to admit of the marriage taking place at Waimea West. Before any answer was received, the day fixed for the marriage arrived, and the Clergyman married them at Waimea West on the supposition that the certificate could be returned amended. This was not done (see over) and accordingly the parties attended at Appleby Church on Thursday the 21st day of April and went through a form, which warranted the Clergman in issueing the usual Certificate of Marriage for Appleby, in addition to that previously issued at Waimea West.[53]

The story handed down repeats that Thomas Knight was very annoyed at having to pay for two certificates! Poor Mr. W. Bell was supposed to have drowned in a flooded river!

The *Colonist* reports that 'on the 14th April 1870 at St. Michael's Church, Waimea West, by the Rev. C.O. Mules, Mr T. Worthington to marry Mary second daughter of Mr E. Tucker'. The marriage certificate gives the date of marriage as 21 April 1870 at St Alban's Church, Appleby.

Thomas and Mary Ann Worthington had seven children: Henry Benjamin Worthington (1871-1935), Francis Hamilton Worthington (1872-1949), Howard Worthington (1874-1951), Percy Knight Worthington (1876-1915), Charles Jennings Worthington (1878-1942), Marianna Katherine Worthington (1881-1947), Adelaide Worthington (1883-1979).

114 Mary Ann Worthington, née Tucker.

The births of two children were announced in the Nelson *Colonist* newspaper: '1st October 1872, at Hamilton, Waikato, Mrs T.K. Worthington of a son' and 'Worthington 29th December 1874, at Charleston, Mrs T.K. Worthington, a son'.

The *Nelson Examiner* also reported the arrival of Francis Hamilton Worthington. His second name is believed to have been given to him because of his birthplace.

During the early months of 1872, Benjamin and Charlotte, and Thomas and Mary Ann left Motueka for the North Island. Thomas took up farming at Ngaruawahia, Waikato, North Island until some time after February 1874 when cousin Benjamin Worthington was drowned in Auckland Harbour. Charlotte Worthington was living with her brother Thomas at this time.

Thomas, Mary Ann and their two sons returned to the South Island for the birth of a third child. Howard Worthington was born at the beachside mining town of Charleston on the West Coast. Mary Ann's father was the editor of a local newspaper in Charleston[54] at this time when about 10,000 men of all nationalities in gold hunting excitement found their way there. Thomas tried his luck at gold mining on the few hundred acres of land adjoining the beach which was found to be rich in fine gold. The fields were soon thoroughly worked and the miners made their way to other fields. All that remains of Charleston in the 1990s is about two buildings, a small wooden hotel and a very small post office.

The family then moved to the Nelson district where Percy Knight Worthington, a fourth son, was born at Marahau on 3 December 1876. Marahau is situated in the Nelson Province and Waimea County and had a population of 44 people in 1952.

While still living in the South Island Thomas Knight Worthington made his will. It is very short and simple and written in his own hand. It is as follows:

MOTUEKA

This is the last Will and Testament of me Thomas Knight Worthington, Pangatotara in the Province of Nelson, New Zealand, labourer. I give, devise, and bequeath all my real and personal estate whatsoever and wheresoever situate unto my wife Mary Ann Worthington absolutely and I appoint my said wife executrix of this my will. In witness whereof I the said Thomas Knight Worthington have hereto set my hand this twenty third day of May 1877. Thomas Knight Worthington.

Signed by the Testator Thomas Knight Worthington as and for his last Will and Testament in the presence of us who in his presence at his request and in the presence of each other have hereunto subscribed our names as witnesses. [Signatures of Elijah Tucker and Arthur Tucker][55]

On 11 September 1878 Charles Jennings Worthington was born at Picton in the South Island, the fifth son of Thomas and Mary Ann. His father gave his profession as labourer. Shortly after this Thomas and Mary Ann decided to return to the North Island and settle in Taranaki.

The family were among some of the first settlers to arrive in Stratford about 1879. A tent village of canvas tops and wooden floors was established on East Road. Little primitive wooden huts were also built. Stratford, described by some as 'The Mountain Town', is situated at the eastern base of Mount Egmont. This dormant volcanic mountain lies on the western promontory of the North Island and rises to a height of more than eight thousand feet.

Originally Stratford was known only to the Maoris who followed a war trail through the dense bush of this area between the northern and southern tribes. There

115 Thomas K. Worthington, Mary Ann Worthington and their seven children taken in Stratford, *c.*1885.

was marked emnity between these two tribes as they defended their territorial hunting privileges. The route they took was destined to become the present highway.
Stratford was originally named 'Whakaahu-rangi' (Whakaahu, to turn upwards; rangi,
the sky) after a Maori chieftainess who slept one night on the present site of Stratford,
on her back with her face to the sky. This site was the resting place for parties of
Maoris for many years.

    The first white men to visit the Stratford area were Messrs. Charles and Francis
Nairn who explored the neighbourhood in 1843. Later in 1866 General Chute marched
with troops from Ketemarae to New Plymouth during the Maori wars, and the track
was reopened. In 1873-4 the land was marked out and purchased from the native
owners. In 1875-6 surveying was carried out to look for a possible road or railway
connection with the Auckland district and Inglewood, a township to the north of
Stratford, was founded in 1875.

    In June 1877 the Taranaki Land Board decided to survey and lay out for sale a
site for a township of 300 acres on the Patea River. The whole area was covered with
dense and heavy forest. The bush was felled and burnt off during 1878.

    On 31 August 1878 the first sale of sections of land was held at the Taranaki
Institute in New Plymouth. A total of 455 sections were offered but only 42 were sold.
Prices of £35-50 were paid for 33-perch sections, but some settlers paid more to

acquire a particular block of land. These first sections were on the northern side of the Patea River. Meanwhile authority had been give for the felling of the bush to the south of the Patea River.

During the last two months of 1878 a store, boarding house and hotel were built. The beginning of 1879 saw the start of through communication north and south. The earliest communication with the Stratford district was by pack horse and bullock wagon. On 17 December 1879 the railway was opened to Stratford from the north and communication with the outside world was established.

Surveying of the land at the southern half of the town began in the autumn of 1880. In May 1881 the population of Stratford was recorded as 97 (56 males and 41 females).[56] Sections were then being bought on the southern side of the river. Thomas Worthington's allotment of land was next to the southern boundary of Stratford, bounded on one side by the main road and the southern boundary by Brookes Road.

Their first house was built of pitsawn timber. It was a very plain little house with a low studd. Off the back verandah, steps down to a small underground cellar led to where the food was kept. The house was originally L-shaped and a wing, later removed, was where the boys of the family slept.[57]

In these early years the family made a living gathering fungus from the bush. The settlement existed for the convenience of men engaged on roads and other developmental work, so unless settlers catered for the wants of these people they had little scope for finding revenue producing employment. A large number of early settlers kept up the instalments on their deferred-payment sections by collecting and selling fungus. Mr. Chew Chong, a Chinese resident, bought and exported fungus, highly prized by the Chinese for making soup. Sixpence a pound (in weight) was paid for dried fungus in the early 1880s, and it was possible to make as much as £1 per day. Mr. Chong later founded the first dairy factory in Taranaki.

Adelaide Jones, née Worthington, told Edgar and Barbara Worthington that her father Thomas Knight was left £800 in his father's will, at about the time her brothers were old enough for secondary school. Mary Ann wanted the money spent on sending the boys to Nelson College but Thomas wanted to buy more land, which he did. A second house was built on Brecon Road, Stratford after that.

Certificates of Title under the Land Transfer Act show that Thomas Knight Worthington purchased two blocks of land on 11 September 1886 from the Land Revenue Office, at New Plymouth (Register Vol. 8. Folio 223). The two blocks of land were in the District of Ngaire, Block I consisting of Section 48 and 50, and Block II, Section 99 and 100. The total area amounted to 35 acres and 8 perches with boundaries on Brecon Road, Warwick Road and Mountain Road. The whole purchase cost was £125 4s. 6d. plus a Grant Fee of £1. More land was bought on 20 April 1887 for the sum of £314. This was payment of Section 83, Block 1 and Section 100, Block 2 in the Ngairi Survey District.

Marianna Katherine, or Kate as she was usually called, and Adelaide were both born in Stratford. Marianna was born on 19 March 1881 and, when Adelaide was born on 26 June 1883, Thomas had to ride a horse 22 miles to the nearest Registrar's Office at Inglewood to register her birth.

The land between their house on Brecon Road and the small township of Stratford was practically empty. Nobody lived there. When Adelaide, the youngest of the family, was a little girl, she used to walk to school. At that time there were wild cattle in that area and she told my father how she would duck from one tree stump to another to avoid them.

The house had a long driveway and stood back from the road. There were macrocarpa trees on the north side of the house, and box hedges bordered each side of the drive which was paved with crushed white seashells. My father and some of his family could remember their grandmother's lovely sitting room. It was furnished with a dull green carpet, antique furniture and pictures which Mary's family had brought with them from England. There was also a Collard & Collard piano that she had arranged for friends to buy for her, while they were visiting England. This purchase was made to ensure that her two daughters received a musical education. A photograph of Katherine Worthington reveals her graduation from a College of Music. My father bought this piano from his Aunt Adelaide when I began having piano lessons from the nuns at Waverley convent at eight years of age. The old family home in Stratford stood empty for many years after Mary Ann's death and was finally pulled down when the land was sold in 1937.

Settlement continued to expand. Through rail connection with Wellington was completed in 1885 when the population increased to 157. More stores and a small school were opened. A post office was situated in the railway station and a town hall was built. Most of these buildings were destroyed by a bush fire in 1885, but in time bigger and better buildings took their place.

With this second start various groups of active Christians planned to build their respective churches. It was during the year 1889 that the leading Anglicans held a meeting to make their dream of the last 10 years come true. Attending the meeting was the Rev. Thomas Farley, M.A.[58] who had succeeded Parson Brown, Charles Curtis, H.N. Liardet, T.K. Worthington, S.H. James, F.G. Arden, George Capper, C.J. Watkins, Thomas Penn and Thomas Henry Penn. These men were all pioneers of Stratford and most of them were members of the 1889 Building Committee.

Plans were submitted by Rev. Farley for a church to accommodate 80 people at a cost of £200. Each gave a subscription of money and Thomas Knight Worthington gave the land on East Road for it to be built on.[59] Brothers Henry, Frank and Howard Worthington helped clear the land for the church to be built. After a long argument as to whether it should be built in concrete or wood it was decided to use the latter. East Road was a muddy track leading into the bush. Beside it ran a light railway along which the pitsawn timber was transported to the site. A year later the building was 'dedicated to the Glory of God' on the last Sunday of July 1890 and named the Church of Holy Trinity by W.G. Cowrie, Bishop of Auckland.

A vestry of six parishioners was elected and Thomas served 1890, 1892 and 1894. Two completely different sources told me a story of how Thomas Knight Worthington always made his sons go to church. He would not go himself, but instead would go down to the back paddock and sit on a stump to read the newspaper. One day the boys set a gunpowder trail to the stump and lit it before they went off to Sunday School. Thomas had a reputation as a vet and that morning somebody called him away to attend to a sick cow. Fortunately he wasn't killed when the stump blew up. The boys still had to go to Sunday School!

By 1893 steady progress was being made in Stratford's development. Farms looked less cluttered with logs. More cows moved in the pastures. The Broadway which was the main street of Stratford carried more gigs and carts. Fashion included bushy side

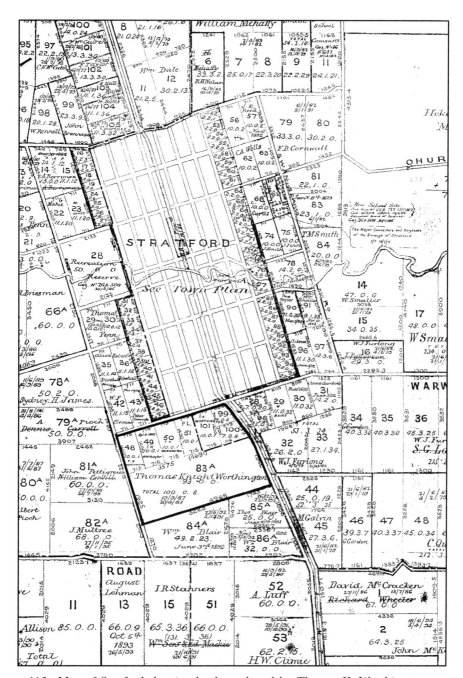

116 Map of Stratford showing land purchased by Thomas K. Worthington.

whiskers for the men and crinoline dresses for the women—long billowy shirts, tight fitting bodices with sleeves to the palm and straw poke bonnets.

Thomas predeceased Mary Ann by 37 years. During August 1896, while visiting his sister Charlotte Morris in Hastings, he suddenly became ill. After a short illness he died in Napier Hospital on 3 September 1896, from uraemia syncope, aged 59 years.

A death notice in the *New Zealand Mail* on 17 September 1896 reported,

> The death is announced of Mr Thomas Knight Worthington of the Brecon Road, Stratford. The deceased was on a visit to Napier when he died. He leaves a widow and family most of the latter grown up. Mr T.K. Worthington was for years a prominent figure in everything that was done in Stratford, but of late his failing health had kept him much in retirement. He was a son of the late Mr T.K. Worthington [incorrect] of Maxton Farm, Dover, Kent.

A snippet from a newspaper says the following: 'The funeral service was conducted by the Rev. John Hobbs who made feeling reference to the sudden decease. Some members of the choir attended and sang the beautiful hymn "When our heads are bowed in woe".' Thomas is buried in Hastings Cemetery.[60] The plot was purchased by Mary Worthington on 14 February 1898.

After Thomas's early death Mary Ann continued to live in Stratford with her children. Mary Ann knew very little about farming but her children assisted her in many ways. The population of Stratford in 1896 was 1,256 and growing. Dairy factories were now operating, a freezing works was opened and the Stratford District High School was constituted. In 1898 the Stratford Borough Council came into existence and the first Mayor was Mr. H.N. Liardet. In 1899 the Electrical Supply Company was established.

Mary Ann was a very strong, independent person and apparently had wonderful health all her life. One of her many skills was lace making and crocheting. She died at 91 years of age, and the only thing she ever complained about in the way of ill health was that her own teeth were getting loose! Not long before she died she was in the Stratford post office and one of the clerks wanted to help her fill in the details on a paper, but she brushed him aside very haughtily and said that nobody helped her, that she was quite 'capable of doing it herself'!

Mary Ann died on 20 April 1933 of respiratory failure and was buried in Stratford Cemetery. Her two sons, Francis Hamilton Worthington of Stratford, farmer, and Howard Worthington of Tauki, farmer, were appointed as executors and trustees of her will which was dated 23 May 1912. Mary Ann Worthington left all her household furniture and effects, piano, phaeton, and all chattels to her two daughters, Marianna Katherine Worthington and Adelaide Worthington, spinsters. After leaving pecuniary legacies to some of her children, namely Francis Hamilton Worthington £200, Marianna Katherine Worthington £100, Adelaide Worthington £100, Charles Jennings Worthington of Ruapekapeka, Bay of Islands £50, the residue of her real and personal estate was divided amongst all of her children with deductions for amounts of money they owed to other members of the family. Provision was also made for the family of Percy Knight Worthington who died quite young leaving his wife, Isabel Agnes Worthington, to raise six children.

A codicil to the will, dated 2 November 1922, was added. Her youngest son Charles Jennings Worthington, one of the beneficiaries under her will, was indebted to her for the sum of £1,640 and interest thereon was to be charged at the rate of '£7 per cent per annum as from the 13 August 1921 until it was repaid'.

Thomas Knight Worthington, his wife and family suffered many pioneering hardships and never returned to their homeland, England. Thomas and Mary Ann's children were not really suited to the farming life most of them pursued. They were described by my father's generation as 'tall, slim, finely built and intelligent people who were also very shy and unassuming'.

Sophia Worthington (1838-1883)

Born in St Mary's Parish, Dover on 18 November 1838, Sophia was the sixth child of Henry and Mary Worthington. Her baptism six days later was recorded in the St James parish register.

Sophia did not marry and moved to Italy for health reasons after contracting tuberculosis. She died in Rome, Italy on 11 December 1883 aged 45 years. Her younger sister, Maria Henrietta Adelaide Worthington, married an Italian in Rome 16 months later, at the age of 44, so perhaps the sisters had moved to Italy together.

Sophia and her sister Maria were well provided for in their single lives by the instructions left in their father's will, which was administered by two of their uncles. They were independent and wealthy while still in their late twenties.

Probate of Sophia's estate was not granted in London until 7 July 1908 when her nephew Harry Edward Worthington M.D. was granted administration. Sophia's effects were valued at £117 14s. 8d. A former grant had been made in August 1907.

Maria Henrietta Adelaide Worthington (1840-post 1895)

Henry and Mary's seventh child, Maria Henrietta Adelaide, was born in St Mary's, Dover on 15 October 1840 and baptised at St Mary's on 2 December 1840.

117 Sophia Worthington (1838-83)   **118** Maria Henrietta Adelaide Worthington.

Maria remained in Rome after her sister Sophia's death and married Dr. Luigi Negri, native of Rome and son of Enrico Negri, on 15 April 1885 when she was 44 years of age. The civil marriage ceremony took place in Rome. They returned to London and were guests at the wedding of Alice Frances Worthington to Captain Charles Sutton Edridge during 1895. Dr. Negri died in London during 1913.

Daines Balderston Worthington (1842-1865)

Born at Alkham on 6 October 1842, in the parish of Buckland, Hougham, Daines was the eighth child and fifth son of Henry and Mary Worthington. He was named after his great-uncle Daines Balderston, son of George and Sarah Balderston, who was christened on 9 June 1726. This line is on his mother's side of the family. His father's occupation at the time of his birth was given as 'Farmer'. At an early age

119   Maria Henrietta Worthington. (Photographed September 1868 by H. Goble, Worthing)

Daines attended a private boarding school with his cousin Edward Worthington, son of Lieutenant Benjamin and Mary Worthington.

In 1859, while still a teenager, Daines travelled to New Zealand where he joined his older brother Thomas Knight Worthington, sister Charlotte and her cousin-husband Benjamin Worthington. A record of Daines's arrival in Nelson, New Zealand can be found in the shipping arrivals column of the *Colonist* newspaper, which states: 'amongst the cabin passengers arriving on the *Golconda* is D.B. Worthington from London, 27th December, 1859. The *Golconda* weighed 688 tons, Master Montgomery.'

Daines and some of his fellow passengers signed a letter of 'approval of the conduct of the surgeon Mr Samuel Harris M.D. towards the patients on board the ship whilst at sea, that he did his duty to them, and was unremitting in his attention and kindness towards them at all times'. The letter was dated 24 December 1859.[61]

Daines was listed in the military settlers rolls for Waikato after he enlisted as a private at Nelson on 1 December 1863. He was 22 years of age, six feet tall and his occupation was given as miner. As gold was discovered in the area late in 1859 he probably worked as a gold miner. Among the earliest recruits, Daines became a member of the 3rd Regiment of the North Island-based Waikato Militia.[62] The New Zealand wars had begun in earnest about five months before, after Governor George Gray issued the following proclamation to the chiefs of the Waikato:

> Europeans living quietly on their own lands in Waikato have been driven away; their property has been plundered; their wives and children have been taken from them. By the instigation of some of you, officers and soldiers were murdered at Taranaki. Others of you have since expressed approval of these murders. Crimes have been

committed in other parts of the island and the criminals have been rescued or sheltered under the colour of your authority.

You are now assembling in armed bands; you are constantly threatening to come down the river to ravage the settlement of Auckland and to murder peaceable settlers. Some of you offered a safe passage through your territories to armed parties contemplating such outrages. The well-disposed among you are either unable or unwilling to prevent these evil acts. I am therefore compelled, for the protection of all, to establish posts at several points on the Waikato River and to take necessary measures for the future security of persons inhabiting that district. The lives and property of all well disposed people living on the river will be protected and armed and evil minded people will be stopped from passing down the river to rob and murder Europeans.

I now call on all well disposed natives to aid the Lieutenant General to establish and maintain these posts and to preserve peace and order. Those who remain peaceably in their own villages in Waikato, or move into such districts as may be pointed out by the Government, will be protected in their persons, property and land.

Those who wage war against Her Majesty, or remain in arms, threatening the lives of her peaceable subjects, must take the consequences of their acts and they must understand that they will forfeit the right to the possession of their lands guaranteed to them by the Treaty of Waitangi; which lands will be occupied by a population capable of protecting for the future the quiet and unoffending from the violence with which they are now so constantly threatened. [63]

Approximately two thousand men, including colonists and Australians, joined the four regiments that served in the militia between 1863 and 1866. A letter from Worthington family archives attributed to Daines would have been written shortly before he joined the militia as in it he contemplates whether he should sign up or not. The 'T.' referred to could be his brother Thomas. The writing is very similar to Thomas Knight Worthington's, but a completely different character and personality shines through. Some of the pages are missing, but the following remains:

The Education rate is collected quarterly here and if you dont pay down at once they'll score a summons. At Alexandra an old man who has passed three score and ten, lives in a shanty the size of flour bins, a poor old man without wife or child but who works and keeps himself from what he makes, works in the bush—well the poor old fellow was called for his rate. 'Shan't pay it. My parents paid my education, let other parents pay for their children or let them go without.'

'Then your goods will be seized.'

'All right. I've an old pan and a billy. They can take them.'

Summonsed to appear at Auckland if he won't hurry up. Refuses to the [?] . 'If they want me let 'em come for me. I don't mind Mount Eden, it'll be very nice for me there three on six months, I'm keeping myself now, I'll be kept by them.' I am not aware if the refractory old gentleman has been sent down by Duck's Creek in charge of a constable to Auckland. The feeling in this province regarding the tax seems to be unlimited aversion and rebellion—the tax collector in this part told me he was threatened with dog, had dishcloths to broomsticks promised him—'shocking arguments' I said. The place is enlivened up about once a week with a quarrel among the navvies who of course drink and then play Old Harry.'

next page ...

I was speaking to T. the other night. 'Well, I've half a mind to join them. Two guineas a week each on dry is not such a bad thing, but the drilling' and here he shook himself like a husky dog, 'Oh, you'll like that, and a fellow nothing like as good as yourself telling you to do 'this' do 'that'. Making you right about face.' 'I would not do it'. 'Oh, but you'd have to, and the more you wise the more drilling you'd get. They'd march you about that ? alone until you give in for the men laughing at you. Perhaps they'd make you a cook and you'd look swell a married man washing up pannikins and plates after a lot of single fellows. And the orderly inspecting them. Oh, you'll like that.' 'Wouldn't do. But it's only three months!' 'Only three months <u>on</u> until you are <u>legally discharged</u>. They'll keep you for ever if they want you—and if you choose to misbehave they'll discharge you after you have been under arrest and taken off a month or twos pay. They don't mind that. Ah; I've tried it!' 'Oh, ho! and how did you like it?' 'Well, there was a fellow sick, so he said, but he was only shamming, he could not be sentry at night, but he could go after the girls, so I was not going to take his night and my own. One night he was sentry, and he comes home after hours, I tell him he was a fine fellow he was, too ill to do anything, but he was well enough to go courting.' 'You can report me to the officer,' he said. I said, 'I will report you! I threw my rifle down, I knew that was a great ... [end of page]

What a pity the letter was incomplete as this writer was quite a story teller.

The enlisting of militia recruits created an acute shortage of labour in the Waikato Province and brought commerce almost to a standstill. The New Zealand Government then proposed that a system of military settlement be formed on land confiscated from the warring tribes. The terms of enlistment for military settlers, as gazetted on 5 August 1863, included the size of the farm sections, allotted according to rank—50 acres for a private such as Daines. Every settler relieved from actual service and who received a certificate of good conduct was also entitled to one town allotment in addition to his farm section. It would have been an enticing offer to young men starting out in life; in fact single men made up the majority of the enlistments.

Passage to the North Island was provided, and men were entitled to pay, 2s. 6d. per diem for a private, rations and allowances until authorised by the Government to take possession of their land, when they would be relieved from 'actual service'. For three years after enrolling in the militia, settlers were not to leave their settlement for more than a month without the leave of the Governor.

By the time Daines enlisted with the volunteers in December 1863, the British had advanced steadily up the Waikato and by the end of 1863 had occupied Ngaruawahia which lies at the junction of the Waikato and Waipa rivers. The Waikato Militia, consisting of the 1st, 2nd and 3rd Regiments along with the 50th Foot, was sent to Raglan on the west coast to establish a supply route. Almost all supplies had to be brought from Australia and then transported to the Front. Because of the nature of the land this involved pack horses, drays, steamers and rowing boats.

In January 1864 General Cameron had built up sufficient reserves to advance further into the Waikato country. Several attacks on Maori Pas were carried out with loss of men on both sides.

During March 1864 the 3rd Waikato Militia was mainly involved in building redoubts and harvesting crops. When the news came that the Maoris were gathering in force at Orakau, plans were made to attack. Captain Blewett's Force from Ragiaohia, consisting of the 65th Regiment and the 3rd Waikato Militia were to approach on the left flank through the swamp and bush to confront the north side of the Maori pa. Another bloody battle took place with heavy loss of life.

120   Church of England, Te Awamutu, New Zealand–burial place of Daines Balderston Worthington.

In May 1864 confiscation of Maori lands began. Cambridge, at the highest point of navigation on the Waikato River was chosen for the 3rd Waikato Regiment, which took up occupation there in July 1864.

Most of the town surveys were completed by the end of 1864 and the soldier settlers drew lots for their one-acre town allotments. Stockades and roads were built. The men were free to build their town houses of whatever materials were available. The Government, embarrassed by a lack of money, pushed the farm surveys so that the militia men could be struck off the pay list.

Many of the 50-acre farm lots were located in swamplands. Daines was given 50-acre Lot 176 in the Bellairs Survey at Pukerimu. Pukerimu, meaning 'Hill of the Rimu Tree', is located in the Waipa County of Auckland Province and is situated five miles south-westwards by road from Cambridge.

Sadly Daines died of 'the fever' in camp at Te Awamutu on Good Friday, 6 April 1865 aged only 22 years. He was buried the next day in the Te Awamutu Church-yard by the camp chaplain, who also wrote to Daines' older sister Charlotte Mary Worthington to inform her of Daines' death. This letter was forwarded to their mother and when it was later needed as proof of Daines' death could not be found.

Letters of administration of Daines' personal effects, valued at under £200, were granted at the Principal Registry to his uncle Robert Finnis Jennings of River House, Kent on 24 May 1866, the same day his father Henry's estate was also granted to Robert. Further grants regarding Daines' estate were made in June 1907 to Elizabeth Worthington, widow. The estate was then valued at £717 11s. 8d.

In July 1906 Charlotte, who was by this time Mrs. William Morris and living in Warren Street, Hastings, Hawkes Bay, had corresponded with the Registrar General and the Defence Office in an attempt to obtain a copy of Daines' death certificate which was 'urgently required'. A letter she wrote on 26 July 1906 says, 'I am sorry to write that the two entries to which you refer do not allude to my brother ...'.[64]

Apparently the authorities had trouble finding a record of his death registration and burial at Te Awamutu, Church of England Cemetery as a death certificate was still being sought in October 1906 when Charlotte's solicitors, Garrick, Cowlishaw & Fisher of Christchurch took up the matter for her. Eventually a few details were found, after which the Registrar General wrote to the Registrar of Deaths at Te Awamutu on 15 October 1906 and said:

> If you will kindly read the accompanying letter you will see the trouble we have had in this office. And the solicitors (very excellent ones) still seem to think I can help them. Can you state if anything by way of evidence is procurable. If there is a Burial Register will not Garrick & C. obtain a copy by applying to cemetery authorities or is there any other way I could indicate to them of obtaining evidence.

Te Awamutu replied: 'The Registrar General, I regret there are no local records further back than 1871 or any trace of what has become of previous records if any were kept. I have searched the tombstones also! but no trace'.[65]

No death registration or burial record was ever found for Daines although his New Zealand Colonial Forces service record shows his date and place of death. The administration of Daines' estate was granted to his nephew Harry Edward Worthington, surgeon, in July 1908. The estate's value had again increased, to £751 6s.

Although Daines was entitled to be posthumously awarded a New Zealand war medal, having actively fought in the New Zealand wars, no record has been found of this occurring.

Elizabeth Harriot Worthington (1843-1906)

Born in Dover during December 1843, Elizabeth Harriot was the ninth child of Henry and Mary Worthington. Throughout her lifetime she was known as Harriot. Perhaps because her parents died during her early twenties, she was adopted by her wealthy spinster aunt, Charlotte Worthington, who left Harriot everything in her will.

At the age of 30 years, Elizabeth Harriot married Dr. John Borthwick Barbour, son of William Barbour, on 6 August 1873 by Licence at St Mark's, Notting Hill in the county of Middlesex. Elizabeth Harriot's address at the time was in the Parish of St James, Dover, while her husband resided at 114 Kensington Park Road, London.

A Doctor of Medicine, John Borthwick Barbour graduated from Glasgow University and obtained a licence from the Royal College of Surgeons, Edinburgh in 1865.

After their marriage Elizabeth Harriot and her husband travelled extensively together and so spent most of her inheritance. Only four years later Dr. Barbour died of consumption at Bournemouth on 12 February 1877, aged 42 years. His brother-in-law George Finch Jennings Worthington was a doctor in Bournemouth so perhaps he tended him during his illness. It is possible Dr. Worthington and Dr. Barbour trained together and perhaps Elizabeth met her future husband through her brother.

John was buried in the Worthington family vault at Buckland after permission was granted by the Secretary of State, Home Department.[66] Beneath an inscription to his memory on one side of the tomb it reads: 'I shall go to him, but he shall not return to me'.

Elizabeth Harriot then married Captain Thomas Clibborn Montano, R.N., in the June quarter of 1878. He was an old admirer who had served his apprenticeship with

121 (*left*) Elizabeth Harriot Barbour, née Worthington. (Photograph by Josiah Russell, Worthing)

122 (*above*) Dr. John Borthwick Barbour (photographed by Lambert Weston & Son, Dover and Folkestone)

her brother, Thomas Knight Worthington, as a Dunbar Cadet. Born in London on 27 July 1833, Thomas Montano was listed in the register of seamen's tickets 1845-1954 as the holder of ticket no.393,144. He had been ticketed as an apprentice at the age of 15 years. According to his records he was still growing in height, his hair was black, complexion sallow, eyes hazel and he had no distinguishing marks. He could write, had not served in the Royal Navy and when unemployed resided at 28 Clements Lane. Thomas received his master's certificate, no.8532, on 5 July 1859. His record of service lists travels to Africa, Columbo, Calcutta, New Zealand, the East Indies and the City of Valparaiso.[67]

After their marriage, the captain, finding most of his wife's money had disappeared, flew into a great rage. He stormed off to Snargate Street, Dover, and bought a dangerous looking blackthorn stick with which he went to see his wife's solicitors in Glasgow. Demanding to know where all her money had gone, and looking the part, Captain Montano declared that he would not leave their office until he had found out. It is recorded that before he left he elicited the fact that there were one or two thousand pounds in a bank in California. This would probably never have been discovered but for the Captain's forceful declamations and the blackthorn supporting his arguments.[68]

Captain Montano died in Dover on 31 October 1899 and probate of his will was granted to Elizabeth Harriot Montano, the sole Executrix, on 23 December 1899. His estate was valued at £2210 4s. 3d. Elizabeth Harriot died on 29 January 1906 at 4 Maison Dieu Road, Dover where she had been living since 1878.[69] She is believed to be buried with her mother in the family tomb at St James' Church crypt in Dover.

123 Elizabeth Harriot and Thomas Clibborn
Montano. (Photographed by A.J. Grossman, Dover)

Elizabeth left a will desiring 'to be buried beside my late dear husband at Copthill Cemetery in Dover and that my wedding rings shall be buried with me and my grave covered with grass'. No record of death registration or burial in Copthill Cemetery could be found for Elizabeth Montano.

Bequests according to her will were, 'my parrot to my friend Mrs. Wood Wood' and if she be deceased the executors were to find a good home for the parrot and her other pets. Legacies were given to Mary Worthington, widow of the late Thomas Knight Worthington £50; to her sister Charlotte Mary Morris £50; to her brother Robert Worthington £50; Ellen Grace Cordeaux who recently resided with her £25; and to her cousin Edward Worthington son of the late Benjamin Worthington £25.

Further bequests were made to her sister-in-law:

> Elizabeth Worthington (widow of my brother George Finch Jennings Worthington) all my wardrobe, wearing apparel and household linen; to my nephew and godson Oscar Clayton Worthington, brother of Harry Edward Worthington, my plain silver teapot, my silver bread basket, four silver salt cellars fitted with glass and antique salt spoons, the pair of antique silver sugar tongs marked B.J.W., my silver milk jug, the miniature likeness of my grandmother Worthington, the picture of Rebecca in Ivanhoe on ivory, the likeness in oils of my great grandfather Worthington, the two large water colours in the recesses of my drawing room, my hall table with marble top, my husband's diamond ring and three Elizabethan chairs in my drawing room.

To her nephew Harry Edward Worthington she left:

> my plated silver sugar basket and plated silver tongs, three sea pictures with steamers, the picture of a Boars Hunt in the Hall, the framed Coat of Arms in Hall, the large picture over the mantelpiece in my dining room, my chess table, the photo likeness of my pet dog Banner, all the books in my library, my gold jubilee medal and the small cabinet and book case over in my library with its contents of curics.

To her cousin Edward Worthington she left:

> five silver table spoons one being marked M.H. and the remaining four having worked edges to the handles, the miniature likenesses of my grandfather and grandmother Worthington, the five china Indian vases on my dining room mantelpiece, my drawing room clock and the vases that correspond thereto, all other ornaments on the drawing room mantelpiece, and the antique cabinet in my drawing room and its contents.

Elizabeth left her sister Charlotte Mary Morris her gold bar brooch set with diamonds and a cluster diamond ring to her niece Katherine Worthington, eldest daughter of 'my late brother' Thomas Knight Worthington. Her niece Alice Frances Edridge received a gold bracelet with watch and niece Elizabeth Mary Worthington was left a diamond hoop ring, all the photographic albums and work baskets, writing desks and also 'the framed screen of needle work in my drawing room'. Niece Charlotte Wilhelmina Worthington received a pair of gold bracelets; nephew George Worthington (a brother of the said Harry Edward Worthington) 'my gold watch with gold face'; nephew Montano Worthington, youngest son of her brother Robert Worthingon, was bequeathed her husband's gold watch with a white face and minute hand and his gold chain.

Miss Pain of 1 Priory Gate, Dover, a 'dear friend' of Elizabeth's, was left an antique china cup and saucer with cover but without handles, and 'my dear friend Miss Jell now residing at 43 London Road Dover my gold brooch with a diamond in

124 Elizabeth Harriot Montano. (Photographed by Lambert Weston & Son, Dover and Folkestone)

the centre; To my friend Mary Elizabeh Boyes my library clock; To my friend Mrs Freeman of Eyam Rectory Sheffield a piece of china to keep in memory of me …'.

Edward Mowll Worsfold received a dining room chime clock and all the remainder of her extensive jewellery and ornament collection was to be divided equally among the daughters of her brother George Finch Jennings Worthington, the two daughters of her late brother Thomas Knight Worthington 'now residing at Taranaki New Zealand' and the two daughters of her brother Robert Worthington residing at 206 Simcoe Street, Toronto, Canada. The remainder of Elizabeth's china and plate and pictures and plated articles was left equally to her sister-in-law Elizabeth Worthington, her nephews Harry Edward Worthington and Oscar Clayton Worthington and her cousin Edward Worthington. Harry Edward Worthington and his mother Elizabeth were also bequeathed the remainder of her household furniture and effects.

A trust fund was to be divided as follows: four fifteenths to her sister Charlotte Mary Morris; four other fifteenth parts in trust to the three daughters of her late brother George Finch Jennings Worthington; four other fifteenths to the two daughters of her late brother Thomas Knight Worthington; and the remaining three fifteenth parts of Elizabeth's trust fund was to remain in trust for her nephew Montano Worthington, youngest son of her brother Robert Worthington. If Robert did not attain the age of 21 years his share was to be divided between his two sisters.

Probate of Elizabeth's will was granted to her executors, Edward Mowll Worsfold, Henry Martyn Mowll and Harry Edward Worthington on 21 March 1906.

Robert Worthington (1845-1916)

The tenth and last child of Henry and Mary Worthington, Robert was born on 12 March 1845 in Dover. Robert is listed in the 1870 Kent 'Post Office Directory' under 'Brewers', at Maxton, Hougham in Dover. In the 1871 census he was listed at Maxton Brewery, aged 27 years and was the unmarried head of the house. His occupation was given as 'Carriers brewer'. Residing with him were Arthur E. Sharp aged 26 years, an unmarried boarder and brewers pupil, and Elizabeth A. Williams, 26 years of age, an unmarried housekeeper originally from Portsmouth.

Robert married Elizabeth Ann Baum, daughter of William Baum, Gentleman, on 6 June 1875 by licence at St Peter's Church, Croydon in the County of Surrey. Both parties were single and residents of South End at the time of their marriage. Their first child Henry Benjamin Worthington was born nearly five months later on 25 October 1875 at Croydon. Robert's occupation was given as brewer on his son's birth certificate and the address of his wife Elizabeth Ann, who reg-

125   Robert Worthington. (Photographed by W.R. Waters, Dover)

istered the birth, was given as 2 Lucena Cottages, Junction Road, Croydon. A market town, Croydon was nine and a half miles from London. There was a large brewery in Croydon which by 1831 had been there for over a century, so perhaps Robert worked there.[70]

During 1878 Robert, his wife Elizabeth, and two children moved to the Province of Ontario, Canada. Henry Benjamin Worthington died during March 1893 at London, Ontario, Canada aged 18 years. A note in Mary Ann Worthington's handwriting is the only record that can be found of his death.[71] Lizzie Worthington was born in England on 31 March 1878 and accompanied her parents to Canada. Two more children were born in Ontario, Sophia A. Worthington on 13 June 1880 and Montano Ophedel Worthington on 1 March 1889. The 1901 census for 206 Simcoe Street, Toronto West City found Robert, Elizabeth, Lizzie and Sophia Worthington in residence. Elizabeth Worthington's mother, Mary A. Williams, an 85-year-old widow born 5 November 1815 in England, was also living with the family, having emigrated in 1884.[72] Robert's first cousin Edward Scott Worthington and family were also in Canada, having moved there before 1876.

126   Montano Ophedel Worthington, Canada.

127 (*right*)   Lizzie Worthington, photographed in Toronto.

Robert died at his home at Rochester Road, Burquitlam, province of British Columbia, Canada on 3 October 1916. He left a will which was drawn up a month before his death appointing his wife Elizabeth Ann of Rochester Road and his son Montano Ophedel Worthington of 327 Blair Avenue, City of New Westminster, Province of British Columbia executors and trustees. He left his estate including the devise left him by his late uncle Robert Finnis Jennings to his wife Elizabeth Ann Worthington.

128   Helen Frances Worthington. (Photographed by Russell & Sons, London)

Chapter 6

Great-Grandchildren
of Benjamin Jelly and Elizabeth Worthington

A select collection of great-grandchildren of Benjamin Jelly and Elizabeth Worthington about whom some information is known:

The Children of Francis Samuel (1836-1912) and Helen Felicite Worthington

Helen Frances Worthington (1864-1920)

Born on 19 July 1864 at Lowestoft, Francis and Helen's eldest child was reputedly a very talented and remarkable woman. Educated at home, Helen Frances later went to Lausanne and spent four years there, finally attending a school in Germany for a year. She was an excellent linguist and spoke Italian, French and German fluently. With her courageous temperament and fondness for animals, Helen was a fearless horsewoman. She was also an excellent dancer. Her chief characteristics were enthusiasm and thoroughness in whatever she undertook, while her sympathy and vivacity brought her many friends.[1]

After returning from Germany to spend a few years at home, Helen went to Italy to study music for a year. Being very fond of travel she then went to the United States of America and to Canada. She became a Professor of Mandoline, known as 'Fiammetta Waldahoff', and on her return to England taught for some years at the Guildhall School of Music at Victoria Embankment, London and was most successful as a conductor of stringed orchestras, often writing the score herself. She also prepared pupils for musical examinations and a speciality of hers was in 'hand callisthenics'. Many press notices were published which paid tribute to her ability including the *Musical Courier, Musical Answers, Musical Times, Globe, City Press* and *The Era,* 21 March 1900:

> At the Guildhall School, on Tuesday evening, Mme. Fiammetta Waldahoff gave a Mandoline Recital, in which many of her pupils distinguished themselves. The recital took place in the pretty new theatre, which was well filled; and, in addition to the solo performances, there was a mandoline orchestra and mandoline quintette, which was very effective, and deserved great credit for the equal balance of tone preserved, and the excellence of the ensemble. The mandoline orchestra was assisted by cello, harp, organ and violins. The combination was a good one, as the organ and cello supplied the sustained and deeper tones required for contrast. Mme. Waldahoff is a very talented lady, who not only proved how well she had taught her pupils, but also displayed great ability in conducting their performances, which gained enthusiastic applause.

Helen was very interested in scientific matters, particularly astronomy, and attended a course of lectures by Professor A. Fowler in 1910. Astronomy became an absorbing interest and she gave up a great deal of her music and social activities in order to devote more time to it. Her indomitable spirit and energy led her to neglect her health, and she often suffered from this lack of care. However, undismayed by the most unfavourable conditions and unwearied by physical weakness, her dauntless spirit often enabled her to achieve success where others would have failed.

Helen sometimes watched the night sky for five or six hours at a time, when only a few stars were visible amid the clouds, but her perseverance was often rewarded by the detection of meteors and other phenomena such as the Aurora Borealis and the Zodiacal Light, about which she published some interesting and useful data.

Between 1910 and 1920 Helen observed some 600 to 700 meteors about which she compiled much data. As these were being doubly observed their real paths were able to be computed. The accuracy of her observations was fully recognised and highly valued on account of her promptness and exactitude. In 1913 she observed the return of Westphal's Comet and duly reported the event; however, an observer abroad had beaten her by a few days. On another occasion in December 1914 she saw a large meteor and immediately despatched details by telegraph to the Planetarium, enabling its real path to be ascertained within two hours of its passage across the sky.

Writing was another skill of Helen's and an excellent paper on 'Clusters and Nebulae visible with small optical means', published in the *British Astronomical Association (B.A.A) Journal*, came from her pen. She also contributed two papers to the R.A.S., one on large meteors she had observed in 1914 and another on the meteor shower of 3 January 1918, besides frequently contributing to foreign journals.

Helen was a member of the Council of the B.A.A., and from 1916 to 1919 was Director of the B.A.A. Meteor Section. Other membership lists in which Helen's name appeared were the Société Astronomique de France, the Societe d'Astronomie d'Anvers, the Commission des Etoiles Filantes, the Leeds A.A. (in 1919) and also the Chaldean Society for Naked Eye Work which she founded with the help of another English astronomer.

Unfortunately Helen never knew she had the honour of being chosen by Harvard College Observatory as the English woman to whom the 'Edward C. Pickering Astronomical Fellowship for Women' for the year 1920-1 had been assigned. This news, which would have greatly pleased and encouraged her, came after she died on 21 July 1920 at Totteridge, Hertfordshire aged 56 years. Helen's health had always given cause for anxiety to her friends as she constantly overtaxed her strength, especially during the First World War. Her work in a canteen and on behalf of prisoners of war occupied many hours of every day and night and was additional to her astronomical labours.

While living at Totteridge in Hertfordshire with her second husband Sidney Wilson, Helen had a wooden platform erected in her garden so that she might have a clear view above the trees. Here on her 'perch' as she called it, she would stand in all night weather, watching and recording with great accuracy and detail the paths of the objects she loved so well.

Eulogistic obituaries appeared in six astronomical journals in England, France and Belgium after Helen's death. In them her attainments as an astronomer were praised and the high appreciation with which she was held in the astronomical world was expressed. In addition there were many from friends and prisoners she had helped during the war. A few tributes extracted from letters to her sister read: 'She was a friend and angel to many of us whilst we were prisoners of war in Germany. I pray God that she will receive the reward which she so merited by her charity, good work and kindly disposition', from Sergeant P. Kelly, Dublin Fusiliers.

A friend wrote:

> But now she is at rest, after a life of kind and gentle love for others for which she was but poorly repaid in this world. She was one of the cleverest and most wonderful women I ever knew; I think THE cleverest, and yet always so modest and humble and so sympathetic in dealing and thinking of others, and so generous in all her thoughts.

Yet another friend wrote: 'For us who loved her there is a blank in our lives that can scarce ever be filled. There was never anyone like her for me.' The Rev. W.R. Fotheringham F.R.A.S. wrote, 'I should like to take this opportunity of expressing the high appreciation in which she was held by Astronomers for her devoted and valuable work'.

Helen married her first husband, H. Webster, sometime between October and December 1889 at St George, Hanover Square, London. Her second husband was Sidney Wilson and there was no issue from either marriage.

Janet Marion Worthington (1870-1953)

The second daughter of Francis Samuel and Helen Felicite Worthington was Janet Marion who was baptised at the Lowestoft parish church on 3 July 1870. Sometime between October and December 1912 she married John J. Jervase Hatt but they had no children. Janet lived at Abbot's Mead, Pettaugh, Suffolk after her husband died. Several interesting bequests were made according to her will after her death on 7 January 1953. The beneficiaries were her godson, Anthony Hunt of 47 Passy Avenue, Belmore, Sydney 'the painting of his mother'; her cousin, Helen Elizabeth Anne Till 'my picture by Benezit'; her maid Alice Mary Merricks 'sufficient furniture to enable her to furnish a bed-sitting room and my fur coat'; her sister Beatrice Cobbold 'my diamond brooch any twelve books she may choose my papers and personal effects and my large blue faience Egyptian brooch'; brother Scott Till Worthington 'my Jacobean cupboard'; niece Mary Wiesner received 'the furniture and pictures I have already lent to her'; niece Helen Olivia Rogerson 'my gold Egyptian bracelets and my ikons'; nephew John Francis Worthington was bequeathed 'my Nelson mirror pair of Sheffield plate vegetable dishes and gold cigarette case'; nephew Francis Richard Worthington 'my carbuncle ring'; her nephew Roger Worthington 'my silver cigarette box', and to her nephew Thomas Worthington 'my silver non-magnetic watch'.

William Scott Till Worthington (1872-1955)

The third child and first son of Francis and Helen was born on 24 May 1872. The 1881 census shows William aged eight years at a school in Brighton, Sussex. The headmaster was William R. Lee.[2] Compulsory education was introduced in England for all up to the age of 10 years. Elementary education did not become free until 1891 and the school boards established Higher Grade Schools where secondary education

129   William Scott Till Worthington.

beyond the age of 10 years was available to all children for the first time. After leaving Charterhouse School and thereby becoming an 'old Carthusian', William completed a three-year course in engineering at University College, London.

Keenly interested in engineering, William devoted some ten years to the study of different branches of the subject. He also spent two and a half years in South Africa. William was not destined to adopt the profession of engineer as a permanent career for in 1902 he joined his uncle's firm, Messrs. Edward Till & Co, pioneers in the rubber trade who were originally known as Jackson & Till, one of the oldest rubber broking firms in London.

William remained with the firm, which became a publicly-listed company in 1916, securing a position as one of the four directors. The company expanded over the years, dealing not only in rubber but also with balata and gutta-percha. William became known as a leading authority on rubber and was Chairman of the Rubber Trade Association in 1923. He was one of the founders of Rubber Settlement House, which dramatically increased the business of everyone in the rubber trade.

On 24 February 1903 William married Mabel Smith, daughter of Major T. Smith of Leek, Staffordshire. They had three sons who were all born at Eltham. The first, John Francis born 8 January 1905, joined his father's firm as a colonial produce broker and at the time of writing is a spritely 91-year-old. He and his wife Sylvia Mary, née Harvey, celebrated their 60th wedding anniversary on 3 October 1996. They have two daughters and a son, all married with children.

William and Mabel's second son, William Roger, born 8 June 1907, attended his father's old school and studied at Jesus College Cambridge before becoming a schoolmaster. William never married and died on 6 April 1978 at Winchester, Hampshire. Their third son, Thomas Scott, born 21 April 1911, trained for the Royal Navy at Dartmouth College. He eventually became an engineer, married Margaret Baird (Madge) Whitton during 1936 and had two sons. Thomas died in London, 18 August 1984.

Interested in all sports, particularly cricket and football, William played regularly. Golf became his chief outdoor exercise as he grew older and he was a Field Marshal of the Royal Blackheath Golf Club in Eltham. He also enjoyed games, shooting, fishing and motoring, being a member of the Royal Automobile Club. In 1925 his family lived at Westwood, Court Road, Eltham.[3] William Scott Till Worthington died 20 November 1955 at Eltham and his wife Mabel died 10 September 1962.

Richard Till Worthington, M.A., M.B., M.D. (1875-1936)

The second son of Dr. Francis Samuel Worthington, Richard Till was born in Lowestoft on 11 August 1875. He was educated at Charterhouse before attending Cambridge University where he studied medicine. Further training took him to St Bartholomew's Hospital, Smithfield, London and to Munich. When fully qualified he joined his father's practice in Lowestoft. He rendered excellent service during the First World War and later gave up his Suffolk practice for a post in the Ministry of Health.

Richard married Edith Marion Hedges between April and June 1904 in London and had four children.

Mary, born 1905 in Suffolk, became a Doctor of Medicine and twice married doctors. She had a son, Jonathan Richard Paul Ruthven Wiesner and a daughter Ruth Weisner by her second marriage to Paul Wiesner. Ruth married a Mr. Lowe and had two children, Emma born about 1971 and James born about 1974.

Francis Richard, born June 1907, married Audrey David De Joux and had four children. One of Francis's sons was a Naval Commander, another became a doctor in the U.S.A. Francis became a Group Captain in the R.A.F. and was killed in a flying acccident during 1950.

Douglas William, born in 1909, married but was separated from his wife for many years. He lived at Warren Bottom, Erwarton, Ipswich, Suffolk and left his whole estate to Margaret Patricia Budd of 49 Shawfield Street, Chelsea, London. Douglas is believed to have had a son.

Helen Olivia, born in 1911, married Commander Rogerson and had one son. She lives at Barfield Cottage, Boxford, Colchester, Essex.

When Richard wrote his will on 10 March 1926 he was living at 27 The Avenue, Bedford Park, Middlesex. He died in Knutsford on 28 September 1936. Richard left his daughter Mary all his microscopes; son Francis his gold watch; son Douglas his silver watch, gold chain and gold links, and daughter Helen £40. He left his double-barrelled shotgun, rifle, revolver, fishing rods and tackle to his sons, and a toss of a coin was to decide who got the gun and who got the rifle, revolver and fishing rods.

To his sister Janet, Richard left any three books including *Johnsons Tour to the Hebrides* (with 6 Errata) 1st edition. His brother William Scott Till Worthington received, 'my brown trout in case' while sister Beatrice Cobbold was left any three

130   Dr. Richard Till Worthington. (Photographed by W. Boughton & Sons, Lowestoft)

books she desired to have. A godson (and nephew) Tom Worthington received £10. Richard left the bulk of his estate to his wife, stating in his will,

> I know full well that my wife will make use of it to her best advantage and in her turn leave it justly distributed amongst our children. I have a great dislike to expensive funerals which to my notion are frequently the source of much needless expenditure but if my wife and executors can get my body transported to Lowestoft and there buried alongside my father and mother for the sum of £50 or under then let it be done.

Edith Marion Worthington, widow, died on 12 November 1944 in the county of Sussex.

Beatrice Worthington (1879-1961)

Beatrice was the youngest child of Francis Samuel and Helen Felicite Worthington born in 1879 at Lowestoft. She married Francis Alfred Worship Cobbold during 1922 and they had no children. Francis Cobbold died in 1947 and Beatrice Cobbold on 17 April 1961. Her estate was divided amongst her nieces and nephews with several monetary bequests to relatives and friends. She bequeathed the portraits of her husband's ancestors, Anthony Taylor, William Taylor, Elizabeth Taylor, née Barnaby and their daughter Elizabeth Worship, née Taylor and her husband John Worship which are mentioned in *Palmers Perlustration of Great Yarmouth*, as well as her copy of this publication, to the Mayor, Aldermen and Burgesses of Great Yarmouth.

The Children of John Scott (1837-1883) and Mary Worthington

William John Worthington (1862-1952)

The first child of John Scott and Mary, William was born in Dunedin, New Zealand on 23 February 1862. A keen sportsman, as a young man he was a member of the Invercargill Football Club and Captain of the city's Rowing Club. William was also a member of the Southland rowing crew who annually competed against Otago for the Edmond Cup.

William spent most of his working life with the Dunedin Post Office as an accountant. According to his obituary in the *Otago Daily Times* on 25 November 1952: 'He was always interested in the territorial movement and started as an ensign of the Queenstown volunteers, later attaining the rank of Major and officer commanding No.4 Company of the P. and T. Engineers. For many years he acted as Secretary to the Otago Officers Club, of which he was a life member.'

Known as 'Will', William married Isobella Elsie (known as Isobel) Preshaw in October 1892. They celebrated their diamond wedding anniversary in 1952 shortly before William's death. Their only child, John Allan Preshaw Worthington, was born on 28 November 1902. During 1938 he obtained a Bachelor or Arts and Teachers Diploma from Otago University and was a teacher at Waimatuku School from 1934-8. He married Lily Kellahan during 1931 and died without issue in 1983.

In later life William was a keen bowler. He was an executive member of the Otago Bowling Council and a member of the Roslyn Bowling Club. William died in Dunedin on 17 November 1952.

Percy James Worthington (1866-1938)

The fourth child of John Scott and Mary, Percy was born in Wakatipu, South Island, New Zealand on 12 September 1866. He was a clerk when he married New Zealand-born Lucy Hare, the daughter of John and Lucy Hare, on 6 September 1889 at St Mathias Church of England, Paddington, Sydney, Australia. They had eight children: Gerald Collins Worthington (1890-1918), Reginald Collins Worthington (1893-1917), Dorothy Dagma Worthington (1897-1987), Frances (Kathleen) Worthington (1899-1972), Clifford S. Worthington (1901-7), Raymond Worthington (1904-90), Percy Worthington (1906), Maxwell Worthington (1909-90).

The two oldest sons, Gerald Collins Worthington and Reginald Collins Worthington, fought and died in the First World War. Gerald, a bedstead maker who lived in Paddington with his wife Annie, enlisted on Monday 27 November 1916, aged twenty-six. He was described as 5 feet 10½ inches, 140 pounds with dark complexion and hair, and brown eyes. He fought in France with the 33rd Battallion of the Australian Infantry Force (A.I.F.) and was 'wounded in action' or 'gassed' at least seven times before he was killed in action on 8 August 1918. He is buried at Villers Bretonneux in France.

Gerald's 'Effects received from the field' and forwarded to his widow at 14 Lambert Street, Erskineville included: '1 Jack knife, 1 metal chain, 1 pocket knife, 1 pipe in case, 1 razor, 1 photo, 1 franc note, 1 purse, 1 bible'.

Gerald's younger brother Reginald enlisted on 3 February 1915 at the age of 21 years. He was 5 feet 10¼ inches, 142 pounds and had a fair complexion with brown

131 *(left)* Gerald Collins Worthington (1890-1918).
132 *(middle)* Reginald Collins Worthington (1893-1917).
133 *(top right)* Dorothy Dagma Worthington (1897-1987).
134 *(bottom right)* Frances Kathleen Worthington (1899-1972).

hair and blue eyes. He was living at Temora at this time and his parents were living at farm 23, Griffith via Walbrigge, New South Wales. Reginald joined the 5th Brigade of the 17th Battalion as a private and had been promoted to Lance Sergeant before he was killed in action in Belgium on 9 October 1917. He is buried at Menin Gate, Panel 17, Ypres, France.

Reginald fought in Gallipoli, suffered dysentery and trench feet and was awarded a Military Medal five days after his death for bravery. The Australian war memorial holds the original recommendation record which states:

> During operations near Westhoek on 20/9/17 this N.C.O. when his seniors had become casualties, took charge of a remnant of his platoon and led them to their objective. On reaching this he carried on with the consolidation despite the enemy artillery, M.G. and sniping fire, showing skill, determination and courage. During the rest of the day he held his post in spite of heavy shell fire, with great tenacity.

These young, strong and handsome men must have been greatly mourned and missed by their families. As my mother Barbara May Worthington wrote many years later, 'War doesn't prove who's right, it just proves who's left!'.

Percy James Worthington died on 18 December 1938 at Lisarow, New South Wales and Lucy died on 9 September 1941 at Sydney.

The Children of Edward Scott Worthington (1840-?)

Colonel Sir Edward Scott Worthington, K.C.V.O., C.B., C.M.G., C.I.E., M.R.C.S., L.R.C.P., M.D., C.M. (1876–1953)

The youngest son of Edward Scott Worthington, Edward was born 24 October 1876 in Montreal, Canada and studied medicine at Toronto University. After obtaining his Chirurgiae Magister (Master of Surgery) degree, he finished his training at a London Hospital where he took his M.D. degree and became a member of the M.R.C.S. and L.R.C.P in 1897. He entered the Royal Army Medical Corps in 1900, became a Captain 1903, Major in 1912 and Lieutenant-Colonel and Brevet Colonel in 1918.

On 31 October 1914 Edward married Winifred Jean Wallace, daughter of the late John Wallace of Glassinghall, Dunblane, Esquire. They had a son, Michael Euan, born 1916 and a daughter, Patricia Marie, born in 1918. Edward was known as 'Teddy' and little can be found about his early life. He apparently ran away from his family and never talked about them to his children.[4] Lady Winifred obtained a divorce from her husband in 1931.

Edward served in South Africa as civil surgeon from 1899 to 1902. He was present at operations in Rhodesia, Transvaal, Orange River and Cape Colonies earning the Queen's Medal with four clasps and Kings Medal with two clasps. He was medical officer on the staff of H.R.H. Arthur William Patrick Albert, Duke of Connaught, third son of Queen Victoria during his visit to South Africa for the opening of the Unions of South Africa Parliament 1911 when he received the M.V.O. 4th class. Edward attended the Duchess of Connaught during her illness in 1913. He again attended H.R.H. during the time he was Governor General of Canada,[5] 1911-14 and when he travelled to India early in 1921 to inaugurate the new Legislatures on behalf of the King.

From 1914 during the First World War Edward served in the R.A.M.C. in England. From 1912 he was Assistant Director General (temp. Lt Col.) of the A.M.S. Edward was appointed Deputy Assistant Director General, War Office in 1917; Assistant Director General, War Office 1918 and was Honorary Physician to the King in 1922.

He was made a Knight of Grace of St John of Jerusalem in 1913 and received the C.M.G. in 1915 when he was also appointed Commandant of the Officers Convalescent Home, Cimiez. He was appointed Deputy Assistant Director-General Army Medical Services or War Office in 1917 and Assistant Director General thereof in 1918.

Edward was awarded a K.C.V.O. in 1918; C.B. (Mil.) 1919; C.I.E. 1921; the D.S.M. (America and the Sacred Elephant (Siam) and Order Leopold and Croix de Guerre (Belgium). He retired from the army in 1926 and by 1949 was a member of the London firm of Messrs Shaw Loebl & Company, Stockbrokers of 148 Leadenhall Street, as was his son Michael Euan Worthington.[6] He was a member of Boodles, Army and Navy Clubs.[7]

At the time he wrote his will on 25 January 1949, Edward was living at 16 Cadogan Square, Chelsea in London. He died there on 5 April 1953 and his son Michael, friend Charles Gregory a solicitor and a Gordon R. Page of Messrs Shaw Loebl & Co were executors of his will. He desired that his body be cremated and that no mourning be worn. Edward left the following 'pecuniary legacies': to his ex-wife, Dame Winifred Jean Worthington, £3,000 and

> my Ming Caledon Dish, my Ch'en Luing Caledon Vase my K'ang-Hsi Caledon Bowl my pair of Blue and White K'ang-Hsi Vases and my small Ming Caledon Vase and I express a wish (but without creating any trust or imposing any obligation) that on her death these Chinese objects d'art should be given to my daughter the said Patricia Marie Drummond ...

His daughter Patricia was also left £1,000; daughter-in-law Venetia £250, son-in-law Lieutenant Commander J.A.L. Drummond R.N. received, 'my Moonstone and diamond set consisting of shirt studs cuff links and waist-coat buttons'.

Sir Edward's 'dear friend' Eric Muirsmith of 32 Davies Street, Grosvenor Square was left his Cartier platinum and gold links. The said Gordon R. Page was left one of his gold cigarette cases, the selection of which was entrusted to Michael Euan Worthington 'whose decision shall be final'. Michael was left all letters, papers, manuscripts, diaries and writings (apart from legal documents, paper money, securities for money and books of account), and was requested by his father's will to destroy any of them which in his opinion should be destroyed. Personal belongings including articles handed down through his family were given to Dame Winifred. The trusts established in the will gave equal share to Michael and Patricia.

The Children of James Copland (1841-1906) and Harriett Worthington

Laura Scott Worthington (1869-post 1906)

Born in Lowestoft and baptised on 16 July 1868 at St John's Church, Laura was the first child of James and Harriett. In 1906, the year both her parents died, Laura was living at the Convent de la Visitation Mont Saint Amand Les Grands in Belgium. Her name at the convent was Soeur Marie Teresa Joseph. She was living in 1906 and it is not known when she died.

George Vigers Worthington, M.A., M.B., B.C., M.R.C.S., L.R.C.P., F.R.G.S. (1870-1942)

Baptised in Lowestoft at St John's on 31 July 1870, George followed his father and grandfather into the medical profession.

George trained at St Bartholomew's Hospital, London and practised for many years at Llandrindod Wells, Wales during summer months and Luxor, Egypt during the English winter. In June 1903 he married Evelyn Maud Le Blond and they had a daughter, Irene Frances Laura who married a Mr. Walsh and had one son named Colin.

George became a member of the British College of Surgeons in 1895 and his listing in the Institute's directory for 1910 and 1915 informs us he was in Rhodesia. By 1920 he was at Llandrindod Wells in the county of Radnor, Wales.

In the 1917 *British Medical Directory* George's listing states:

'Mangalore', Llandrindod Wells (Tel 39 May-Oct), & Luxor, Upper Egypt (Nov-March), M.A., M.B., B.C. Cambridge 1895; M.R.C.S., L.R.C.P. London 1895; (Camb. & St. Bart.) Brackenbury Surgical School 1896; Superintendent Medical Officer Luxor Hospital for Natives; F.R.G.S.; Fellow Society Tropical Medicine & Hygiene, & Royal Society of Medicine; Late Senior Hospital Surgeon St Bartholomew Hospital; Surgeon Wenlock Hospital & Womens and Childrens Hospital Mangalore; Surgeon Princess Christian Hospital South Africa (Medal & Clasp). Author 'Sulphur & other baths & water in skin disease.'; 'Llandrindod Wells: its climate and waters'; 'Spa treatment of Rheumatoid Arthritis'; 'Spa treatment of Gout'; 'Obesity & its treatment'; 'Prognosis of Tetanus' St Bartholomew Hospital Reps. 1895; 'Streptomycosis treated with Antistreptococcic Serum', Ib 1896; 'Princess Christian Hospital in South Africa', British Medical Journal 1901; &c.

George was still living at 'Mangalore' when he wrote his will on 29 November 1940. He died on 8 July 1942 and appointed his brothers John Vigers Worthington and Frank Vigers Worthington as executors and trustees, for which they received £10 each. Lady Hailsham (formerly Mrs. Clive Lawrence) was also left £10 so she could purchase 'some small article in recognition of the kindness shown to me in years gone by'.

George bequeathed to his trustees the furniture and household effects in his flat at 'Fairhaven', Llandrindod Wells to be dealt with in accordance with instructions written at the foot of the inventory accompanying his will.

He directed his trustees to allow his wife and daughter to choose any furniture and other articles 'to the value not exceeding £40 which they would like to keep in my memory'.

Trusts were established so that £250 was paid to his daughter Irene Frances Laura Walsh, 'for the education and or advancement of her son Colin'. The remainder of the trust fund was to provide an income for his wife and after her death, for his daughter, grandchildren, godchild and niece Muriel Hepburn, daughter of his sister Rubie and his niece Peggy Chappe-Hall, daughter of his sister Dulcibella. As regards the sale of his house and practice George directed, 'that my Trustees shall consult the Solicitors of the Medical Defence Union as to the advisability of immediate sale and as to selling the house and practice separately or together and whether the sale shall be entrusted to the British Medical Association Bureau or other Agents ...'. It was also his desire that his Trustees–'shall take opinion as to the sale of his postage stamps, pictures, china, bronzes and other works of art with view to obtaining the highest price'.

Sir John Vigers Worthington, M.D., M.R.C.S. (1872-1951)

Known as 'Jack', the fourth child of James Copland and Harriett was baptised in Lowestoft during March 1872. Educated at Woodbridge and Haileybury, John continued the growing family tradition by becoming a Doctor of Medicine. He trained at London Hospital where he was house surgeon and later travelled as medical attendant to Mr. and Mrs. Du Cros who eventually persuaded him to give up medicine and go into business.

John then worked with the Dunlop Rubber Company from 1901-21 (technical support and director 1919). He was Parliamentary Private Secretary to the Prime Minister 1931-5 and then to Lord President of the Council. He sat as Member of Parliament for Forest of Dean Division of Gloucestershire (National Lab.) from October 1931 until November 1935 when he was defeated. He received his knighthood in 1935 and according to the 1947 British publication of *Who's Who*, John remained a director of the Moran and Rajmai Tea Companies.

A member of the College of Surgeons (M.R.C.P) by 1895 and L.R.C.P. London by 1895, he was listed in the *College Directory* for the years 1910, 1915 and 1920 as living in Acton. In June 1904 he married Agnes Janet Edwards, daughter of Elisha John Edwards of Assam and they had a son, John Benjamin Scott Worthington, and daughter, Dorothy Mary Elizabeth. Sir John's address in the 1937 *Debrett's* was listed as Queen Anne's Mansions, S.W.1. His will states he was 'Knight of Queen Anne's Lodge, Lyme Regis in the County of Dorset'.

Sir John died on 16 June 1951 in Dorset. His wife, son and Lloyds Bank were appointed executors and trustees of his will. £1,000 was left to each of his children and £500 each to his son-in-law Captain John Ronald Stewart Brown, and daughter-in-law Eve Worthington. A grandson–David Worthington Brown–was also left £500. His wife Agnes was provided for during her lifetime, and after her death a trust Sir John established divided his estate into equal shares to be distributed to his two children and/or grandchildren. His daughter Dorothy was married to Godfrey Lias at the time of Sir John's death.

Frank Vigers Worthington, F.R.G.S., F.Z.S., O.B.E., C.B.E. (1874-1964)

Born in Lowestoft between July and September 1874, Frank was the sixth child of James and Harriett Worthington.

Frank was educated at Repton and served in the African Matabeleland Rebellion of 1896 for which he received a medal. He entered the Rhodesian Civil Service in the same year. He became Secretary for Native Affairs in Northern Rhodesia and a Judge of the Administrators Court from which he retired in 1914.

In March 1912 he married Gladys Elma Maclachlan (died 1940), only daughter of Major K.F. Maclachlan, R.H.A. and it is not known whether there was any issue of this marriage.

His listing in the 1921 *Debrett's* reads: '... Deputy Chief (Postal) Censor at War Office (1915-19), a F.R.G.S. & F.Z.S., Deputy Director of Awards of Ministry of Pensions 1919, and a Fellow of Zoological, African Sos. and of Royal Colonial Institute, Officer d'Academie; cr. O.B.E. (Civil) 1918, C.B.E. (Civil) 1920. Address 20 Montpelier Square, SW7; St James's Club.'

Frank was also Chief Postal Censor 1939-40; Member of Standing Interdepartmental Committee on Censorship, Committee of Imperial Defence, 1938-40; Member of Linguistics Committee, Ministry of Labour since 1939; Palmes d'Officer de l'Academie Francais, 1920.[8]

Another aspect of Frank's ability was that of author. He published several books and plays:

Chiroma the Witch Doctor (Field Pr.), 1923; The Little Wise One (Williams & N.), 1924; Illustrated edition published by Collins, 1929; The Zoo on Sunday (illus) (do.) 1925; Plays: The Dancing Poisoners (1 act); Mavana (3 acts); I.D.B. (3 acts) (all African subjects); Kalulu the Hare (Illus.) (Collins), 1930; C XIXth Century, Dearborn Ind. (U.S.A.), Patches (Pittsburg), Morning Post, Field, Illustrated London News, Evening Standard.[9]

Frank's address in 1937 was still 20 Montpelier Square, Knightsbridge, London S.W.7 and Yellow Chimneys, Angmering-on-Sea, Sussex. He was a member of the Titmarsh, Savage and St James's clubs. Between 1957-60 he was known to be living at Westerfield Hall, Ipswich, Suffolk with his widowed sister, Dulcibella Chappe-Hall. He died on 29 January 1964 at Ipswich. His will requested that he be cremated 'and its ashes scattered to the four winds' and 'that the seat (for which I have paid during my lifetime) in the National Theatre yet to be built dedicated to the memory of my late wife shall bear a plate if such be allowed inscribed as follows "In Memory of Mrs Frank Worthington and her Special Matinees for Charities" '. Various legacies included

To Peter Waterfield (son of Jean Truscott) of 51 Hartford Drive, Watford, Hertfordshire the gold watch with chain attached which belonged to my father and my gold cuff links; To my said sister Dulcibella Chappe-Hall all my table silver bearing the Worthington Crest together with the silver rose bowl presented to me on my marriage by the British South Africa Company and the pair of three branch candle sticks bearing the Worthington Crest and in the event of her predeceasing me then to Honor Gasston now in Nairobi, Kenya. In the event of both the said Dulcibella Chappe-Hall and Honor Gasston predeceasing me then I bequeath the same to my nephew Benjamin Worthington.

Benjamin[10] Worthington was also left the three silver salvers bearing the Worthington Crest and Dulcibella Chappe-Hall the copyright of his books and all his papers, sketch books, etc. 'to read through or destroy as she may think fit'. His wearing apparel was left to the Seamen's Friendly Society for distribution to needy members.

Rubie Elisabeth Worthington (1877-1963)

Rubie or Ruby[11] Elisabeth Worthington was born at Lowestoft during the first quarter of 1877, the daughter of James Copland and Harriett Worthington. She married Malcolm Langton Hepburn, ophthalmic surgeon of Harley Street and had four children, Rosalind Dorothea Hepburn, Jean Meta Waterfield, née Hepburn, Muriel Linnet

Felling, née Hepburn and Ian Malcolm Coryndon Hepburn. In 1941 Rubie and Malcolm were living at Triginta, Watford Road, Kings Langley, Hertfordshire. Malcolm Hepburn died on 2 January 1942 leaving a will. Rubie died between October and December 1963.

Phyllis Mary Worthington (1880-?)

Born in Lowestoft during 1880, Phyllis was 28 years of age when she married Robert Thorne Coryndon, a 38-year-old civil servant in the colonial office, at St Margaret's Church, Lowestoft on 3 March 1909. Phyllis' address at the time was 4 Victoria Mansions, Lowestoft while Robert was residing in Dewerston House, Cheltenham. Robert was the son of Selby Coryndon, a solicitor of Plymouth and Kimberley, Cape Colony South Africa. The couple spent their married life in South Africa where they had four children; John born 1910, Roger born 1911, Peter born 1913 and Honor born 1917.

An extract from a history of British East Africa in the Macmillan Library, Nairobi reveals the following about Phyllis's husband, Sir Robert Thorne Coryndon:

> K.C.M.G. cr. 1919 C.M.G. 1911; Governor and Commander-in-chief Kenya and High Commission of Zanzibar since 1922. He was born at Queenstown, Cape Colony, 2 April 1870, the son of Selby Coryndon of Plymouth. After being educated at Cheltenham College he joined the Bechuanaland Border Police under British South Africa Company on 9 November 1889 and was part of the Pioneer Force for the occupation of Mashonaland from June 1890-1. He was Private Secretary to the Premier of the Cape Colony, the Right Honorable Cecil John Rhodes during 1896-7 and the Parliamentary Inquiry into the Jameson Raid when Rhodes was forced to resign because of his complicity. Robert served in the Matabele Rebellion 1896 (medal and clasp). He was British resident with Lewanika, and B.S.A. Company's representative in Barotseland June 1897. During the same year he took an expedition to Lealui, Upper Zambesi River. Robert became administrator of North Western Rhodesia September 1900; Resident Commissioner for Swaziland 1907-16 and Basutoland 1916; Chairman of the Southern Rhodesia Native Reserves Commission 1914-15, and Governor and Commander-in-Chief Uganda 1917-22. He was also awarded the rank of Commander, Crown of Belgium. Died 10 February 1925.

Dulcibella Mary Gooch Worthington (1885-1976)

The ninth and youngest child of James Copland and Harriett was born in Lowestoft, June 1885. She married a 34-year-old Clerk in Holy Orders, John Obiot de Collancy Chappe-Hall after banns at All Saints Church, Margaret Street, Marylebone, London on 1 June 1910. John was the son of John Hall, a physician. The marriage was witnessed by her mother and brother, George Vigers Worthington. John and Dulcibella Chappe-Hall are known to have had a daughter, Peggy. Dulcibella died on 14 February 1976.

The Grandchildren of Henry (1803-1866) and Mary Worthington

The children of Henry and Mary Worthington are to be found in England, Australia, New Zealand and possibly Canada.

The Children of George Finch Jennings (1833-1898) and Elizabeth Worthington

Harry Edward Worthington, M.D., M/R.C.S., L.R.C.P. (1867-1936)

135   Dr. Harry Edward Worthington.

136   Mrs. H.B. Worthington, England–believed to be Muriel Rose Worthington, wife of Dr. Harry Edward Worthington.

Baptised on 14 February 1867 at Worthing in Sussex, Harry Edward followed his father into the medical profession and became a doctor and surgeon. Harry remained at home with his family in Foots Cray and then Sidcup in Kent during his education and medical training, travelling daily to Guy's Hospital in London.

In the medical register for 1893 Harry's address is given as Thorncliff, Poole Road, Bournemouth, the same address as his father. He was registered as a doctor on 15 February 1892 and admitted as a member of the Royal College of Surgeons and licensed by the London Royal College of Physicians the same year. Harry bought his own medical practice in 1895 in Birchington, Kent, a parish within the cinque-port liberty of Dover, of which it was a member, though locally in the hundred of Ringslow, or the Isle of Thanet, three and a half miles from Margate.

The 1900 *Medical Directory* includes this listing for Harry Edward: 'Birchington, Thanet–M.R.C.S., L.R.C.P. Lond 1892; (Guy's); Mem. British Medical Association; Surg. Odd Fells; Surg. Police; late Surg. B.I.S.N. Co.'.

Harry married Muriel Rose Morice during the March quarter of 1904. The *Dover Telegraph* announced the birth of a daughter to the couple on 17 June 1912 at The Sycamores, Birchington.[12] After his mother's death in 1908, Harry was granted administration of both his parents' estates and also that of his aunt, Sophia Worthington.

He became known in his later life as an artist and an exhibition of his paintings was held in 1925. He is listed in the *British Index to Artists* by Daniel Trowbridge and also the *British Who's Who in Art, 1927-1934.*

On retiring in 1927 after 32 years of untiring labour, he was presented with a cheque for £250 and a handsome testimonial signed by 530 of his patients, their names inscribed in a gilt-edged leather album. The first page of this album reads: 'Presented to Dr H.E. Worthington on his retirement from the practice, by the inhabitants of Birchington and the neighbourhood, in token of their esteem, affection and gratitude for his ungrudging services during the years 1895-1926'. A small gift was also presented to Mrs. H.E. Worthington for her helpfulness and devotion at all times.

Harry died on 17 May 1936 at Birchington, Kent and left a will, which was signed on 2 July 1924, appointing his wife Muriel Worthington and Lloyds Bank Limited executors and trustees. He gave his drawing by Gainsborough and his watercolour by David Cox to his daughter Elizabeth Mary Morice Worthington; furniture, plate and plated articles, linen, china, glass, books, pictures, prints (except those already given to his daughter Elizabeth), musical instruments and all other articles of personal, domestic or house use or ornament to his wife. Real and personal property was left to his trustees for disposal.

Oscar Clayton Worthington, M.D. (1869-1958)

Born in Heene, Sussex on 11 February 1869 and christened there on 17 March that year, the second son of George Finch Jennings and Elizabeth Worthington was named after a great friend of his father's, Sir Oscar Clayton, Surgeon, who was knighted by King Edward VII.

Oscar also lived with his family at Sidcup while he trained at Guy's Hospital. After becoming qualified as a doctor in 1899, Oscar joined his father in the Sidcup practice. In the 1901 *Medical Directory* Oscar is listed in the provincial section at Birchington-on-sea, Kent. Later he had a practice in the West End of London for seven years.

A very handsome man, Oscar knew a number of the aristocracy and wealthy, important people. Oscar never gave his patients prescriptions, but, having a dispensary in the basement of his practice, made up medicines himself. By these methods he kept his patients from going elsewhere or lending his prescriptions.

In the March quarter of 1908 Oscar married Louisa Jane Peacock of

137 One of George Finch Jennings Worthington's sons. (Photographed by Josiah Russell, Worthing)

138   Group of Finch Jennings Worthingtons at Birchington Hall.

Birchington Hall, Birchington, Kent. From 1916 to 1919 Oscar was practising at Guildford and was a member of staff at the Surrey County Hospital and of the Clandon Park Military Hospital in Guildford.

Oscar retired from medical work in 1919, owing to a serious illness which incapacitated him. For many years he resided in Folkestone. His wife Louisa died on 7 June 1932 and on page seven of the *Folkestone Herald*, 11 June 1932, her obituary reads: 'Died suddenly at home … She was niece of Mrs Susan Gray of Birchington Hall, Thanet and had lived in Folkestone for 11 years'.

Her will was signed on 28 October 1925 when she was living with Oscar at 'Fairlawn', Castle Hill Avenue, Folkestone. She appointed her husband and Arthur Ernest Burton of 10 Norfolk Street, Strand, London, solicitor trustees and executors of her will. The following bequests were made:

    To my sister Mary Gray Letord–£10,000
    To Dr Harry Worthington–£500
    To Arthur Ernest Burton–£500
    To Miss Etty Lyon–£200
    To Mrs Elizabeth Colbert–£200
    To Mrs Marion Toulmin–£200
    To Miss Florence Bradwell–£200
    To George Toulmin–£200

To Miss Ellen Edwards–£100
To Elizabeth Burleigh–£100
To Annie Bishop–£100
To Mrs Bishop–£50
To Edward Bishop–£50 annuity for life
To Mrs Baker (cook)–£50
To Edith Janes (housemaid)–£50
To Society for the Prevention of Cruelty to Animals–£200
To the Poplar Hospital to found a bed which bed shall be called 'The Susan Gray'–£1000

When the chapel of the church of St Andrew, Buckland was restored in 1932, Oscar paid for a new sacristy to be erected. A plaque in his memory reads: 'Oscar Clayton Worthington and Louisa Jane his wife June 7th 1932'. Until July 1940 when it was destroyed by enemy action, the east window in the Worthington Chapel had a memorial dedication to a member of the Worthington family.[13]

Prior to renovations in the 1930s the south-east end of the aisle was known as the 'Worthington Chapel' and contained the following memorial plaques on the south wall: 'Benjamin Jelly Worthington (d.1822) and Elizabeth his wife'; and 'Thomas Knight Worthington, Surgeon, Third son of the above (d. 1856)'.

Oscar died on 24 September 1958 at 'Fairlawn', 13 Castle Hill Avenue, Folkestone aged 89 years and was buried three days later in a Worthington family vault at Buckland Church, Dover.[14]

In his will written on 30 October 1959, Oscar appointed Cecil Burton, solicitor and Harry Joseph Purchase as trustees. He bequeathed his wife's jewellery to Mrs. L.M. Purchase and his silver and silver plate to his nephew Hugh Sutton Worthington-Edridge, who also received £5,000. Oscar left £150 to the vicar and churchwardens of Buckland Church, Dover upon trust to invest in order to receive an annual legacy, on the condition they kept the Worthington family vaults in the churchyard at Buckland and the tomb of Thomas and Susan Gray in the Kensal Green Cemetery in due order and proper repair. If the church failed in its obligations for 12 months, then the legacy was to be transferred to the Royal Air Force Benevolent Society.

Oscar refers in his will to a Settlement, of which he was Settlor, which was made between his brother George Benjamin Worthington and the Public Trustee on 14 November 1930. Provided George had no children, the property and funds

139 Dr. Oscar Clayton Worthington.

comprised in the Settlement were to be held upon trust for his great nephew, Oscar Charles Worthington-Edridge, until he reached 21 years of age. If Oscar Charles died before attaining a vested interest in the funds, they were to be held for and shared equally between the siblings of Oscar Charles.

Additional bequests were left to his housekeeper Annie Hockam–£1,000 and an annuity of £104 to be paid quarterly during her life. Another codicil left, 'My twin beds at present located as to one bed on each of the first and second floors of my house and … my dinner service on the kitchen dresser in the basement'. Annie's husband was left Oscar's grandfather clock which was standing in the basement. Harry Joseph Purchase and John William Purchase were left Oscar's home, 'Fairlawn' and £1,300 for repairs and improvements to the property. His estate was valued at £63,970 16s. 6d.

140 Hillside tomb of Oscar and Louisa Worthington.

Alice Frances Worthington (1872-1930)

The fourth child of George F.J. and Elizabeth Worthington, Alice Frances, was baptised at Heene, Sussex on 20 November 1872.

On 19 December 1895 Alice married Captain Charles Sutton Edridge of the 8th, 'The King's' Regiment, eldest son of Colonel F.L. Edridge, late 20th Regiment of Orwell Lodge, Bournemouth, at St Peter's Church in Bournemouth.

Alice lived at Thorncliff in Bournemouth at the time of their wedding. A newspaper clipping found in family archives reveals details of the wedding which was a very large and grand affair and must have been highlight of the year:

> … The service which was fully choral, was conducted by the Rev.Canon Fisher, Vicar of St Peter's Bournemouth, assisted by the Rev. P.M.C. Johnstone. There were three bridesmaids, Miss Elsie Worthington and Miss Charlotte Worthington (sisters of the bride) and Miss Mary Isabel Edridge (sister of the bridegroom). They wore dresses with cream satin skirts, primrose coloured silk bodices and large black velvet 'picture' hats. They carried pretty shower bouquets composed of golden brown chrysanthenums and wore gold bangles, the gift of the bridegroom. Mr Hugh Lockwood Edridge, brother of the bridegroom, was best man. The bride was given away by her father. She wore a very handsome dress of ivory satin, with full court train of white velvet, embroidered with pearl and ostrich feather trimming. Her dress was prettily adorned with the same trimming, and looped with sprays of orange blossom. Her veil was of

Brussels net worked in silk, which was fastened by a pearl star, the gift of the bridegroom and she carried a shower bouquet of exotics with streamers. A reception was held after the ceremony, at Thornecliffe, at which many relatives and friends were present. The bride and bridegroom left early in the afternoon for London. The bride's travelling dress was of burgundy alpaca, with white serge and silk cord trimming, and a front of white China silk, accordion pleated, with a large black 'picture' hat trimmed with black feathers. Her travelling cloak was old gold velvet, trimmed with ostrich feathers. The dresses were designed and made by Giles Jefferys, Streatham. Amongst those invited were the following:- Col & Mrs F.L Edridge, Dr Harry Worthington, Mr Oscar Worthington, Mr George Worthington, Mr Edward Worthington, Dr & Mrs Negri, Mr Robert Jennings, Captain & Mrs Montano, the Rev. & Mrs H.P. Edridge, Capt & Mrs Sutoon, the Baroness Van Aerssen, Miss Jones, Miss F. Jones, Dr & Mrs Frank Worthington, Dr & Mrs James Worthington, Mr & Mrs Edward Fairthorne, Mr & Mrs Roberts, Miss Fairthorne, Miss Augusta Fairthorne, Mr & Mrs Wetton, Miss Hamond, Mrs Lauriston Kneller, Miss Gordon, Colonel & Mrs Eyre Williams, the Officers of the 8 40 [sic] Regimental District, Major & Mrs Grattan, Major & Miss Lowndes, Canon Fisher, Captain & Mrs Campbell, Sir Edmund De la Pole, Bart. & Lady De la Pole, Mr F De la Pole, Mr & Mrs Swinburne, Mr & Mrs Butler, Mrs Gilbert Cooper, Mr, Mrs & Miss Stevens, Mr & Mrs Alexander Duncan, Mr & Mrs Clarke, Mr & Mrs Lloyd, Miss Duncan, Mr, Mrs & Miss Stephens, Mr & Mrs Goldway(?), Mr & Mrs Gotton(?), Mr A Erskine Barrett, Capt Alexander Barrett, Miss Barrett, Mr & Mrs Lyne, Mr, Mrs & Miss Feiling, Mrs & the Misses Foster, Sir Digby Murray, Bart. Mr, Mrs & Miss Desprey, Dr & Mrs Hibbard, Miss Cornish, Mr, Mrs & the Misses Watts, Mr & Mrs Hampden Pye, Dr & Miss Abraham, Mr O Campbell Clark, Mr, Mrs & the Misses Cottall, Dr & Mrs Les, Admiral & Mrs Mead, Major & Mrs Hamilton Spooner, Mrs Spooner, the Misses Clayton, Colonel & Mrs Colthurst, Mrs Clayton, Lieutenant de Conrey Dashwood R.N. & Mrs Dashwood, Miss K Symonds, Miss Daisy Marten, Major Phibbs, R.A., Mr, Mrs & Miss Bidben, Colonel, Mrs & the Misses McLeod, the Rev & the Misses Williams, Dr & Mrs Hodson, Mrs & Miss Bishop, Miss Mainwaring, Mrs Clover, Mr & Mrs Jackman, Dr & Mrs Davison, Mr, Mrs & Miss Welchman, Mrs Walker, Mr & Mrs J Druitt, the Rev & Mrs Hodgkins, the Rev & Mrs Loy, Mr & the Misses Hughes, Mrs Wynne, Mr, Mrs & the Misses Methold, Mrs & Miss Hull, Mr & Mrs Mayor, Mr & Mrs Jardine, Rev. P.C.M. Johnstone, Mr & Mrs Ward, Miss Barton, Dr & Mrs Knight Holt.

Alice and Captain Edridge had several children, one of whom, Hugh Sutton Worthington Edridge, was an heir to his uncle, Oscar Clayton Worthington's estate. Hugh's son, Oscar Charles Worthington Edridge, was left the bulk of his great-uncle and namesake's estate. Alice died between October and December 1930 at Camberwell aged 58 years.

George Benjamin Worthington (1875-1957)

Born during the December quarter of 1875 in Islip, Oxfordshire, George Benjamin Worthington was the fifth child and third son of George Finch Jennings Worthington and Elizabeth Worthington. He married Gertrude Adeline Little, daughter of Richard Little 'of independent means' on 15 March 1913 in the Chertsey Register Office, Surrey. He was aged 35 years and his bride 24 years. George was described as a farmer and he and Gertrude were living at Lightwater Farm, Bagshot, Windlesham. He was believed to have emigrated to Australia but no record has been found of him in the Pacific region. He died in England during 1957.

The Children of Thomas Knight (1836-1896) and Mary Ann Worthington

Henry Benjamin Worthington (1871-1935)

141 Mary Ann Worthington holding Henry Benjamin Worthington, 1872.

Henry Benjamin Worthington was the eldest son and first child born in Nelson, New Zealand to Thomas and Mary Ann. Henry began farming at Mangatoroto at about 16 years of age, and by 1896 was farming at Stratford.

Henry was a slim man about six feet tall, of fair complexion and a quiet, gentlemanly manner. He wore a moustache most of his life. Henry married Isobel/Isabella McKenzie at Stratford during 1897 and had six children: Henry Thomas Knight Worthington (1898-1967), James Worthington (1899-1916), Roy Worthington (1903-81), Annie Isabell/Isobel Worthington (1906-95), Ian Hamilton Worthington (1910-73), Jessie Adeline Worthington (1912-....).

After their marriage Henry and Isobel moved to a farm at Puniwhakau near Strathmore. Once a year the family travelled to Stratford to their townhouse in Warwick Road for a few months. This property backed onto land originally owned by Thomas and Mary Worthington. It was a two-day drive from the farm and the family would stay overnight at a boarding house at Douglas. The same distance can today be covered by car in one and a half hours.

Jessie, the youngest in the family, had frequent visits to stay with her grandmother and aunts in Stratford as she was always in trouble on the farm. Jessie was often in trouble wherever she was and recalled that once while walking with her grandmother in Stratford she smiled at the butcher's boy and was admonished with the words, 'you don't recognise the butcher's boy when you are out!'.[15]

Life on a farm at Puniwhakau in the early part of this century meant isolation. The family seldom ate beef as there was no refrigeration. Lighting was provided by lamps and candles and Isobel did all the cooking. Wool was taken into town by bullock wagon and foodstuffs and other supplies would be brought back. In 1920 a neighbour bought a truck but horses were regularly required to tow it as it would get bogged in the muddy tracks.

The children rode to school on ponies, a distance of five miles. The school was comprised of 11 students. Dances were often held at the school and everyone in the family would attend. Music was provided by an accordion and people would come in buggies from miles around.

Christmas on the farm was a traditional occasion. Oranges, bananas, sweets, hair ribbons and a doll for the girls. Jessie can remember receiving a doll while her brother Ian received a pocket knife with which he chopped off her doll's head.

The family's evening meal was always served at the table by Henry. Isobel was served first and then the children, in order of age. Jessie's meal was always cold as she was the youngest.

A family social highlight occurred when the Prince of Wales visited Stratford on 3 April 1920 and Henry and Isobel attended the reception held in his honour.

Henry gave up farming through ill health and moved to Stratford about 1932. He died of arterio sclerosis and uraemia on 18 March 1935 aged 64 years. He was buried two days later in Koputana Cemetery. Annie, his eldest daughter, continued to care for her mother who lived for

142 Henry Thomas Knight and James Worthington.

another fifteen years before she died on 31 March 1947.

My father, Edgar Worthington, was very fond of his uncle Henry. Edgar and he used to go walking together and everybody thought Henry was Edgar's father because of their resemblance.

Francis Hamilton Worthington (1872-1949)

The second son of Thomas Knight and Mary Ann Worthington, Francis, known as Frank, was, like most of his family, tall, upright and slim with a very fair complexion and blue eyes. He had a white moustache and was always neatly dressed, often in a medium-grey suit. His very quiet manner could have been shyness as he could be difficult to communicate with.

Frank never married and lived with his mother, who spoilt him, and two younger sisters. He was known by various members of the family as 'Eb'—short for Ebenezer Scrooge because he was mean. If he gave anything away it was to the Salvation Army. Whenever his sister Kate gave her nieces and nephews turkey eggs, Frank would try to get them back so he could take them to the market to sell them.

He would often give his nieces and nephews hidings when they stayed with their grandmother and was a most unpopular man. His nieces were frightened of him and would hide in the raspberry bushes near the washhouse when Frank chased them. Frank would take beautiful meat home for his mother and complain about how it was cooked. He did not often think of others and it never occurred to him to cut some wood for his mother who would have to go down the back of the farm to collect pine cones at 80 years of age.

Frank eventually bought a dairy farm at Te Aroa by himself. He owned several houses and farms and retired to Papatoetoe, Auckland where his sister Adelaide nursed him before he died on 10 August 1949.[16] He suffered angina pectoralis and died of a thrombosis following 10 years of myocarditis. He was buried on 13 August at Purewa.

Howard Worthington (1874-1951)

143   Howard Worthington.

The third son of Thomas Knight and Mary Ann Worthington, Howard's birth was announced in the local paper, the Nelson *Colonist* after he was born on 29 December 1874 at Charleston, New Zealand. Thomas and Mary Ann had moved to Hamilton in the North Island in 1972 but returned prior to Howard's birth so that Mary Ann could be with her mother during her pregnancy.

Thomas tried his luck at gold mining and his occupation is given as miner on Howard's birth certificate. About 1878 Howard, his parents and four brothers moved to Stratford, Taranaki on the west coast of the North Island.

Among Howard's earliest memories of his home here was the fact that if you wanted to see Mt Egmont you had to climb a hill on the opposite side of the road. The land between the town and the mountain was covered in tall standing bush at that time, but it did not take long for the axe, slasher and fire in the hands of the settlers to demolish the growth of centuries.

The Worthingtons lived on the main road where bullock teams regularly passed, and it was custom to give their drivers a cup of tea with bread and treacle. Treacle was known in Australia and New Zealand as 'Bullocky's Joy'. Fruit for making jam was scarce and sugar expensive so this was a luxury and kept only for special occasions, family and friends.[17]

Like other members of the family, Howard would have done his share of gathering fungus, clearing bush and milking cows. In February 1881 the Education Board agreed to build a school in Stratford as soon as funds were available and Fenton Street school was opened on 6 April 1882 with facilities to accommodate 60 pupils. Among the first names in the official register of admissions were those of Henry, Frank and Howard Worthington.[18]

South African Experiences

In 1901 Howard borrowed some money from his younger sisters and set off for Wellington to look around the capital city. While there he got a job on a ship sailing for the Argentine where he stayed for only a few weeks. From South America he managed to get a job on a boat taking horses to South Africa for the British troops who were fighting in the Boer War.

While in South Africa Howard saw his first snake and got off his horse to take a closer look at it. His horse promptly bolted and left him standing there, or so he told his daughter-in-law Barbara Worthington.

Howard's letters to his mother and sisters during the few years he was away reveal him as a warm, caring and humorous man. He had a very close relationship with his mother and also had an eye for the girls! Parts of these letters are faded and the words indistinct. Some spelling errors have been corrected where they confuse the reader but others remain as originally written:

Pier Hotel
Wellington, N.Z.
Oct 1st 1901
Mrs M A Worthington

Dear Mother,
I will be in Monte Video tomorrow about three o'clock and then I am going to Buonos Ayres the same night by another steamer, about twelve hours run. I have had a slendid trip it has taken 23 days to get there. I saw about twenty iseburgs some as high as the steamer and they looked splendid. I wish the girls could have seen them for they won't see things like that ? ? I am posting this letter on the steamer so as you will get it by the first male they have to go to Teneriffe. I expect it will take about four weeks to get to you. I will write again in about a weeks time and then you will know what I am doing. I think this trip has saved my life for I feel as fresh as a lark and getting as fat as porpoises. Tell the girls I will write to them as soon as I get a job. Tell Addy to ride the tail of old Dandy and she'd ? ? she sees ? ? remember me to Dot
So goodbye
Hoping this letter will find you all well

H Worthington

* * * * *

Dec 25/01
Natal.

Dear Mother,
I must say I am sorry for not writing before but things are all right with me now. I had no idea of landing here when I left home that morning. I had few weeks in South America and it is the worst place in the world I think. I wouldn't like to see any lady I know in such a place. Well wages well nigh nothing in fact but murders. So I thought I would try South Africa and I came over in a cattle boat with 400 mules, 300 horses, 200 bullocks and now I am looking ? ? take horses I have ? ? and one white roan. What with breaking in horses and swearing at the natives I have my work cut out. I am putting through 20 a week and I have them all to ride myself. Today is Christmas day but I have no holiday but I hope you are enjoying yourselves. My boss is a horse dealer in a large scale. He puts through about 100 a month and in a fortnight I might be boss over the whole thing as he knows nothing about a horse and I have crawled up his sleeves a little bit but not enough yet for my liking. I hope to get out riding.

I hope the cows are doing alright with you ? about Frank's foal. Tell Frank to do whatever he likes about things but I would give him the straight tip to get married sooner than to tackle this game the second looks rougher. Did you get the letter I wrote from the Wakanui?. I think I will come back to Stratford to get married (what about Page Street and ? the girls can tell I am in the ? looking at the Boer girls.) I am sending a ??? ten pounds ??? rents will be ??? as you write I will send some over. I think I ought to have a nice little walk by that time and I wish you all merry Christmas and a happy New Year. I do give my love to the girls XXXXXX
goodbye
Your son
H Worthington

H Worthington
Durban Natal
South Africa

see you soon

* * * * *

c.1901-2

Dear Mother,
Sisters and brothers I hope this letter will find you all well at home where I ought to be If I had any senses at all but you know I lost them in the last storm. I am doing fine here, three meals a day a be that ??? and is it in a new country. I wont ?? the work I am doing or you would laugh at me when you see me again. My next ?? (shift?) in ?

   I am beginning to think I will have to get a Dutch gal with a farm for my missus if my luck doesnt soon change of all the places I have seen Johannesburg is the best. Tell Frank ... if he likes and ??? what was my share of the money it might get him drunk. I don't suppose he has much of it later. He earned enough of it but this beats it by one hell and I cant get over it. The heat is about a thousand in the shade here I supppose you get the ??? I ??? you on the 14th December and the cheque ? pounds. I haven't had my answer yet. I thought the girls might have written a line or two dear Addie I will be home for your next birthday and I will have a drive on the carriage together and then I will ???

   I will have to wish you all good bye
H Worthington
Durban, Natal
South Africa

* * * * *

Durban
Natal,
Sth Africa
June 4th 02

My dear mother,
I was very glad to here from you and see you are all well—by your letter it is nothing but peace, peace, peace here now but I suppose it is worse where you are, you hear more about the war in Stratford than I do here. I will soon know whether I am going to stop here or not. You can tell A Thomas he is far better where he is than Africa at the present time if a lot of them could see both sides of the globe at once then they would know when they were well off.

   I met Charlie Till and Black and a few more of New Zealanders they were quite taken back when they saw me ride up to them. I sent you a cheque for 10 pounds last

December 24th but you didn't say you got it in your letter. I am sending a cheque now and could you go to the bank with it and draw what money there is if any. I am writing to Mr Bayley about it so it will be alright. There would have been more there but owing to a smash up I had a little while ago but I am about alright again and bossing up Caffers in a bakehouse now so I wont starve yet. My boss got marrried this morning and ??? at me ??? to her fathers and demands Kate ??? scarce here as in Stratford but now the war is finished I might be able to get you some—will have to wait to get up to Johannesburg. I got mothers letter one other day the only one I have had. Old Dick Seddon was here but didn't go to see him. I suppose Kate is a ? taller now she is twenty one and as for Addie she must feel small and bony side of Kate. Never mind Adie we will make a back seat in the carrriage when I come home wont we. So good bye all
XXXXXXXX

I remain your loving brother
H Worthington

I say Addie if you see Miss Walsh or Miss F.A. Potts you can tell them I am still living and single.

* * * * *

Pretoria
Aug 4-1902

Dear Mother,

It is about six weeks since I have written to you or heard anything of you, I have been shifting about so much that I haven's had five minutes to myself to write you a line. I am in Pretoria most of my time now. I go into Johannesburg about once a fortnight to bring horses and mules over here for sale. It is not bad game shifting about but your money doesn't last till the next month that is the worst part about it. I don't think I shall ever save enough money to see N.Z. any more but I will have to see you at Mus next this country suits me. We haven't had rain for five months now you tell the girls I was at a dance last week and it wasn't so bad dancing with the Dutch girls. I think it will be a Dutch gal I will be marrying after all and not a N.Z. I often think of F. and that bush farm. If we had the bush over here we wouldn't have to work any more. You don't see a tree for thousands of miles here nothing but grass but you never see any English grass. The country is over run with men and the wages are so low that a man has to work for 5/ shillings a day, no eight hours here six to six thats a day in this country, but I suppose we will soon have the eight hour system when Dick Seddon lives in Johannesburg. I will never work in the mines for 5/ per day, so if you here of any of the boys coming over here you can tell them the wages they will get, and you can't start farming here on nothing. Is old Dandy dead yet? If not tell the girls to ride him to death and I will get them another.

   How are the girls getting on with Ping Pong? I often have a game with myself. How are the sisters-in-law gettting on with their families. I suppose Percy is six inches tall now, with his baby girl. I say girls that we ask Miss Walsh down and we will all go to dance together. Remember me to all and Miss Gibson.
So goodbye all
Love from
Howard Worthington
Pretoria
Transvaal
South Africa

Write soon and I will answer. Did you get the cheques? I corner Durban Caffe.[19]

Everyone was very glad when Howard returned home safely from his adventures. He finally arrived back in Stratford after two years and wondered why his mother had been so worried about him! Howard became a farmer and helped his mother on the farm until he married. As his father had died quite a few years earlier everybody in the family helped on the farm.

Howard was always a very practical man. He was an excellent horseman and was very strong in his youth. He also had skills as a water diviner. A big, broad shouldered, loose limbed man of 5ft. 10in. tall, with fair skin and blue eyes. He was not like his brothers Henry and Frank. Henry, Frank and his eldest son Edgar were taller, slimmer, very upright and straight.[20]

Howard and Florence

Howard was nearly 30 years old when he married Florence Amy Potts, the Miss F.A. Potts mentioned in his letters, on 20 December 1903 in Eltham, Taranaki. Florence, who worked for a Dr. Paget before her marriage, was about 5ft. 2in.-5ft. 3in. tall, had beautiful auburn wavy hair, hazel eyes and a florid complexion.

Born on 23 October 1878 at Carterton in New Zealand, Florence was the daughter of Charles and Emily Sophia Potts (née Gearing). Charles Potts was a carpenter by trade and built many houses in Carterton. He was a very well respected man and owned several hotels in various parts of New Zealand. As a girl Florence had a kiwi as a pet after the bird had been accidentally caught at Otaki. When the bird died she had it stuffed and years later I rescued it from being thrown into a bonfire during one of Florence's spring cleans.

After their wedding Howard and Florence put all their goods on a pack horse, including a blue and white willow pattern dinner set, and rode out to Puniwhakau to start their married life. It wasn't long however before they moved to a farm at Uruti, north of Waitara. Over the next seven or eight years the family moved from Waitara to Sentry Hill, then to Smart Road, Fitzroy and Ratapiko. Six children were born during these years: Edgar Charles Worthington (1904-74), Cecil Howard Worthington (1905-95), Mildred Louise Worthington (1907-), William Henry Worthington (1909-75), Edith May Worthington (1910-86), Felicity Adele Worthington (1912-).

Life was hard. Like other New Zealand farms, the land around Stratford was very poor and not well cultivated. The family moved again in 1913, to a house on the corner of Regan and Miranda Streets in Stratford. Shortly after settling in Stratford, Howard bought a livery stable. Many beautiful horses came to be fed or shod while their owners attended stock sales. The stock yards were situated on land where the Memorial Hall, R.S.A. and County Offices now stand. There were still many more horses than cars at the time and Howard also had a horse cab for hire.

During the First World War Howard was busy with his stable and taxi business. About this time there was a very severe influenza epidemic and Howard helped the undertakers remove the bodies to the Town Hall until they could be buried. Florence's old employer Dr. Paget warned Howard not to work long hours without a meal, and the children had little camphor bags hung around their necks. Sulphur was sprinkled on hot embers and burned in the rooms of the house. Although hardly a home escaped the dreaded sickness; fortunately the Worthington family was one of them. Mothers got out of bed to attend to children suffering a relapse and dying. My aunt Edie related to me how her mother was talking to a neighbour one morning who died the next day, leaving a grieving husband to manage a family of young children.

Howard would harness two black horses to his cab for funerals and two white horses for weddings. While the family was still living in Miranda Street Howard was asked if he was interested in taking a franchise for Ford cars. Because he was not a businessman he did not accept the offer which in retrospect was a pity, because not long after these cars became plentiful.

Brecon Road South

In September 1918 Howard sold the livery stable and the family moved from Miranda Street to Mary Ann Worthington's 50-acre farm on Brecon Road South. This farm had a six-roomed house with a separate dairy and wash-house. There was also a well and pump in the backyard.

After the war Howard bought two four-horse teams and block drays for metal carting and transporting bricks from the railway to building sites.

Lepperton

When it came time for Edgar, Howard and Florence's eldest child, to go to school, they bought him a bicycle. Edgar would travel to Stratford from the farm at Lepperton on the train in the mornings and cycle home at night. By doing this he could get home a lot more quickly in the afternoon to help milk the cows, which was done by hand.

144 Left to right: Cecil, Florence, Edith, Felicity, William, Howard and Mildred Worthington photographed by Edgar Worthington at Brecon Road, Stratford, c.1917.

Bill, Edie and Phyll all went to school at Lepperton. Their headmaster, Mr. Gilmore, made Edie stay behind after school one cold winter's day in order to finish a story. It became dark and she became very frightened sitting there by herself, as Mr. Gilmore had forgotten all about her. When he came back after his dinner and discovered Edie was still there, he sent her off home in a hurry. Poor Edie, aged then about seven or eight years, had to walk a mile home in the dark–something she has never forgotten.

After this Edie begged her mother to let her attend school at Huirangi where two women taught pupils in two rooms. Edie loved them. Miss Joyce played the violin and the other teacher played the piano. The children enjoyed their singing lessons and sang songs such as 'Men of Harlech', 'Do ye ken John Peel' and 'Johnny so long at the fair' with great gusto.

141 Brecon Road

In 1921 Howard bought 20 acres of land adjoining a swamp in Brecon Road for £2,000. A wooden four-bedroom house on the property was extended, another three rooms being built onto it. The home had an open fireplace, a wood and coal range and was in walking distance from Stratford.

Cecil, Howard and Florence's second son bought a Rimu tree from Lepperton and planted it by the front gate. This tree grew almost thirty feet high.

Saturday was town shopping day, when Florence and Edie would carry a basket of eggs to the egg circle. Each egg had an individual number stamped on one end and only clean and fresh eggs were accepted. On the return journey home they carried groceries. Butter was bought at the dairy factory, 6lbs at a time. A seven-

145   Left to right: Cecil, Edgar, William and Howard Worthington with cocky in the cage.

146 *(left)* Florence Amy Worthington, née Potts and Mary Ann Worthington.
147 *(middle)* Edgar Charles Worthington, *c.*1917.
148 *(right)* Left to right: Edith, Howard, Felicity and Florence Worthington.

pound tin of golden syrup cost 1s. 9d. and a 60lb tin of honey cost £3. Bread was bought for school lunches but never cake or scones.

Florence would arrive home exhausted after these shopping trips. There were no footpaths, only loose metal roads to walk on. She would flop on her bed for half an hour before getting ready to milk the cows. The heat of the sun on the tin cowshed roof, the smelly breath of cows chewing their cud and then the effort of carrying buckets of milk to the cans on the milkstand made the slow, hard work of milking even more difficult. This was followed by the preparation of the evening meal for her husband, six children, and the men employed to drive the horse team.

In later years the mail, newspaper and milk were all delivered together and the grocer and butcher had vans which would stop at the front gate once a week. Travelling hawkers visited once a month with horse covered wagons and they sold linen and clothes.

The family always had a large vegetable garden. Peas were picked by the bucket and enough potatoes, carrots, parsnips and onions were grown to last the whole year. Lamb was usually on the menu with mint sauce and for Christmas dinner there were new potatoes and peas followed by fruit salad and jelly. Christmas cake with fresh cream from their own cows was served with the evening meal.

Fruit was preserved by the open pan method. Rows and rows of jars stood on shelves to be used in winter. Beans were salted in stone crocks and boxes of fruit were bought at auction sales. The household water supply came from tanks and a spring before borough water was piped to the house. Water for washing and baths was heated in a fuel fired copper in the washhouse. This room contained the tubs, bath and the handwringers used after boiling and bluing the clothes, another hot and tiring job.

Soap was made from the fat rendered down after killing sheep. Candles were bought by the packet and kerosene lamps were used in the kitchen and dining room. Electricity was a welcome arrival, followed by the purchase of a large heavy electric iron.

After the depression Howard bought a Studebaker car from Newton King and started Stratford's first taxi stand. It was the first car in the family. An employee called Perce Collins (Paddy) drove the taxi. Later Howard bought a Ford for the mail run and it was driven by Ernie Heal. Edie recalled a trip when she accompanied her mother, sister Phyl and Howard, who was taking a couple to Auckland. Chains had to be used over steep Mount Messenger and a punt took the cars over the Mokau River. Later a bridge was built with gates at each end to keep rabbits from crossing it. Te Kuiti was the first stop if one was lucky enough to avoid punctures and being stuck in the mud. Extra petrol was carried in tins on the running board of the car. It was a hard and gruelling trip.

Family Life

Christmas in Howard Worthington's household was an exciting time. Cakes and biscuits were baked on the coal range and sealed away in tins and Christmas puddings were hung. Plum duffs with money to be found inside were eaten with relish. Florence would make all the girls a new dress and socks were hung on the bed-ends for Father Christmas to fill. Wonderful goodies were found inside, sweets, nuts and an orange stuffed well down in the toe. A new hair ribbon, a pretty hair clip and other small presents such as small kewpie dolls made of celluloid filled the sock.

Howard loved to play draughts and he and a neighbour spent long evenings playing the game. There was also a piano and portable gramophone. Edie bought a zither but said she was never very good at playing it.

Engaged couples were always given a 'kitchen tea' and in this way gathered a good many useful articles for their future home. After the wedding a 'tin-kettling' was always held. This was supposed to be a surprise party but the couple always enjoyed it. Music was usually a mouth organ and piano and everyone sang and danced. Alcohol was seldom served at these parties but everyone enjoyed themselves.

Florence was a very strong character and would overide Howard. He just gave in for peace. Florence usually dealt out the punishment to the children, not Howard. Cecil remembers he was threatened once by his father when he was six years old and was so scared he hid in the dog box and stayed there until it was dark.

Howard had very good ideas. He was interested after the First World War in buying houses around Stratford which at this time could be bought for £300-400. Florence would not allow him to do this but Howard told Edgar when he was a boy that he should save his money and buy houses as it was a way to get rich. Howard would often want to do things Florence did not agree with. She would just put her foot down and refuse to have anything to do with it.

Florence read the newspaper thoroughly and was a staunch nationalist. Nothing the Labour Party did was any good. She was absolutely bigoted as far as politics were concerned. She was also a wonderful pioneer cook and could cook anything under any conditions, whether on a camp fire or in an old coal range. Nobody could make a better jellied chicken or pigs-head brawn. The favourite Saturday night dish was boiled rice and sausages. Florence was also fond of recitations and ditties. She had a scrapbook and liked to press plants. Her own cough mixture recipe has been used successfully by several members of the family. The recipe is as follows: 5 oz. vinegar;

½ lb honey; ¼ lb golden syrup or treacle and one dessertspoon paregoric elixor. Simmer a few minutes and when cold add paregoric.[21]

Other old home-remedies were crushed garlic for clearing the throat and to stop the choking associated with whooping cough; and sulphur and treacle, Bertram's pills and castor oil for constipation. Diluted Condy's crystals were used to treat rheumatism.

Later Years at Brecon Road

Howard gradually lost his hearing as he aged and also suffered from Parkinson's disease. He came to life, however, at 2 p.m. on afternoons when Parliament was broadcast and he would turn the volume up as loud as he could.

After Howard's death on 4 April 1951 at the age of 76 years, Florence continued to live by herself at Brecon Road. Howard left his estate to his wife and appointed his sons as executors. Edie did not inherit any of his estate as she had been assisted

149 Florence Amy Worthington's 70th birthday family gathering in 1948. Top row from left: Edward Worthington, William Worthington, Arthur Watson, John Trigg, Donald Worthington, Jack Worthington, Cecil Worthington; 2nd row: Barbara Worthington, Mildred Hart, Edgar Worthington holding Garth Worthington, Frederick Trigg, Felicity Trigg, Jean Worthington, Eileen Worthington; 3rd row: Howard Hart, Marjorie Hart, Edith Watson, Janet Worthington; 4th row: Colleen Worthington, James Watson, Nancy Worthington, Howard Worthington, Susan Worthington leaning on Howard, Florence Worthington holding Bernard Watson and Robert Trigg.

financially during his lifetime. She and her family lived next door. Florence remained vital and independent with excellent sight and hearing although she suffered from a heart condition. She continued to cook, look after chooks and cut the lawns until well into her eighties. Florence died of a heart attack on 13 May 1967 aged 88 years and was buried beside Howard at Stratford Cemetery.

Howard and Florence were my grandparents and their eldest son, Edgar Charles Worthington was my father. I fondly remember visiting Brecon Road with its hessian backed wallpaper that flapped in the breeze, the cockys beak on the mantelpiece (which my brother has), the rolled wallpaper and bead curtain in the hallway and my good natured, smiling grandmother who always had her apron on. My grandmother's favourite plant, a South American succulent (nopalx ochia) which she kept in the hallway, lives happily with her grandson Jack Worthington.

Percy Knight Worthington (1876-1915)

The fourth son born to Thomas and Mary Ann, Percy was born at Marahau, Nelson. On his birth certificate his father gives his profession as mariner. A tall, frail man of six feet, Percy married Isabel Agnes Sinclair and became a farmer. Percy and Isabel, who was always known as 'Mum Dot', had six children: Mary Frances Worthington (1902-19..), John Newton Worthington (1903-83), Joan Catherine Worthington (1903-19..), Edward Montano Worthington (1904-19..), Adelaide Hilary Worthington (1905-19..), Bernard Lindsay Worthington (1907-1980).

Between 1900 and 1902 Percy farmed land and milked cows at Waitara, but after Percy's death in 1915 Isabel had to sell the farm.

150   Percy Knight Worthington and Isabel Agnes Worthington.

In 1912 the family lived for nine months at New Plymouth. The children went to Onehunga school for 12 months and then to Pahi, near Paparua for a year or two. All the children received two years of high school. At Helensville Percy and Isabel farmed 30-40 acres; however Percy was not strong enough to be a farmer and fainted many times before he died in 1915 aged 38 years.

Percy's second son Edward Montano Worthington, known as Ted, was born in Waitara. He remembers spending 1912-13 Christmas at Grandma's (Mary Ann Worthington). The boys were given carpenter's sets and the girls a doll. One cousin lost his carpenter's set so he took Ted's.[22]

The family was very poor and, according to Ted, 'the church mice had nothing on us!'. On the children's birthdays their mother's sister, Auntie Jean, would give them half a crown. Percy had a ledger into which he would enter this amount with a flourish and the children never saw their money again. If Percy got himself into financial trouble he went to court and acted as his own lawyer. He was often in court.

As young men Ted and Bernard milked cows for their uncle Frank (Francis Hamilton Worthington) for three months. Because their father had borrowed £80 at one time Frank never paid them, so Percy's debt could never be reduced.

After Percy died the children were divided amongst family and friends. Mary and Joan went to live with Gran Sinclair, Bernard worked for a neighbour, Ted went to Waitara, Hilary lived with a family called Chambers. Joan went on to train as a nurse at Taumarunui Hospital and graduated in 1924. She described her family as 'a wild lot!'.[23]

Charles Jennings Worthington (1878-1942)

Charles Jennings Worthington was the fifth child born to Thomas and Mary Ann. As a child he was stricken with infantile paralysis or poliomyelitis and was paralysed down his right side. An operation on his feet enabled him to walk when he was about 15 years old. His education suffered because of this handicap but he could mentally work out a problem faster than someone with a pen and paper.

During 1909 Charles married Annie Grace Jameson, a spinster with two children. The family lived on a farm north of Auckland at Kawa Kawa and also farmed near Ruapekapeka Pa and at Maromaku. They relied on horses and Annie Grace was an excellent horsewoman. Her horse Jep, a trotter, showed a clean pair of hooves at all corners. Going home one night Jep refused to go the usual way home which was down a gully and across a bridge, so Grace dropped the reins and let him go in the direction he wanted. It was quite dark by the time they arrived home which was of some concern to Charles. The next morning they were called on by a local farmer who informed them that there was a dangerous wild bull on the loose in the area. One fine horse, don't you think![24]

At times the family struggled financially and to supplement their income they dug for kauri gum and sold dressed lamb. A large piece of kauri gum is still treasured by the family. During 1919, Charles, Annie and six of their children moved to Gordon Road, east of Stratford, to take up dairy farming. A large swamp area was drained and a dam built. Charles was very good at choosing the best bulls and a Jersey cow herd was begun. The whole family hand-milked in a slabbed floor cowshed and supplied their produce to nearby Gordon Road creamery. After the creamery closed, cream was transported to the Stratford butter factory.

The children attended Toko School and were active members of sports teams and boys' and girls' agriculture competitions. All the boys served in the armed forces during the Second World War and Snowy served four years in the Middle East.

Charles died on 2 April 1942 aged 62 years and his youngest son, Percy, continued to farm successfully at Gordon Road, steadily increasing stock numbers and production. In 1975, Graeme, youngest son of Percy and Molly Worthington, took over the 80-acre family farm, milking 90 cows in a walk-through cowshed and the following year converted the shed to a herringbone. In 1991 Worthingtons purchased the neighbouring 100-acre Stanford property on Gordon Road and further major developmental work was done. The farm currently allows for 200 Jersey cows to be milked, along with a beef cattle unit. Annie died on 19 November 1972 aged 88 years.[25]

Marianna Katherine Worthington (1881-1947)

Marianna Katherine was a very talented and musical woman who had a lovely contralto voice and played the piano. She sang in operas and often went to Wellington to sing with overseas visitors. She would wear a red gown and looked very regal, especially with her hair dressed. She was a very good looking woman in her youth.[26]

Unfortunately as a young woman she suffered a tragic accident when she hit her head during a fall at a local dance in the Tututawa Hall. She was unconscious for two days and only partially recovered from this accident, requiring care for the rest of her life. She never married. Doctors later declared it a terrible tragedy that she hadn't been taken to a specialist when she had the fall; however, at the time her mother refused to admit that there was anything wrong.

While her mother was still alive Kate was cared for at home and would make butter for pocket money. Later she was taken to a hospital where she was cared for. Marianna's extended family were not kept informed of her whereabouts and she died at Ngawhatu mental hospital in Nelson on 10 November 1947 aged 67 years, of acute cardiac failure, unresolved pneumonia and senile decay. It is believed nobody ever visited her in hospital.

151 Adelaide and Marianna Katherine Worthington.

152   Adelaide and Marianna
Worthington.

Adelaide Worthington (1883-1979)

A tall, slim woman who had a good figure into her nineties, Adelaide was a very upright, prim, egotistical type with no sense of humour. She had very fair skin, blue eyes and wavy hair.

Adelaide married Joseph Jones and went to live on the West Coast of New Zealand's south island. She had some strong, strange religious beliefs such as women not being allowed to wear 'trousers' in her presence! After spending many years in an Auckland Nursing Home, she died on 6 September 1979.

Adelaide bequeathed her estate to various relatives as follows:

Allan Hall, nephew of my late husband $4,000; Doris Hall, niece of my late husband $5,000; Margaret Hall, niece of my late husband $5,000, Jean Burges, niece of my late husband $2,000; Mildred Harris, niece of my late husband $1,000; my nephew, Cecil Worthington $2,000; Eileen Worthington, widow of the late William Worthington $3,000; my great nephew Jack Worthington $1,000 and 109 shares in The Christchurch Press Company Ltd; my great nephew Garth Worthington 101 shares in The Christchurch Press Company Ltd; my great nephew James Watson $2,000 and 30 shares in The Christchurch Press Company Ltd; my great nephew Bernard Watson 130 shares in The Christchurch Press Company Ltd; my niece Edith Watson $2,000; and my niece Felicity Trigg $1,000.

The remainder of estate was divided equally between The Bible Society of New Zealand Incorporated, The Mission to Lepers (N.Z.) and The St John Ambulance Association 'Auckland Centre' Trust Board. She directed that her body be cremated.

Chapter 7

Cousins of Benjamin Jelly Worthington

John Worthington (1716-....)

John Worthington was Benjamin Jelly Worthington's uncle and his father's younger brother by two years. He was a cooper and after his marriage to Mary Fryar on 15 October 1749 in St Mary's Church, Dover, nine children were born to them (see Chart 6). Most of the following information on this branch of the Worthington family was supplied by Ann Facey, Darfield, New Zealand, Lynda Cumming, Kawakawa, New Zealand and David P. Hill, New Zealand, descendants.

William Worthington (1758-1821/8)

William was the fifth child born to John and Mary Worthington and baptised at St Mary's on 22 September 1758. He was a mariner and became a Freeman of Dover by birth on 3 December 1779. During his sea voyages he met Sarah Johnson and they were married at St Thomas' Church, Portsmouth, Hampshire on 4 April 1782. Seven children were born and baptised at St Mary's, Dover. They were: William Worthington (1783-....), Edward (Victor) Worthington (1785-1865), Mary Ann Worthington (1787-....), Susanna Worthington (1789-....), Elizabeth Worthington (1797-....), John Worthington (1800-....), Ann Worthington (1804-1854).

William took an active part in Dover affairs and was on the voters list for Mayor of Dover in 1813. William was either buried 26 August 1821 or 12 August 1828 at St James', Dover. Sarah was buried 26 September 1834 in the same place.

William Worthington (1783-....)

William Worthingtons appear frequently in east Kent records and it was probably the William baptised in 1783 who became a Freeman of Dover by birth on 24 October 1806. The Deal censuses 1841-61 lists William Worthington, who was born in St Mary's parish, Dover about 1784 and his wife Elizabeth who was native of Deal and born about 1796. William was a mariner and the family lived at 15 Princess Street, Deal. In the 1841 census their daughter Mary aged 20 years and born in Kent was a bonnet maker. James Worthington their son aged 14 years, was not born in Kent and William, aged 10 years, was born in Kent.

The Bishops Transcripts for St Leonard's, Deal record the marriage by banns of William Worthington bachelor of the parish to Mary Buttress spinster on 4 October 1804. Witnesses were Wm Kennet, Ann Goodchild and Mary Ann Worthington, his sister. This was William's first marriage as he was a widower when he married Elizabeth May, spinster by banns on 30 December 1814. The marriage was witnessed by James Bowbyes and Edward Foreman.

The Poll of Two Barons to serve in Parliament 1880 lists two William Worthingtons, one a wine merchant in Dover and the other a mariner in Deal. The *Kentish Gazette* newspaper on 20 November 1818 reported that a William Worthington was involved in a smuggling case (spirits) at Deal. On 31 March 1818 a long, detailed newspaper report gave an account of William Worthington and others of Deal and their smuggling activities.

Edward (Victor) Worthington (1785-1865)

Born in Dover on 26 April 1785 and baptised on 22 May 1785 at St Mary's, Edward was the second son of William and Sarah Worthington. He entered the Royal Navy in 1796 under the patronage of his maternal uncle Edmund Johnson, then First Lieutenant of the *Emerald*, and served until about 1810. After leaving the Royal Navy he served on ships some of which visited Calcutta, India for the East India Company.

Edward served on the *Emerald* as a midshipman, able seaman and clerk from 29 January 1796 until 16 January 1801 and was present at the blockade of Cadiz, Alexandria, Malta and Brest. He was at Tenerife with Lord Nelson and assisted in the capture of many of the enemy ships and fitting out of the captured ships at Aboukir. On 17 January 1801 he transferred to the *Achilles* as an able seaman until 1 March when he joined the *Edgar* from 2 March until 22 August 1801. He had followed his uncle and Captain G. Murray from the *Achilles* on to 74-gun HMS *Edgar* in which battleship his uncle was killed at the Battle of Copenhagen in 1801.[1]

Edward Worthington's Naval General Service Medal with Copenhagen Clasp is on display at the Royal Naval Museum at Portsmouth.

His next ship and position was on the *London* as a midshipman from 23 August 1801 until 31 January 1802. He joined the *Albatross* as a midshipman 9 November 1803 after passing his lieutenant exams in February 1802.[2] If a position of rank was not available to an eligible seaman, he accepted a lesser rank until one was available.

Edward was paid off on the Peace of Amiens but joined *Arrogant* and *Albatross* in India. He was present at the capture of the Isle of France (Mauritius) and commanded two of the Colonial government vessels there. After leaving the Navy he settled in Mauritius where he was Captain of Vessels and Trade at Port Louis. *The East India Register and Directory* lists him from 1831 until 1837 as a mariner except for the years 1834 and 1835 when he was

153 Polymnie Worthington, née Durup and Emma Worthington.

154 Captain Edward Worthington (1785-1865).   **155** Polymnie Worthington, née Durup.

commander of the ship *Ann*. He was a master mariner and merchant at Port Louis and through his business expertise became a wealthy stockholder and a man of 'independent means'.

Edward married Laurence Louise Polymnie Durup, known as Polymnie, after banns on Saturday afternoon 8 August 1840 at Port Louis, Mauritius. The marriage was witnessed by Robert Frith, Edouard Hugon, Jules Deschambeaux and Andre Labauve d'Arifat. This event took place after the births of six children, which Edward legally acknowledged as his own;[3] four more children were born after this date. The children were: Louise Anne Felicie Worthington (1829-1915), Victorine Leonide Mary Worthington (1831-....), Victor William Edward Worthington (1833-64), Louis Leonard Worthington (1834-....), William Worthington (1837-....), Sarah Worthington (1838-....), Clara Worthington (1840-....), Robert Worthington (1844-1920), John Worthington (1846-1928), Emma Worthington (1853-....).

Polymnie was born in the Colony of Mauritius on 28 January 1813, the eldest natural daughter of Laurence Melanie Victorine Durup who was deceased by 1840. She is believed to have been related to a noted wealthy French family and is known to have had a brother, Jean Leonard Victor Deveaux, and sisters Eucharis Deschambeaux, who died 18 October 1871 at Pondicherry, India and Juliette Jersey who died before 1876.

About the year 1843 the family moved to 4 rue Saint-Etienne, Tours, France where they lived until after 1846 when they moved again to Guernsey in the Channel

Islands. In 1853 Edward was described as a retired master mariner. Captain Worthington spoke nine languages, his daughter Louise Anne could speak six and Polymnie could only speak French. According to Guernsey directories Captain Worthington and family were living at Couture in 1859, Rozel Road 1862 and 10 Union Street 1865. There is information that Edward lived at Rozel House, Rozel Road but this could have been Rozel Terrace off Mt Durand Road. Rozel House was built by Thomas Carey in 1804 and was in the possession of Thomas Godfrey Carey at the time of Edward's death in 1865. He was probably a guest or a tenant of Carey's in 1862.

Edward Worthington died at 10 Union Street, Newtown, St Peter Port, Guernsey on 22 October 1865[4] aged 80 years. 'Mrs Worthington' was living at 10 Union Street in 1866. Edward's last will and testament bequeathed all his estate and effects with the exception of his household property to Joseph Collings Esquire of Grange Road, St Peter Port, Victor Deveaux of St Jacques, Guernsey, gentleman and William Smith late of Stow Villa, Bath, gentleman now residing at 3 College Terrace, Guernsey. His estate was to be converted into cash and be invested in securities of the Government of Great Britain, or the Government of the East Indies or in Railway Debentures or Preference Shares in the Railways of Great Britain. The interest and dividends and proceeds arising from these investments was to be paid to his wife, Polymnie Worthington.

The daughters still unmarried at the time of his decease were Mary, Sarah, Clara and Emma Worthington. Emma later married James J. Thomas and had a son, Edward S. Thomas, born 1880 at Westbury on Trym, Bristol. Edward's daughter, Louise Ann(e), was a Professor of the French Language and is believed to have corrected Victor Hugo's manuscripts. Victor Hugo lived in Guernsey from 1855 until 1870 when he returned to France. He wrote some of his most famous poetry and novels while living at Hauteville House in St Peter Port. It is generally thought that

156 Louise Anne Felicie Worthington photographed at Guernsey.

157 Clara Worthington.

158 Sarah Worthington.

Hugo's mistress, Juliette Drouet, read and corrected all his manuscripts. Louise Ann, or Anne as she was known, married Anthony Isemonger, a bailiff's clerk of St James Place, St Jacques, St Peter Port, Guernsey. They had three children: Anthony Isemonger born 9 August 1858 Guernsey who married Rebecca Hazard 1887 at Wellington, New Zealand. He served in the Permanent Militia and was a Sergeant in the New Zealand Police Force. He died 4 September 1920 Auckland, New Zealand. Florence Emily Isemonger born 8 March 1860 Guernsey was a musician who was unmarried and died 22 May 1914 Guernsey; and Walter Leonard Isemonger born 20 April 1862 Guernsey served in the U.S. Navy and died 1906 in Chicago, United States of America.

Anthony Isemonger was born on 21 October 1831 at Guernsey, the son of Anthony Isemonger and Isat Isemonger, née Scadding. He died on 5 February 1906 aged 74 years at 2 George Place, Union Street, St Peter Port. Louise Anne Felicie Isemonger died on 3 March 1915 at St Martin's, Guernsey aged 85 years.

Victor William Edward Worthington (1833-1864)

Born 26 February 1833, the son of Edward and Polymnie Worthington at Port Louis, Victor married Amanda, surname unknown. He is probably the 'E. Worthington' who appears in 1853 as a volunteer in the Bengal Marine establishment 30 August 1849 and in 1860 as mate in H.M. Bengal Pilot Service, India. He drowned in the Hooghli River, India on 5 October 1864 and a tablet was erected by a number of his brother officers, 'In memory of Edward Victor Worthington, H.M. Bengal Pilot Service, who unfortunately lost his life by drowning from the ship *Ally* during the cyclone of 5 October 1864. Aged 31 years.'

Louis Leonard Worthington (1834-....)

Louis was born at Port Louis on 25 August 1834, the third son of Edward and Polymnie Worthington. He was merchant seaman–third mate and in 1853 was cited for bravery during the wreck of the barque *Meridian* of London off the island of Amsterdam. The Port Louis newspaper reported the events surrounding the wreck when the *Meridian* on a voyage from London to Sydney with 79 passengers on board struck a rock on the night of 24 August 1853 and began to sink. After 12 days on the rugged and almost perpendicular cliffs of the island the crew and passengers were rescued by an American whaling ship and conveyed to Mauritius, with the exception of two, who with the captain had been drowned. Leonard, as he was known, was awarded a gold medal plus £50 for an outfit by the Chamber of Commerce. On his return to England five years later he was presented with another gold medal by the Duke of Marlborough. Leonard passed his Master's Certificate Exam during 1860 in London.

Robert Worthington (1844-1920)

The eighth child of Edward and Polymnie Worthington, Robert was born 12 February 1844 at Tours, France. He was educated at Elizabeth College, Guernsey. On 26 November 1861 he and his brother John Worthington arrived as second-class passengers at Port Chalmers, Dunedin, New Zealand on board the 522-ton ship *Derwentwater* which had sailed from London.

Robert was a farmer and married Catherine, known as Kate, Jaggar at St Mary's Church, Timaru on 24 June 1869. Catherine was a school teacher and the daughter of the headmaster of Timaru Public School. She began teaching at Pleasant Point School in 1868 when she was 17 years of age. Robert became a member of the first Pleasant Point School committee which dated from 1870. Robert and Catherine Worthington had 11 children: Anthony Henry Devaux Worthington (1870-1954), Leonard Edward John Worthington (1872-1948), Laurence Arthur Robert Worthington (1873-1936), Herbert William Jaggar Worthington (1875), Bertha Polymnie Worthington (1875-1943), Sydney Arthur Worthington (1877), Catherine Edith Worthington (1879-82), Maude Annie Worthington (1880-2), Lily Evelyn Worthington (1881), Claude Turnbull Worthington (1883-1930), Violet Worthington (1887).

Robert Worthington died at Christchurch on 7 August 1920 aged 76 years. He was buried on 9 August 1920 in Waimairi Cemetery.

John Worthington (1846-1928)

Born in Tours, France on 4 August 1846, son of Edward and Polymnie Worthington, John was educated at Elizabeth College, Guernsey. He spoke fluent French, being bilingual from childhood. Enid Hawker remarked,

> I can remember him saying that when he first attended Elizabeth College he was asked if he had learnt French and thinking that the Master meant French as a subject, he said 'No'. Later in class he prompted a boy who was having difficulty with his French lesson and the Master brought him out in front of the class calling him a liar— he said he hated school after that.

John arrived in New Zealand on board the *Derwentwater* with his brother Robert, 26 November 1861. Enid Hawker says that,

> their father sent them to New Zealand to farm as some of the older sons had been lost at sea. Captain Edward Worthington had decided not to allow Robert and John to join the Navy and sent them with guardian to New Zealand where the guardian was to buy them farms. A man on the ship persuaded Robert and John to give their guardian the slip and buy land at Pleasant Point. This was a grave mistake for the land at Pleasant Point was poor and they were deprived of further money from their father.

John is recorded between 1876-8 as having a freehold section number 16803 at Pleasant Point. In 1879 it had 12 sheep and by 1881 20 sheep. The Return of Freeholders of New Zealand records him as owning 82 acres worth £806.

John met Dorothea Caroline Wilhemina Bremer who lived in George Street, Dunedin. He thought nothing of walking from Pleasant Point to Dunedin to see his future bride, a distance of many miles. They were married at her father, Jacob Bremer's house in Dunedin on 3 August 1881 and had four children: Minnie Mary Polymnie (May) Worthington (1882-1950), Lily Henrietta Anne Worthington (1883-1973), Edward Victor Worthington (1887-1918), Mary Enid Worthington (adopted) (1906-84).

John and Minnie lived in a 10-bedroom, two-storey house at 62 Tengawi Road, Pleasant Point which they probably rented. Enid said that 'life was hard at Pleasant Point for John and Minnie who had no farm experience and had both been used to servants. When there was a slump in farming John took on any work available such

159   Left to right: Mary Enid Worthington, Annie Bremer, Dorothea Caroline Wilhelmina Worthington née Bremer, Minnie May Worthington, John Worthington.

as driving sheep and acting as poundkeeper and Minnie taught music at the local Waitohi School.'

John went back to Guernsey for a holiday, but when this was is not clear. After Minnie died in 1926 he seemed to age and during the Christmas holidays of 1927 he fell and badly sprained his leg. He did not recover and died several months later on 22 April 1928 at his residence 'Willowbank', 231 Waimakariri Road, Harewood, Christchurch. He was in his 82nd year when he was buried at St James' churchyard, Harewood Cemetery in front of the large Wellingtonia tree. It was his express wish that he have no headstone, just the tree, but Edgar Bray, descendant of John Worthington (1846-1928), has now put a headstone there.

Mary Ann Worthington (1787-....)

Mary Ann was the third child born on 25 January 1787 to William and Sarah Worthington. She was baptised at St Mary, Dover on 18 February 1787.

On 4 February 1812 she married Thomas White at St James' Church of England, Dover. Witnesses to this event were Ann Holmes and Susanna Worthington, her sister.

Mary Ann White left a will at the time she died which mentions her sister, Elizabeth Cole of London; her nieces Mary-Ann Cole of London, Mary Ann Norman of Dover and Esther Longley of Dover; great-niece Mary Ann Norman of Dover and nephew Samuel Cole.

Hythe Worthingtons

Hythe is a parish, borough and one of the Cinque Ports situated 33 miles from Maidstone and 67 miles from London. It is probable that a branch of the Dover Worthingtons moved to live in this area as several records can be found for them.

The East Kent Poll Book records William Worthington of Elm Terrace, Hythe and of East Street, Hythe 1868. Joseph Worthington married Sarah Street by licence at Hythe on 21 January 1820 and this William may be one of his children. So may the John Worthington aged 15 years, agricultural labourer who was found with Mary Steel and family at Windmill Row, Hythe in the 1841 Census.

William Worthington, wheelwright, aged 20 years was found to be living at Hardways End, Hythe in 1841 with Jesse Wanstall, a 35-year-old carpenter and his family. Next door was 25-year-old William Evenden who was a wheelwright. William Worthington was born in Hythe about 1821 and in 1871 was a coachbuilder living with his wife Blanche Worthington on The Avenue, Hythe. Blanche was born at Boughton under Blean about 1820.

William and Blanche Worthington baptised a daughter, Elizabeth at Hythe on 7 January 1844. William was described as a wheelwright at that time. By 1871 Elizabeth had either died or left home as the 1871 census records six other children who were all born in Hythe: Robert a coach painter aged 25 years, Jane aged 23 years, William an apprentice coach builder aged 16 years, Emeline aged 13 years, Lucy aged 11 years and Frederick aged seven years. The 1881 census recorded the family at Tanners Hill, Saltwood, Hythe.

Worthington Brothers, coachbuilders, painters and writers could be found at East Street, Hythe in 1902.[5] They were first-class coachbuilders and built a coach for the Prince of Siam. The Worthington coach building business continued until about the beginning of the First World War when they built an early motor car called the 'Worthington Flyer'. It was described in *Motor Cycling* as

A Cycle-Car with Flat Belt-Drive—First Illustrated Description of the Worthington Duocar. A 4½ inch flat belt running on large pulleys is a feature of the transmission of the Worthington four-wheeled cycle-car built by Worthington Bros., Ltd., East Street, Hythe, Kent. By means of the system of belt drive and free wheel clutches in the back hubs, the need for a differential is done away with. The machine has gears of 4½ to 1 and 10 to 1, which have been proved in tests to be capable of giving a high speed and making the machine a good hill climber. The engine is an 8 h.p. J.A.P., which is supplied with gas by a J.A.P. automatic carburettor and cooled by a fan. Lubrication is through an automatic sight feed, and there is an auxiliary hand pump on the dashboard. Transmission is by chain from the engine to the countershaft, and thence by the flat belt mentioned. A hand lever enables the belt to be tightened when running if required. The clutch is of the multiple-disc type. Steering is by worm and sector, and the 16 in. wheel is mounted on a well raked pillar. Band brakes on the back hubs are operated by pedal, while a side lever operates shoe brakes on the back wheels.

The frame of the Worthington cycle-car is of armoured ash, and is carried on three-quarter elliptic springs in front and behind. The two-seater body with scuttle dash

A CYCLE-CAR WITH FLAT BELT-DRIVE.
First Illustrated Description of the Worthington Duocar.

A 4½ in. flat belt running on large pulleys is a feature of the transmission of the Worthington four-wheeled cycle-car, built by Worthington Bros., Ltd., East Street, Hythe, Kent. By means of the system of belt drive and free wheel clutches in the back hubs, the need for a differential is done away with. The machine has gears of 4½ to 1 and 10 to 1, which have been proved in test to be capable of giving a high speed and making the machine a good hill-climber. The engine is an 8 h.p. J.A.P., which is supplied with gas by a J.A.P. automatic carburetter and cooled by a fan.

Lubrication is through an automatic sight feed, and there is an auxiliary hand pump on the dashboard. Transmission is by chain from the engine to the countershaft, and thence by the flat belt mentioned. A hand lever enables the belt to be tightened when running if required. The clutch is of the multiple-disc type. Steering is by worm and sector, and the 16 in. wheel is mounted on a well-raked pillar. Band brakes on the back hubs are operated by a pedal, while a side lever operates shoe brakes on the back wheels.

The frame of the Worthington cycle-car is of armoured ash, and is carried on three-quarter elliptic springs in front and behind. The two-seater body with scuttle dash gives plenty of leg room, and there is ample accommodation for luggage on the tool locker at the rear. Severe tests have been imposed on the Worthington, and it has survived them successfully.

The weight is approximately 4½ cwt., the wheelbase is 8 ft., and the price 95 guineas.

A side view of the Worthington cycle-car. - It is fitted with an 8 h.p. J.A.P. engine which is fan-cooled.

160   Advertisement for Worthington Bros., Carriages, 1902.

161   Worthington Bros., Duocar in *Motor Cycling*, 18 June 1912.

gives plenty of leg room, and there is ample accommodation for luggage on the tool locker at the rear. Severe tests have been imposed on the Worthington and it has survived successfully. The weight is approximately 4½ cwt., the wheelbase is 8 ft., and the price 98 guineas.[6]

During the First World War Robert Worthington had a heart attack in a bus and died. He had a son, Leslie Worthington. William Worthington committed suicide on the Hythe railway line after learning that his eldest son was killed early in the First World War. William's son, Donald Worthington died during the early 1980s and left a widow living at Hythe. The youngest son, Frederick Worthington was a coach painter and died about 1946. His daughter, Miss Worthington, was living at Hythe in 1983. His son was apprenticed as carpenter and joiner and left Hythe many years ago.[7]

Chapter 8

Related Families

The Jelly Family

Henry Jelly (*c.*1700-1755)

Henry Jelly was born in the parish of St Lawrence, Thanet, of unknown parents, around the turn of the century. The earliest reference to Jellys in Dover St Mary's parish records was the marriage of Wyllyam Jellye to Annys Wiles on 26 September 1580. Another early record was the baptism of Richard, son of Robert and Ann Jelly, on 4 June 1682 and William, son of William and Aphry Jelly, on 15 August 1689 both at Dover St Mary's. There were Jellys in east Kent at least a hundred years earlier as Henry Jeely [*sic*], son of John, was baptised at Goodnestone by Sandwich on 6 December 1564.

Henry was a bachelor on 2 July 1722 when he married Aphra [*sic*] Rouse, spinster daughter of William and Affry Rouse[1] at St Mary's, Dover, by licence. The marriage

Jelly Descendants Chart

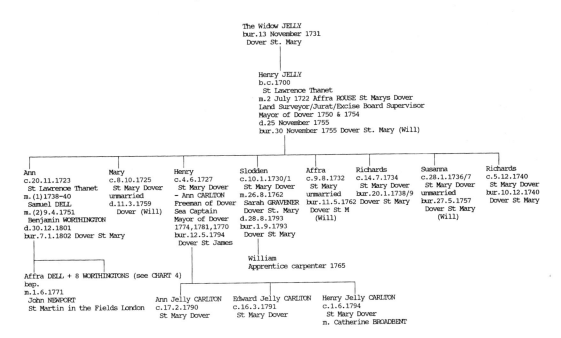

*N*overint *Universi per præsentes*, Nos *Henricum Jelley S. Laurantij in Insula Tanat & Com Cant Gen & Richum Love City Cant Barber Chirurgeon to nie firmæ obligari Rev.mo in X̃po Patri ac Dno Dno Gulmo providentia Dia Cant Archiepo totuj Angliæ Primati & Metropano*

in *Ducentij* libris bonâ & legalis Monetæ Magnæ Britanniæ, *solvend'* eidem *Rev.mo Patri* aut *suo certo* Attornato, Executoribus, Administratoribus, vel *Assignatis suis* : *Ad quam quidem solutionem bene & fideliter faciend'* Obligamus nos & *utrumque nostrum per se pro toto & in solido*, Hæredes, Executores, & Administratores *nostros firmiter per præsentes*. *Sigillis nostris Sigillat'* Dat' *8.vo die Junij*

Anno Dni 1722

*T*HE Condition of this Obligation is such, That if there shall not hereafter appear any Lawful Lett or Impediment, by reason of any Pre-contract, Consanguinity, Affinity, or any other just Cause whatsoever ; But that *y.e above Pomidon Henry Jelley Batch: aged 25 years & Affra Rouse of S.t Mary in Dover Spinster aged 25 years*

may Lawfully Marry together ; And that there is not any Suit depending before any Judge Ecclesiastical or Civil, for, or concerning any such Pre-contract ; And that the Consent of the Parents, or others the Governors of the said Parties be thereunto first had and obtained ; And that they cause their said Marriage to be openly solemnized in the face of the Parish-Church of *in y.e Licence specified* between the Hours of Eight and Twelve of the Clock in the Forenoon ; And do and shall save harmless, and keep indemnified the above-named *Archbyshop his Comisary or* his Surrogates, and all other his Officers, and Successors in Office, for and concerning the Premises ; That Then this Obligation to be Void and of none Effect, or else to remain in full Force and Virtue.

Henry Jelley

Signat' Sigillat' & Deliberat'
in præsentia

Jo: Goatley N. Pub.   *Rich.d Love*

162   Marriage licence for Henry Jelly and Aphra Rouse

licence allegation dated 8 June 1722 stated that this event could also take place in the parishes of St James or Charlton.

Henry and Affra Jelly had eight known children. The eldest, Ann, was baptised on 20 November 1723 in the parish of St Lawrence, Thanet. She was the only one of four daughters to marry. Her first husband was Samuel Dell, and after his death she married Benjamin Worthington.[2]

Henry and Affra's third child, Henry junior, was baptised on 4 June 1727 at St Mary's. He was a Freeman of Dover and a Mariner. Henry was Captain of the Customs cutter *Tartar* in the period immediately prior to his nephew, Benjamin Jelly Worthington. He retired from the Customs Service in 1784 due to ill health and was presented with a silver cup in appreciation of his services. He became 211th Mayor of Dover in 1774, was elected again during 1781 and was elected for a third period of office in 1790. In 1790 the *Kentish Gazette* reported that 'Henry Jelly Esq. was chosen Mayor for the ensuing year'.[3] (The same paper had been used in 1788 to advertise the sale of his house, see illustration 56.) On 12 July 1792 and 8 October 1793 he presided with his colleagues at the Court of Lodemanage of the Cinque Ports and was described as 'Henry Jelly, Esquire Captain of Archcliffe Fort'.[4] Archcliffe Fort had been built by Henry VIII for the military as part of the defence of Dover.

Henry junior, although unmarried, appears to have been the father of three children born to Ann Carlton and baptised in St Mary's, Dover: Ann Jelly Carlton, 17 February 1790; Henry Jelly Carlton, 16 March 1791; and Edward Jelly Carlton, 1 June 1794. On 9 June 1819 Henry George Carlton was baptised at St Mary's, Dover, son of Henry Jelly Carlton and Catherine Jelly, née Broadbent, his wife. Henry Jelly, a Jurat of Dover, was buried at St James's, Dover, 12 May 1794.

Henry and Affra's second son, Slodden Jelly, was baptised on 10 January 1730/1 at St Mary's, Dover, and married Sarah Gravener by licence at the same church on 26 August 1762. William Jelly, son of Slodden Jelly, gentleman, was apprenticed for seven years to John Gibson, a Master Carpenter of Dover, on 5 September 1765 for a fee of £15.[5] Slodden died on 28 August 1793 aged 62 years and was buried on 1 September in the altar tomb near the east door of St Mary's Church.[6]

Of their daughters, Mary was baptised on 8 October 1725, Affra on 9 August 1732 and Susanna(h) Jelly on 28 January 1736/7. They all remained spinsters and all left wills. Mary Jelly died on 11 March 1759, Susanna, on 27 May 1757 and Affra, who was buried with her two sisters, her parents and members of the Rouse and Worthington families in the altar tomb near the east door of St Mary's Church, on 11 May 1762.[7] All three girls left their estates to their siblings.

After Henry senior's return from sea, where he 'had been abroad up the Straights for six years and two months',[8] he was the land surveyor of the Dover Customs House. The building of Castle Jetty was commenced during his first mayoralty in 1750.[9] A boundary stone on the front of a house in Athol Terrace bears the Coat of Arms of Dover and underneath 'HJ'. Some local historians believe that Henry Jelly made efforts to change some of the boundaries in Dover. To date no documentation has been found to support this.

Henry senior was appointed Common Councilman by a majority of votes at the Dover Assembly, being sworn in on 8 May 1754.[10] In 1754 he was the occupier of a house owned by Place Green of Dover.[11] In 1750 he became the 194th Mayor of Dover and was re-elected again by a majority of votes of assembly and sworn in on

8 May 1754.[12] The Corporation or Town Council consisted of a Mayor and 12 Jurats. A Common Council of 37 Freemen was elected and from this a Mayor was chosen for a term of one year. The Mayor chose his own Jurats who were responsible for apprenticing poor children, orphans and blue coat boys to tradespeople of Dover. From the medieval period a Freeman who was chosen as Mayor by the Council but turned down the office was punished by the demolition of his house.[13] After Henry's death in 1755, Henry Jelly junior was recommended to succeed him by the Corporation, but this was objected to by the Treasury–'that the son could not succeed the father'. Michael Russell was elected by the Corporation and sworn in as Mayor on 2 February 1756.[14]

The Jelly family were comfortable financially and owned property in Dover. In the Weald, brick town houses were virtually unknown, but new houses in north and east Kent were increasingly being built with this material during the 17th and 18th centuries.[15] The 'For Sale' advertisement of a 'modern, genteel and commodious dwelling house' placed on page one of the *Kentish Gazette* between 7-11 March 1788 supports this assumption of position and wealth.

Affra Jelly predeceased her husband and was buried on 23 August 1754. Henry died a little over a year later on 25 November 1755 and left a will leaving property in Dover to his family.[16] He was buried with his wife and children in the altar tomb in St Mary's churchyard on 30 November 1755.[17] Also interred in the family tomb are the remains of William Richard Jelly and John Slodden Jelly.

An extract from the Excise Board minute books, dated Tuesday 2 December 1755, shows that 'Samuel P. Warren, Supervisor of Sandwich District, is appointed

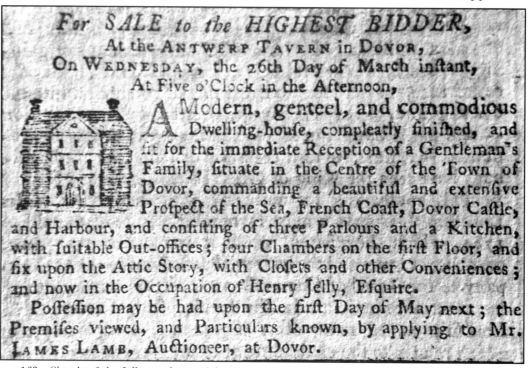

163 Sketch of the Jelly residence. Advertisement from the *Kentish Gazette*, 7-11 March 1788.

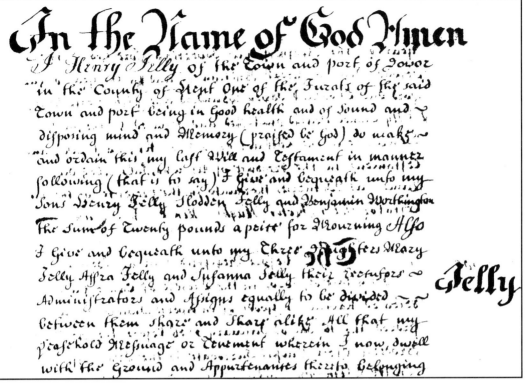

164 Will of Henry Jelly.

to replace Henry Jelly, Senior, deceased, as the Supervisor for Exciseable imported Liquors at the Port of Dover'.

Jelly Coat of Arms

The Kent Family History Society's microfiche publication of *St James's Dover Additional Monumental Inscriptions* drew my attention to the Jelly Coat of Arms. The Coats of Arms listed in this publication have been gathered from Rev. John Lyon's *Dover*, published in 1813, and Douglas Welby's *Dover's Tidy Ruin*, published in 1976. A letter to P. Ll. Gwynn-Jones, Lancaster Herald at the College of Arms, requesting some research into their official records drew the response: 'I find no trace of any Armorial Bearings ever having been granted or confirmed to anyone of the surname of Jelly. At the same time I do not find that any Jelly pedigrees have ever been registered here.'

Searches at the College of Arms were extended beyond official records to private papers and pedigrees and once more nothing was found. They reported that:

Only one Shield of Arms on the official registers bore similarity to the Arms attributed to the Jellys. These same Arms were borne and used by a Mediaeval family of Ashbroke and may be blazoned as:−Vair argent and sable a chevron gules. This family who would seem to have become extinct in the male line during the fourteenth century, when one Christiana alias Felicia, sister and heir of Thomas Ashbroke of Kinsbury in the County of Warwick, married one John de Flandres. The Arms of

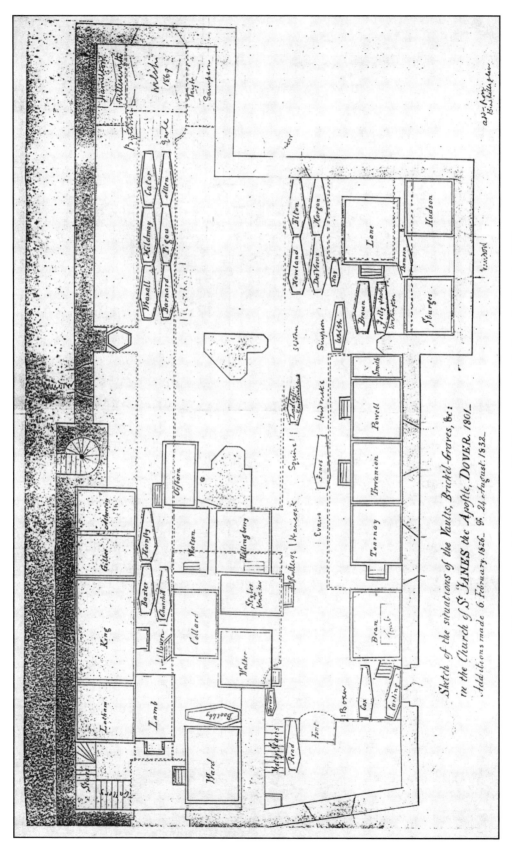

165 Positions of the vaults and bricked graves in St James's Church, 1801.

Ashbroke were subsequently quartered by her de Flandres descendants. The diagram of Arms is weak in indicating tinctures. Had a chevron gules (i.e. red) been intended this might have been indicated by hatching with small vertical lines. As the chevron is left clear of any hatching, it may well be argent or white.

Unofficial works of reference list a second Coat of Arms where the chevron is white and not red as is the case with the Arms of Ashbroke. These second Arms are attributed to a family of Apsey. The full Armorial Bearings listed for such a family may be blazoned as:- Vair a chevron argent; and for the Crest:- A dove with an olive branch in its beak volant over water proper. The Armorial Bearings of Apsey found in unofficial armories first make their appearance therein towards the end of the eighteenth century. There was a gentry family of Apsey established in Ely during the eighteenth and early nineteenth centuries. It is possible that this is the family who made use of the Armorial Bearings in question.

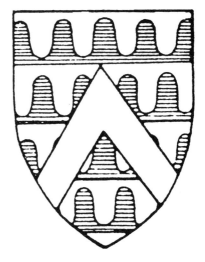

166 Jelly shield.

No apparent relationship has been found between the Jelly and Ashbroke or Apsey families. Therefore we can assume that the Arms were either unofficially adopted by the Jelly family or have been erroneously attributed to them.

The Collins Family

Elizabeth Collins (1768-1845)

Elizabeth Collins was baptised at St Mary's, Dover, on 10 September 1768, the third child of Knight Knight Collins, brewer, and Elizabeth Collins formerly Novice.

Her eldest brother, William Collins, was baptised on 22 April 1764 at St Mary's. During 1778 William Collings [*sic*] was apprenticed at the age of 14 years to his father Knight Collings of Dover, brewer.[18] He married Ann Brown and they do not appear to have had any children. William was buried on 31 July 1831[19] at the old cemetery of St James's, Dover, and a plaque commemorates this event:

> Beneath this Tomb are interred the remains of Mr William Collins who departed this life 31 July 1831 aged 67 years. Also of Ann Collins relict of the above who departed this life 12 January 1839 aged 74 years. Also of Mary Ann Brown niece of the above who departed this life 17 November 1854 aged 56 years.

Old St James's Church

Pigot's Directory of 1839 records under Dover 'Gentry, Nobility - Mrs Collins, Biggin Street, Dover'. Under 'Gentry and Clergy' in the Folkestone section of the directory appears 'William Knight Collins, Esq., Prospect House' and this could have been a grandson.

Elizabeth's other brother, Thomas Collins, was named after his grandfather Thomas Collins, and baptised on 27 April 1766 at St Mary's. He was aged 50 years when he

The Collins Family Chart

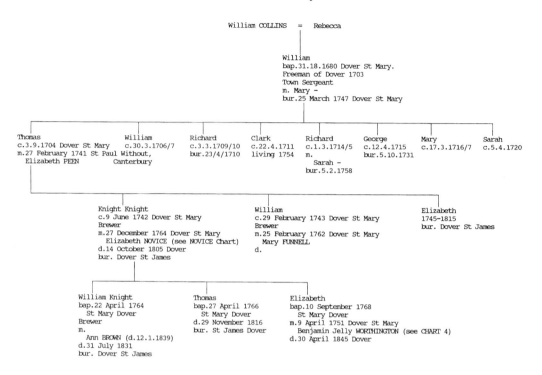

William COLLINS = Rebecca

William
bap.31.18.1680 Dover St Mary.
Freeman of Dover 1703
Town Sergeant
m. Mary -
bur.25 March 1747 Dover St Mary

Thomas
c.3.9.1704 Dover St Mary
m.27 February 1741 St Paul Without,
  Elizabeth PEEN   Canterbury

William
c.30.3.1706/7

Richard
c.3.3.1709/10
bur.23/4/1710

Clark
c.22.4.1711
living 1754

Richard
c.1.3.1714/5
m.
  Sarah -
bur.5.2.1758

George
c.12.4.1715
bur.5.10.1731

Mary
c.17.3.1716/7

Sarah
c.5.4.1720

Knight Knight
c.9 June 1742 Dover St Mary
Brewer
m.27 December 1764 Dover St Mary
  Elizabeth NOVICE (see NOVICE Chart)
d.14 October 1805 Dover
bur. Dover St James

William
c.29 February 1743 Dover St Mary
Brewer
m.25 February 1762 Dover St Mary
  Mary FUNNELL
d.

Elizabeth
1745-1815
bur. Dover St James

William Knight
bap.22 April 1764
  St Mary Dover
Brewer
m.
  Ann BROWN (d.12.1.1839)
d.31 July 1831
bur. Dover St James

Thomas
bap.27 April 1766
  St Mary Dover
d.29 November 1816
bur. St James Dover

Elizabeth
bap.10 September 1768
  St Mary Dover
m.9 April 1751 Dover St Mary
  Benjamin Jelly WORTHINGTON (see CHART 4)
d.30 April 1845 Dover

was buried with his parents on 29 November 1816 at St James's, Dover. He does not appear to have married.

Knight Knight Collins (1740-1805)

Knight Knight Collins was born in 1740 and baptised on 9 June 1742 at Dover St Mary's, the son of Thomas Collins and Elizabeth Collins, née Peen. He married Elizabeth Novice, daughter of Thomas and Elizabeth Novice, on 27 December 1764 at St Mary's witnessed by Jonathan Finnis and Thomas Peen, both relatives. When Knight Collins died he was a man of substantial property and investments. His will left his estate to his wife Elizabeth Collins, his two sons, daughter Elizabeth Worthington and son-in-law Benjamin Jelly Worthington. He also left annuities to the Worthington grandchildren.[20] A plaque at the old cemetery of St James's reads:

> Here are deposited the remains of Mr Knight Collins of this town, Brewer, who departed this life 14 October 1805 aged 63 years. Also of Elizabeth Collins relict of the above who departed this life 16 January 1813 aged 70 years. Also of Thomas Collins son of the above who departed this life 29 November 1816 aged 50 years.

Thomas Collins (1710-....)

Kentish marriage licences show that a licence was issued on 27 November 1741 to Thomas Collins, a bachelor aged 30 years and Elizabeth Peen, a spinster aged 26 years, both parties being of St Mary the Virgin, Dover. Elizabeth Pean [*sic*] was baptised at St James the Apostle, Dover, on 2 November 1715. She was the daughter of William Peen and Mary Peen, née Knight, who were married on 12 January 1714/5 at Dover St Mary's.

William Collins (1680-1747)

William is believed to have been baptised on 31 October 1680, the son of William and Rebecca Collins. He became a Freeman of Dover by birth in 1703. About this

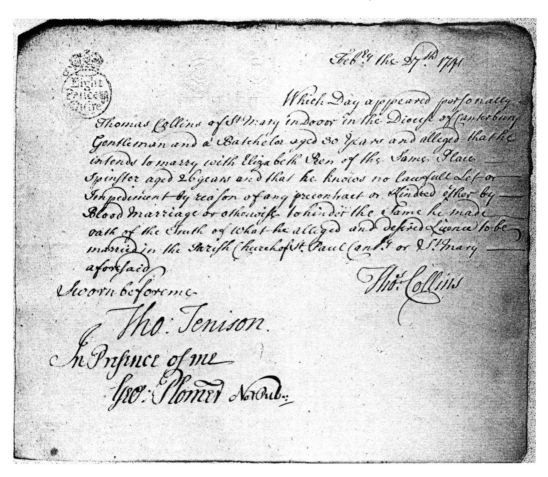

167 Marriage licence for Thomas Collins and Elizabeth Peen, 1741-2.

time he married Mary (surname unknown) and their first child, Thomas, was baptised on 3 September 1704 at Dover St Mary's.

William was the Town Sergeant and he and Mary had several other children who were all baptised at Dover St Mary's: William on 30 March 1706/7; Richard on 3 March 1709/10, who was buried on 23 April 1710; Clark on 22 April 1711 (he most probably had a son by the same name as a Clark Collins was apprenticed to Richard Baker of Dover, tinplate worker, during 1763 for a fee of £20[21] and occupied a house in 1754 in Dover, freehold owned by Thomas Elgar of Dover[22]); Richard on 1 March 1713/4 who married Sarah–she was buried with their daughter Mary on 28 September 1746 followed by her husband on 5 February 1758; George on 12 April 1715, who was buried on 5 October 1731; Mary on 17 March 1716/7; Sarah on 5 April 1720.

William was one of five Churchwardens and Overseers of the Poor of the parish of St Mary's, responsible amongst other things for organising the apprenticeship of poor children with consent of Her Majesty's Justices of the Peace. By indenture dated 22 June 1710 'Henry Simms aged 10 years in February next, a poor child of the said parish, apprenticed to John Joll of Dover, cordwainer until the said Henry Simms attain his full age of one and twenty years'.[23]

Coat of Arms

168   Collins family shield and crest.

The Collins family inherited a Coat of Arms. The Armorial Bearings were established by Robert Cooke, Clarenceux King of Arms, in 1589 to John Collins of Barneshill. There would also seem to have been an extension of limitation to cover not only John Collins and his descendants, but also the descendants of his half-brother Thomas Collins of Offwell in the same county of Devon. These same Armorial Bearings may be blazoned as: Azure three firebrands gold enflamed proper; and for the Crest: a cubit arm proper grasping a firebrand gold enflamed proper.

The Visitations of the County of Devon, carried out by the Heralds in 1620, produced two pedigrees which incorporated the above mentioned persons; these pedigrees were subsequently reproduced in Vivian's *Visitations of Devon*, a copy of which is shown.

Thomas Collin [*sic*], son of Thomas, was found to have been baptised on 10 April 1603 at Dover St Mary's. Another early Dover Collins record is that of William Collins, a postman, who was buried on 25 July 1623 at St Mary's. John Collins was also buried there on 19 February 1681.

Amongst marriages found in Dover pre-1700 was that of Elizabeth Collins to Stephen Cassell, on 3 November 1692 at St Mary's.

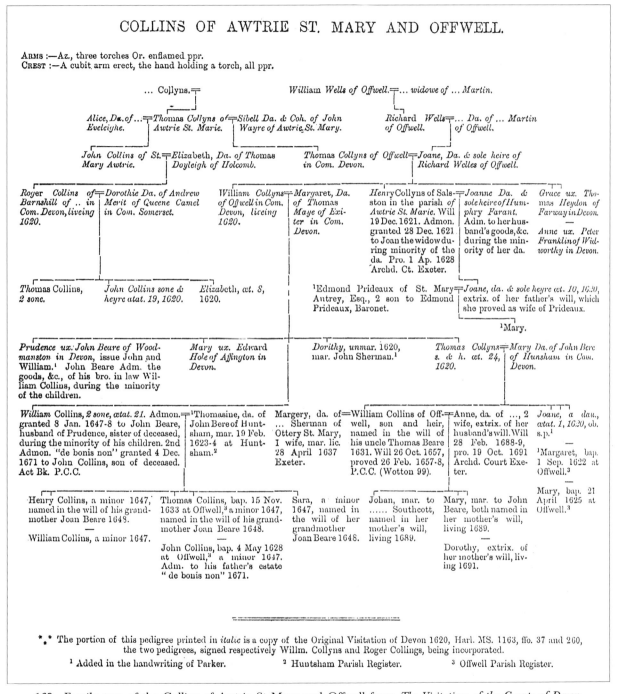

COLLINS OF AWTRIE ST. MARY AND OFFWELL.

ARMS :—Az., three torches Or. enflamed ppr.
CREST :—A cubit arm erect, the hand holding a torch, all ppr.

... Collyns.

William Wells of Offwell.═ ... widowe of ... Martin.

Alice, Da. of ...═Thomas Collyns of═Sibell Da. & Coh. of John
Eveleiyhe.   Awtrie St. Marie.   Wayre of Awtrie St. Mary.

Richard Wells═ ... Da. of ... Martin
of Offwell.   of Offwell.

John Collins of St.═Elizabeth, Da. of Thomas
Mary Awtrie.   Doyleigh of Holcomb.

Thomas Collyns of Offwell═Joane, Da. & sole heire of
in Com. Devon.   Richard Welles of Offwell.

Roger Collins of═Dorothie Da. of Andrew
Barnshill of .. in   Merit of Queene Camel
Com. Devon, liveing in Com. Somerset.
1620.

William Collyns═Margaret, Da.
of Offwell in Com. of Thomas
Devon, liveing   Maye of Exi-
1620.   ter in Com.
*   Devon.*

Henry Collyns of Sals-═Joanne Da. &
ston in the parish of   sole heire of Hum-
Awtrie St. Marie. Will phry Farant.
19 Dec. 1621. Admon.   Adm. to her hus-
granted 28 Dec. 1621   band's goods, &c.
to Joan the widow du-   during the min-
ring minority of the   ority of her da.
da. Pro. 1 Ap. 1628
Archd. Ct. Exeter.

Grace ux. Tho-
mas Heydon of
Farway in Devon.

Anne ux. Peter
Franklin of Wid-
worthy in Devon.

Thomas Collins,   John Collins sone &   Elizabeth, æt. 8,
2 sone.   heyre atat. 19, 1620.   1620.

[1]*Edmond Prideaux of St. Mary═Joane, da. & sole heyre æt. 10, 1620,*
Antrey, Esq., 2 son to Edmond   extrix. of her father's will, which
Prideaux, Baronet.   she proved as wife of Prideaux.

[1]*Mary.*

Prudence ux. John Beare of Wood-
manston in Devon, issue John and
William.[1] John Beare Adm. the
goods, &c., of his bro. in law Wil-
liam Collins, during the minority
of the children.

Mary ux. Edward
Hole of Affington in
Devon.

Dorithy, unmar. 1620,
mar. John Sherman.[1]

Thomas Collyns═Mary Da. of John Bere
s. & h. æt. 24, of Hunsham in Com.
1620.   Devon.

William Collins, 2 sone, ætat. 21. Admon.═[1]*Thomasine, da. of*   Margery, da. of═William Collins of Off-═Anne, da. of ..., 2   Joane, a dau.,
granted 8 Jan. 1647-8 to John Beare,   *John Bere of Hunt-*   ... Sherman of   well, son and heir,   wife, extrix. of her   ætat. 1, 1620, ob.
husband of Prudence, sister of deceased,   *sham, mar. 19 Feb.* Ottery St. Mary, named in the will of   husband's will.Will   s.p.[1]
during the minority of his children. 2nd   *1623-4 at Hunt-*   I wife, mar. lic.   his uncle Thomas Beare   28 Feb. 1688-9,
Admon. "de bonis non" granted 4 Dec.   *sham.[2]*   28 April 1637   1631. Will 26 Oct. 1657,   pro. 19 Oct. 1691   [1]*Margaret, bap.*
1671 to John Collins, son of deceased.   Exeter.   proved 26 Feb. 1657-8,   Archd. Court Exe-   1 Sep. 1622 at
Act Bk. P.C.C.   P.C.C. (Wotton 99).   ter.   Offwell.[3]

Mary, bap. 21
April 1625 at
Offwell.[3]

Henry Collins, a minor 1647,   Thomas Collins, bap. 15 Nov.   Sara, a minor   Johan, mar. to   Mary, mar. to John
named in the will of his grand-   1633 at Offwell,[3] a minor 1647,   1647, named in   ...... Southcott,   Beare, both named in
mother Joan Beare 1648.   named in the will of his grand-   the will of her   named in her   her mother's will,
                                 mother Joan Beare 1648.   grandmother   mother's will,   living 1689.
William Collins, a minor 1647.   Joan Beare 1648.   living 1689.
                                 John Collins, bap. 4 May 1628   Dorothy, extrix. of
                                 at Offwell,[3] a minor 1647.   her mother's will, liv-
                                 Adm. to his father's estate   ing 1691.
                                 "de bonis non" 1671.

. The portion of this pedigree printed in italic is a copy of the Original Visitation of Devon 1620, Harl. MS. 1163, flo. 37 and 260,
the two pedigrees, signed respectively Willm. Collyns and Roger Collings, being incorporated.
[1] Added in the handwriting of Parker.   [2] Huntsham Parish Register.   [3] Offwell Parish Register.

169 Family tree of the Collins of Awtrie St Mary and Offwell from *The Visitations of the County of Devon.*

Novice Descendants Chart

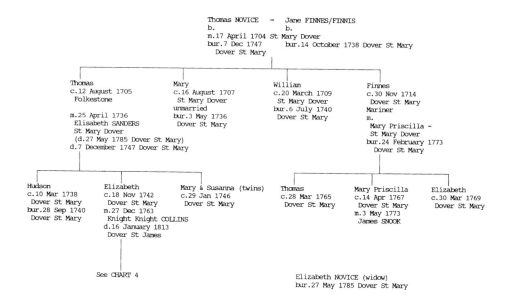

The Rouse Family

The surname Rouse and its spelling variants can be found in Dover for many centuries. Edmundus Rowse 'miles' (term equivalent to a knight) was elected as Member of Parliament for Dover in 1555.

Affry Rouse, who was buried at St Mary's on 1 November 1719, could be the mother of William Rouse who apparently found a bride outside the parish of Dover St Mary's as no record of his marriage can be found there. They may have come from the parish of Ospringe as the Bishops' transcripts there record a Richard Rouse marrying an Elizabeth Jennings on 16 April 1691.

William Rouse (1660-1738)

Nine children are known to have been born to William and Affry/Affra Rouse and baptised in St Mary's, Dover. William Rouse junior was baptised on 18 August 1689 and became Master Cooper of the Victualling Office. Upon his death in 1752 he was succeeded by his sister's son-in-law, Benjamin Worthington. It is likely that he married and had a family, as an indenture for John Rouse, son of William Rouse cooper of Dover, dated 18 June 1729, apprentices John to William Richards, tailor of Dover, for seven years. Two years later an indenture dated 31 August 1731 reveals possibly three generations present by the same name when William Rouse, son of William Rouse cooper of Dover is apprenticed to his father and enrolled by his grandfather,

William Rouse, Jurat.[24] Another William Rouse was a wine merchant in Dover and the occupier of a property in or near Limekiln Lane. He was involved in the sale of Ropewalk Vaults,[25] caves in the cliffs which were used to store the wine at an even temperature. Business could not have been going well as he received a creditors' notice issued by a solicitor four years later.[26]

Little is known of John, who was baptised on 2 July 1693 and buried on 21 September 1712 at Dover St Mary's aged 19 years.

Affra[27] Rouse was baptised at St Mary's, Dover, on 8 September 1695. She married Henry Jelly on 8 June 1722 and together they had eight children.[28]

Francis was baptised on 14 November 1697, married Susanna and had three children: Francis junior, baptised on 18 September 1726, who married Ann Goodwin and had descendants; Mary, baptised on 1 May 1729; and Susanna who was buried on 7 November 1731. Francis senior was buried six months after his youngest child on 20 April 1732, and his wife seven years later on 13 September 1739.

Richard(s) was baptised on 9 March 1701/2 and became a Commoner and Jurat of Dover. In 1732 he and Edward Worthington were Overseers of the Poor of the parish of St Mary. Richard married Susanna and they are known to have had at least two children: a daughter named Susanna was buried on 24 April 1734 and a son, Richard, was baptised on 31 July 1737. Richard Rouse senior was a wine merchant

Rouse Descendants Chart

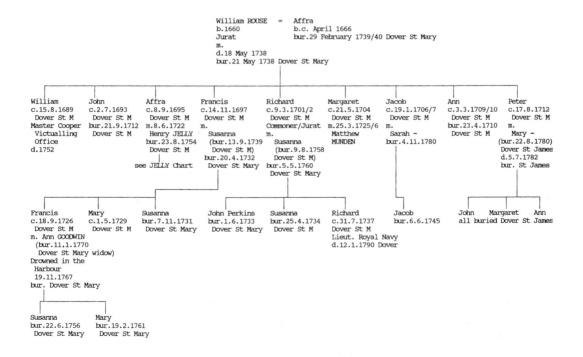

and resided at Archer's Court when he became Mayor of Dover in 1748.[29] He was still the occupier of a house in Dover in 1754.[30] Richard was buried at Dover St Mary's on 5 May 1760 two years after his wife who was buried there on 9 August 1758. His son, Richard, became a Lieutenant in the Royal Navy and as Deputy Lieutenant of Dover Castle from 1763 to 1767 sat at the Court of Lodemanage, which met at the Church of St James the Apostle, with Jacob Rouse, Captain of Archcliffe Fort from 1763 to 1778, and others.[31] He died at Dover on 12 January 1790.[32]

The first Court of Lodemanage was set up by the Lord Warden in 1526 to organise and regulate pilotage on a proper basis, the organisation itself being called the Trinity House of the Cinque Ports. However, a few years later the words Trinity House seem to have been discarded and the name 'Cinque Ports Pilots' came into general use. The controlling Court of Lodemanage admitted only suitable and knowledgeable pilots, who were designated lodesmen, and regulated their services and the fees they charged.[33]

Margaret was baptised on 21 May 1704 and married Matthew Munden on 25 March 1725/6.

Jacob Rouse was baptised on 19 January 1706/7 and married Sarah. He was a Mariner and party to an indenture from Robert Balderston to himself on 22 September 1766. This indenture was 'Confirmation of the mortgage of the reversion of a messuage, malthouses, lands and premises in Biggin Street in Dover for securing the payment of £300 and interest at £4 percent per annum'.[34] A son, Jacob, was buried on 6 June 1745.

Ann Rouse was baptised on 3 March 1709/10 and buried seven weeks later. Peter was baptised on 17 August 1712 and buried on 8 July 1782, all at Dover St Mary's. The altar tomb near the disused doorway of St Mary's Church records the interment

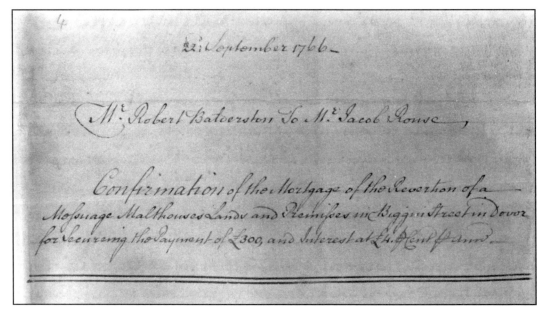

170   An indenture of confirmation of mortgage of property between Jacob Rouse and Robert Balderston, 1766.

of Peter who died in 1782, aged 69 years. He was buried three days after his death with his wife, Mary 'who departed this life the 22 August 1780 aged 69 years. She was a sincere friend and very agreeable companion'. In the same vault are interred John, Margaret and Ann, three of their children.

Rouse was also found as a middle name when the christening of Affra Rouse Elsted, daughter of Edward and Affra Elsted, took place in the parish of New Romney on 30 March 1772.

William was a Jurat of Dover and as such was part of the old order of Magistrates responsible for administering justice. The ancient mode of election was for the Mayor to be chosen by the burgesses from amongst themselves and, after he had taken oath, the Mayor selected from the burgesses 12 men to assist him in his office. Once they had taken the oath they were called Jurats. This system gradually changed over the years with parliamentary and municipal reform. In 1832 the Corporation was deprived of the privilege which had existed since the 13th century of sending burgesses to represent the town and port in the House of Commons. The style of the Corporation, which had been 'Mayor, Jurats and Commonalty', was changed to 'Mayor, Aldermen and Burgesses'.[35]

Mr. William Rouse was one of the Jurats present on 23 November 1721 when William Rouse, son of William Rouse, labourer of Dover was apprenticed to Thomas Smith, the older of Dover, tailor. There was no apparent relationship between this father and son and the Jurat. However in 1731 all three generations are found together as mentioned earlier. William, senior, continued to appear in these records as a Jurat until 1732.[36]

William and Affra Rouse were also interred in the altar tomb with the Jellys and the Worthingtons. The inscription reads: 'Mr William Rouse one of the Jurats of this town departed this life the 18 May 1738 (buried 21 May) aged 78 years. Here also lieth the body of Mrs Affra Rouse, the wife of the above William who departed ye life ye 25 February 1739 aged 72 years 9 months.'[37]

Descendants probably continued to live in Dover as Thomas Rouse of Limekiln Street was the occupier of a house to be sold by auction in 1838.[38]

The Jennings Family

George Jennings (c.1723-1809)

The Jennings family became closely linked with the Worthingtons from the 1820s when two Jennings siblings married two Worthington siblings in Dover. Four generations before, George Jennings, a bricklayer of Canterbury, was the earliest George Jennings found on the ancestral line. His marriage has not been found. He became a Freeman of Canterbury during 1747. His son, George Jennings, was apprenticed in Dover and it appears that George Jennings, senior, also moved to Dover as he was buried at St Mildred's, Canterbury on 19 May 1809 aged 86 years after being removed from St Mary's parish, Dover.

George Jennings (1752/3-....)

Young George was apprenticed to Benjamin Vernon of Dover, a plumber and glazier on 4 April 1767 for a fee of £16.[39] George finished his apprenticeship and married

Jennings Descendants Chart 1

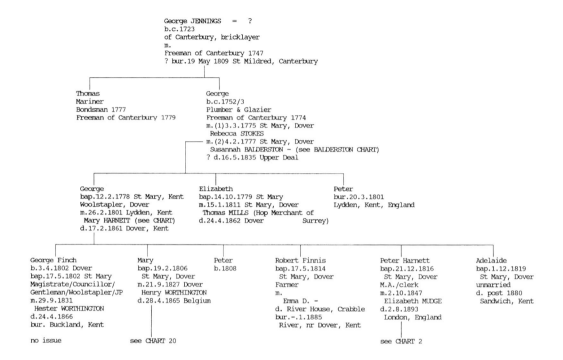

```
                        George JENNINGS   =   ?
                        b.c.1723
                        of Canterbury, bricklayer
                        m.
                        Freeman of Canterbury 1747
                        ? bur.19 May 1809 St Mildred, Canterbury


        Thomas                          George
        Mariner                         b.c.1752/3
        Bondsman 1777                   Plumber & Glazier
        Freeman of Canterbury 1779      Freeman of Canterbury 1774
                                        m.(1)3.3.1775 St Mary, Dover
                                          Rebecca STOKES
                                        m.(2)4.2.1777 St Mary, Dover
                                          Susannah BALDERSTON - (see BALDERSTON CHART)
                                        ? d.16.5.1835 Upper Deal


        George                      Elizabeth                   Peter
        bap.12.2.1778 St Mary, Kent bap.14.10.1779 St Mary      bur.20.3.1801
        Woolstapler, Dover          m.15.1.1811 St Mary, Dover  Lydden, Kent, England
        m.26.2.1801 Lydden, Kent      Thomas MILLS (Hop Merchant of
          Mary HARNETT (see CHART)   d.24.4.1862 Dover              Surrey)
        d.17.2.1861 Dover, Kent
```

```
George Finch          Mary            Peter         Robert Finnis       Peter Harnett       Adelaide
b.3.4.1802 Dover      bap.19.2.1806   b.1808        bap.17.5.1814       bap.21.12.1816      bap.1.12.1819
bap.17.5.1802 St Mary  St Mary, Dover                St Mary, Dover       St Mary, Dover      St Mary, Dover
Magistrate/Councillor/ m.21.9.1827 Dover            Farmer              M.A./clerk          unmarried
Gentleman/Woolstapler/JP Henry WORTHINGTON         m.                  m.2.10.1847         d. post 1880
m.29.9.1831          d.28.4.1865 Belgium             Emma D. -           Elizabeth MUDGE     Sandwich, Kent
  Hester WORTHINGTON                                d. River House, Crabble d.2.8.1893
d.24.4.1866                                         bur.-.1.1885          London, England
bur. Buckland, Kent                                  River, nr Dover, Kent

no issue             see CHART 20                                                          see CHART 2
```

Jennings Descendants Chart 2 (from Jennings Chart 1)

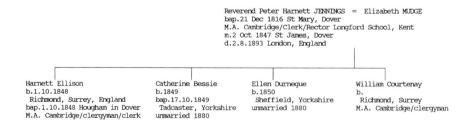

```
                        Reverend Peter Harnett JENNINGS  =  Elizabeth MUDGE
                        bap.21 Dec 1816 St Mary, Dover
                        M.A. Cambridge/Clerk/Rector Longford School, Kent
                        m.2 Oct 1847 St James, Dover
                        d.2.8.1893 London, England


  Harnett Ellison          Catherine Bessie        Ellen Durneque        William Courtenay
  b.1.10.1848              b.1849                  b.1850                b.
    Richmond, Surrey, England bap.17.10.1849       Sheffield, Yorkshire  Richmond, Surrey
  bap.1.10.1848 Hougham in Dover Tadcaster, Yorkshire unmarried 1880    M.A. Cambridge/clergyman
  M.A. Cambridge/clergyman/clerk unmarried 1880
```

his first wife Rebecca Stokes by licence on 3 March 1775 at St Mary's in Dover. Rebecca was a minor when she married, her mother Benedicta standing surety. She must have died soon after the marriage, perhaps in childbirth, because on 4 February 1777 not two years later, George Jennings, widower, married Susannah Balderstone (*sic*) aged 21 years by licence at St Mary, Dover. The bondsman was Thomas Jennings of Dover.

The Balderston Family

Baptised on 7 September 1755 at St Mary's, Susannah Balderston was probably the youngest child of Robert and Elizabeth Balderston. Her grandmother, Sarah Balderston, née Taylor, had a cousin Robert Daines of Well Court Manor, in the parish of Ickham near Littlebourne, who left his manor to her son, Daines Balderston, in 1733. Daines then passed this estate to his father, George Balderston who died in 1751 leaving the property to his wife Sarah. In 1775 her trustees sold it to Sir Philip Hales, Bart.[40] Daines Balderston Worthington (1842-1865) was named after Daines Balderston, his great uncle (see Balderston Chart).

George and Susannah Jennings

To make matters more confusing, the first child of George and Susannah Jennings was also named George Jennings. He was baptised on 12 February 1778 at St Mary's, Dover. Their second child, Elizabeth, married Thomas Mills on 15 January 1811 by licence at St Mary's, Dover witnessed by George Finch and Elisa Neales. Thomas was a hop

Balderston

171 The Balderston Coat of Arms.

Balderston Descendants Chart 1

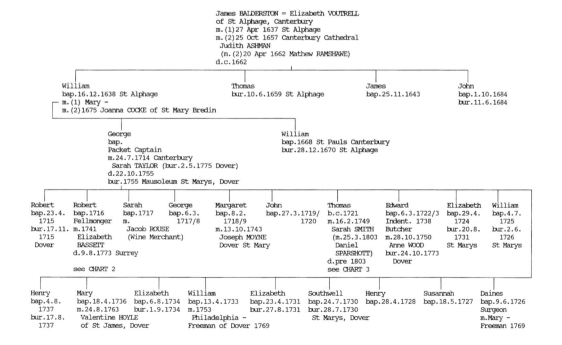

Balderston Descendants Chart 2 (from Chart 1)

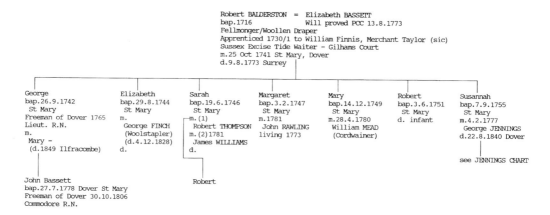

Balderston Descendants Chart 3 (from Chart 2)

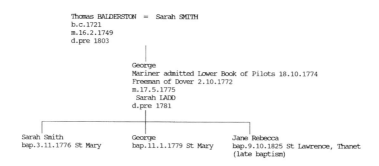

merchant of the parish of St Mary, Lambeth and Surrey. Elizabeth lived her married life in Surrey and after the death of her husband returned to Dover where she died on 24 April 1862.

The name Jennings was common in the East Kent area with several people living with the same name at the same time. In 1790 George Jennings was listed in the Poll for Members of Parliament to represent the city of Canterbury. George and Susannah Jennings may have retired to Upper Deal where George died in 1835 and Susannah died in 1840.

George Jennings (1778-1861)

George Jennings was baptised at St Mary's Dover on 12 February 1778, son of George Jennings and Susannah Jennings, née Balderston. He became a woolstapler and married Mary Harnett, daughter of Peter and Elizabeth Harnett on Thursday 26 February 1801 by licence at Lydden. The Rev. M. Sayer officiated at the marriage.[41]

The Harnett Family

A Peter Harnett came to Lydden parish in the early 1700s where he became the owner of a house and land in the parish of St Peter, Broadstairs near Margate.[42] He farmed extensive lands and in 1732 acquired all the Osborn property from the widow of George Osborn, who had died in February of 1728.[43]

Lydden was a small town four and a half miles from Dover. It was from Lydden Hill that the first view of Dover, its castle and the sea could be acquired. The historical records of this parish go back to the Norman Conquest when there were three principal manors, one of which, Cocklescombe, became the Harnetts' home in 1791 after it was bought with accompanying lands by Peter Harnett. The surname Harnett appears in the Lydden baptismal registers from 1737 and prior to that the family may have been in Thanet, as 'The Poll for the Knights of the Shire to represent the County of Kent, 1734' records Peter Harnett as living in Liddon (*sic*) with freehold land in St Lawrence.

Cocklescombe was apportioned at the Conquest as a Dover Castle Knight's fee,[44] before it became the property of the Knights of St John of Jerusalem in the reign of Edward I. At the time of the Reformation the Manor was sold by the Crown to Mr. Edward Monins of Waldershare, from whom it passed to Sir Henry Furness of Waldershare. Later Viscount Bolingbroke acquired it by marriage and in turn sold it to Peter Harnett. The manor no longer exists.

Harnett Descendants Chart (from Jennings Chart 1)

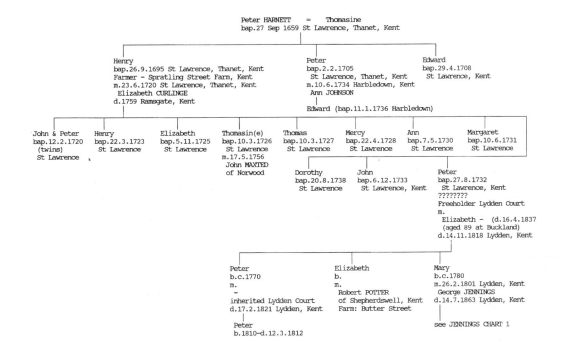

Mary Harnett's sister Elizabeth married Robert Potter who owned large areas of land in Lydden including Lydden Court Farm, Bell Farm, Cocklescombe Farm, Warren Farm, Upper Farm, Cannons Land and cottages which he sold at auction in September 1846.[45]

A mural tablet in the Lydden Church on the north side of the chancel is dedicated to the memory of Peter Harnett, his wife Elizabeth and their descendants. Included on the tablet are George and Mary Jennings, née Harnett.

George and Mary Jennings

George and Mary Jennings settled in Lydden and had five children: George Finch Jennings (1802-66), Mary Jennings (1806-65), Robert Finnis Jennings (1814-85), Peter Harnett Jennings (1816-93), Adelaide Jennings (1819-post 1880).

George continued to work as a woolstapler and in December 1802 engaged an apprentice, Thomas Knott.[46] On 2 February 1837 Armorial Bearings were granted to 'George Jennings of The Shrubbery in the Parish of Buckland near Dover'. These bearings may be blazoned as: Azure a chevron engrailed ermine between three golden fleeces proper; and for the crest: A dragon passant vaire the wings gold the dexter forepaw resting on a shield azure charged with a golden fleece proper; the motto being 'Conservabo ad mortem'.[47]

The rating list for Dover, 1838-9 lists rates paid for the following property owned by the Jennings family: a warehouse in St Mary's Town Ward, Church Place owned by George Jennings valued at £21 with annual rates of 7s.; a house in St Mary's 'Pier' Ward, Strond Lane owned by George Jennings valued at £13 10s. with annual rates of 4s. 6d.; a house in Council House Street valued at £15 with annual rates of 5d. also owned by George; a house and garden in St James' parish owned by George Finch Jennings, valued at £100 the rates for which were £1 13s. 4d., and a house in Charlton Parish, Victoria Crescent owned by Miss Jennings valued at £12 for which she paid annual rates of 4s.

The 1841 census lists the George Jennings family at Shrubbery House. Present at the time was Katharine Finnis, born in Kent and aged 90 years, of independent means; George Jennings aged 60 years of independent means; Peter Jennings and Adelaide Jennings, both aged 20 years and of independent means; and Elizabeth Worthington aged 12 years, not born in Kent. Elizabeth was the daughter of William Collins and Sarah Worthington and was born in Suffolk.

The Shrubbery, near Crabble Hill in Dover, was a large house and had been the residence during the 18th century of Vice Admiral Sir John Bentley, for whom it was probably built.

George was very involved in his community and was a politically active, vocal and enthusiastic gentleman. He was also a loyal friend as seen in a report in the *Dover Chronicle* of the farewell dinner and plate presentation to Mr. William Prescott on his departure from Dover with his family. Mr. Prescott was leaving for South Australia. After several speeches were made,

172 George Jennings (1778-1861).

173 Mary Jennings, née Harnett (1780-1863).

Mr Jenings returned thanks. He felt highly gratified at being able to attend that day, to meet his worthy friend Mr William Prescott. He [Mr Jennings] was certainly not younger than he was thirty years ago; but he conceived his desire to aid the Cause of Reform by honest means was as strong as ever; but he deplored to observe that practices were still had recourse to at elections that every honest man must desire to see abolished. After condemming the bribery system in the most unequivocal terms, Mr Jennings sat down amid loud applause.[48]

Another example of the support George gave his friends can be found in the 1841 'Roll Book for Two Barons, Dover'. It was written that George Jennings, Senior Esquire proposed the candidate Alexander Galloway, Esq. Stepping forward, Mr. Jennings observed that he:

174 The Jennings Coat of Arms.

had the honour on a former occassion to propose Mr Thompson—a man who, he was happy to say, had not only signalized himself in the councils of the nation, but had also been the pacificator of Canada (Cheers). It was that day his pleasing duty to propose to their notice an old, tried, firm and steady friend of the people, Mr Alexander Galloway, (Cheers) who was a man that came forward as the friend of liberty, and not like some, to aggrandize himself. (Cheers) Mr Galloway wanted neither place nor peerage. He came to them not scraping and bowing. He solicited their suffrages solely that he might faithfully represent them in the Commons House of Parliament, and benefit the people's cause. Mr Galloway's liberal conduct was before the public in the proceedings of the Common Council of the City of London; and he had suffered four years imprisonment in a dungeon at the hands of a Tory Government for his devotion to the cause of Reform. He (Mr Jennings) would therefore call on those he addressed to stick to this man, and he would stick to them. (Cheers) Mr Galloways's practical experience as an engineer would be of great service to them in connection with the Harbour, did they return him as one of their representatives; and he had therefore much pleasure in proposing him. (Loud cheers)

George died of senile debility on 17 February 1861 at The Shrubbery, Buckland aged 84 years. His effects were valued under £12,000 and the executors of his estate were his three sons. At that time George Finch Jennings Esquire was living in Dover, Robert Finnis Jennings lived at Little Betshanger, Kent and the Reverend Peter Harnett Jennings lived at Palestine Place, Cambridge Heath, Middlesex. He bequeathed 'to my dear wife Mary, my horses, carriages, furniture, plate, linen, china, books, pictures and household provisions, chattels and effects of every description'. He also left extensive property to Mary, including the freehold estate at Buckland; his estate called Butterfield situated in Romney Marsh occupied at the time by Edward Smith and William Green, a farm called Paynden at Horsemonden occupied by Joseph Williams; a house at Otham occupied by Mrs. Chambers, a property called Dunning

175   The Shrubbery, London Road, Crabble Hill, Dover.

in Cornwall; and a freehold house called East Brook Cottage and garden in St James' parish, Dover occupied by George Finch Jennings.

George Jennings also owned Oakleigh, 73 London Road, Deal which was occupied at one time by Rattery Brown, Vincent Cornwell, Edward Williams and Mrs. Watson. After his death the property was put up for auction on 20 January 1864 at the *Clarendon Hotel*, Deal, by his three executors and sold for £460 to Emanuel Solomon. The property was described as:

all those two messuages tenements or dwelling houses with outhouses buildings land or garden ground and appurtenances belonging containing by estimation 1 acre in Middle Deal abutting on one side to the Turnpike Road on another side to a garden and land of Lancelot Hayward and then of John Rothschild Edwards and on other sides thereof to land then late belonging to or occupied by Richard Chitty and then by George William Chitty then formerly in the occupation of Joseph Bell and James Farendon afterwards of Edward Williams and Vincent Cornwell and then or late George Pittock and William Nethersole together with the rights etc.

George also left his children generous bequests of money and made special provisions for his spinster daughter Adelaide Jennings. George stipulated in his will, however, that his children were to forfeit their inheritances if they did not remain resident in England. On 5 March 1861 Mary renounced, by deed poll, her part as executor of her husband's estate.

Two years after her husband's death Mary Jennings died on 14 July 1863 at the Shrubbery, Buckland of senile debility aged 83 years. She did not leave a will but Letters of Administration were granted on 3 November 1863 to George Finch Jennings and Robert Finnis Jennings. Her effects were valued at under £4,000. After Mary's death the mansion house, well laid out grounds and three-stall stable and coach-house were advertised for sale by private contract in the *Dover Telegraph* on 13 February 1864. Comprising three and a half acres, the Shrubbery had a frontage to the Turnpike Road. The advertisement read:

A very desirable and eligibly situated residence at East Brook, Dover with the Conservatories, and large well stocked and tastefully laid out garden, now in the occupation of G.F. Jennings Esquire.

The garden has a frontage to East Brook Place of upwards of 100 feet, and to Ashentree Lane of upwards of 180 feet.

The residence is replete with every convenience, it having been fitted up by the

present occupier regardless of expense, and is in admirable repair.
Possession of the above properties may be had at an early day.

Enquiries regarding purchase of the properties were to be directed to Robert Finch Jennings at the Shrubbery or James Stilwell his Dover solicitor.

George Finch Jennings (1802-1866)

Born on 3 April 1802 and baptised at St Mary's on 17 May 1802, the eldest child of George and Mary Jennings became a councillor and magistrate of Dover. George was also described at times as a woolstapler,[49] gentleman, Justice of the Peace and Pavement Board Commissioner. Paving Commissioners dealt with most of Dover's sanitation and the control, drainage, maintenance and general improvement of the streets.

George Finch Jennings was named after his great uncle George Finch who was the son of Peter Finch, blacksmith of Chartham. He had been apprenticed firstly to Thomas Godden, fellmonger and glover of Dover on 4 January 1757 and later transferred during 1764 to Robert Balderston of Dover, fellmonger, with the consent of his father and Susanna Godden, widow of Thomas.[50] George Finch married Elizabeth Balderston, his master's daughter, and became a prominent citizen of Dover. He lived in Biggin Street, Dover and was a joint executor for the estate of Lieutenant Richards Rouse.[51] Various wills, indentures and abstracts of title survive between George Finch, Elizabeth Finch, George Balderston, Daines Balderston, William Balderston, Margaret Rawling, Mary and Susannah Balderston, witnessed by Jacob Rouse and John Smith, all of whom were related. George Finch, woolstapler left a will dated 16 November 1828, proved 21 January 1829, bequeathing £50 to the minister and church wardens of the parish of Temple Ewell, near Dover, to be invested so the interest and dividends could be used to purchase bread in every winter season for the poor of the parish.[52]

At the age of 29 years George Finch Jennings married Hester Worthington, Lieutenant Benjamin Worthington's daughter and his brother-in-law Henry Worthington's sister, on 29 September 1831. Hester lived at Charlton at the time of her marriage and was 31 years of age. They married by licence, issued two days before their marriage.

George died on 24 April 1866. A five-sided Worthington family memorial headstone in the Buckland churchyard reads on one side, 'Sacred to the memory of George Finch Jennings Esquire, Justice of the Peace of the town of Dover who died 24 April 1866 aged 64 years. Unto thine hand I commit my spirit. Thou hadst redeemed me O Lord God of truth. Also of Hester wife of the above who died at Dover, Feb 16 1871 aged 76 years.'

Mary Jennings (1806-1865)

Mary Jennings was baptised at St Mary's Church on 19 February 1806. Twenty-one years later she married Henry Worthington of Charlton, son of Benjamin Jelly Worthington, on 21 September 1827. They married by licence, which was granted on 3 September 1827. Their family life is recounted in the chapter on Henry Worthington (1803-1866).

Robert Finnis Jennings (1814-1885)

Baptised at St Mary's on 27 May 1814, Robert became a farmer. By 1836 Robert had moved to Berkshire, and as he had no intention of returning to Dover it was decided, against his wishes, that he should not remain on the Dover Freemans list.[53]

Robert married Emma D., surname unknown, who was born in Reculver. In 1871 they were living at River House, Crabble, in the River parish of Dover with one servant. Robert was aged 56 years and retired, and Emma was 53 years. They had one unmarried cook and servant, Frances A. Gorden aged 35 years.[54]

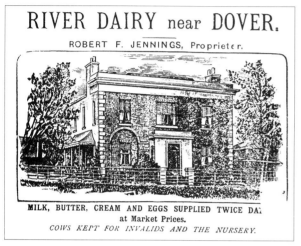

RIVER DAIRY near DOVER.

ROBERT F. JENNINGS, Proprietor.

MILK, BUTTER, CREAM AND EGGS SUPPLIED TWICE DAI
at Market Prices.
COWS KEPT FOR INVALIDS AND THE NURSERY.

176 Advertisement for the River Dairy, near Dover, Robert Finnis Jennings, Proprietor.

The pretty village of River, two miles from Dover, was reached by either of two roads which converged at Buckland Bridge. The one on the right was the only one available for vehicles and was by way of Crabble Hill, a long and steep ascent from which wonderful views of the variegated valley of the Dour could be enjoyed. Crabble Hill was in the parish of River, and on it were built several very pretty villa residences.

An advertisement in a local directory, post 1875, advertises the River Dairy, near Dover, of which Robert F. Jennings was the proprietor. Milk, butter, cream and eggs were supplied twice daily, with cows kept for invalids and the nursery. Mr. R.F. Jennings was also a churchwarden of the local parish church, River-Cum-Guston.

Robert died at River House, Crabble and was buried at River in January 1885.

Reverend Peter Harnett Jennings (1816-1893)

Baptised on 21 December 1816, Peter obtained a Master of Arts degree from Corpus Christi College, Cambridge and became Rector of Longfield School, Kent.

From the *Dover Telegraph* of 2 October 1847 we learn that the 'Reverend Peter Harnett Jennings of Richmond, Surrey this morning at St James Church married Elizabeth Mudge, eldest daughter of Lieutenant Mudge, R.N., Commander of Her Majestys Packet *Onyx*'.[55]

In 1851 Peter was living with his wife, three children and three servants at 70 Maitland Place in the parish of All Saints', Southampton. Peter and Elizabeth's son Harnett Jennings was aged two years, daughter Catherine Bessie Jennings was aged one year and Ellen Durnegue Jennings was aged five months.[56] A fourth child, William Courtenay Jennings, was born in Richmond, Surrey. Both Harnett and William Jennings are listed in the 1902 *Crockford's Clerical Directory* as ministers, having followed their father's career path by first attending Corpus Christi College at Cambridge and both acquiring B.A and M.A. degrees. Harnett received a B.A. in 1871 and M.A. in 1875 and was living in the parsonage at St Clement's from 1902 until at least 1930. A Courtenay Balderston Jennings, who is mentioned in his aunt

Adelaide's will, was living at the Hose vicarage, Melton Mowbray in 1902. He obtained a B.A. at Cambridge in 1884 and M.A. in 1900.

Peter died at Notting Hill Square, London on 2 August 1893 in his 76th year.

Adelaide Jennings (1819-post 1880)

The fifth child of George and Mary Jennings, Adelaide was baptised on 1 December 1819 at St Mary's. Adelaide never married and was well provided for by her family. She died post-1880 at Cypress House, Sandwich, Kent. Peter Harnett Jennings was appointed executor of her will.

Beneficiaries included her brother Robert Finnis Jennings, £100; her cousin Mrs Soley, £100 and household furniture, linen and wearing apparel; Peter Harnett Jennings received their mother's gold wedding jewellery and gold seal; her

177 Reverend Peter Harnett Jennings (photographed by Mowll & Co., London).

nephew Harnett E. Jennings received her silver tea service, books and pictures; nieces Sophia and Maria Worthington were left the silver and plated articles to be divided between them; nephew William Mudge Jennings received Adelaide's telescope, marble clock and horse shoe clock; nephew Courtenay Jennings a barometer, thermometer, silver watch and field glasses; niece Catherine Bessie Jennings received a travelling trunk, photo albums, a topaz and diamond ring and tea caddy. Adelaide's niece Ellen D. Jennings received a silver inkstand, gold senaccole work table and lock-up writing case, Mrs Barbour was left a gold watch and gold sleeve buttons; and to her friend Miss J.A. Lord, a machine for making 'Tear Malevace'.

Adelaide left half her property to her brother Peter Harnett Jennings and the other half to be divided among the four daughters and three sons of 'my dearest sister Mary Worthington.'

Appendix 1

Report upon Jelly-Worthington Research at the Public Record Office, Kew

From David Villers to Jan Worthington, Summer 1986

It must be stressed at the outset that this report deals only with the research possibilities at Kew and does not include consideration of those existing elsewhere. I believe, in fact, that one could profitably continue the research in repositories like the Chancery Lane branch of the Public Record Office, the National Maritime Museum at Greenwich, as well as the Kent Record Office at Maidstone and in local libraries. But for the present assignment I judged all places other than Kew outside my terms of reference.

Kew yielded a great deal of information, most notably on Benjamin Jelly Worthington, as the enclosures make clear, and one of my problems was to decide how much of it you would want. I hope you will approve of my 'saturation' coverage and the choice of photocopies. Let me say straightaway that I was most grateful for the material you provided at the start of this inquiry; it gave me the necessary framework from which it was possible to expand in depth. When I struck a rich vein, I had to persevere until it was exhausted because I believe we have here a biographical profile of real interest, apart from a fascinating insight into the way the local Customs Service worked in the 18th and early 19th centuries.

Nevertheless there were limitations to the research at Kew. The Jelly-Worthington families were obviously prominent in the political and social life of Dover–truly local 'characters' in the best sense of the word. Yet the material unearthed here only advances our knowledge of the subject's professional career and sheds no light upon his municipal activities or personality: for his immersion in town affairs and the impact he made upon his contemporaries in a non-professional capacity we would have to turn to the local sources. We do, however, catch a fleeting glimpse of the 'private man' when illness prevented him from carrying out the duties annexed to his employment.

Equally, there were disappointments when the results accruing from likely-looking sources proved to be minimal or negative. We have just the solitary reference to Henry Jelly senior to show for a search extending over 363 volumes of the Excise Board & Secretariat Minute Books, from 1740 to 1823, in Cust.47. The relevant Home Office papers (H.O.43) could have been more revealing about smuggling in the Dover and Deal vicinity and the actions taken by individual Revenue cutter commanders to suppress it. The rapidly decaying Seamen's Wills (ADM, indexed in ADM 48), the Register of Lieutenants applying for employment (ADM 6), the Register of Naval Pensions after 1814 (ADM 22) and the Admiralty Correspondence (ADM 106) produced absolutely nothing, while the ships' muster books (ADM 36) and captains' logs (ADM 51) next to nothing. The Lieutenants' log books–well worth inspection–can be found at the National Maritime Museum. Regrettably the Coastguard Records of Service (ADM 175) begin too late to be of value for Benjamin Jelly Worthington (about whom there is a plethora of material in any case), and anyway, as you know, the Worthingtons in the 19th century were enlisting in the Royal Navy.

You will see from the material gathered that the Customs Records, especially Cust.54 (1-49), gave me the greatest joy. These records together with the complementary series Cust.31 (2-10 and 271-280) enable us to follow closely the career of Benjamin Jelly Worthington in the Revenue Service from the time he assumed command of the *Tartar* cutter in September 1786 until he was superannuated in June 1816. It might be as well, at this point, to say something about these two important series, as so much of my information is drawn from them.

Cust.54 consists essentially of letters and various communications from the Collector, who was responsible for, amongst other things, all the Customs business at the Port of Dover, to the Commissioners of Customs (the Board) sitting in London. The Collector was accountable to the Board for a wide variety of matters, ranging from moneys paid for Customs and other duties to making sure that the Revenue vessels were properly manned and officered and efficient instruments of government policy. The correspondence that passed between the local Collector and the London based Board of Customs was, by the standards of that day, voluminous. In 1792, for example, no fewer than 746 letters went out from the Dover Customs House to the Commissioners in the capital. Indeed, the Collector was the pivot upon which turned the whole relationship between the local port and the Board. He had to manage the Commissioners' business, but in doing so he was deeply involved with subordinates paid, like himself, to discharge it. No one was better placed to comment upon the personnel and general conditions at the port of Dover. The local scene emerges less clearly and intimately from the correspondence in reverse, namely that between the Board and the Collector (Cust.31), but without doubt the orders, inquiries and responses that flowed from the Commissioners to the port often illuminated matters that had otherwise seemed obscure or unexplained.

Another set of Customs Records I found useful but rather tedious to use was the Register of Seizures (Cust.21), especially 66-83 which cover the years 1763-80. For our purposes, the register exclusively concerned Henry Jelly junior and demonstrated, to a quite remarkable degree, his zeal in bagging contraband goods. This appears to be a subject sadly neglected by historians of the 18th century; it is the law-breakers—the smugglers—who continue to monopolise the attention of students and writers. In the 18th century the populace and the smuggling fraternity both shared a dislike of the Revenue man on land and sea and made his calling a particularly hazardous one. Once a Mariner on the *Tartar* under Henry Jelly was killed in the line of duty, and it is no less significant that Captain Dubois Smith, Commander of the *Lively* cutter and Benjamin Jelly Worthington's colleague of long-standing, was wounded three times during his career.

And so, in a popular climate generally hostile to the efforts of Revenue men, Henry Jelly junior, compiled a record of seizures that commands admiration. Between 1763 and 1780 his name is mentioned 188 times in the Register of Seizures; according to my shaky arithmetic, he confiscated, during that 17-year period: 93,006 quarter-pounds of tea assessed at £20,165 11s., 58,784 three-quarter-gallons of geneva (gin), together with 2qts, 14pts and 'several parcels' worth £12,565 1s. 6d., 17,886 half-gallons of brandy appraised at £4,791 19s. 9d., and 2,043 gallons of rum valued at £414 5s. 3d. Added to this haulage, he impounded 60 vessels (48 'boats', 2 sloops, 7 galleys and 3 cutters), some of which were claimed for immediate use in the Revenue Service. The aggregate value of the impounded vessels was £1,770 13s. 3d. These details I took down in pencil—all of them—and if you would like them in their rough state, I'll gladly send them on. But I must not be held responsible for the totals, worked out with nothing more sophisicated than a pocket calculator. It would do no harm for somebody to check my figures.

After finding myself almost buried under lists of goods and columns of figures, it was a relief to get back to the human dimension. The records which you will examine yourself are filled with accounts of damaged bowsprits, lost anchors and broken cables. When one reflects upon these and other seemingly mundane preoccupations of a sea captain (only mundane to those who know little about the sea), you will realise what monumental importance they assume in the mind of a person charged with the responsibility of maintaining the efficient running and safety of the vessel. Matters which some people are tempted to dismiss as boringly technical or inconsequential take on an altogether different complexion when they directly impinge upon the normal pattern of the individual. The 18th-century sea captain's reliance upon sound equipment was just as absolute as that of the modern racing driver or long distance trucker. So I make no apologies for introducing so much material relating to the *Tartar* cutter's various component parts. For Captain Benjamin Jelly Worthington, as for Henry Jelly junior before him, the need to keep the *Tartar* afloat and seaworthy was a dominant professional and personal concern. Of course one would have liked to come across official confirmation of Captain Worthingtion's colourful escapades as narrated in the *History of Deal* and to learn much more, in particular, about his service in the war against France when he was seconded to the Admiralty, which commended his patriotic labours. But in essence seafaring was a tough, daily grind in which men battled the sameness of things and the tyranny of routine; for the most part, not a great deal seemed to be 'happening'. We find it difficult today to appreciate the rigours of a life at sea in the 18th century, particularly for a conscientious captain of a Revenue cutter whose task it was to be eternally vigilant. At the close of a 42-year long career in the Revenue Service similar to Benjamin Jelly Worthington's, Captain Dubois Smith was practically blind. He attributed his greatly impaired eye-sight to constant 'watching at sea'.

DAVID VILLERS
6 September 1986

Appendix 2

Buckland Paper Mill

Ann Worthington, elder sister of Benjamin Jelly Worthington married Thomas Horn, owner of the Buckland paper mill.

A brief history of Buckland paper mill, believed to have been written by a recent mill manager, records that the 'The very early history of Buckland Mill is rather obscure. It is known however that Buckland Mill was one of a number of mills operating in the Dover district during the 18th and 19th centuries'. It still exists today, although much altered with the passage of time. In 1770 paper was made by hand and Buckland mill would have been a small place, producing only a few hundredweight of paper in a week.

The paper industry was late in becoming established in England most of the supply being imported from Europe until at least two or three decades after 1600. Brown paper manufacture rapidly spread during the early 17th century, but the more complicated process involved in the making of the finer white papers needed for writing and printing took far longer to gain a hold and it was not until after 1670 that English manufacture began to satisfy demand to any large extent.[1]

About 1700 Kent shared first place with Buckinghamshire as the leading paper-producing county. Many rags were brought to the mills by local collectors–no doubt the presence of most mills near the medium-sized and larger towns such as Dover owed much to there being a useful source of raw materials. For brown paper old ropes and sails were used, and clearly the Kentish ports provided a plentiful supply of these.[2]

In the year 1699-1700 increasing amounts of brown paper were leaving the ports of Faversham and Dover. At his death in 1696 Thomas Hatton of Buckland mill had 'in ye ragghouse twenty three hundred [weight] of paper stuffe,' worth £4 8s. 2d., 'stuffe ready beate to make twenty-one reame of paper' (£1 11s. 6d.), and 'one reame of paper a drying in ye lodge' valued at £2 8s.[3]

According to the paper written on Buckland mill, 'In 1777 Ingram Horn, a land owner in the parish, was the owner of Buckland Mill and making paper there'. Hasted in his book of Kent states that in 1790 the mill was very much enlarged.

In 1799, Thomas Horn, probably son of Ingram Horn, was mentioned as the owner of Buckland mill. Then on 6 January 1814 the mill and the dwelling house were burned down. They were rebuilt that same year by Thomas Horn, whose keystone with initials and the date 1814 was put over the great water wheel and is still on site. At that stage the mill was still producing hand-made paper.[4]

In 1822 Thomas Horn contemplated installing a patent machine at Buckland mill and a plan of the mill of that year shows the position it was to occupy. It is of interest to note that the mill was then a two-storey building, with brick up to the first floor and wood above this, the roof being composed of tarred paper. The layout consisted of the beaterroom and, workroom, over which were the drying lofts, the gelatine preparation room, the counting house and, strangely, another room as large as the counting house called the wine cellar. There was also a vacant site marked for the erection of an open copper tank for the boiling of rags.

It was about this time, in 1823, that the present Buckland House was built by Thomas Horn. Sometime between 1825 and 1828 the mill passed into the hands of George Dickinson, a brother of John Dickinson who founded the well-known firm of papermakers based in London. This would have followed the death of Thomas Horn in December 1823, his only son Thomas Horn junior having died on 22 March 1807 aged 27 years.

1. Chalklin, *op. cit.*, p.151.
2. Chalklin, *op. cit.*, p.152.
3. Chalklin, *op. cit.*, p.153.
4. *The Dover Express.*

178 Buckland paper mill. The original mill from a painting by T. Forrest, 1770.

179 Horn family monument, Buckland churchyard.

Appendix 3

St Mary's Church, Dover

The first mention of this church dates from 1203 in Henry III's reign, when it was a parsonage and established for the accommodation of priests, pilgrims and strangers in conjunction with the Maison Dieu Hospital. A parsonage meant that a house, lands and tithes were set apart for the support of the priest. St Mary's Church was given by Henry VIII to the inhabitants of Dover. From 1549 to 1558 there were six hired ministers at St Mary's, all laymen of the town. They were styled 'Sir' instead of Reverend. Money was scarce in Henry VIII's time. In the month he died in 1547 the vestry ordered the church plate, valued at £9 8s. 4d., to be sold to pay their debts. At Easter 1547 the chalice was missing and it was discovered that John Hibbing, the parish clerk, had pawned it because he could not get his wages. The churchwardens had to pay 20s. to redeem it for use at the Easter Festival.

After the Conquest there were seven churches in Dover of which only one now remains. Church attendance was a strictly enforced duty of rich and poor, old and young, bound and free, so many churches were required. At the time of the Commonwealth, 1649 to 1660, the old authorities of church and state were swept aside and an opportunity made for the uprising of nonconformity. The incumbents of St Mary's and St James's were ousted and Presbyterian ministers installed by order of Parliament. Protestant meeting houses were opened in town. This arose from the greater religious liberty and partly from the opposition to any form of state religion, even that carried on by the clergy officiating at the parish churches by order of Parliament.

The Dover Corporation did not approve of the change and the minister of St Mary's was requested to be present at all their meetings and open the proceedings with prayer. The ministers who were elected by the parishioners had no easy time. One preached a vehement sermon against Parliament which was much to the liking of the congregation. For his temerity, his house was ransacked, all his books and papers seized and he was imprisoned in Dover Castle. Charles I had him liberated and gave him the rectory of Chartham, near Canterbury. The Commons vetoed the appointment. Other priests were appointed but none were allowed to enjoy the living, their stay in Dover being mostly in the Castle prison and not in the rectory. At the Restoration of Charles II in 1660 the old rector was reinstated. He stayed at St. Mary's until 1662, at which point he went to Chartham an old and worn out man.

When Charles II had landed at Dover in 1660 there had been great rejoicings and festivities. He went first to St Mary's to return thanks and was shown his seat in the Corporation pew. This was over the altar and in front of the east window. He refused to occupy it, saying that he would not darken the shadow of the Almighty and took the front seat in the nave.

The nave in St Mary's in those days was half the length it is now. It was extended and the low Norman arches copied and made to correspond with the old work. These low arches shut out the light from the galleries above and so several of the Norman arches were removed and four lofty arches in the Early English style replaced them.

St Mary's was rebuilt in 1843 (except the tower). The restoration was most faithfully carried out, each stone being numbered to ensure accuracy.

The church suffered damage in the Second World War from enemy bombing and subsequent restoration included the fitting of the present east windows. No ancient glass survives.

The entrance lobby at the base of the tower and the west gallery over it are both modern. On the front of the gallery are the royal arms of William and Mary, the arms of the Trinity House and of the Dover Harbour Board, the last two marking the close association of St Mary's with both the Harbour Board and the Cinque Ports Pilots.

The Seafarers' window in the chancel shows the T.S.S. *Invicta*, and the devices of the Royal Navy, the Merchant Navy, the Dutch Navy, the Southern Railway, Trinity House and the Cable Ships, all of which had operational associations with the town and harbour.

Among the flags is the personal flag of a famous Dover mariner, Captain H.L. Payne, Master of the *Invicta* and Commodore of the Southern Fleet, and that of the ship *Lady Brassey* of the Dover Harbour Board.

During my several visits to St Mary's I have found memorials inside the church, and headstones and tombs outside the church, all in memory of Worthingtons and related families.

Appendix 4

Bastardy Bond
From Dover Sessions of Peace 1706-13 held at the Dover Library, Kent

July 1710. 'Ann Brooks single woman delivered of a male bastard child in the parish of St James Dover on oath charged Bartholomew Worthington the younger of Dover, cooper, with the begotting of the said bastard child. The said Bartholomew Worthington is therefore judged by this Court to be the father of the male bastard child and is ordered that for the relief of said parish in part as also forward the maintenance of the said bastard child he shall not only forthwith pay unto the Churchwardens and overseers of St. James the sum of 10/- towards lying in of said Anne Brooks but also he shall pay the Churchwardens and Overseers of the said parish of St James for the time being for every week from henceforth so long as the said bastard child shall be chargeable, 1/6d of lawful British money; and is likewise advised it is ordered that the said Anne Brooks the mother shall pay from the birth of the said child for every week and weekly afterwards for so long as the said bastard child shall be chargeable to the said parish or she shall not keep the same 1/- of like money and lastly it is ordered that the said Bartholomew Worthington shall upon notice forthwith shall give sufficient security to the Churchwardens and Overseers of St James: The Recogca [recognizance: bond by which person engages before court or magistrate to observe some condition] of Bartholomew Worthington forefeited ...'.

Appendix 5

The following wills are transcribed from the originals. Any minor alterations arise from occasional problems inherent in the original script.

Will of Bartholomew Worthington of Dover 1718, PRC 32/59/495

In the name of God Amen
I Bartholomew Worthington of the Town and port of Dover in the County of Kent being weak in body but of sound mind and memory and mindfull of my Mortality do make and ordain this my last Will and Testament in manner and form following

Impris I give and bequeath my Soul into the Hands of Almighty God my maker trusting to receive the pardon of my Sins and the Salvation of my Soul through the Mercies of God and the alone merits of my Lord and Saviour Jesus Christ my body I commit to the Earth to be decently interred at the discretion of my Executrix hereafter named ...

As to that portion of goods it hath pleased God to bless me with I give and bequeath the same as follows

Item I give and bequeath to my Three Sonns, Bartholomew, Elias and Edward my Lease of the moiety of the House at the Pier that Nicholas White now lives in being Harbour Lease and all arrears of Rent which shall be due thereon at the Time of my Death equally to be divided between them upon this Express Condition that they give my Executrix full discharge of that Note which I sometime since gave my Mother herefor Ten pounds which I obliged my Selfe to pay them at my Death and not otherwise

Item I give to my Loving Wife Wilmet Worthington all the rest of my Estate both real and personall to her own use and behoffe and after her death to my Children John and Susan Worthington in Such Share and proportion as she shall by her last Will and Testament or any other Writing under her hand and seal signed in the presence of two or more Credible Witnesses limit proportion or appoint And I do hereby Consititute and appoint my said loving Wife Sole Executrix of this my last Will and Testament hereby revoking all former Wills.

In Witness Whereof I have hereunto set my Hand and Seale this one and twentieth day of December Anno Domini 1717 Bartholomew Worthington Signed sealed and published and declared by the said Bartholomew Worthington to be last Will and Testament ...

The above written will of Bartholomew Worthington late of Dover deceased, whose goods were in divers dioceses, was proved the 6th day of November in the year of our Lord 1718 in the rightful court where Simeon D'Enereme, legal surrogate clerk of the venerable man Thomas Bourchrie, Doctor of Law, was truly and legitimately appointed Commisary General of the City and Diocese of Canterbury and made administration of all and singular the goods of the said deceased and his will howsoever concerning Wilmett [sic] Worthington widow of the said deceased and executrix named in the aforesaid will and sworn on oath.

Appendix 6

Will of Edward Worthington 1719, Kent Archives, PRC 32/59/495

In the Name of God Amen

I Edward Worthington the Elder of the Town and port of Dover in the county of Kent, Cooper, being of sound mind and memory praised be to Almighty God for the same do make and ordain this my last Will and Testament in manner following

First and principally I commend my Soul to God who gave it hoping by and through the meritts and mercy of Jesus Christ my Saviour and Redeemer to inheritt eternall life and my body I committ to the Earth to be interred at the discretion of my Executor hereafter named

Item I give and bequeath to my son Thomas Worthington of Dover aforesaid Cooper and to his heirs and assigns forever All that my estate right title property claim interest and demand whatsoever of in and unto All that Messuage or Tenement with the Stable, Outhouses, Yard, Garden and Appurtenances thereunto belonging or appertaining Scituate lying and being in Biggon Street in the parish of St Mary's in Dover which is now in possession of the said Thomas Worthington To have and to hold to him the said Thomas Worthington and to his heirs and assigns forever

Item I give and bequeath unto my Said Son Thomas Worthington All my goods and chattels whatsoever and debts that shall be due to me and owing at the time of my decease and I do hereby make nominate and appoint my Said Son Thomas Worthington Sole Executor of this my last Will and Testament hereby revoking all former Will or Wills by me heretofore made and thus I conclude the same

In witness whereof I have hereunto set my hand and seal this tenth day of October Anno Domini 1719. E Worthington signed sealed published declared and delivered by the said Edward Worthington to be his last Will and Testament in the Presence of the Witnesses hereunder written who have Subscribed their Names in the Presence of the said Testator ... Jonas Botting, John Griggs, William Lamb. Not Published.

Examined by me Mark Upton N.P.

PROBATUM in Latin - testator died 1720.

Appendix 7

Will of Bartholomew Worthington 1724, PCC 32/60/90

In the Name of God Amen
I Bartholomew Worthington Eldest Son now living of Bartholomew Worthington late Master Cooper at his Majesties' Victualling Office at Dover in the County of Kent being weak in body but of Sound Mind and Memory do make this my last Will and Testament in manner following:

First I commend my Soul to almighty God who gave it and my body to the Earth to be decently buried near my late dear wife in the Church Yard of St Mary the Virgin in Dover aforesaid And as to my worldly estate I dispose thereof as follows:

Imprimis. I will that my Debts Legacies funerall charges with the probate of this my will be first paid.

Item I give to my Eldest Son Robert Worthington my Gold mourning Ring one piece of Gold Swedish Coin his own Silver Spoon marked R W one wrought Silver Spoon marked B W with a small silver spoon. Also the half of my wearing apparell both Linen and woollen and the other half I give unto my Son Richard Worthington to whom I also give one Corral Sett in Silver with Silver Bells and the Gold ring which was the Wedding Ring of my Said late Dear Wife's Mother with the Silver Spoon marked R L.

Item I give unto my Daughter Mildred Worthington the bed and furniture whereon I now lye in the Great Chamber with the Bolster two pillows one pair of Pillow Coats and one pair of good Holland sheets and I do give unto my said Daughter Mildred one plain silver spoon marked B W, her little Silver Tankard Little Gold Ring and all her late Mother's wearing apparell of what Nature soever with all her Childbed Linnen her late Mother's Gold Wedding Ring and the Chest or Case of Drawers now standing in my said Great Chamber.

Item I give to my dear brother Edward Worthington now Master Cooper of his Majesty's said Victualling Office the Gold Ring which I now wear Also my Fowling piece and the Gilt Image of the Lady on the Moon with the pedestall on which it now stands.

Item I give unto my loving brother in Law Richard Larkins a Gold Ring of the same value with that I have given my brother Edward And I do hereby Nominate and appoint my said Brother Edward Worthington and my said Brother in Law Richard Larkins my Trustees and Joint Executors of this my will to whom I do also give all other my Estate or what Nature soever whereof I shall die possessed or be entitled to and not herein before given or disposed of (that is to say) All my ready money plate Rings household goods and Debts due to me by bond, bill, Book or otherwise upon trust and confidence never-the-less in them reposed And to the Intent and purpose that my Said Trustees and Executors and the Survivor of them do sell and dispose of my said household goods and Estate for and towards the bringing up and maintenance of my said three Children as much in proportion to each of them as their respective Circumstances will from time to time permit And lastly I do hereby revoke and make void all former wills by me at any time heretofore made And do declare this and no other to be my last Will and Testament. In Witness whereof I have to this my last Will and Testament set my hand and seal this twenty first day of January in the year of our Lord Christ one thousand seven hundred and twenty four ... Wm Richardson, Cornelius Baker, James Ellis.

The above written will of Bartholomew Worthington late of Dover in the diocese of Canterbury, deceased, was proved the 29th day of January in the year of our Lord 1724 in the rightful court where Thomas Johnson, legal surrogate clerk of the venerable man Richard Chicheley, Bachelor of Law, was truly and legitimately appointed Commissary General of the City and Diocese of Canterbury and made administration of all and singular the goods, rights and dues of the said deceased and of his will however concerning Edward Worthington and Richard Larkins executors named in the aforesaid will and sworn on oath.

Appendix 8

Will of Andrew Worthington of Dover 1748, Liber 63, No.236, PRC 32/63/236

In the Name of God Amen

I Andrew Worthington Marriner of the Town and Port of Dovor in the County of Kent being of sound disposing mind and Memory and considering the Perils and Dangers of the Seas and other uncertainties of this transitory Life do for avoiding controversies after my decease make publish and declare this my last Will and Testament in manner following that is to say

First I recommend my Soul to God that gave it and my Body I commit to the Earth or Sea as it shall please God to order and as for and concerning all my Pay Wages Sum and Sums of Money Lands Tenements Goods Chattels and Estate whatsoever as shall be anyways due owing or belong unto me at the Time of my decease I do give and bequeath the same unto my loving Sister Sarah Davis of the Town and Port of Dovor [*sic*] in the County of Kent and do hereby nominate and appoint the said Sarah Davies [*sic*] Executor of last [will] and Testament hereby revoking all former and other Wills Testaments and Deeds of Gift by me at any Time heretofore made and I do ordain and ratify these Presents to stand and be for and as my last Will and Testament.

In Witness whereof I have hereunto set my Hand and Seal the Twenty Seventh day of September one Thousand and Seven Hundred and Forty Eight and in the Twenty Second Year of the Reign of our Sovereign Lord George the Second by the Grace of God of Great Britain France and Ireland King Defender of the Faith and so forth.

Andrew Worthington–Signed and Sealed published and declared in the Presence of Us - Edward Atherden, Ben Vernon. Examined W. Cullen.

The before Registered Will of Andrew Worthington deceased was proved the Seventh day of November in the Year 1749 before the Reverend William Gurney Clerk Surrogate to the Worshipful George Paul Doctor of Laws Commissary General of the City and Diocese of Canterbury lawfully constituted by the Oath of Sarah Davis Sole Executrix named in the said Will To whom Etc. She being first Sworn duly to Execute the same.

Appendix 9

Will of John Worthington of Dover 1747, Liver 63, No.108, PRC 32/63/108

In the Name of God Amen

I John Worthington of the Town and Port of Dover in the County of Kent Cooper being Aged but in good state of health and of sound and perfect mind and memory praised be God for the same and knowing the certainty of death but not knowing how soon do therefore make and ordain this my Last Will and Testament following First and Principally Recommend my Soul to God who gave it trusting through the Merits of Jesus Christ my Saviour and Redeemer to be made partaker of Everlasting Life and my Body I commit to the Earth to be Interred at the Discretion of my Executors hereafter named

Item - I give and bequeath unto my Loving Daughter Sarah Worthington All that my Messuage or Tenement Yard Garden Ground and Premises with the Appurtenances belonging lying and being in Biggin Street in Dover aforesaid and now in my own Occupation And all and every the household Goods Implements of household Bedding Linnen Brass and Pewter now standing and being in the aforementioned Messuage or Tenement and Premises for and during the Term of her natural Life committing no waste She my said Daughter Sarah permitting and suffering my Daughter Elizabeth Worthington to have her dwelling and living in the said Messuage or Tenement and Premises with the said Sarah so long as she the said Elizabeth shall remain Single and Unmarried if she shall think fit and convenient and no longer and from and after the decease of the said Sarah and Marriage of the said Elizabeth then I give and bequeath the said Messuage or Tenement Ground and Premises and all and every the said household Goods and Implements of household Bedding Linnen Brass and Pewter unto all and every my sons and daughters As shall be then living Anne, Mary, Richard, Andrew, John and Benjamin and to their heirs executors administrators or assigns for ever equally to be divided between them share and share alike

Item - I give and order my Son John to have and take such of my Working Tools as he shall have occasion for and the New Saw that is his own that I make use of And all the rest of my Tools to be equally divided between my said Sons Richard and Benjamin

Item - I give and and bequeath unto my daughters Sarah and Elizabeth Worthington the sum of Ten Pounds each to be paid by my Executors hereafternamed within three Months next after my decease

Item - All the rest and residue of Money and Securitys Plate Rings and other Goods and Chattels not hereinbefore given after my Debts Funeral Expenses and Charges of Probate of this my Will are paid and satisfied I give and bequeath unto my said Sons and Daughters, Sarah, Anne, Mary, Richard, Andrew, John, Benjamin and Elizabeth Worthington equally between them share and share alike And I hereby appoint my said sons Andrew and John Worthington full and sole Executors of this my said Will and thus I conclude the same revoking all former and other Will or Wills by me heretofore made

In witness whereof I the said John Worthington have to this my last Will contained in two Sheets of Paper to the first thereof set my hand and to the Last my hand and seal this first day of August in the Eighteenth Year of the Reign of Our Sovereign Lord George the [Second] by the Grace of God of Great Britain France and Ireland King Defender of the Faith etc. and in the Year of our Lord One Thousand Seven Hundred and Forty Four. Jn. Worthington Signed sealed published and declared by the said Testator as and for his last Will and Testament in the presence of Us who in his presence have subscribed our names as Witnesses hereunto S. Lambe, Wm. Lambe, Sampson Farbrace. Examined W. Cullen.

Appendix 10

Renunciation of Probate by Mary Worthington, 15 March 1757, before the Reverend William Broderip, Clerk Surrogate

Appointed personally George Plomer Notary Public one of the Proctors of this Court and Exhibited a Proxy under the hand and seal of Mary Worthington widow and Relict of Edward Worthington late of Dovor in the Diocese of Canterbury deceased by virtue whereof the said Plomer in the Name of the said Mary Worthington Renounced the Letters of Administration of the said deceased's Goods then appeared Personally–Bartholomew Worthington Natural and lawful Son of the said deceased and prayed that Letters of Administration of the said deceased's goods might be granted to which whereupon the said Surrogate in the Presence of the said Plomer [illegible] committed the Letters of Administration to him the said Bartholomew he being first sworn well and truly to Administer the same bound with him Edward Pain and William Iverson both of the City of Canterbury Victuallers in £200.

Appendix 11

Will of Elias Worthington of Dover 1773, PRC 32/65/585

In the Name of God Amen
I Elias Worthington of the Town and port of Dover in the County of Kent Cooper being aged and infirm of Body but of sound and disposing mind and memory praised be God do make and declare my last Will and Testament in manner following that is to say I give and bequeath unto my Nephew Robert Worthington his executors admons or Assigns the Sum of Twenty Pounds to be paid to him immediately after my decease. Also I give and bequeath unto my Kinsman Elias Worthington Son of Bartholomew Worthington deceased my Leasehold Messuage or tenement with the Ground and Appurtenances thereunto belonging (part of the Lands and Tenements belonging to the Harbour of Dover aforesaid) Situate lying and being in the Town and port of Dover aforesaid at or near a certain Street or Lane at the Pier there called Limekiln Lane and now in the Tenure or Occupation of [space] Rigden or his Assigns Together with the Lease thereof and also all the Estate Interest and Term of years which I shall have therein to come and be unexpired at the Time of my decease. Also All that my Workshop in the Back street and the Ground and Appurtenances thereunto belonging in Dover aforesaid late in the occupation of John Archer and now of the said Elias Worthington or his Assigns And also my two Messuages or Tenements in four several Dwellings Situate in the Town and Borough of Deal in the [   ] County of Kent and now or late in the several Occupations of the Widow Thompson and said Hayman and others To hold the same unto my said Kinsman Elias Worthington his Executors Administrators and Assigns Together with the several Leases thereof and also all the Estate Interest and Term of years therein respectively which I shall have to come and be unexpired at the time of my Decease. And as to all my Ready Money and Securities for Money, Goods, Chattels, Debts, Effects and all other my Personal Estate whatsoever Except the Legacy of Twenty Pounds hereinbefore given to the said Robert Worthington I Give and bequeath the same and every Part thereof unto the said Elias Worthington his Executors Administrators and Assigns And I do make and appoint the said Elias Worthington to be sole Executor of this my last Will and Testament And I do hereby revoke and make void all former Wills by me made and do publish and declare this only to be my last Will and Testament.

In Witness whereof I have to this my last Will and Testament contained in two Sheets of Paper set my hand to the first Sheet thereof and to this Second and last Sheet my hand and seal the Tenth day of May in the Thirteenth year of the Reign of our Sovereign Lord George the Third by the Grace of God King of Great Britain etc. And in the year of our Lord One thousand seven hundred and seventy three. Elias Worthington his mark Signed sealed published and delared by the said Elias Worthington the Testator as and for his last Will and Testament in the Presence of us who Subscribed our Names as Witnesses thereunto in the Presence of the said Testator. Thomas Bateman Lane, Abraham Obree, Phineas Kennett. Examined by W. Cullen.

Appendix 12

Will of Benjamin Worthington of Dover 1779, PCC Const. (PROB B11/1107) folio 326

In the Name of God Amen

I Benjamin Worthington of the Town and Port of Dover in the county of Kent Master Cooper of his Majesty's Victualling Office at the said port being of sound and disposing Mind and Memory praised be God for the same but considering the uncertainties of this mortal life do make and ordain this my last Will and Testament in manner and form following that is to say

I Give and |Devise all and singular my Messuages Lands Tenements and Hereditaments now situate whatsoever and wheresoever as well in possession as in reversion remainder or expectancy with their and every of their appurtenances to my beloved Wife Ann Worthington and her Heirs to the only use and behoof of her the said Ann Worthington her heirs and assigns for ever.

And I do also give and bequeath unto my said Wife Ann Worthington All my Leasehold Estate and all and singular my Personal Estate of every nature kind and quality whatsoever to have and to hold the same as her own proper Goods Chattels and Estate for ever and I do constitute and appoint my said Wife Ann Worthington sole Executrix of this my Will and do declare this and none other to be my last Will and Testament In witness whereof ... this sixteenth day of June 1779. Benjamin Worthington signed sealed and published by the said Benjamin Worthington the Testator as and for his last Will and Testament in the presence of us who at his request and in his presence have subscribed our Names as witnesses John Wellard - George Shaw - Wm. Morphew.

Appendix 13

Will of Edward Worthington 1812, PRC 32/68/168

In the Name of God Amen.

I Edward Worthington of Dover in the county of Kent being ill of Body but of sound mind memory and understanding thank God for the same do make this my last Will and Testament in manner and form following

I give unto my dear Wife Sarah Worthington all my Money, Stock, Furniture, Apparel together with all the Debts due to me to her and her Heirs for ever

I Give also unto my said Wife the House which I now live in And also my House joining the same built by me on the same Premises together with all the Ground and Appurtenances thereunto belonging during the Term of her Natural Life And after her decease I Give the said two Houses with the Ground and Appurtenances thereunto unto my Daughter Susannah Worthington and her Heirs for ever. But in Case my said Daughter Susannah Worthington should die before my Wife then and in that Case I give the said two Houses with the Ground and Appurtenances thereunto belonging which said two Houses are situated in Fifteen Post Lane in or near Paradise Pent, Strond Street, unto my said Wife Sarah Worthington to her and her heirs for ever.

I desire after my decease that all my just Debts and Funeral Expenses may be paid And I do hereby nominate constitute and appoint my dear Wife Sarah Worthington whole and sole Executrix of this my last Will and Testament. In Witness whereof I the said Edward Worthington have hereunto set my Hand and Seal this tenth day of December in the year of our Lord One thousand and eight hundred. The mark of X Edward Worthington Signed sealed and declared by the aforesaid Edward Worthington as and for his last Will and Testament in the presence of us who in the presence of each other have subscribed our names as witnesses thereto in his presence ... William Polhill, pawnbroker Dover. Sarah Goddin.

The before registered will of Edward Worthington deceased was proved the twenty first day of December 1812 before the Reverend John Francis Clerk Surrogate to the Right Honorable Sir William Scott Knight, Doctor of Laws, Commissary General of the City and Diocese of Canterbury lawfully constituted by the Oath of Sarah Worthington Widow the Relict and sole Executrix named in the said Will she being first sworn well and truly to perform the same.

Appendix 14

Will of Benjamin Jelly Worthington 1822
Proved 19 November 1822 PCC London (original in possession of the author)

Extracted by Jn Wills
Proctor, Doctors Commons

This is the last Will and Testament of me Benjamin Jelly Worthington of the Parish of Charlton in the Liberty of the Town and Port of Dover in the County of Kent Gentleman First I Give and Bequeath unto my beloved wife Elizabeth for her own use the sum of Two hundred pounds sterling to be paid to her immediately after my decease Also I give and bequeath unto my said Wife during the term of her natural life the free Use and Enjoyment of all and every of my Household Goods Furniture Plate Linen China Books and all and singular other my Household Effects and do authorize and empower her in case she shall after my death remove into a smaller house or shall give up housekeeping to sell and dispose of the same or such parts thereof as she may think proper together with the fixtures of my present dwelling house and the Monies to arise by any such Sale I direct shall go and be applied in the same manner as the monies to arise from the Residue of my Estates and Effects Also I give and devise unto my said Wife during her life All that my freehold Messuage or Tenement with the Coachhouse Stable Buildings Garden Land and Appurtenances thereunto belonging situate in the parish of Charlton aforesaid and now in my own occupation she keeping the Messuage and Buildings in tenantable repair and paying all Taxes and outgoings in respect of the said Premises And as to my said Dwellinghouse and premises and household furniture and effects subject to the said devise and Bequest to my said Wife And all and every other my Freehold and Leasehold Estates and all and singular other my Goods Chattels Monies in the Public Stocks or Funds Debts and Securities for money and all and singular other my property Estate and Effects whatsoever and wheresoever I give devise and bequeath the same and every part and parcel thereof unto my said Wife and to my Brother in Law William Collins of Dover aforesaid Brewer / whom I do hereby nominate and appoint Executrix and Executor of this my Will / their Heirs Executors and Administrators subject with respect to my personal Estate to the payment of my just debts funeral Expenses and the charges of proving and executing this my Will / Upon Trust that they or the survivor of them her or his Heirs Executors or Administrators shall and do dispose of such parts thereof as shall not consist of Ready money or be already invested in the funds and call in such Monies as shall be due to me on Mortgage or otherwise and do and shall lay out the monies which shall so come to their Hands in the purchase of Stock in the public Funds or upon good private securities at interest and do and shall stand possessed thereof and of all such other Stocks Funds and securities whereon any part of my Property shall at the time of my Death be invested Upon Trust to pay the annual Interest Dividends and Proceeds thereof unto my said wife during her life and after her decease Upon Trust to pay share and divide all the capital of such Stock Funds and securities unto and amongst all and every such children as I may leave or whereof my said Wife may be encient at the time of my Death in equal parts and proportions share and share alike The parts of such of them as shall be sons to be paid and assigned to them when and as they shall attain the age of twenty one years and of such of them as shall be daughters at the like age or on the days of their respective marriages before that age with the consent of my said Executrix and Executor or of the survivor of them her or his Executors or Administrators whichever shall first happen And in case of the Death or Deaths of any of my children before his her or their share or shares shall become payable then the same to go to the survivors or survivor of my said children and the issue of any of them that shall then be dead such issue to take only the share or shares to which his her or their deceased parent or parents would have been entitled if living Provided always that it shall be lawful for my said Executrix and Executor or the survivor of them her or his Executors or Administrators to sell and dispose of either by public sale or Private contract of my said Dwelling house Coachhouse Buildings Stable Garden Land and Appurtenances at Charlton aforesaid and to lay out and invest the monies arising thereby in the purchase of another Dwellinghouse either Freehold or Leasehold for the Residence of my Wife and Family or upon Government or Private Securities at their or her or his Discretion Upon the same or like trusts as before declared concerning the Residue of my Property and Effects And upon any Sale or Sales of my said Dwelling house and

Premises I declare that the Receipts or Receipt of my said Executrix and Executor or of the survivor of them her or his executor or administrators whichever shall first happen And in case of the death or deaths of any of my children before his her or their share or shares shall become payable then the same shall go to the survivors or survivor of my said children and the issue of any of them that shall then be dead such issue to take only the share of shares to which his her or their deceased parent or parents would have been entitled if living provided always that it shall be lawful for my said Executrix and Executor or the survivor of them her or his Executors or Administrator to sell and dispose of either by public sale or private contract of my said Dwellinghouse Coachhouse Buildings, Stable Garden Land and Appurtenances at Charlton aforesaid and to lay out and invest the monies arising thereby in the purchase of another Dwellinghouse either freehold or Leasehold for the Residence of my Wife and family or upon Government or private Securities at their or her or his Discretion Upon the same of life trust as before declared concerning the Residue of my property and Effects And upon any Sale or Sales of my said Dwelling house and premises I declare that the Receipts or Receipt of my said Executrix and Executors or the survivor of them her or his executors or administrators shall sufficiently discharge the purchaser or purchasers thereof without he she or they being liable to see to the application or being answerable or accountable for the misapplication or nonapplication of the purchase money or any part thereof Provided also and I do hereby authorize my said Executrix and Executor her or his Executors or Administrators by and out of the monies which shall come to their hands to lay out and advance such sum of money as may be required for the purchase of the outstanding part or share of my Stable and Garden adjoining my Dwelling house in Charlton aforesaid and of such other part of the Ground and premises belonging to my said Dwellinghouse and Buildings or whereon any part thereof hath been erected as such outstanding part or share may relate to or affect And when and so soon as the same shall be so purchased I direct that it may be conveyed to my said Executrix and Executor their Heirs and Assigns Upon such and the like trusts intents and purposes as are hereinbefore mentioned expressed and declared concerning my said Dwellinghouse and Appurtenances Provided also that in case the annual interest and dividends of my property shall be found insufficient to maintain my wife and to provide for the maintenance education and bringing up of my children I do in such case authorize and empower my said Executrix and Executor and the survivor of them her or his executors or administrators to apply a competent part of the Capital of the said trust funds for those purposes Provided also that in case my said Wife shall find that the annual income arising from my property shall be insufficient to maintain her comfortably I do in that case authorize and require my said Executor to join with her in raising any sum not exceeding eight hundred pounds sterling to be laid out in the purchase of an Annuity during the Life of my said Wife either in the Bank of England or such public or private Company or individual or individuals as my said Wife shall judge best such annuity when purchased to be for the absolute use and benefit of my said wife during her life Provided also that if my said Wife shall die leaving any of my Children in his her or their minority it shall be lawful for my Executor his Executors or Administrators to apply as well the Annual Dividends and interest as also the capital if necessary of the share or shares of such Children for their better maintenance education and support and for the putting out apprentice or otherwise advancing him her or them in life Provided also that my Executrix and Executor shall not be answerable the one for the other of them or for the Acts Deeds Receipts or defaults of the other of them but each of them for her and his own acts Deeds Receipts and defaults only And that they shall be at Liberty to deduct retain and to reimburse themselves all such charges expenses as they shall necessarily be put to or sustain in or about the execution of the Trusts hereby in them reposed In witness whereof I the said Benjamin Jelly Worthington the Testator have to this my last Will and Testament contained in four sheets of Paper to the first three sheets thereof set my hand and to this fourth and last sheet thereof set and affixed my Hand and Seal this fifteenth day of January in the year of our Lord one thousand eight hundred and twenty two–B.J. Worthington Signed sealed published and declared by the said Benjamin Jelly Worthington the Testator as and for his last Will and Testament in the presence of us who in his presence at his request and in the Presence of each other have hereunto subscribed our names as witnesses–Michael Moses, Dover, gentleman–Wm. Shipden of Dover, gentleman–John Shipden, solicitor, Dover.

Appendix to this the last will and testament of me Benjamin Jelly Worthington

Charles by divine providence, Archbishop of Canterbury, Primate of all England, and Metropolitan, do by these presents make known to all Men, that on the nineteenth Day of November in the Year of our

Lord, One Thousand Eight Hundred and Twenty-Two at London, before the Right Honorable Sir John Nicholl Knight, Doctor of Laws, Master, Keeper, or Commissary of our Prerogative Court of Canterbury, lawfully constituted the last Will and Testament of Benjamin Jelly Worthington late of Charlton in the Liberty of Dover in the County of Kent, Gentleman deceased hereunto annexed, was proved, approved, and registered; the said Deceased having whilst living, and at the time of his Death, Goods, Chattels, or Credits, in divers Dioceses or Jurisdictions, by reason whereof the proving and registering the said Will, and the granting Administration of all and singular the said Goods, Chattels, and Credits, and also the auditing, allowing, and final discharging the Account thereof, are well known to appertain only and wholly to us, and not to any inferior Judge; and that Administration of all and singular the Goods, Chattels, and Credits of the said Deceased, and any Way concerning his Will was granted to Elizabeth Worthington, widow, the Relict of the Deceased and William Collins the Executors named in the said Will they having been already sworn by Commission well and faithfully to administer the same, and to make a true and perfect Inventory of all and singular the said Goods, Chattels, and Credits, and to exhibit the same into Registry of our said Court, on or before the last Day of May next ensuing, and also to render a just and true Account thereof. Given at the time and place above written and in the eighteenth year of our Translation. (Three signatures of Deputy Registrars)

Sworn under Two Thousand Pounds.

180   The last will and testament of Benjamin Jelly Worthington.

Release of Legacies and Indemnity to Executors 1845, Dated 21 August
(original in possession of author)

The Residuary Legatees under the will of the Mr Benjamin Jelly Worthington deceased and the Executors of the surviving Executor

THIS INDENTURE made the twenty first day of August One thousand eight hundred and forty five between Benjamin Worthington of Dover in the County of Kent a Lieutenant in Her Majesty's Royal Navy, Benjamin Fairthorne of Shrivenham near Farringdon in the County of Berks and Harriot his wife (late Harriot Worthington Spinster), Charlotte Worthington of Dover aforesaid Spinster, George Finch Jennings of Dover aforesaid Esquire and Hester his Wife (late Hester Worthington Spinster), together with Robert Potter of Lydden in the County of Kent Esquire, and Henry Worthington of Dover aforesaid Esquire, which said Robert Potter and Henry Worthington are Trustees of and under the Marriage Settlement of the said George Finch Jennings and Hester his Wife as hereinafter recited, William Collins Worthington of Lowestoft in the County of Suffolk, Surgeon, Thomas Knight Worthington of Dover aforesaid Surgeon, and the said Henry Worthington of the first part, Henry Fairthorne of Brightwell near Wellingford in the County of Berks Esquire of the second part, the said Benjamin Fairthorne together with Mary Anne Fairthorne, Elizabeth Fairthorne, Charlotte Fairthorne, Hester Sophia Fairthorne, Edward Fairthorne and Augusta Fairthorne (which said last mentioned seven parties are the only Children of Elizabeth the late deceased Wife of the said Henry Fairthorne who was formerly Elizabeth Worthington Spinster) of the third part, and the said Benjamin Worthington and Charlotte Worthington of the fourth part. WHEREAS Benjamin Jelly Worthington formerly of the Parish of Charlton in Dover aforesaid Gentleman by his Will bearing date the fifteenth day of January one thousand eight hundred and twenty two after certain specific legacies and directions therein contained Gave and devised all the residue of his estate and effects unto his Wife Elizabeth and his Brother in law William Collins of Dover aforesaid Brewer whom he thereby appointed Executrix and Executor of that his Will Upon trust of his said Wife during her life And after her decease Upon trust to pay and divide the Capital unto and amongst all and every such Children as Testator might leave or whereof his said Wife might be encient at the time of his decease in equal parts and proportions share and share alike the parts of such of them as should be Sons to be paid and assigned to them when and as they should attain the age of Twenty one years and of such of them as should be daughters at the like age or on the days of their respective marriages before that age with the consent of Testators said Executrix and Executor or of the survivor of them his or her executors or administrators whichever should first happen And in case of the death or deaths of any of his said Children before his or her share or shares should become payable then the same to go to the survivor or survivors of his said Children and the issue of any of them who should be then dead Such issue to take only the share or shares to which his her or their deceased parent or parents would have been entitled if living AND WHEREAS the said Benjamin Jelly Worthington the Testator departed this life on the twenty seventh day of October One thousand eight hundred and twenty two and his said Will was duly proved in the Prerogative Court of Canterbury on the nineteenth day of November one thousand eight hundred and twenty two by Elizabeth Worthington the Widow of the deceased and William Collins the Executors named in the said Will AND WHEREAS the said William Collins departed this life on the thirty first day of July One thousand eight hundred and thirty one—AND WHEREAS the said Elizabeth Worthington departed this life on the thirtieth day of April one thousand eight hundred and forty five having by her Will appointed the said Benjamin Worthington and Charlotte Worthington her Executors who both proved the same in the Prerogative Court of the Archbishop of Canterbury on the [blank] day of May last AND WHEREAS the said Benjamin Worthington left surviving him eight Children namely Elizabeth Fairthorne (late the wife of the said Henry Fairthorne) the said Benjamin Worthington the said Harriot Fairthorne (the Wife of the said Benjamin Fairthorne) Charlotte Worthington Hester Jennings (the Wife of the said George Finch Jennings) William Collins Worthington Thomas Knight Worthington and Henry Worthington all of whom attained the age of twenty one years AND WHEREAS the said Elizabeth Fairthorne departed this life on the third day of April one thousand eight hundred and twenty eight leaving her Husband the said Henry Fairthorne and seven Children being the parties hereto of the third part her surviving AND WHEREAS by an Indenture bearing date the twenty seventh day of September one thousand eight hundred and thirty one (being a settlement made on the occasion of the marriage of the said George Finch Jennings and Hester his wife) made between the said George Finch Jennings of the first part the said Hester Jennings (by her then description of Hester Worthington (Spinster) of the second part and the said Benjamin Worthington and Robert Potter (the deceased father of the said Robert Potter party hereto) together with John Pembrooke since deceased of the third part and by one or more Indenture or Indentures appointing new Trustees subsequent thereto and by the deaths or resignation of Trustees all the estate and interest of the said Hester Jennings under the said recited Will of the said Benjamin Jelly Worthington deceased is now vested in the said Robert Potter (party hereto) and Henry Worthington with full power for them to receive and give valid discharge for the same AND WHEREAS the said Benjamin Worthington and Charlotte Worthington as the acting Executors of the Will of the said Benjamin Jelly Worthington deceased have produced an account of the property of the said Testator by which it appears that after payment of all debts funeral expenses probate charges legacy duty and other expenses the residue of the said Testators estate now consists or recently consisted of the following property namely a few articles of furniture together with the sum of Nine hundred and seventy eight pounds eleven shillings and seven pence sterling AND WHEREAS the said parties hereto have examined or are satisfied with the accounts as they severally testify by executing these presents AND WHEREAS to settle any differences that may exist respecting the construction of the said Will the property so constituting the residue has been paid and divided immediately before the execution of this Indenture (with the mutual consent of all the said parties hereto) in manner following namely one eighth share thereof to the said Benjamin Worthington one eighth share thereof to the said Benjamin Fairthorne and Harriot his Wife one eighth share thereof to the said Charlotte Worthington one eighth share thereof to the said Robert Potter and Henry Worthington as Trustees under the Marriage Settlement of the said George Finch Jennings and Hester his Wife one eighth share thereof to the said William Collins Worthington one eighth share thereof to the said Thomas Knight Worthington one eighth share thereof to the said Henry Worthington and the remaining one eighth share unto and equally between the said parties hereto of the third part as the children of the said Elizabeth Fairthorne deceased And the said several parties hereto in consideration of such payment and division the receipt and payment whereof they hereby respectively acknowledge have agreed to execute the Release and Indemnity hereinafter contained NOW this Indenture WITNESSETH that in pursuance of the said recited agreement and in consideration of the payments and divisions so made as hereinbefore recited It is hereby declared and agreed by and between the several persons parties hereto of the first part in the respective characters and capacities aforesaid each of them for himself or herself his and her respective heirs executors and administrators and as far as they can or may be interested or entitled (except that the said Robert Potter and Henry Worthington as such Trustees as aforesaid are to be answerable for their own acts only) and in particular it is agreed by the said George Finch Jennings in respect of the share so to be paid or divided to the said Robert Potter and Henry Worthington as such Trustees as aforesaid and in respect of any further shares or property (if any) to which they the said George Finch Jennings and Hester his Wife or the said Robert Potter or Henry Worthington or either of them (as such Trustees for the said George Finch Jennings and Hester his Wife as aforesaid) are or may be in any wise entitled under the said Will of the said Benjamin Jelly Worthington deceased And it is also expressly agreed by the said parties hereto of the second and third parts jointly and severally and for their and each of their heirs executors and administrators in respect of the shares so to be paid or divided to the said parties hereto of the third part and in respect of any further shares or property (if any) to which the said parties hereto of the second and third parts or any of them are or may in any ways interested or entitled under the said Will of the said Benjamin Jelly Worthington deceased That they the said Benjamin Worthington and Charlotte Worthington and each of them and their respective heirs executors and administrators and the heirs executors and administrators for the time being of the said Benjamin Jelly Worthington and Elizabeth Worthington deceased and every of them shall be for ever discharged and indemnified from and against all actions suits accounts and claims both at law and in equity which they the said several parties hereto or either of them in any such characters or capacities as aforesaid or otherwise howsoever or their respective heirs executors administrators or assigns now have or but for these presents could or might have or enforce concerning the several sums of money or property so paid or divided or agreed to be paid or divided as aforesaid and from and against all claims damages and expenses on account thereof by any person whomsoever claiming or pretending to claim under the said Will of the said Benjamin Jelly Worthington deceased IN WITNESS whereof the said parties to these presents have hereunto set their hands and seals the day and year first above written.

Signatures and seals:

Benjamin Fairthorne	Harriot Fairthorne
George Finch Jennings	Hester Jennings
Robert Potter	Henry Worthington
William Collins Worthington	Thomas Knight Worthington
Henry Fairthorne	Mary Anne Fairthorne
Elizabeth Fairthorne	Charlotte Fairthorne
Hester Sophia Fairthorne	Edward Fairthorne
Augusta Fairthorne	Benjamin Worthington
Charlotte Worthington	

The 'Instructions' stated 'This Deed to be signed by each party where their names are written in pencil; each party to put a stamp on the wax and say "I deliver this as my deed"–this to be done in the presence of an impartial witness, who must sign a proper attestation (according to the form of the other attestations) on the back of the Deed the names of the parties executing being properly introduced in such attestation'.

William Collins Worthington, Thomas Knight Worthington, George Finch Jennings and Hester, his wife and Charlotte Worthington all signed in the presence of James Hukes, Surgeon, 5 Lower Seymour Street, Portman Square, London.

Benjamin and Harriot Fairthorne signed in the presence of John Bradford, Gentleman, Shrivenham, Berkshire.

Benjamin Worthington, Henry Worthington and Robert Potter signed in the presence of Edward Elwin, Solicitor, Dover.

Henry, Mary Anne, Elizabeth, Charlotte, Hester Sophia, Augusta and Edward Fairthorne signed in the presence of John Dearlove, Farmer of Brightwell, Berkshire.

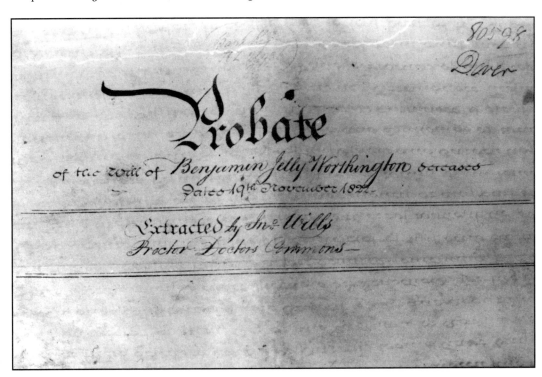

181 Will of Benjamin Jelly Worthington.

68 Signatures and seals on release of legacies and indemnity to executors, 1845.

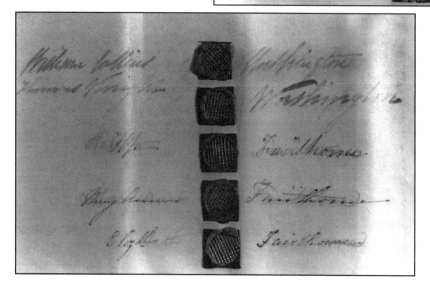

Appendix 15

I Elizabeth Worthington of Dover in the County of Kent Widow declare my Will to be as follows. I appoint my son Benjamin and my daughter Charlotte Worthington Executors of this my Will and direct that their receipts and the receipts of my executors for the time being shall fully discharge any persons paying them any money under this my Will from sealing to the application thereof

I bequeath my wearing apparel unto and equally between my three daughters Harriot the Wife of Mr Benjamin Fairthorne the said Charlotte Worthington and Hester the Wife of Mr George Finch Jennings

I bequeath my Carriage and the furniture harness and implements in uses therewith or adjoining thereto unto my daughters the said Charlotte Worthington and Hester Jennings absolutely

And I bequeath all my furniture plated goods and household effects (except my linen china and a glass) unto my said daughter Charlotte for her absolute use

I bequeath my linen china and glass unto and equally between all my children equally and if any difference arises respecting the division thereof I direct that the same shall be divided in such manner as my executors may think just and equitable

I direct that a Marble tablet be erected in Buckland Church to the memory of my late dear husband and myself and that my executors shall appropriate the sum of about fifty pounds or such further sum as they shall find necessary for such purpose

And I bequeath all the Residue of my property as to six seventh shares thereof unto and equally between my children Benjamin Worthington Charlotte Worthington Hester Jennings William Collins Worthington Thomas Knight Worthington and Henry Worthington as tenants in common for their absolute benefit and as to the remaining seventh share thereof I direct that the same shall be retained by my executors and be invested in some or one of the public funds of this Kingdom upon trust to allow my said daughter Harriot Fairthorn to receive the annual income thereof for her separate use during her life or otherwise to [*illegible*] and pay the same to such person or persons and for such purposes as she shall whether married or single by writing under her hand from time to time appoint but so as not to charge alias or anticipate the same free from the control of any husband to whom she may be married and for which her receipts alone or the receipts of her appointees for the time being that be a sufficient discharge and immediately after her decease upon trust for my granddaughter Elizabeth Harriot the of eldest child of my said Mary for her absolute benefit with power for her executors to apply the annual income thereof towards the maintenance of my said granddaughter till she attains the age of twenty one years but in case my said granddaughter shall die before me or under the age of twenty one years then such seventh share shall be divided after the decease of the said Harriot Fairthorne among my other six children or their representatives

In Witness my hand this twenty second day of May one thousand eight hundred and forty four. Elizabeth Worthington (sgd) Signed by the said Elizabeth Worthington the Testatrix and acknowledged by her to be her Will in the presence of us who in the presence at the same time and in the presence of each other here unto subscribe our Names as Witnesses [*illegible*]

Proved at London 22nd May 1845 before the Judge by the Oath of Benjamin Worthington the Son and Charlotte Worthington Spinster the Daughter the Executors to whom Administration was granted having first sworn duly to administer.

Appendix 16

Will of Henry Worthington of Dover 1866

THIS IS THE LAST WILL AND TESTAMENT of me HENRY WORTHINGTON of Dover in the County of Kent Esquire I Devise and bequeath to my brothers in law the Reverend Peter Harnett Jennings Clerk and Robert Finnis Jennings Esquire all my freehold Estate situate at Maxton in the Parish of Hougham in the said County of Kent as the same is now in the tenures or occupations of George Hammins & William Brazier with its rights members and appurtenances to hold the same unto and to the use of the said Peter Harnett Jennings and Robert Finnis Jennings their heirs and assigns Upon the trusts hereinafter declared that is to say Upon trust to pay and apply the yearly rents assets and profits of my said Estate as the same shall become due after payment of the annual Insurance of the Buildings against fire and all other landlords charges affecting the said Unto and equally between my two daughters Sophia Worthington and Maria Henrietta Worthington so long as they shall both remain single and unmarried and from and immediately after the marriage or death of one of them whichever shall first happen upon trust to pay and apply the whole of the said yearly rents taxes and profits subject as aforesaid to the other of them until she shall be married or die and from and immediately after the marriage or decease of my said two daughters upon trust with all convenient speed to sell and dispose of my said Estate at Maxton by Public Auction or Private Contract to any person willing to become the purchaser or purchasers thereof for such price or prices as to my said trustees shall seem reasonable and for the purpose of promoting and facilitating such sale I direct my said Trustees to enter into make and execute all such contracts conveyances assurances acts and deeds which they shall deem proper And I declare that the receipt and receipts of my said Trustees for any money payable to them or any amount whatsoever under the trusts of this my Will shall effectually discharge any purchaser or other person or persons paying the same from being answerable or accountable for the misappropriation or nonapplication thereof or of any part thereof or to inquire into the necessity or propriety of any sale or sales made under this my Will I direct my said trustees to stand possessed of any Interest in the monies arising from such sale after paying all necessary expenses of the said sale and incidental thereto Upon trust to divide and pay the same equally between and amongst my sons George Finch Jennings Worthington Thomas Worthington Robert Worthington and my daughter Charlotte Worthington and also to my said daughters Sophia and Maria Henrietta if they my two last mentioned daughters or either of them shall still be living and the survivors and survivor of all my said Children and the lawful child or children of any one of them who may be then dead such child or children taking his her or their parents share in such parts shares and proportions that they may take per stirpes and not per capita I give and bequeath all my goods chattels money and securities for money and other my personal Estate unto my said Trustees their executors administrators and assigns Upon trust with all convenient speed after my decease to call in and convert into money all my said personal estate or such part thereof as shall not consist of money and with and out of the monies arising from such calling in and conversion of my said personal Estate to pay satisfy and discharge all my just debts funeral and testamentary expenses and then to divide and pay the residue of the produce of my said personal Estate unto and equally between my said Three Sons George Thomas and Robert and my said daughters Sophia Maria and Charlotte or to such of them as shall be living at the time of my decease and in case any one or more of my said last mentioned children shall die in my lifetime leaving any lawful issue living at his or her decease or born in due time afterwards then I direct the share or shares of my said son or sons daughter or daughters so dying shall be and remain in trust for such issue of my said Son or Sons or daughter or daughters so dying as aforesaid who shall be living at the death or respective deaths of his her or their parent or respective parents or be born in due time afterwards and in such parts shares and proportions that such my grandchildren may take per stirpes and not per capita And I hereby declare that if the Trustees hereby appointed or to be appointed as hereafter is provided or either of them shall die or be desirous of being discharged or refuse or become incapable to act then and so often as the said Trustees or Trustee (and for this purpose any retiring Trustee shall be considered a Trustee) may appoint any other fit person or persons to be a Trustee or Trustees in the place of the Trustee or Trustees so dying or desiring to be discharged or refusing or becoming incapable to act And upon every such appointment the said trust premises shall be so transferred that the same may become vested in the new Trustee or Trustees jointly with the surviving or continuing Trustee or Trustees or solely as occasion may require and every such new Trustee shall have the same powers authorities and discretions as if he had been hereby originally appointed a Trustee And I declare that the Trustees or Trustee for the time being of this my Will shall be chargeable only for such monies only as they or he respectively shall actually receive And shall not be answerable the one for the other of them nor for any Banker broker or other person in whose hands any of the trust monies shall be placed nor for involuntary losses And that the said Trustees or Trustee for the time being may reimburse themselves or himself out of the monies which shall come to their or his hands under the trusts aforesaid all expenses to be incurred in or about the execution of the aforesaid trusts I appoint the said Peter Harnett Jennings and Robert Finnis Jennings EXECUTORS of this my Will In witness whereof I the said Henry Worthington the Testator have to this my last Will and Testament contained in three sheets of paper hereunto set my hand the Sixteenth day of December One thousand eight hundred and sixty five   HENRY WORTHINGTON signed and declared by the said Henry Worthington (the testator) as and for his last Will and Testament in writing in the presence of us both present at the same time who in his presence at his request and in the presence of each other have hereunto subscribed our names as witnesses WM HUGH DENNETT Worthing Sussex Solcr HORATIO LUCKETT his clerk

PROVED at London 7th March 1866 by the Oaths of the Revd Peter Harnett Jennings Clerk and Robert Finnis Jennings Esquire the Executors to whom Administration was granted.

Appendix 17

Will of Henry Jelly senior, 1756, PRC 32/64/65

In the Name of God Amen I Henry Jelly of the Town and Port of Dover in the County of Kent One of the Jurats of the said Town and port being in Good health and of sound and disposing mind and Memory (praised by God) do make and ordain this my last Will and Testament in manner following (that is to say) I Give and bequeath unto my Sons Henry Jelly, Slodden Jelly and Benjamin Worthington the sum of Twenty pounds a piece for Mourning. Also I Give and bequeath unto my Three Daughters Mary Jelly, Affra Jelly, and Susanna Jelly their Executors Administrators and Assigns equally to be divided between them share and share alike All that my Leasehold Messuage of Tenement wherein I now dwell with the Ground and Appurtenance thereto belonging and the Tenement or Laundry adjoining thereto with the Appurtenances situate and being in or near Snargate Street in Dover aforesaid together with the Lease and Leases thereof and all the Estate Term and Terms of years and Interest I shall have therein at my Death. Also I give devise and bequeath unto them my said Three Daughters Mary Jelly, Affra Jelly and Susanna Jelly their Heirs Executors Administrators and Assigns equally to be divided between them share and share alike All my Real Estate whatsoever ... and all my Ready money and Securities for money Household Goods Plate Linnen and other my Personal Estate whatsoever and I do nominate and appoint them my said Three Daughters to be Executors of this my Last Will and Testament and I hereby revoke all former and other Wills by me made and do publish and declare this only to be my last Will and Testament.

In Witness whereof ... the twenty ninth day of August in the twenty eighth year of the Reign of Our Sovereign Lord George the Second King of Great Britain etc. and in the year of Our Lord One Thousand Seven hundred and Fifty Four ... Witnessess Peter Fector, Hughes Minet, Wm Lane.

The before Registered Will of Henry Jelly late of Dover in the Diocese of Canterbury deceased having Goods etc. in diverse Dioceses was proved the 16 day of January 1756 before the Rev. Wm. Broderip Clerk Lawful Surrogate to the Worshipful Edward Simpson Doctor of Laws Commissary General of the City and Diocese of Canterbury ... and his Will was committed to Mary Jelly, Affra Jelly, and Susanna Jelly Executrixes ... .

Appendix 18

Will of Knight Collins 1805, PRO (PROB 11/1433)

This is the last Will and Testament of me Knight Collins of the Town and Port of Dovor [sic] in the County of Kent, Brewer in manner following that is to say, I give devise and bequeath unto my beloved wife Elizabeth The Rents and Profits of all and every my Messuages Lands Tenements and Hereditaments together with the profits arising from my Brewing Trade And also the Interest dividends and profits of all and every my Monies Stocks Funds and other Securities or Money And the Use Profit and advantage of all and singular my Household Goods Furniture Plate Linen and Gilt and of all other my Estate and Effects whatsoever and wheresoever that I shall be possessed interested in or intitled unto at the time of my decease whether in Possession Reversion Remainder Expectancy or otherwise To hold in the same to her my said wife Elizabeth and her assigns for and during the term of her natural Life and for her own proper use and benefit she and they keeping my said Messuages and Buildings in good and tenantable Repair and Condition and paying thereout all and every my just Debts Funeral Expenses Charges of proving this my Will and other incident charges And from and immediately after the decease of my said wife Elizabeth then I give devise and bequeath All and every my said Messuages Land Tenements and Hereditaments Goods Chattels Farming Stock Stock in Trade Monies Securities for Money my Monies in the Public Funds of five per Cent Bank Annuities and my Leasehold Messuages hereinafter mentioned excepted and all other my personal estate whatsoever and wheresoever Unto my Son William Collins for and during the term of his natural Life And from and immediately after his decease I give and bequeath the same and every part thereof my Leasehold Estate and Monies in the Fund of five per Cent Bank Annuities as aforesaid excepted unto and equally between such Child and Children of my said son William Collins lawfully to be begotten as shall live to attain the age of twenty one years and to his her or their Heirs Executors Administrators and Assigns for ever And my Mind and Will is that if my said son William Collins shall depart this Life without leaving any such Child or Children or shall not live to attain the Age of twenty one years as aforesaid Then and in that Case I give and bequeath All and every my said Messuages Lands Tenements and Hereditaments Goods Chattels Farming Stock Stock in Trade Monies Securities for Money except my Monies in the five per cent Bank Annuities and Leasehold Estate aforesaid and all other my Personal Estate unto and equally between each Child and Children of my son Thomas Collins lawfully begotten as shall live to attain the age of twenty one years to his her or their Heirs Executors Administrators and Assigns for ever And in case both my said Sons shall depart this Life without such Issue as aforesaid Then I give and bequeath All and every my said Messuages Lands Tenements and Hereditaments Goods Chattels Farming Stock Stock in Trade Monies Securities for Money except as before excepted unto and among all and every the Child and Children of my Daughter Elizabeth Worthington wife of Benjamin Jelly Worthington of Dover aforesaid Mariner equally to be divided between them as Tenants in Common and not as joint Tenants and to their several and respective Heirs Executors Administrators and Assigns for ever And from and after the Decease of my said wife Elizabeth I give devise and bequeath the Interest Dividends and Proceed of the Sum of three thousand pounds five per Cent Bank Annuities standing in my own Name in the Books at the Bank of England amounting to the Sum of one hundred and fifty pounds per annum Unto my said Son Thomas Collins for and during the term of his natural Life the first payment to be made to him when the dividends shall become due next after the decease of my said wife And from and after the decease of my said Son Thomas Collins I give and bequeath One Annuity or Yearly Sum of Twenty pounds Stirling to be paid and payable out of the Interest Dividends and Proceed of the said Sum of Three thousand pounds five per Cent Bank Annuities unto the wife or widow of said son Thomas Collins for and during such time and term as she shall remain a widow and unmarried and no longer and from and after the decease of my said Son Thomas Collins I give and bequeath the said principal sum of Three thousand pounds Stock subject to the payment thereout of the annual sum of Twenty pounds to the wife or widow of my said son Thomas Collins during her widowhood as aforesaid unto and among the Child or Children of my said Son Thomas Collins lawfully begotten in equal shares and proportions if more than one at their respective ages of twenty one years the Interest Dividend and Proceed thereof in the mean time to be applied toward the Maintenance and Education of such Child or Children during their Minority to and for their own proper and respective use and benefit and to his her or their Executors Administrators and Assigns And in Case my said Son Thomas Collins shall happen to die without leaving any such Child or Children lawfully begotten or shall or may leave any who shall die under the Age of twenty one years Then I give and bequeath the said Principal Sum of three thousand pounds Stock subject to the payment thereout of the annual sum of twenty pounds as aforesaid to the Widow of my said Son Thomas Collins in case he should leave such Widow him surviving unto and amongst the Child or Children of my said Daughter Elizabeth Worthington in equal shares and proportions at their respective ages of twenty five Years and to his her or their Executors Administrators and Assigns Also I give devise and bequeath the Interest Dividends and Proceed of the further sum of three thousand pounds five per Cent Bank Annuities unto my said Daughter Elizabeth Worthington and the said Benjamin Jelly Worthington her husband for and during the term of their joint natural Lives and the life of the longer liver of them And from and immediately after the decease of both of them the said Elizabeth Worthington and Benjamin Jelly Worthington Then I give and bequeath the said last mentioned Sum of three thousand pounds Stock unto and among all the Child or Children of the said Benjamin Jelly Worthington and Elizabeth his wife in equal shares and proportions at their respective ages of twenty five years the Interest Dividends and Proceed thereof in the mean time to be applied towards the Maintenance and Education of such Child or Children during their Minority and to his her or their Executors Administrators and Assigns Also I give devise and bequeath All that Leasehold Messuage or Tenement situate in Snargate Street in Dover aforesaid and now in the occupation of the said Benjamin Jelly Worthington unto the said Benjamin Jelly Worthington and Elizabeth his wife for and during the term of both their joint natural Lives and the Life of the longer liver of them And from and immediately after the decease of the longer liver of them Then I give and bequeath the said Leasehold Messuages and premises unto Thomas Knight Worthington Son of the said Benjamin Jelly Worthington and Elizabeth his wife at his Age of twenty five years And to his Executors Administrators and Assigns to and for his own proper Use and benefit But in case the said Thomas Knight Worthington shall depart this Life before he attains the said Age of twenty five Years Then I give and bequeath the said Leasehold Messuages and Premises unto and among the other Child and Children of the said Benjamin Jelly Worthington and Elizabeth his wife equally to be divided between them at their respective Ages of twenty five Years and to their several and respective Executors Administrators and Assigns also from and after the decease of my said wife Elizabeth I give and bequeath unto the Children of my said daughter Elizabeth Worthington namely as follows The Sum of one thousand pounds five per Cent Bank Annuities standing in my Name in the Books of the Bank of England Unto Elizabeth Worthington daughter of my said daughter Elizabeth Worthington The sum of one thousand pounds five per cent Bank Annuities unto Benjamin Worthington The sum of one thousand pounds five per cent Bank Annuities unto Harriot Worthington The sum of one thousand pounds five per cent Bank Annuities unto Charlotte Worthington The Sum of one thousand pounds five per cent Bank Annuities unto Hester Worthington The sum of one thousand pounds five per cent Bank Annuities unto William Collins Worthington The sum of one thousand pounds five per cent Bank Annuitiies unto the said Thomas Knight Worthington and The sum of one thousand pounds five per cent Bank Annuities unto Henry Worthington which said several sums I do hereby direct to be assigned and transferred unto each and every of them when and as they shall respectively attain the age of Twenty five years and not before And I hereby give and bequeath the Interest Dividends and profits of the said several Sums of One thousand pounds or such part thereof as shall not have been assigned or transferred unto my said Son William Collins his Executors Administrators and Assigns to and for his own proper use and benefit and my Mind and Will further is that in case any or either of the said Children above named of my said daughter Elizabeth Worthington shall happen to die before they attain the age of twenty five years and without issue Then I do hereby give and bequeath the part and share or parts and shares of him or her so dying unto such Child or Children as may be born (if any) of the body of the said Elizabeth Worthington my daughter after my decease in the same way and manner I have bequeathed the same to the Children of my said daughter as are now living it being my desire that all and every the Children of my said daughter should be equally interested under and by virtue of this my Will And if there should be no Child or Children born after the making of this my Will or they should die under the Age of twenty five years and without issue Then I give and bequeath the part and share or parts and shares of him or her so dying unto the Survivor and Survivors of them and the Issue of such of them as shall be then dead leaving Issue lawfully begotten equally between them as aforesaid and to their Executors Administrators and Assigns such Issue to take only what would have been the share of his her or their deceased parent therein Provided also and I do hereby declare my mind and will to be That in case my

Executors herein after named or the Survivor of them his or her Heirs Executors and Administrators shall at any time after my decease be desirous of parting with my Brewing Business and shall think it proper and necessary to sell and dispose of my said Freehold and Personal Estate either by public or private Sale as to them or either of them shall seem moot it shall be lawful for them or either of them so to do and to enable them thereto I do hereby in that Case and for that purpose only give devise and bequeath All that my present dwelling house with the Brewhouse adjoining and Ground thereunto belonging together with all that public Alehouse called the Queens Head with Buildings Ground and Appurternances thereunto belonging and now in the Occupation of Richard Sawry [?Harvey] As also all that Messuage Butchers Shop and Ground thereunto belonging and now in the Occupation of Christopher Wood together with the Malthouse and Ground thereunto adjoining All which premises are situate lying and being in Biggin Street in Dover aforesaid in the said County of Kent As also All that Messuage or public Alehouse called the Dublin Man of War with the Ground and Appurternances thereunto belonging and now in the Occupation of John Brockman situate in the Parish of River in the said County of Kent Together with all my Brewing Utensils Farming Stock Stock in Trade Household Goods Plate Linen and China and All other my Personal Estate whatsoever and wheresoever (my Leasehold Estate in the occupation of my Son in Law Benjamin Jelly Worthington and my Monies in the Public Funds excepted) Unto my said wife Elizabeth Collins and my said Son William Collins or the Survivor of them their Heirs Executors Administrators and Assigns for ever And the Monies arising thereby after adjusting the necessary expenses attending the said Sale together with my Monies on Private Securities I give devise and bequeath the same unto my said wife Elizabeth Collins and my said son William Collins their Executors Administrators and Assigns Upon this special Trust and Confidence that they the said Elizabeth Collins and William Collins and the Survivor of them shall and do place out the same Monies on Government Securities in their Names or in the Name of the Survivor of them his or her Executor and Administrators Upon Trust to permit and suffer my said wife Elizabeth to receive the Interest Dividends and Proceed arising thereby for and during the term of her natural Life to and for her own proper Use and Benefit And from and immediately after her decease The Interest Dividends and Proceed of such Stock I direct to be paid and received by my said Son William Collins for and during the term of his natural Life to and for his own proper use and benefit And after his decease I direct the Interest Dividends and Proceed arising thereby with the Stocks or Funds wherein it may be invested shall be paid and applied in the same way and manner I have hereinbefore in the first part of this my Will Given my said Messuages Lands and Tenements Goods Chattels Farming Stock Stock in Trade Monies Securities for Money and other my personal Estate And I do hereby direct that the Receipt and Receipts of my said Executors and the Survivor of them his or her Heirs Executors and Administrators shall be a good and sufficient discharge and good and sufficient discharges to the purchaser or purchasers of such part or parts of my said Estate and Effects for so much Money for which such Receipt and Receipts shall be given And that such purchaser or purchasers shall not be answerable or accountable for the Misapplication or Nonapplication of such purchase Monies to be by him her or them paid or any part thereof and that they my said Executors shall not be answerable or accountable for any more Monies than they respectively shall actually receive under and by virtue of this my will nor for any loss that may happen of my said Estate and Effects ...

Whereof the said Knight Collins ... my Hand and Seal the sixteenth Day of May in the forty fifth year of the Reign of our Sovereign Lord George the Third by the Grace of God of the United Kingdom of Great Britain and Ireland King Defender of the Faith And in the year of our Lord one thousand eight hundred and five ... Witnesses, Wm Brockman, Thomas Farmar and Thomas Marsh.

This Will was proved at London the nineteenth day of November in the year of our Lord One thousand eight hundred and five before the Right Honorable Sir William Wynne Knight Doctor of Laws ... lawfully constituted at the Oaths of Elizabeth Collins widow and Relict of the deceased and William Collins the son of the said deceased the Executors to whom Administration was granted ...

Appendix 19

Abstracts of Title & Various Wills 1733-1830
(Original copies held by the author)

ABSTRACT of the Title of The Devisees In Trust for sale under the Will of Mr. George Finch deceased to a messuage or tenement storehouses coachhouse outhouses edifices and buildings to same belonging situate lying and adjoining to Biggin Gate in Parish of St. Mary the Virgin in Dover in Kent the late residence of Mr. Finch.

16th & 17th December 1754.
INDENTURES of Lease and Release made between Daines Balderston of Parish of Minster in Isle of Sheppey in County of Kent Surgeon of one part and William Balderston of City of Canterbury Gentleman of other part IT IS WITNESSED that in consideration of £165 to said Daines Balderston paid by said William Balderston The said Daines Balderston Did grant bargain sell alien release and confirm unto said William Balderston (in his peaceable possession etc. and to heirs and assigns of said William Balderston <u>ALL THAT Revenue or Remuneration then expectant upon death of George Balderston of Town and Port of Dover in said County of Kent Gentleman and Sarah his Wife of and in</u> ALL THAT messuage or Tenement with the Malthhouses oasts stowages stable coachhouse oasthouses edifices and buildings to same belonging situate and adjoining to Biggin Gate in Parish of St. Mary in Dover aforesaid And also the yard garden orchard and meadow land to same belonging and adjoining containing by estimation one acre and a half be that more or less with Appurtenances then in the occupation of said George Balderston [*sid*] his assigns or undertenants TO HOLD same unto said William Balderston his heirs and assigns TO the only Proper use and behoof of said William Balderston and of his heirs and assigns for ever

COVENANTS by said Daines Balderston that he was lawfully seized of revenue expectant as aforesaid in fee had not done any act to incumber - for quiet enjoyment - free from all incumbrances and for further assurances

EXECUTED by said D. Balderston in presence of 2 Witnesses and receipt for consideration money indorsed signed and Witnessed

[*Back of page 1*] 8th Oct. 1733 (Office Copy) - Will of Robert Daines of the Town and Port of Dover in the County of Kent Gent and one of the Jurats of the same Town and Port whereby (amongst other things) he gave and bequeathed unto George Balderston Sarah his wife the said Testator's House and Malthouse next adjoining to Biggin Gate in Dover aforesaid with the stable yard backside garden ground and appurtenances To hold unto the said George Balderston and Sarah his wife for and during their natural lives and the life of the longer liver of them and from and after the decease of the longest liver of them said Testator gave said House Malthouse and Premises with the appurts unto Daines Balderston son of said George Balderston Sarah his wife and to his heirs assigns forever

Duly executed by said Robert Daines attested by 3 witnesses. Proved the 2nd December 1734 by Bryan Pybus one of the Executors in the Prerogative Court of Canterbury

23 & 24 April 1759
INDENTURES of Lease & Release made between said William Balderston of one part & Robert Balderston of Dover aforesaid Woollen draper of the other part

IT IS WITNESSED that in consideration of £203 to said William Balderston paid by said Robert Balderston The said William Balderston Did grant bargain sell alien release and confirm unto said Robert Balderston (in his peaceable possession etc.) and to heirs & assigns of said Robert Balderston

ALL THAT the Revenue etc. (expectant on death of said Sarah Balderston widow of said George Balderston) of and in said Premises mentioned in hereinbefore abstracted Indentures

TO HOLD same unto said Robert Balderston of his heirs and assigns To only proper use and behoof of said Robert Balderston of his heirs and assigns for ever

COVENANTS by said William Balderston that he was lawfully seized in fee - had not done any act to incumber - for quiet enjoyment - free from all incumbrances - and for further assurance

EXECUTED by said William Balderston in presence of 2 Witnesses and receipt for consideration money - signed & witnessed

1st May 1759

INDENTURE made between said Robert Balderston of one part and Jacob Rouse of Dover aforesaid Mariner of other part

IT IS WITNESSED that in consideration of £200 to said Robert Balderston paid by said Jacob Rouse The said Robert Balderston DID bargain & sell demise grant & to farm let unto said Jacob Rouse his Executors administrators and assigns

Said Revenue (expectant on decease of said Sarah Balderston widow as aforesaid) of and in Premises partly described by him before abstracted Indentures of 16th & 17th December 1754

TO HOLD same unto said Jacob Rouse his Executors Administrators and Assigns from day next before day of date of now Abstracted Indenture for term of 500 years at a pepper corn rent if demanded

PROVISO that if said Robert Balderston his heirs should pay unto said Jacob Rouse his Executors said sum of £200 together with Interest for same after rate of £4 per centum per annum on 1st November then next ensuing date of now abstracted Indenture then same to be void

COVENANTS by said Robert Balderston for payment of said £200 together with Interest at rate day & time mentioned in proviso - that he was lawfully seized in fee (expectant as aforesaid) had good right to demise - in default of payment of said £200 and Interest thereof on day and time stated in Proviso - Power for said Jacob Rouse to enter said premises and receive rents etc. - free from all incumbrances (rents to chief Lord only excepted) and for further assurance

AGREEMENT between said parties to now Abstracted Indenture that until default should be made in payment of said £200 and interest thereof it should be lawful for said Robert Balderston quietly to enjoy said Premises

Executed by said Robert Balderston in presence of 2 Witns and rect. for Cons: Money indorsed - signed and witnessed

22nd September 1766

INDENTURE made between said Robert Balderston of one part and said Jacob Rouse of other part RECITING hereinbefore Abstracted Indenture of Mortgage of 1st May 1759

AND ALSO RECITING that said £200 then remained due unto said Jacob Rouse upon said therein recited security all interest then being paid off to date thereof and said Richard Balderston being in want of further sum of £100 had requested said Jacob Rouse to advance him same on security of said Premises which said Jacob Rouse had consented to do

IT IS WITNESSED that said Robert Balderston in consideration of said £200 due unto said Jacob Rouse upon said therein recited security & of said further sum of £100 to him said Robert Balderston then paid by said Jacob Rouse He said Robert Balderston DID release and quit claim unto said Jacob Rouse his executors administrators and assigns Proviso in said therein recited Indenture and all equity by reason thereof And for considerations aforesaid He said Robert Balderston DID ratify and confirm unto said Jacob Rouse his executors administrators and assigns

ALL and singular thereinbefore mentioned and expressed messuage or tenement malthouses out-houses edifices buildings Lands and premises & every part thereof with their appurtenances

AND all full and whole estate etc. TO HOLD same unto said Jacob Rouse his Executors Administrators & Assigns from thenceforth for remainder of said term of 500 years discharged from Proviso in said therein recited Indenture contained

PROVISO that if said Robert Balderston should pay unto Jacob Rouse £300 with Interest for same after rate of £4 for £100 by the year upon 23rd March then next ensuing date of now Abstracted Indenture then said Jacob Rouse his Executors Administrators & Assigns should at costs of said Robert Balderston his heirs executors administrators or assigns assign said Premises to him his heirs and assigns or to such other person as he should appoint

COVENANTS by said Robert Balderston for payment of said £300 and Interest for same at rate day and time mentioned in Proviso in default thereof that he said Robert Balderston would execute any further assurance

EXECUTED by said Robert Balderston in presence of two Witnesses and Receipt for £100 indentured signed and witnessed

9th August 1773

Probate produced 8th October 1830

WILL of said Robert Balderston of this date (then of Gilhams Court in parish of St. Mary Magdalen Bermondsey in Co. of Surry Excise Tide Waiter) executed in presence of three witnesses Whereby he gave devised and bequeathed all his estate and effects both real and personal whatsoever and wheresoever unto his beloved Wife Elizabeth Balderston and his Son in Law George Finch their executors administrators and assigns

TO HOLD same unto said Elizabeth Balderston and George Finch their heirs executors administrators and assigns

IN TRUST nevertheless that as soon as conveniently might be after his decease they said Elizabeth Balderston and George Finch should sell same for most money that could be gotten And after payment of his lawful debts and funeral expenses [sic] to pay and apply money produced by such sale in manner therein directed

AND he thereby appointed his said Wife Elizabeth Balderston and his said Son in Law George Finch joint Executors of that his Will

Proved in Prerogative Court of Canterbury 13th August 1773 by said Executors thereof

19th and 20th October 1773

Originals produced 8 October 1830

INDENTURES of Lease and Release made between said Elizabeth Balderston of Gilhams Court aforesaid Widow and George Finch of Town and port of Dover in County of Kent Merchant Executors of last Will and Testament of said Robert Balderston And also Trustees named in said Will of 1st part said Jacob Rouse of 2nd Part Sampson Farbrace of Dover aforesaid Jurat of 3rd Part and William Lambe of Dover aforesaid Gentleman of 4th Part

RECITING hereinbefore abstracted Indentures of 1st May 1759 and 22 September 1766 ALSO RECITING that said principal sum of £300 together with £84 18 4 for Interest thereof making together £384 18 4 then remaining due to said Jacob Rouse upon said therein reciting security ALSO RECITING hereinbefore Abstracted Will of said Robert Balderston AND ALSO RECITING that said Elizabeth Balderston and George Finch as Trustees as aforesaid pursuant to direction of said Will caused said premises to be advertized for sale on 27th September then last past at which time same premises were exposed to Public Sale And said George Finch bidding sum of £500 for same and being highest bidder became purchaser thereof for that sum upon which it was agreed between all said parties to now abstracting Indenture that out of said purchase money said sum of £384 18 4 so due to said Jacob Rouse upon said therein recited security should be paid off and discharged And that residue of said purchase money should remain in hands of said Elizabeth Balderston and George Finch as Executors and Trustees and to be applied by them according to directions of said Will And that thereupon fee simple inheritance etc. of and in all singular said premises expectant upon death of said Sarah Balderston should be conveyed and assured unto said Sampson Farbrace his heirs and assigns Upon Trusts thereinafter mentioned And also that residue of said Term of 500 years in said Premises should be assigned unto said William Lambe his executors administrators and assigns In Trust as was thereinafter mentioned

IT IS WITNESSED that in pursuance of said Agreement and in consideration of £384 8 4 (in part of said sum of £500 to said Jacob Rouse paid by said George Finch And also in consideration of £115 1 8 residue of said purchase money aforesaid then remaining in hands of said Elizabeth Balderston and George Finch as Executors and Trustees aforesaid and of 10% to them or one of them paid by said Sampson Farbrace They said Elizabeth Balderston and George Finch Did each of them grant bargain sell alien release and confirm direct limit and appoint unto said Sampson Farbrace his heirs and assigns

ALL THAT the Reversion or Remainder expectant upon death of said Sarah Balderston of and in

ALL AND SINGULAR thereinbefore mentioned and expressed Messuage or Tenement malthouses oasts stowages coachouse oasthouses edifices buildings yard garden orchard lands hereditaments and premises and of and in every part and parcel thereof with their and every of their appurtenances (all which said Premises were in actual possession of said Sampson Farbrace by virtue etc. And all full and whole Estate etc. Together with all Deeds TO HOLD same unto said Sampson Farbrace his heirs and assigns UPON TRUST nevertheless as to the estate and interest of said Sampson Farbrace and his heirs of and in all and singular said premises with their and every of their appurtenances To and for several uses intents and purposes thereinafter mentioned expressed and declared of and concerning same (that is to say)

To use and behoof of such person and persons and for such Estate and Estates use and uses intents and purposes and subject and liable to and under such powers processes conditions limitations and charges with or without power of revocation and in such sort manner and form as he said George Finch should from time to time and at all times thereafter during his natural life by any deed or deeds writing or writings under his hand and seal attested by two or more credible Witnesses or by his last Will and Testament in Writing or by any writing purporting to be his last Will and Testament to be by him duly executed in the presence of 3 or more credible Witnesses convey and assure direct limit and appoint or give devise and bequeath same or any part thereof And for want or in default of such conveyance assurance direction limitation or appointment gift or devise And in mean time until such conveyance assurance direction limitation or appointment gift or devise should be made Or if any such conveyance etc. should be made Then and in such Case as and when several Estates and Interests thereby to be limited should respectively cease end or determine

TO THE ONLY PROPER USE AND BEHOOF of said George Finch and of this Heirs and Assigns for ever And to and for no other use trust intent or purpose whatsoever

To be holden of Chief Lord etc.

IT WAS BY NOW ABSTRACTING INDENTURE FURTHER WITNESSED that said Jacob Rouse in consideration of said £384 18 4 paid unto him by said George Finch and in Consideration of 10% to him paid by said William Lambe He said Jacob Rouse at request of said George Finch DID bargain sell assign and set over unto said William Lambe his Executors Administrators and Assigns

Said reversion (expectant as aforesaid) of and in said premises And all full and whole Estate etc. Together with said therein recited Indenture and all other Deeds etc. To hold same unto said William Lambe his Executors Administrators and Assigns from thenceforth for residue of said term of 500 years by said first therein recited Indenture granted

IN TRUST to attend inheritance etc. COVENANT by said Jacob Rouse that he had not incumbered

EXECUTED by said Elizabeth Balderston, George Finch, Jacob Rouse, Sampson Farbrace and William Lambe in presence of two witnesses and Receipt and acknowledgement for consideration money indorsed signed and witnessed

Sarah Balderston, widow was buried at St. Mary's Church Dover 2nd May 1775 -

16 November 1828.

Attested copy produced 8 October 1830

WILL of said George Finch (executed by him in presence of three Witnesses) Whereby he gave and devised unto Thomas Spencer of Shalford in county of Surry [sic] Gentleman George Finch Marsh of White Hart Court in City of London Clothier and Samuel Marsh of Great Prescott Street in City of London Clothier their heirs and assigns for ever

ALL AND SINGULAR his freehold and copyhold messuages lands tenements and hereditaments and real estate whatsoever and wheresoever and every part thereof with their and every of their rights members and appurtenances

TO HOLD same (according to several tenures or qualities thereof respectively unto and to the use of said Thomas Spencer, George Finch Marsh and Samuel Marsh their heirs and assigns for ever

NEVERTHELESS upon Trusts and for ends intents and purposes thereafter expressed and declared concerning same (that is to say) Upon Trust that they said Trustees or Survivors or Survivor of them his heirs or assigns did and should as soon as conveniently might be after his decease make sale and absolutely dispose of said Messuages and other hereditaments thereinbefore devised with the Appurtenances and fee simple and inheritance thereof and in such lots or parcels and either by Public Auction or by Private Contract or partly by Public Auction and partly by Private Contract as they his said Trustees or survivors or survivor of them his heirs or assigns should think fit or advisable and convey and surrender or otherwise assure same when sold (according to several tenures or qualities thereof respectively) unto person or persons who should agree to become Purchaser or Purchasers thereof his her or their Heirs and Assigns or to such other person or persons or to for such uses trusts intents and Purposes as he she or they should direct or appoint AND Testator did direct and appoint that person or persons respectively who should become purchaser or purchasers of said Estates and Premises thereby directed to be sold as aforesaid or any part thereof his her or their heirs executors administrators should not be obliged or required to see application of money to be paid or advanced by him her or them respectively as consideration of such purchase or purchasers or be answerable or accountable for misapplication or nonapplication of same money or any part thereof after same should have been paid to or to order of his said Trustees or Survivors or Survivor of them his Executors or Administrators And that every receipt which should be given by his said Trustees or Survivors or Survivor of them his executors or administrators for such purchase money or any part thereof should be a good valid and sufficient acquittance and discharge for Sum or Sums of money which therein or thereby respectively should be acknowledged or expressed to be received and said Testator appointed said Thomas Spencer, George Finch Marsh and Samuel Marsh Executors of his said Will

Proved in Prerogative Court of Canterbury the 21st day of January 1829 by said Thomas Spencer, George Finch Marsh and Samuel Marsh the Executors thereof - (N.B. Mr Finch died Thursday 4th December 1828 and was buried Thursday 11th December 1828 at Friends burying ground in Dovor)

Appendix 20

Indenture between Daines Balderston & William Balderston 1754
(from original copy held by the author)

THIS INDENTURE made the Sixteenth Day of December in the Twenty Eighth Year of the Reign of our Sovereign Lord George the second by the Grace of God of Great Britain France and Ireland King Defender of the Faith and in the Year of our Lord One Thousand Seven Hundred and Fifty four BETWEEN Daines Balderston of the parish of Minster in the Isle of Sheppey in the County of Kent Surgeon of the one part and William Balderston of the City of Canterbury Gentleman of the other part WITNESSETH that for and in Consideration of the sum of Five shillings of lawful money of Great Britain to the said Daines Balderston in hand at or before the sealing and Delivery of these Presents by the said William Balderston well and truly paid the receipt whereof he the said Daines Balderston doth hereby confess and acknowledge He the said Daines Balderston HATH Granted Bargained and Sold and by these Presents Doth Grant Bargain and sell unto the said William Balderston ALL that the Reversion or Remainder expectant upon the death of George Balderston of the Town and Port of Dover in the County of Kent Gentleman and Sarah his Wife of and in ALL that Messuage or tenement with the Malthouses Oasts Stowages Stable Coach House Outhouses Edifices and Buildings to the same belonging situate and adjoining to Biggin Gate in the Parish of Saint Mary in Dover aforesaid AND ALSO the Yard Garden Orchard and Meadow Land to the same belonging and adjoining containing by Estimation one acre and an half be thereof more or less with the Appurtenances and now in the tenure or occupation of the said George Balderston his Assigns or Undertenants TO HAVE AND TO HOLD the said Reversion or Remainder of and in the said Messuage or tenement Lands Hereditaments and all other the premises by these presents Granted Bargained and Sold or mentioned or intended so to be with the Appurtenances unto the said William Balderston his Executors Administrators and Assigns from the Day next before the Day of the Date hereof for and during and unto the full End and Term of One whole Year from thence next ensuing and fully to be compleat and ended At and under the Rent of One Pepper Corn at the End of the said Term if the same shall be lawfully demanded TO the Intent and purpose that by virtue of these presents and of the Statute made for transferring Uses into Possession the said William Balderston may be in the actual Possession of the said Reversion or Remainder hereby Granted Bargained and Sold as aforesaid and be thereby enabled to take and accept a Grant and Release of the same unto and to the use of him the said William Balderston his Heirs and Assigns for ever as in and by one Indenture of Release intended to bear date the Day next after the Day of the Date of these presents and to be made between the said the Day next after the Day of the Date of those presents and to be made between the said parties to those presents IN WITNESS whereof the said parties to these presents have to these present Indentures Interchangeably set their Hands and Seals the day the year first above written.

DAINES BALDERSTON

Appendix 21

Indenture between Daines Balderston & William Balderston 1754
(from original copy held by the author)

THIS INDENTURE made the Seventeenth day of December in the Twenty Eighth year of the Reign of our Sovereign Lord George the second by the Grace of God of Great Britain France and Ireland King Defender of the Faith etc. and in the Year of Our Lord One Thousand Seven Hundred and Fifty four BETWEEN Daines Balderston of the parish of Minster in the Isle of Sheppey in the County of Kent Surgeon of the one part and William Balderston of the City of Canterbury Gentleman of the other part WITNESSETH that for and in Consideration of the sum of one hundred and sixty five pounds of good and lawful money of Great Britain to the said Daines Balderston in hand well and truly paid by the said William Balderston at or before the sealing and delivery of these presents the receipt whereof he the said Daines Balderston doth hereby acknowledge and thereof and of every part thereof doth exonerate acquit and discharge the said William Balderston his Heirs Executors and Administrators and every of them by these presents He the said Daines Balderston HATH Granted Bargained Sold Aliened released and Confirmed and by these presents doth Grant Bargain Sell alien release and Confirm unto the said William Balderston (in his peaceable and quiet possession seizin thereof now being by virtue of one Bargain and Sale to him thereof made by the said Daines Balderston by Indenture bearing date the day next before the day of the date of these presents for the term of one whole year commencing from the day next before the day of the date of the same Indenture and by force of the statute made for transferring Uses into Possession) and to the Heirs and Assigns of the said William Balderston ALL that the Reversion or Remainder expectant upon the Death of George Balderston of the Town and Port of Dover in the said County of Kent Gentleman and Sarah his Wife of and in ALL that Messuage or Tenement with the Malthouses Oasts Stowages Stable Coach House Outhouses Edifices and Buildings to the same belonging situate and adjoining to Biggin Gate in the Parish of St Mary in Dovor aforesaid AND ALSO the Yard Garden Orchard and Meadow Land to the same belonging and adjoining containing by Estimation one acre and a half be thereof more or less with the appurtenances and now in the tenure or occupation of the said George Balderston his Assigns or Undertenants TO HAVE AND TO HOLD the said Reversion or Remainder of the said Messuage or Tenement Lands Hereditaments and all other the premises with the appurtenances unto the said William Balderston his Heirs and Assigns TO the only Use and behoof of the said William Balderston and of his Heirs and Assigns forever AND THE SAID Daines Balderston for himself his Heirs Executors and Administrators and for every of them doth Covenant Promise and Grant to and with the said William Balderston his Heirs and Assigns and to and with every of them by these presents in manner and form following (that is to say) that he the said Daines Balderston now is and standeth lawfully Rightfully and absolutely Seized of the Reversion or Remainder expectant as aforesaid of and in the said Messuage or Tenement Lands Hereditaments and all other the Premises before mentioned to be hereby Granted and Released with the Appurtenances of a good sure perfect lawful absolute and Indefeazible Estate of Inheritance in Fee Simple to him and his Heirs without any manner of Alteration Condition Trust Power of Revocation Limitation or any other Use or Uses Restraint Matter or Thing whatsoever to alter or change the same AND ALSO that he the said Daines Balderston hath not at any time heretofore made committed done or suffered any Act Deed matter or thing whereby or wherewith or by reason or means whereof the said Messuage or Tenement Lands Hereditaments and all other the premises with the Appurtenances now are or at any time hereafter shall or maybe incumbered in by or with any Estate Right Title Charge or other Incumbrance whatsoever AND ALSO that the said William Balderston his Heirs and Assigns shall and lawfully may from time to time and at all times hereafter peaceably and quietly have hold possess and enjoy the said Messuage or Tenement Lands Hereditaments and all and singular other the premises with the appurtenances without the Let Suit Trouble Interruption or Disturbance of the said Daines Balderston his Heirs or Assigns or of or by any other person or persons claiming or that shall claim from by or under him or them and also free and clear and freely and clearly acquitted and discharged of and from all former and other Gifts Grants Bargains Sales Leases Estates Rights Titles Jointures Dowers Fines Forfeitures Mortgages Statutes Recognizances Judgements Executions Rents Annuities Charges Burthens and Incumbrances whatsoever had made done committed or suffered by the said Daines Balderston or by any person or persons claiming or that shall claim from by or under him AND LASTLY that he the said Daines Balderston his Heirs and Assigns shall and will from time to time and at all times hereafter at the request costs and charges of the said William Balderston his Heirs and Assigns make do acknowledge Levy execute and suffer all and every such further and other lawful and reasonable Act and Acts Thing and Things Devices Conveyances and Assurances in the Law whatsoever for the further better more perfect and absolute Conveying and Assuring of the said Messuage or Tenement Lands Hereditaments and all and singular other the premises herein before Granted and Released or mentioned or intended to be hereby Granted and Released with the Appurtenances unto and to the use of the said William Balderston his Heirs and Assigns for ever as by the said William Balderston his Heirs or Assigns or by his or their Counsel learned in the Law shall be reasonably devised or advised and required IN WITNESS whereof the said parties hereunto have to these present Indentures Interchangeably sett their Hands and Seals the day and year first above written

DAINES BALDERSTON

ON THE BACK OF THIS INDENTURE
Received the day and year first within written of the within named William Balderston the within mentioned Sum of One Hundred-Sixty five pounds being the full of the Consideration money within mentioned to be paid by him to me - Witness hereunto
    DAINES BALDERSTON

    JACOB ROUSE
    JOHN SMITH

SEALED AND DELIVERED (BEING FIRST DULY STAMPED) IN THE PRESENCE OF JACOB ROUSE   JOHN SMITH

Appendix 22

Indenture between Robert Balderston & Jacob Rouse 1766
(from original copy held by the author)

THIS INDENTURE made the twenty second Day of September in the sixth year of the Reign of our Sovereign Lord George the Third by the Grace of God of Great Britain France and Ireland King Defender of the Faith and in the Year of our Lord One Thousand Seven hundred and Sixty Six BETWEEN Robert Balderston of the Town and Port of Dover in the County of Kent Fellmonger of the one part and Jacob Rouse of the same place Mariner of the other part WHEREAS by Indenture of Lease Mortgage bearing date on or about the first Day of May which was in the year of our Lord One Thousand Seven hundred and Fifty nine made or mentioned to be made between the said Robert Balderston by the name and Description of Robert Balderston of the Town and port of Dovor in the County of Kent Woollendraper of the one part and the said Jacob Rouse of the other part he the said Robert Balderston in Consideration of the sum of Two hundred Pounds of lawful money of Great Britain to him in hand then paid by the said Jacob Rouse DID Bargain Sell Demise Grant and to Farmlett unto the said Jacob Rouse his Executors Administrators and Assigns ALL that the Revertion or Remainder Expectant upon the death of Sarah Balderston Widow and Relict of George Balderston late of Dovor aforesaid Gentleman Deceased of and in ALL that Messuage or Tenement with the Malthouses Oasts Stowhouses Coachhouse Outhouses Edificies and Buildings to the same belonging Situate and then adjoining to Biggin Gate in the parish of St. Mary in Dovor aforesaid AND ALSO of and in the Yard Garden Orchard and Meadow Land to the same belonging and adjoining containing by Estimation one Acre and a half be thereof more or less with the Appurtenances then in the Tenure or Occupation of the said Sarah Balderston but now in the Tenure or Occupation of the said Robert Balderston or his Assigns or Undertenants AND of and in all Ways paths passages Waters Watercourses Lights Easements Libertys Rights privileges and appurtenances to the same or any part thereof belonging or in anywise appertaining AND the Revertion and Revertions Remainder and Remainders Rents Issues and profits thereof and of every part and parcel thereof TO BE HAD AND HOLDEN unto the said Jacob Rouse his Executors Administrators and Assigns from the day next before the day of the date of the said recited Indenture for and during and unto the full end and Term of five hundred years from thence next ensuing and fully to be compleat and ended without Impeachment of Waste under the Annual Rent of a pepper corn payable as therein mentioned and under acertain proviso or Condition therein contained for making void the same by the said Robert Balderston his heirs Executors Administrators or Assigns paying unto the said Jacob Rouse his Executors Administrators or Assigns full Sum of Two Hundred Pounds with lawfull Interest for the same at the Rate of four pounds per Cent per Annum of lawfull Money of Great Britain at or upon the first Day of November thou next ensuing As in and by the said Recited Indenture Relation being thereunto had more fully and at large appears AND WHEREAS The said Principal Sum of Two hundred Pounds now wholly Remains due oweing and payable unto the said Jacob Rouse by and upon the said recited Security All Interest being paid off and discharged to the day of the date hereof AND the said Robert Balderston being in want of the further Sum of One hundred pounds hath requested the said Jacob Rouse to lend and advance the same unto him on Security of the said premises which he the said Jacob Rouse hath consented and agreed to do NOW THIS INDENTURE WITNESSETH that the said Robert Balderston in Consideration that the said Sum of Two hundred pounds wholly remains due and oweing unto the said Jacob Rouse by and upon the said recited Security and in Consideration of the said further sum of one Hundred pounds to him now in hand well and truely paid and satisfied by the said Jacob Rouse at or before the Ensealing and Delivery of those presents the Receipt whereof he the said Robert Balderston doth hereby confess and Acknowledge and thereof and of and from every part and parcel thereof doth Acquit Release and discharge the said Jacob Rouse his Executors Administrators and Assigns by those presents He the said Robert Balderston HATH Released and quitclaimed and by these presents DOTH Release and Quit Claim unto the said Jacob Rouse his Executors Administrators and Assigns the Condition or Proviso in the said recited Indenture contained and all Equity and benefit of Redemption to be had or taken thereby or by reason or means thereof and for the Consideration aforesaid he the said Robert Balderston

HATH Ratified and confirmed and by these presents DOTH Ratifie and confirm unto the said Jacob Rouse his Executors Administrators and Assigns ALL and Singular the aforementioned and expressed Messuage or Tenement Malthouses Outhouses Edifices Buildings Lands and Premises and every part and parcel thereof with their and every of their appurtenanances AND ALL the full and whole Estate Right Title Interest Reversion Expectant Claim and Demand whatsoever of him the said Robert Balderston of in and to or out of the same premises every or any part thereof with the Appurtenances TO HAVE AND TO HOLD The said Messuage or Tenement Malthouse Outhouses Edifices Buildings Lands Hereditiments premises and every part and parcell thereof with their and every of their Appurtenances unto the said Jacob Rouse his Executors Administrators and Assigns from henceforth for and during all the Rest Residue and Remainder of the said Term of five hundred years in and by the said recited Indenture Granted and demised now to come and unexpired without Impeachment of or for any manner of Waste absolutely freed and Discharged of and from the Proviso or Condition in the said Recited Indenture contained and all Equity and benefit of Redemption to be had or taken thereby But Subject nevertheless to and under the Following Proviso or Condition for Redemption of the said Premises (that is to say) PROVIDED always and these presents are upon this express Condition nevertheless that if the said said Robert Balderston his heirs Executors Administrators and Assigns or any of them shall and do well and truely pay or cause to be paid unto the said Jacob Rouse his Executors Administrators or Assigns the full Sum of Three Hundred Pounds with lawfull Interest for the same at the rate of four pounds for an hundred pounds by the Year of lawfull money of Great Britain at or upon the twenty third Day of March next ensueing the date of these presents without fraud or further delay and Without any Deduction or Abatement out thereof or any part thereof for any Taxes Aids or Assessments whatsoever parliamentary or otherwise Taxed Charged or Imposed or to be Taxed Charged or Imposed on the said premises or any part thereof or on the said Jacob Rouse his Executors Administrators or Assigns for or in Respect thereof or for or in respect of these presents That then he the said Jacob Rouse his Executors Administrators or Assigns shall and will at the Request Costs and Charges in the Law and otherwise of him the said Robert Balderston his heirs Executors Administrators or Assigns Assign Surrender or otherwise reconvey All and Singular the said premises and every part and parcell thereof with their and every of their Appurtenances And all his and their Estate Right Title Interest Claim and Demand whatsoever of in and to the same unto the said Robert Balderston his heirs and Assigns Or to such other person or persons as he or they shall direct and appoint freed and discharged of and from all Incumbrances made done or committed by him the said Jacob Rouse his Executors Administrators or Assigns AND THE SAID Robert Balderston for himself his heirs Executors and Administrators and for every of them doth Covenant Promise and Grant to and with the said Jacob Rouse his Executors Administrators and Assigns and to and with every of them by these presents in manner following (that is to say) That he the said Robert Balderston his heirs Executors Administrators or Assigns or some or one of thou shall and will well and truely pay or cause to be paid unto the said Jacob Rouse his Executors Administrators or Assigns the full and just Sum of Three Hundred Pounds with Interest for the same at the rate aforesaid of lawfull Money of Great Britain at the day and time and in manner and form hereinbefore limited and Appointed for payment thereof and that without any Deduction or Abatement whatsoever AND That if default shall happen to be made of or in payment of the said Sum of Three hundred pounds with Interest for the same at the rate aforesaid of lawfull Money of Great Britain at the day and time and in manner of form herein before Limited and Appointed for Payment thereof and that without any Deduction or Abatement whatsoever AND that if default shall happen to be made of or in payment of the said Sum of Three Hundred Pounds with Interest for the same at the rate aforesaid of lawfull Money of Great Britain or any part thereof contrary to the Proviso or Condition and Covenant aforesaid He the said Robert Balderston his heirs Executors Administrators or Assigns and All other persons haveing or lawfully Claiming or that can shall or may have or lawfully claim any Estate Right Title or Interest of in to or out of the aforementioned and expressed Messuage or Tenement Malthouses Outhouses Edifices Buildings Lands and Premises or any part thereof shall and will upon the request of the said Jacob Rouse his Executors Administrators or Assigns But at the only proper Costs and Charges in the Law or otherwise of the said Robert Balderston his heirs Executors Administrators or Assigns make do acknowledge Levy Execute and Suffer or cause and procure to be made done Acknowledged Levied Executed and Suffered all and every such further and other lawfull and reasonable Act and Acts Deed and Deeds Conveyances and Assurances in the Law whatsoever to and for the further better more perfect and absolute Conveying and Assureing Suremakeing Ratifieing and confirming of the said Messuage or Tenement Malthouses Outhouses Edifices Buildings Lands

Hereditaments and Premises and every part thereof with their and every of their Appurtenances unto the said Jacob Rouse his Executors Administrators and Assigns for and during all the rest residue and Remainder of the said Term of five Hundred Years in and by the said recited Indenture Granted and which shall be then to come and unexpired Absolutely freed and discharged of and from the said last mentioned Proviso or Condition and all other Provisoes or Conditions whatsoever and all Equity and Benefit of Redemption to be had or taken thereby Be it by funds Feofment Recovery Release Confirmation or by all and every or any of the said Ways and Means or by such other lawfull and reasonable Ways and means as by the said Jacob Rouse his Executors Administrators or Assigns or his or their Council learned in the Law shall be reasonably Devised or Advised and required IN WITNESS whereof the parties first named to these present Indentures their Hands and Seals Interchangeably have sett and affixt Dated the Day and Year First above Written

ROBERT BALDERSTON

Appendix 23

Will of Robert Balderston 1773
(from original copy held by the author)

IN THE NAME OF GOD AMEN

The Ninth Day of August in the year of our Lord One thousand seven hundred and seventy three I
<u>ROBERT BALDERSTON</u> now of Gilhams Court in the Parish of St Mary Magdalen Bermondsey* in
the County of Surrey Excise Tide Waiter but late of the Town and Port of Dover in the County of Kent
Merchant being Weak in Body but of sound and disposing Mind Memory and understanding (praised
be God) Do make and ordain this my last Will and Testament in manner following that is to say FIRST
and principally I surrender up my soul into the Hands of Almighty God my Creator hoping to be saved
by the Merits and satisfaction of Jesus Christ my Saviour and Redeemer and my Body I commit to the
Earth to be decently Interred by and the discretion of my Executors hereafter named and as for my
Worldly Estate wherewith it hath pleased God to bless me I Give and dispose thereof as follows that
is to say I give and bequeath unto my son George Balderston the sum of five shillings of Lawful Money
of Great Britain to be paid him in twelve Months next after the decease of my dear and loving wife
Elizabeth Balderston by my Executors hereafter Named Also I give and bequeath unto my daughter
Elizabeth Finch five shillings of like Money to be paid at the time and in manner as aforesaid Also I
give and bequeath unto my three other Children Margaret, the Wife of John Rawling, Mary and
Susannah Balderston and my Grandson Robert Thompson fifty pounds a piece of lawful Money of
Great Britain to be paid to them within Twelve Months next after the decease of my said Wife in case
they shall be then living and if any of my said Three Daughters or my said Grandson shall dye [*sic*]
during the Lifetime of my said Wife having any Child or Children living at the time of the Death of
my said Wife Then I give and bequeath the part or share of either or any of them so dying unto the
Child or Children of either or any of them so dying to be equally divided between them share and share
alike Also I give devise and bequeath all my Estate and Effects both real and personal whatsoever and
wheresoever unto my said Beloved Wife Elizabeth Balderston and my Son in Law George Finch of
Dover aforesaid their Executors Administrators and Assigns To have and to hold the same unto them
the said Elizabeth Balderston and George Finch their Heirs Executors Administrators and Assigns In
trust nevertheless as follows and my Will is That as soon as rconveniently may be after my decease they
shall sell and dispose of the same for the most Money or best price that can be gotten and after Payment
of my lawful debts and Funeral expences I direct that my said Wife Elizabeth from the produce thereof
shall have receive and retain for her sole use and benefit the sum of Fifty pounds of lawful Money of
Great Britain which I hereby give and bequeath unto her to put her into any way of Trade or Business
she shall think most proper and advisable to enter into And I also direct and appoint and my Will is
that the remaining produce of all my said Real and Personal Estate after payment of my Debts, funeral
Expenses and the said sum of fifty pounds unto my said Wife Elizabeth as aforesaid shall by my said
Wife Elizabeth and George Finch be put and placed out in some of the Government Funds or Securities
or upon some such Real Security or Securitys as shall be approved of by Council Learned in the Law
and my Will is that my said Wife shall receive the Interest of such remaining produce of my said Estate
for and during the Term of her natural Life and from and after the decease of my said Wife Then I give
devise and bequeath the same residue and remaining produce of my said Estate unto and amongst my
five Children (that is to say) George Balderston Elizabeth Finch Margaret Rawling Mary Balderston and
Susanna Balderston and my said Grandson Robert Thompson to be equally divided amongst them share
and share alike But in case any of my said Children or my said Grandson should happen to dye before
he she or they shall be intitled to the Legacy or Legacys hereby given that then and in such case my
will and Mind is and I do hereby direct and appoint that the share or shares of him her or them so dying
shall go and be divided to and amongst the Child or Children of him her or them so dying and in case
any of my said five Children or my said Grandson shall dye without Issue Then I do hereby Give and
bequeath the part or share or parts or shares of him her or them so dying without Issue unto the
Survivors or Survivor of them and unto the Child or Children of such of my said Child or Children
as shall be living at the time of my said Wife's decease to be equally divided amongst them share and
share alike And Lastly I do hereby Nominate and Appoint my said loving Wife Elizabeth Balderston

---

* [parish 1548 Surrey 1-½ miles s.e. London population 29,741 archd Surrey dioc. Winchester.]

and my said Son in Law George Finch Joint Executors of this my last Will and Testament hereby Revoking and making void all former Wills by me heretofore made IN WITNESS whereof I the said Robert Balderston the Testator have to this my last Will and Testament contained in two sheets of Paper to the first sheet thereof set my Hand and to the last my Hand and Seal the day and year in the first sheet mentioned Robert Balderston Signed Sealed Published and Declared by the said Robert Balderston the Testator as and for his last Will and Testament in the presence of us who in his presence and in the presence of each other have subscribed our Names as Witnesses thereunto Sarah Balderston - Sarah Davis - Wm. Balderston

Appendix to IN THE NAME OF GOD AMEN
FREDERICK by Divine Providence Archbishop of Canterbury, Primate of all England, and Metropolitan, do by these Presents make known to all Men, that on the THIRTEENTH Day of AUGUST in the Year of our Lord One Thousand Seven Hundred and Seventy THREE at London, before the WOR-SHIPFUL FRANCIS SIMPSON DOCTOR OF LAWS-SURROGATE OF THE RIGHT WORSHIP-FUL GEORGE HAY Doctor of Laws, Master, Keeper, or Commissary of our Prerogative Court of Canterbury, lawfully constituted the last Will and Testament OF ROBERT BALDERSTON LATE OF THE PARISH OF ST MARY MAGDALEN BERMONDSEY IN THE COUNTY OF SURREY DECEASED hereunto annexed, was proved, approved and registered; the said Deceased having whilst living, and at the Time of HIS Death, Goods, Chattels or Credits, in divers Dioceses or Jurisdictions, by reason whereof the proving and registring the said Will, and the granting Administration of all and singular the said Goods, Chattels and Credits, and also the auditing, allowing and final discharging the Account thereof, are well known to appertain only and wholly to us, and not to any inferior Judge; and that Administration of all and singular the Goods, Chattels and Credits of the said Deceased, and any way concering HIS Will was granted to ELIZABETH BALDERSTON WIDOW THE RELICT OF THE SAID DECEASED AND GEORGE FINCH THE EXECUTORS NAMED IN THE SAID WILL THE SAID ELIZABETH BALDERSTON HAVING BEEN ALREADY SWORN AND THE SAID GEORGE FINCH HAVING ALREADY MADE A SOLEMN AND SINCERE DECLARA-TION OR AFFIRMATION ACCORDING TO ACT OF PARLIAMENT––––––well and faithfully to administer the same, and to make a true and perfect Inventory of all and singular the said Goods, Chattels and Credits, and to exibit the same into the Registry of our said court on or before the last Day of FEBRUARY next ensuing, and also to render a just and true Accompt thereof. GIVEN AT THE TIME AND PLACE ABOVE WRITTEN AND IN THE FIFTH YEAR OF OUR TRANSLATION.

JOHN STEVENS
G. GOSTLING   } Deputy
HENRY STEVENS   Registers

Appendix 24

Other Dover Worthingtons

Worthingtons of Dover and surrounding parishes who cannot be reliably connected at this time:

Ann	Burial at St Leonard's, Deal, on 10 November 1831 of Ann Worthington of Princes Street, Lower Deal, aged nine years (burial register).
Ann Jane	Baptism on 21 January 1827 at St James's, Dover, of Ann Jane, daughter of John Worthington of Dover Heights, private in 85th Regiment, and Catherine.
Bartholomew	Buried on 15 October 1734 at St James's, Dover (burial register).
Bebe	Burial on 25 May 1863 of Bebe Worthington, single woman aged 54 years, of St James's parish (cemetery list).
Catharine	Baptism on 27 April 1739 of Catharine, daughter of Henry Freeman and Susanna Worthington, at Ewell parish, near Dover.
Catherine	Baptism on 28 August 1732 at Dover St Mary's of baseborn daughter of Susanna Worthington (parish registers).
Edward	A young child, with no parents' names given, buried on 8 November 1721 at Dover St Mary's (burial register).
Elizabeth	Administration of her brother John Leverland's estate of South Kyne, Lincs. 27 September 1623 (f.42) (Prerogative Court of Canterbury Administrations 1620-30, p.119, 4474).
Henry	Baptism on 6 July 1733 of Henry, illegitimate son of Henry Freeman and Susanna Worthington, at Ewell parish, near Dover. Child died on 16 July 1733.
Henry	Baptism on 22 April 1736 of Henry, illegitimate son of Henry Freeman and Susanna Worthington, at Ewell parish, near Dover. Child buried.
Henry	Baptism in 1737 of Henry, the son of Henry Freeman and Susanna Worthington at Ewell parish, near Dover. Child buried.
John	Indenture on 1 March 1724 of John Campbell of Dover to John Worthington, joyner of Dover, for eight years (Dover Borough Records, Apprenticeship Enrolment - Indentures 1673-1788, Kent Archives Service, Maidstone).
John	Burial on 15 May 1803 (Charlton by Dover, Bishop's Transcripts, Box 78).
John	Administration of estate on 30 August 1625 at St Anne Blackfryers. Left to relative Jane Worthington (Prerogative Court of Canterbury Administrations 1620-30, p.119, 8070 ref. f.5).
John	Owner of freehold land and house in own occupation at St Mary's, Dover (1754 poll book of Dover residents).
John Cotton	Birth of daughter on 28 August 1817 to John Cotton Worthington at Speldhurst (*Kentish Gazette*, 5 September 1817, back page, col.5).
Mary	Burial on 29 April 1777 of Mary Worthenton (Charlton by Dover, Bishop's Transcripts, Box 78).
Mary	Burial on 31 July 1770 of Mary Wotherington (St Alphage, Canterbury, burial lists).
Mary	Burial at St Leonard's, Deal, on 19 May 1814 of Mary Worthenton of Beach Street, Lower Deal, aged three years (burial register).
Mary	Licence for Mary Worthington of St Mary Bredman, to marry John Wallis bachelor of All Saints, Canterbury, at St Mary's, either at Patrixbourne or Barham, dated 17 July 1736 (Cowper's Marriage Licence Book, 1726-50).
Mary Ann	Death on 13 March 1860 at 31 Castle Street, Dover, of Mary Ann Worthington aged 53 years (*Dover Express*, 17 March 1860). Single woman buried on 19 March 1860 (St James's, Dover, burial list). One upright stone in St James's cemetery, Dover, records 'Sacred to the memory of Mary Ann eldest daughter of Thomas and Mary

	Worthington who died 13 March 1860 aged 53 years also Bebe Worthington only sister of the above who died 20 May 1863 aged 54 years'. Mary was a schoolmistress living at Trapham Lane, Margate, with her sister Bebe (1841 census).
Richard	Settlement on 23 January 1729 at Dover of Richard Worthington from Elham (Dover St Mary's settlements U3/30, 13/1-3).
Richard	Burial at Dover St Mary's on 23 October 1713 of son of Bartholomew and Elizabeth (burial register).
Robert	Pipe-maker of Folkestone, apprenticed to Paul Parker of Canterbury in 1741 (Freeman of Canterbury by apprenticeship, Canterbury Cathedral Archives).
Sarah	Baptism on 24 December 1710, daughter of Sarah and Andrew Worthington (St Mary's, Northgate, Canterbury).
Sarah	Buried on 8 November 1783 (Buckland by Dover, parish registers).
Sarah	Buried on 18 January 1786 (Buckland by Dover, Bishop's Transcripts).
Sarah	Buried on 25 October 1807 (Buckland by Dover, Bishop's Transcripts).
Susan	Marriage on 25 February 1696 to John Watts at St Mary's, Dover.
Susanna	Marriage on 2 January 1698 to William Steward/Stuard at St Mary's, Dover.
Susanna	Marriage on 27 December 1836 to Henry Freeman at Ewell parish, near Dover.
Susanna	Licence for Susanna Worthington, spinster, to marry Henry Freeman, bachelor of Ewell, at Ewell, dated 23 December 1735 (Cowper's Marriage Licence Book 1726-50).
Thomas	Died on 23 July 1835 at Margate, aged 61 years. Many years in Post Office service at Dover (*Dover Telegraph*, 25 July 1835, p.8, col.5).
Thomas	Marriage on 6 October 1730 to Ann Gibbons at St James's, Dover (marriage register, St James's parish, ref: U3/26/1/2).
Thomas	Burial on 12 August 1755, Dover St Mary's, drowned (burial register).
Thomas	'In memory of Thomas Worthington who died 20 October 1808 aged 36 years' (St James's Church Monumental Inscriptions, Dover Library).
William	'Sacred to the memory of William Worthington who departed this life 12 August 1828? aged 64 years also of Sarah his wife who departed this life Dec ... aged 82? years also of Ann Worthington daughter of the above who d... Oct... aged 30? years ...' (St James's Monumental Inscriptions, Dover Library).
William Edward	Burial on 15 May 1831 of William Edward Worthington of Peter Street, Lower Deal, aged 15 years (burial register, St Leonard's, Deal).

Withington/Withrington extracted from indexed transcripts of registers for Boughton-under-Blean, near Faversham, Kent:

Abigail	Burial 28 October (no year) infant.
Edward	Baptism 1630s 'of Henry'.
G.	Baptism 5 May 1656, son of H. and Elleded Withington.
H.	Marriage 24 March 1633/4 Susan Taylor.
H.	Marriage 16 July 1655 Elleded Gates, widow.
H.	Burial 3 August 1659.
James	Baptism 1630s 'of Henry'.
Margaret	Baptism 1630s 'of Henry'.
Susanna	Burial 4 April 1655, wife of H. Withington.

* * * * *

Collins of Dover who cannot be connected at this time:

William	Monumental inscription at St James's Church, 'Sacred to the memory of William Collins of the town of Dover who departed this life ... 1830 aged 63 years. Also of Elizabeth his wife who departed this life 28 January 1852 aged 77 years. 23rd Psalm' (Dover Library).

Notes

Chapter 1: Early Worthingtons of Dover

1. For further information see *The Worthington Families of Medieval England* by Philip M. Worthington, Phillimore.
2. PRC 32/11, f.90.
3. St Alphage, Canterbury Registers.
4. Chalklin, C.W., *Seventeenth Century Kent*, Introduction.
5. Chalklin, *op. cit.*, p.192.
6. Chalklin, *op. cit.*, p.2.
7. Stretch of water off the coast from Deal used as a naval anchorage and a naval station.
8. Dover District Council Information Leaflet, Sheet 1, 1 September 1993.
9. Canterbury Marriage Records.
10. Fitzhugh, Terrick V.H., *The Dictionary of Genealogy*, p.78.
11. An oath taken by every man of 18 years and over 'to live and die for the true Protestant religion, the liberties and rights of subjects, and the privilege of Parliaments'. Lists were made of those who signed and of all who refused to sign.
12. Kent Protestation returns 1641/2 (House of Lords R.O.), folios 8 & 9.
13. A note was added to the Freeman Records entry for Roger–'Obit, 1616'.
14. Details from unpublished family history, date and author unknown.
15. Chalklin, *op. cit.*, p.113 & Appendix B, p.269.
16. Smith, Frank, *The Lives and Times of Our English Ancestors*, Vol. II, p.182.
17. The *London Daily Chronicle*, 30 September 1926.
18. Data collected in the parish of Sevenoaks in 1695 by famous demographer, Gregory King.
19. Chalklin, *op. cit.*, pp.36-7.
20. Chalklin, *op. cit.*, pp.38-9.
21. Two changes were made to the English calendar in 1752, one being a change of system from the Julian to the Gregorian when 2 September 1752 was renumbered 14 September and the other being when the commencement of that year was brought forward from 25 March to the preceding 1 January. Therefore pre-1752 dates between January and March can use both new and old reckonings, e.g. 1687/8.
22. See Appendix 4 for full story.
23. St Alphage, Canterbury Registers, 1558-1800.
24. Ref: U3/173/13/3 CCL.
25. See Appendix 7.
26. 1754 Kent Poll Book of Dover Residents.
27. See Appendix 11.
28. Dover Apprentice Enrolments.
29. Mary Worthington, widow of Edward Worthington, renounced the Letters of Administration of the deceased goods and appointed personally Bartholomew Worthington son of the deceased. He was granted Letters of Administration (see Appendix 10).
30. Freemen Rolls, folio 19.
31. Freemen of Dover Rolls, folio 30.
32. Canterbury Marriage Licences (3rd series) 1661-76, edited by Joseph Cowper.
33. A bond was a binding engagement with a penalty for non-performance.
34. Canterbury Freemen 1650-99, FA27, 345.
35. Canterbury Freemen 1650-99, AC6, 28; FA28, 151.
36. See Appendix 6.
37. The baptismal entry for Thomas has been transcribed as Thomas Northington and indexed under 'N'.
38. The Freemen of Dover records incorrectly describe his claim by birth as 'son of Bartholomew', when in fact he was the son of Edward.
39. Dover Borough Records Apprenticeship Enrolment–Indentures 1673-1788, Kent Archives Service, Maidstone.
40. Whitfield Burial Register U3/66 1/1.
41. Whitfield Bishop's Transcripts.
42. Dover Freemen Rolls.
43. Dover Borough Records Apprenticeship Enrolment–Indentures 1673-1788, Kent Archives Service, Maidstone.
44. Dover Freemen Rolls, folio 62.
45. Dover Freemen Rolls, folio 81.
46. See Appendix 8, p.106.
47. Chalklin, *op. cit.*, p.172.
48. Mary is probably John's first cousin despite the variance in spelling of Fryer/Fryar.
49. PRO Inland Revenue Records Kent 1763-74, 24/46.
50. See Appendix 13.
51. Will of Sarah Worthington of Dover, 1834, Liver 70, No.138 (Catalogue mark: PRC 32/70/138).
52. Dover Chamberlain's Accounts 1700-84, vol.7.
53. Also called the Pepper Charity.
54. See Appendix 9.
55. Dover Freemen Rolls, 'Benjamin, by birth, son of John (Cooper) F.108 admitted 26 October 1739'.
56. Dover Apprentice Enrolments, Kent County Archives.
57. Jones, John Bavington, *Annals of Dover*, pp.288-90.
58. Willis's Printed Books, *Canterbury Marriage Licences Granted*.
59. It is not known how he died, and his burial is not recorded at St Mary's.
60. See Appendix 2.
61. Originally found hidden amongst the holly bushes in 1986 but since restored.
62. Dover Corporation Records, microfilm, Dover Library.
63. Monumental Inscription, St Mary's Dover.
64. See Appendix 12.
65. Chalklin, *op. cit.*, p.24.
66. Jones, John Bavington, *Dover*, pp.113-15.
67. The section headed 'The Worthingtons' on p.114 of John Bavington Jones' book is inaccurate.
68. *Ibid.*, p.115.
69. Town Council's year book, 1897.
70. *Idem.*

Chapter 2: Benjamin Jelly Worthington–His Early Life

1. See Chapter 8.
2. See Appendix 3.
3. O'Byrne, William R., *A Naval Biographical Dictionary*, p.1092. William Sidney Smith entered the Navy in June 1777 on board the *Tortoise*. He was removed in January 1778 to the *Unicorn* under Captain Ford.
4. PRO, Muster & Pay Books *Unicorn*, ADM34/802, ADM36/10018.
5. PRO, Muster Book of Ships at Home 1779, ADM7/427, ADM36/9238, ADM36/9239.
6. PRO, Musters & Pay Lists *Brilliant*, ADM36/9239.

7. PRO, Musters & Pay Lists *Dragon*, ADM36/8775.
8. PRO, Muster Book *Dragon*, ADM36/8682.
9. PRO, Pay Book *Nymphe*, ADM34/537; Log *Nymphe*, ADM51/518.
10. Index of Registers of Freemen from 1664, folio 493. Extracts from Dover Freemen Lists–microfilm in Dover Library.
11. PRO Cust. 54, Vol. 1, No. 252.
12. Jones, John Bavington, *The Cinque Ports*, p.41.
13. Chatterton, E. Keble, *King's Cutters and Smugglers*, p.122.
14. Chatterton, *op. cit.*, p.122.
15. Chatterton, *op. cit.*, pp.403-4.
16. Chatterton, *op. cit.*, p.123.
17. Chatterton, *op. cit.*, p.124.
18. Chatterton, *op. cit.*, p.124.
19. Chatterton, *op. cit.*, p.158.
20. 'Falding' was a coarse cloth. Chaucer, *The Canterbury Tales: Prologue*.
21. Chatterton, *op. cit.*, p.125.
22. David Villers' report–see Appendix 1.
23. Cust. 21, Vol. 67, p.62, Vols. 68, 71, 80, 83.
24. Cust. 21, Vol. 67, p.62, Vols. 68, 71, 80, 83.
25. Douch, John, *Smuggling Rough, Rude Men*, pp.79-81.
26. Chatterton, *op. cit.*, p.113.
27. Cust. 54, Vol.1, no.236
28. Chatterton, *op. cit.*, p.114.
29. H.O. 43, Vol. 1.
30. Cust. 54, Vol. 1, No. 266.
31. Kenneth Worthington, son of Henry Thomas Knight Worthington (1898-1967), New Zealand.
32. Cust. 54, Vol. 1, No. 409.
33. Cust. 54, Vol. 1, Nos. 293 & 317.
34. Cust. 54, Vol. 2, No. 397.

Chapter 3: Commander Benjamin Jelly Worthington of the *Tartar* Cutter
1. Cust. 54, Vol. 2, No. 420.
2. Cust. 54, Vol. 2, No. 503.
3. Chatterton, E. Keble, *King's Cutters and Smugglers*, p.125.
4. Willis's Printed Books, *Canterbury Marriage Licences Granted*, and letter from Ted Hughes, Rector of St Mary's, Dover, 1984.
5. Jones, John Bavington, *The Dover Express*, Friday 13 February 1881.
6. Jones, John Bavington, *Dover*, p.333.
7. Cust. 54, Vol. 3, No. 423.
8. Cust. 54, Vol. 3, No. 426.
9. Cust. 31, Vol. 3, p.273, no date.
10. Cust. 31, Vol. 3, p.31.
11. Cust. 31, Vol. 3, p.192.
12. Cust. 54, Vol. 4, No. 291.
13. Cust. 54, Vol. 4, No. 189.
14. Cust. 54, Vol. 4, Nos. 389 & 439.
15. Cust. 54, Vol. 5, No. 558.
16. Effectively this list serves as a census of all Officers employed in the service of the Customs at the Port of Dover on 19 April 1791.
17. Cust. 54, Vol. 5, No. 451.
18. Mowll, J.H., *Royal Visitors at Dover*, p.32.
19. In a later paper there is some dispute about her birth date, which is put at ten years previously!
20. The current custodian (1996) is Garth John Worthington of New Zealand.
21. See illustration 37.
22. Cust 54, Vol. 6, No. 567.
23. Cust. 54, Vol. 6, No. 568.
24. *Tartar* cutter, Dover Road, 7 February 1792. Cust. 54/6, 101612.

25. The Gore Channel and anchorage lies to the westward of the South Channel approach to the Thames Estuary, between the Margate Hook and the Thanet coast around Birchington.
26. Cust. 54, Vol. 6, p.155-6.
27. Chatterton, *op. cit.*, Chap. 17.
28. Cust. 54, Vol. 6, Nos. 288, 363 and 493.
29. Cust. 54, Vol. 6.
30. Cust. 54, Vol. 7 and letter written by Benjamin from *Tartar*, loaned by Ramsgate Museum to Dover Museum for an exhibition October/November 1992.
31. Cust. 54, Vol. 7, No. 157.
32. Cust. 54, Vol. 8, p.57.
33. Cust. 54, Vol. 8.
34. Cust. 54, Vol. 8.
35. Profit from employment, salary. Chart from PRO Cust. 54/12, 102000.
36. By the authority of the Warden of the Cinque Ports as stated in Cust. 54, Vol. 9, p.186.
37. Cust. 31, Vol. 5, p.392, letter dated 5 March 1796.
38. Cust. 31, Vol. 5, p.237, no date.
39. Cust. 54, Vol. 9, p.137.
40. Watts, Christopher T. and Michael J., *My Ancestor was a Merchant Seaman*, p.11.
41. Cust. 54, Vol. 8, p.330.
42. Cust. 54, Vol. 9, p.196 & 197.
43. Cust. 31, Vol. 6, p.146, letter dated 12 May 1796.
44. Cust. 54, Vol. 10, No. 51.
45. Chatterton, *op. cit.*, Appendix III, p.407.
46. Chatterton, *op. cit.*, pp.139 & 140.
47. Cust. 54, Vol. 6, No. 34.
48. Letter dated 24 January 1797, loaned by Ramsgate Museum to Dover Museum Exhibition October/November 1992.
49. Mowat, R.B., *A New History of Great Britain*, pp.559 & 560.
50. *Kentish Gazette*, Dover, 4 September 1798, p.4, col.4.
51. Cust. 54, Vol. 10, Doctors' certificates, 22 November 1797, p.303.
52. Cust. 54, Vol. 11, p.101.
53. Cust. 54, Vol. 12, pp.48-9.
54. Cust. 54, Vol. 12, p.53.
55. Cust. 54, Vol. 12, p.92.
56. Cust. 54, Vol. 12, letter dated 16 January 1800, p.133.
57. Cust. 54, Vol. 12, letter dated 28 January 1800, p.135.
58. Cust. 54, Vol. 12, p.164.
59. Hester Nye was Benjamin's sister.
60. Cust. 54, Vol. 11, p.232.
61. Cust. 54, Vol. 12, letter dated 15 February 1800, p.187.
62. Cust. 54, Vol. 12, letter dated 19 April 1800, p.215.
63. Cust. 54, Vol. 12, letter dated 1 March 1800, p.303.
64. Cust. 54, Vol. 16, p.146-8.
65. Cust. 54, Vol. 13, letter dated 11 December 1800, p.150.
66. Cust. 54, Vol. 13, letter dated 25 February 1801, p.238.
67. Cust. 54, Vol. 12, letter dated 29 March 1800, p.204.
68. Cust. 54, Vol. 12, letter dated 9 April 1800, p.207.
69. Cowes, Isle of Wight.
70. Cust. 31, Vol. 7, p.113, no date.
71. Cust. 31, Vol. 7, p.173, no date.
72. Cust. 54, Vol. 13, p.39.
73. Cust. 31, Vol. 8, p.40, no date.
74. Cust. 31, Vol. 8, p.139, no date.
75. Douch, John, *Smuggling Rough, Rude Men*, p.71.
76. Cust. 54, Vol. 10, No. 66, letter dated 28 Nov. 1801.
77. Son of Dubois and Ann Smith, christened on 21 March 1787 at Greensborough. Also Richard and Mary Smith had a son, Dubois, christened on 10 August at

Greenwich, St Alphage.
78. Cust. 54, Vol. 10, letter dated 22 December 1801.
79. Cust. 54, Vol. 8, p.281, letter dated 9 February 1802.
80. Cust. 31, Vol. 8, p.344, letter dated 6 March 1802.
81. Cust. 54, Vol. 15, p.111.
82. Cust. 54, Vol. 14, No. 63.
83. Cust. 54, Vol. 10, No. 65.
84. Extracts from the diary of Thomas Pattenden of Bench Street, Dover. Daily occurrences and remarks on Dover affairs commenced on 7 March 1797. He was regarded as the authority on Dover affairs.
85. Jones, John Bavington, *Dover*, p.144.
86. According to Bavington Jones, Jonathan Osborne [*sic*] was Mayor of Dover in 1803 and 1816. An iron founder, he bought and melted down the historic three guns from the dismantled Three Gun Battery.
87. Cust. 54, Vol. 15, No. 278, letter dated 31 May 1802.
88. Cust. 54, Vol. 15, pp.47 & 58.
89. Cust. 54, Vol. 15, p.149.
90. Cust. 54, Vol. 16, p.21.
91. Cust. 54, Vol. 15, p.145 and Vol. 16, p.263.
92. Cust. 54, Vol. 15, p.326.
93. Cust. 54, Vol. 16, p.44.
94. Cust. 54, Vol. 16, p.145.
95. Cust. 54, Vol. 17, No. 7, letter dated 7 January 1805.
96. Cust. 54, Vol. 17, pp.85, 228 and 234.
97. The Revenue men found in her hold 665 casks of brandy, 237 casks geneva, 118 casks rum, 119 bags tobacco, 6 packages of wine and 43 pounds of tea.
98. Cust. 54, Vol. 18, letter dated 12 March 1805.
99. Cust. 54, Vol. 18, p.307.
100. Cust. 54, Vol. 18, pp.180-1.
101. Atton, Henry and Holland, Henry Hurst, *The King's Customs*, Vol. II, 1910, p.97.
102. The surname Burwash, probably a surname variant, was found in Kent.
103. The Nuckel family appear in the parish registers of St Peter's, Thanet.
104. A large family in Kent. Two marriages recorded in the 1988 IGI for John Finn to Grace Brown at Woodchurch 1804, and John Finn to Mary Brown at Lewisham 1813.
105. No McCordials in 1988 IGI Kent but could be McCordell or McCordall of whom there were several.
106. A frequently occurring surname in Kent.
107. Two Isaac Jennings were found living in the 1600s in Kent according to the 1988 IGI.
108. Three Richard Andrews married between 1807 and 1811 in Kent according to the 1988 IGI.
109. His marriage could have taken place on 22 October 1797 at Tonbridge to Sar. Wood.
110. Could be the son of Edward Norwood and Frances Earle, baptised on 20 August 1786 at St Mary the Virgin, Dover.
111. A George Gladman married Elizabeth Cleverly on 24 September 1807 at St Mary the Virgin, Dover.
112. Cust. 54, Vol. 18, No. 196, The Collector's letter dated 26 June 1805.
113. Cust. 31, Vol. 9, p.18, no date.
114. Cust. 54, Vol. 21, p.278.
115. Cust. 54, Vol. 19, pp.5, 99 and 109.
116. Cust. 54, Vol. 19, p.170.
117. Cust. 54, Vol. 19, p.326 and Vol. 20, p.128.
118. Correspondence from David Villers, 6 September 1986.
119. One quire equals 24 sheets of writing paper.
120. Cust. 54, Vol. 18, No. 197, letter dated 26 June 1805.
121. Will of Knight Collins 1805–see Appendix 17.

122. Cust. 54, Vol. 20, No. 150, letter dated 15 April 1807.
123. Cust. 54, Vol. 20, No. 150.
124. Cust. 54, Vol. 20, pp.143, 153, 154 and 324.
125. Cust. 54, Vol. 20, p.324.
126. Cust. 54, Vol. 21, pp.259, 273 and 277.
127. Cust. 31, Vol. 9, p.250, letter dated 21 September 1807.
128. Cust. 54, Vol. 21, No. 140. The Collector's letter 6 May 1808.
129. Chatterton, *op. cit.*, pp.176-7.
130. Cust. 54, Vol. 22, pp.5, 56, and 164.
131. Cust. 54, Vol. 22, p.246.
132. Cust. 54, Vol. 23, p.3.
133. Cust. 54, Vol. 22, p.121.
134. Cust. 54, Vol. 23, p.207.
135. Cust. 54, Vol. 23, p.318.
136. Cust. 54, Vol. 24, pp.29, 36 & 137.
137. Chatterton, *op. cit.*, p.177.
138. Chatterton, *op. cit.*, pp.177-8.
139. Cust. 31, Vol. 32, No. 443.
140. Cust. 54, Vol. 27.
141. Cust. 54, Vol. 24.
142. Cust. 31, Vol. 271.
143. Cust. 31, Vol. 271, p.25, letter No. 127 dated 7 April 1812, Yarmouth.
144. Cust. 31, Vol. 271, p.167, letter No. 176 dated 20 May 1812, Yarmouth.
145. Cust. 31, Vol. 271, p.321, letter No. 229 dated 30 June 1812, Yarmouth.
146. Cust. 31, Vol. 271, p.353, letter No. 240, 7 July 1812, Yarmouth.
147. Cust. 31, Vol. 272, p.38, undated letter No. 24.
148. Cust. 31, Vol. 273, No. 179, letter dated 16 June 1814, Yarmouth.
149. Cust. 31, Vol. 275, No. 56, pp.406-7, Yarmouth.
150. Cust. 31, Vol. 277, No. 190, p.31, letter dated 6 July 1815, Yarmouth.
151. Cust. 31, Vol. 277, No. 215, p.177, letter dated 21 July 1815, Yarmouth.
152. Cust. 31, Vol. 279, No. 18, p.129, letter dated 11 January 1816, Yarmouth.
153. Cust. 31, Vol. 280, letter dated 20 June 1816, Yarmouth.
154. Cust. 31, Vol. 281, Yarmouth.
155. Cust. 54, Vol. 38, p.151.
156. Cust. 54, Vol. 43, p.320.
157. Bonython, William, *Bonython's Dover Guide*, p.16.
158. Cust. 54, Vol. 49, p.105.
159. Buckland church is dedicated to St Andrew. Some twelve Worthington ancestors have been buried in the old churchyard and the adjoining cemetery. During 1880, when Buckland church was restored, a large and ancient yew tree had to be either cut down or removed. This huge tree was moved a distance of 60 feet, together with a ball of soil weighing 56 tons, by a firm from the Midlands. It suffered no after effects and has continued to thrive thanks to the financial generosity of Oscar Clayton Worthington.
160. See Appendix 14.
161. See Appendix 15.

Chapter 4: Children of Benjamin Jelly and Elizabeth Worthington
1. Willis's Printed Books, *Canterbury Marriage Licences Granted*.
2. See Appendix 14–Benjamin Jelly Worthington's will.
3. ADM 107/43, Folio 162
4. ADM 107/43, Folio 160.

5. Ellis, M.H., *Lachlan Macquarie his life, adventures and times*, 3rd ed. Angus & Robertson, Sydney, 1958, pp.167-8.
6. Ship or property captured in naval warfare.
7. Huey, Alexander, *Journal aboard H.M. Store Ship Dromedary, from Yarmouth to Port Jackson, May 1809-April 1810*, CY Reel 1388, Mitchell Library, Sydney, B1514.
8. Captain Pasco to Commodore Bligh, *Historical Records of Australia*, 1810, Series 1, Vol, 7, p.211.
9. Mr. Pritchard to Captain Pasco, *Historical Records of Australia*, 1810, Series 1, Vol. 7, p.211.
10. *Ibid.*, p.211.
11. ADM 107/43, p.89.
12. ADM 107/43, p.92.
13. Rodger, N.A.M., *Naval Records for Genealogists*, HMSO, London, 1988, p.18.
14. ADM 196/1, 44321, PRO Kew.
15. ADM 51/2089, Captain's log of the *Ajax* dated 17 March 1814 describes *Alcyon* as a brig with 18 guns.
16. O'Byrne, William R., *O'Byrne's Naval Biography*, John Murray, London, Publisher to the Admiralty, 1849, p.1327.
17. *Dover Telegraph*, p.8, col.2.
18. *Pigot's Directory*, 1839, 'Nobility, Clergy and Gentry'.
19. Family history believed to have been written by a member of the Till family.
20. Keyes, Robert, *Dover; A Reminiscence of the Past, by an Ancient Freeman*, 1904, p.3.
21. Hasenson, Alec, *The History of Dover Harbour*, Ayrum Special Editions, London, 1980, pp.81-2.
22. From *Extracts from Evidence given before a committee of The House of Commons appointed to enquire into the State of Dover Harbour 1836*.
23. Jones, John Bavington, *Annals of Dover*, Dover, 1916, pp.131-5. John Bavington Jones was Honorary Librarian of the Corporation.
24. 'Dover Cameos XXXI–The Worthingtons', *Dover Express*, 5 October 1906.
25. Jones, *Annals of Dover, op. cit.*, p.128.
26. 'Dover Cameos', series in *Dover Express*, May 1906-April 1907. Scrap book ref: CUT/R/3.1-58.
27. Report of Dover Humane Society Meeting, *Dover Telegraph*, 19 November 1836, p.8, col.4.
28. LSNP, 50/2, Nos. 178, 179, 180, 181 & 1501.
29. New Plymouth History, Taranaki Files, Vol. 1001, pp.297-347.
30. See Appendix 14.
31. *Melville Directory*.
32. St James Monumental Inscriptions at Dover Library, no.376.
33. 1841, 1851 & 1861 censuses.
34. *1835 Post Office Directory*, Dover and *1855 Court Directory*.
35. 1851 census, Dover.
36. Cemetery transcription.
37. 1851 census, Dover.
38. *1839 Dover Directory*, 'Miscellaneous Trades'.
39. 1851 census, Dover.
40. 1851 census, Dover.
41. *Dover Telegraph*, 19 July 1835.
42. Jones, Bavington, *Annals of Dover*.
43. Jones, Bavington, *Annals of Dover*.
44. Lewis, Samuel, *A Topographical Dictionary of England*, Vol. III-IV, p.172.
45. *Op. cit.*
46. *Plarr's Lives of the Fellows*, College of Surgeons, London, pp.549-50.

47. *Morris & Co's Commercial Directory and Gazetteer of Suffolk*, Nottingham, 1868, p.400.
48. From unpublished anonymous Worthington family history *c.*1928.
49. *Medical Directory 1882*, p.79.
50. International Genealogical Index.
51. Unpublished anonymous family history.
52. *Op. cit.*
53. 1851 census, Lowestoft, Suffolk.
54. *Op. cit., Morris & Co Directory*, p.402.
55. *Ibid.*, pp.397-8.
56. *Ibid.*
57. Rose, Jack, *Lowestoft Then and Now–A Walk in the Past*, Lowestoft Archaeological and Local History Society, Lowestoft, 1973.
58. Information supplied by John Francis Worthington (1905-).
59. Jones, John Bavington, *Annals of Dover*, p.427.
60. Kathleen Hollingsbee to author. 1883 letter with extracts from Willis's printed books–*Canterbury Marriage Licences Granted*.
61. In the 1841 census, ages were to the nearest fifth year for adults and no place of birth was given, only whether they were born in Kent or 'elsewhere'. The word 'sole' means pond.
62. Alkham tithe map 1842 (U3/267/27/1).
63. Hasenson, Alec, *op. cit.*, p.88.
64. *Ibid.*
65. *Ibid.*
66. *Ibid.*, p.90.
67. *Ibid.*
68. *Ibid.*
69. *Dover Telegraph*, 16 January 1826 & 20 February.
70. *Dover Telegraph*, 13 August 1836, p.8.
71. Letter from Kathleen Hollingsbee to author, source of information Ivan Green.
72. *Ibid.*, p.92.
73. David, Elizabeth, *English Bread and Yeast Cookery*, 1977, p.40.
74. Harman, *loc. cit.*
75. Dover library reference: Eng/L/66.
76. *Dover Telegraph*, 22 November 1834.
77. *Dover Telegraph*.
78. *Dover Telegraph*, Saturday, 23 January 1836.
79. Kathleen Hollingsbee to author 1983. Extracts from Mowll, *Royal Visitors to Dover*, p.37.
80. Harman, *loc. sit.*
81. Letter from Kathleen Hollingsbee to author.
82. From unpublished research on Dover pubs by Barry Smith, 1990.
83. Messuage–a house, its outbuildings, yard and sometimes garden.
84. Hollingsbee to author. Letter from Whitbread Fremlins.
85. Church records for the parish of Hougham 1730-1863.
86. Jones, John Bavington, *Dover–A Perambulation of the Town, Port and Fortress*, Dover, 1907, pp.277-8.
87. Church records for the parish of Hougham 1730-1863.
88. *Ibid.*
89. Miss Hams-Hopkins to author, 1983. Extract from a letter.
90. L.D.S., *loc. sit.*
91. Church records for the parish of Hougham 1730-1863.
92. *Ibid.*
93. *Dover Express*, 17 April 1908.
94. Hollingsbee to author. Letter from Whitbread Fremlins.
95. Letter to author from local historian Jim Barter, Worthing, Sussex, 5 December 1985.

Chapter 5: Grandchildren of Benjamin Jelly and Elizabeth Worthington

1. Sir Morrell Mackenzie (1837-92) was one of the founders of the science of laryngology and worked at the London hospital. He was most probably referred to him by either William Collins Worthington or Thomas Knight Worthington, both of whom were Doctors of Medicine.
2. 1871 census.
3. *Cambrian News*, 25 May 1883.
4. *Cambrian News*, 25 September 1885.
5. From the *Cambrian News*, date of publication unknown but believed to be 1927.
6. Alfred appears in a photograph of the lifeboat crew.
7. *Cambrian News*, 9 October 1885.
8. Lord, Peter, *Artisan Painters*, The National Library of Wales, June 1993, pp.63 & 65.
9. Funeral notice *Cambrian News*, 12 February 1925.
10. Nelson *Columnist* newspaper.
11. From 'A Narrative of Events' for the province of Nelson, *Southern Province Almanac 1860*.
12. Lowther Broad, *A Jubilee History of Nelson*, Nelson, 1892, p.152.
13. Algar, F., *Colonial Handbook*, Auckland, 1870.
14. *Auckland Herald*, Saturday, 14 February 1874.
15. Coroners Inquests, JL-1874/559, N.Z. Archives, Vivian Street, Wellington.
16. Burials Book, Buckland parish, Dover, No. 437.
17. Original letter deposited Mortlock Library, Adelaide, South Australia by Miss Emily Bateman, ref: D4922(L). This information was supplied by Peter Barwick, 111 Main Street, Mornington, 3931, to Stephen Murray-Smith, Department of Education, University of Melbourne and the letter is from his own family. From letter to author, 4 February 1987.
18. FHL Reel 1341388, 1622/159/14.
19. *Morris & Co. Comm. Directory 1868*
20. *Freeholders of New Zealand 1883* and death certficate.
21. John Scott Worthington's will at Dunedin High Court Q6/83.
22. *Post Office London Directory 1846*, p.187.
23. PRO BT 122/20 & BT 122/18, Navy List 1858.
24. India Office Records, SLC FHL Reel 523919.
25. *The Medical Register 1893*.
26. 1871 census.
27. Royal College of Surgeons Library, London.
28. The South Australian *Register* newspaper, Saturday, 17 March 1877.
29. British Museum Catalogue of Printed Books.
30. *The Medical Directory 1882*.
31. Census returns.
32. Conversation with Edith Watson, Stratford, New Zealand, 1984.
33. Reid, J.C., *A Book of New Zealand*, 1964, p.51.
34. Broad, L., *The Jubilee History of Nelson*, Nelson, 1892, p.123.
35. PRO BT 151/2, London, 29 August 1850, T.K. Worthington. Only some of these records were retained–records for four out of five years were destroyed.
36. PRO Ref: BT 114/22, also William Worthington, born Dover, Ticket No. 204872.
37. PRO Ref. BT 98/2600, A List of Crew.
38. Brett, Henry, *White Wings*, Immigrant Ships to New Zealand 1840-1902, Chapter 13, pp.25-8.
39. PRO Ref: BT 98/3878, Release at the Termination of the Voyage & Crew List.
40. PRO Ref: ADM 101/253, Surgeon Superintendent's Journal for the *Phoebe Dunbar*–Jn. W.M. Bowker.
41. PRO Kew, BT 98/4237. Crew List and Log Book for the *Nile*.
42. PRO Ref: BT 98/4237, Official Log of the *Nile*.
43. Card Index to Adelaide Hospital Admissions, & *Adelaide Hospital Admission Register* Ref: GRG 78/49.
44. PRO Kew, BT 98/4605.
45. PRO, Kew, *The Register of Seamen, Series III*, 1853-7, BT 116/105.
46. PRO Ref: BT 98/2658, Official Log Book for the *Sea Park*.
47. Sailor's word for penis.
48. PRO Ref: BT 98/4605, Crew List & Official Log of the ship *Sea Park*.
49. PRO, Kew, BT 98/4625, Crew List for the *Charlotte*.
50. Taranaki Museum, New Plymouth, microfilm of *Taranaki Herald* newspaper arrivals 1856.
51. *London Post Office Commercial Directory*, 1853.
52. Stratford newspaper obituary 1894. The author is researching and writing the family history of the Tucker family for future publication.
53. Original letter in possession of the author.
54. Scholefield, Guy, *Newspapers in New Zealand*, Wellington, 1958, p.159.
55. Original in the Registry of the Supreme Court, New Plymouth.
56. *Straford Jubilee 1878-1928*, pp.8, 13-16, 37-40.
57. Cecil Worthington to author, 1986.
58. Taranaki Missioner 1889-91.
59. *The Church of the Holy Trinity Stratford, Diamond Jubilee, 1890-1950*, p.5.
60. Hastings Cemetery, Church of England Section, Block A, Plot 336.
61. Turnbull Library, Wellington, N.Z., Ref: IMN 9/1.
62. National Archives, Wellington, AD 76/3 (Repro 14 & 15) 3rd Waikato Militia. Daines recorded as Daniel, Regimental number 950.
63. Sir George Grey, Governor of New Zealand, Auckland, 11 July 1863.
64. Copies of letters deposited in Alexander Turnbull Library, Wellington, N.Z.
65. *Op. cit.*
66. Buckland Burial Register 17.2.1877.
67. PRO, Kew, England.
68. Anonymous unpublished family history, *c.*1928.
69. *Post Office Directory Kent 1878*, Private Residents.
70. Samuel Lewis, *A Topographical Dictionary of England*, originally published 1831, London, p.555.
71. Original in possession of author.
72. 1901 census, Toronto West City, Ward 4, Enumeration district B13, FHL Reel 1843581.

Chapter 6: Great-Grandchildren of Benjamin Jelly and Elizabeth Worthington

1. Author unknown, unpublished Worthington family history, *c.*1928.
2. SLC FHL Reel 1341258, Roll 1094, Folio 83, p.19.
3. Author unknown, *Notable Men of Affairs*, 1925, p.561.
4. Letter to author from Evelyn Venetia Worthington, London, England, 16 September 1996.
5. Lemieux, L.J., *The Governors-General of Canada 1608-1931*, pp.277-97.
6. Anonymous unpublished family history *c.*1928, *Debrett's Knightage*, London, 1928, p.1280 and *Whittaker's Peerage*, London, 1916, p.827.
7. *Debrett's Peerage, Baronetage, Knightage & Companionage*, 145th year, edited by C.F.J. Hankinson, Odhams Press Ltd., London, 1947.

8. *Who's Who*, A. & C. Black, London, 1947, p.3025.
9. *Who's Who in Literature*, 1932 edition, edited by Mark Meredith, published by the Literary Year Books Press Ltd., Liverpool, p.476.
10. John Benjamin Scott Worthington, son of John Vigers and Agnes Janet Worthington.
11. Registered as Rubie at the time of her birth but her name was found later spelt Ruby.
12. *Dover Telegraph*, Wednesday, 6 June 1912.
13. Letter to author from Mrs. L.M. Catt, St Andrew's Church member, Dover.
14. Buckland Parish Burials Book, Dover, No. 6959.
15. Jessie Adeline Vezic to author.
16. R.G.O. Death Certificate, New Zealand.
17. Barbara Worthington to author.
18. *Stratford Primary School 1882-1957*, 75th Anniversary Celebrations, p.2.
19. Copies from original letters held by Mildred Hart.
20. Phyllis Jeans to author.
21. Jean Iva Worthington to author.
22. Edward Montano Worthington to author about 1982.
23. Joan Laverty, née Worthington, to author about 1982.
24. Story told by Connie Leeming.
25. Stratford Cemetery, headstone.
26. Letter to Barbara Worthington from Edith Watson, née Worthington 1983.

Chapter 7: Cousins of Benjamin Jelly and Elizabeth Worthington
1. From undated, unfinished letter written by Edward Worthington to Admiral Sir James A. Gordon, Governor, Royal Hospital, Greenwich soliciting a presentation to the Upper School for his son Robert. Original letter held by Mrs. Margaret Gudex.
2. Records held at the PRO, Kew.
3. Deed registered at Court 17 May 1833, Mauritius, Vol. 1, folio 149.
4. *Star* newspaper, Guernsey, Tuesday, 24 October 1865.
5. Pike's *Folkestone, Hythe and Sandgate Directory 1902-3.*
6. *Motor Cycling*, 18 June 1912, p.166. From BP Library of Motoring, The National Motor Museum, Beaulieu, Hampshire.
7. Family information from a local resident whose father worked for the firm. Letter from Kent County Library 1983.

Chapter 8: Related Families
1. From Canterbury (Cowper's) Marriage Licence Book.
2. See Chapter 1.
3. *Kentish Gazette*, 7 October, p.4, col.4.
4. Minute Book of Dover Court of Lodemanage, p.121.
5. PRO Inland Revenue Records, Kent, Vol. 1763-74, 24/156.
6. St Mary's, Dover, Church Monumental Inscriptions.
7. St Mary's, Churchyard Monumental Inscriptions.
8. *The Dover Express*, 1 August 1748.
9. Jones, John Bavington, *Annals of Dover*, p.338.
10. Dover Corporation Minutes, Microfilm at Dover Library.
11. Kent Poll 1754.
12. Jones, John Bavington, *op. cit.*, p.338.
13. Dover District Council Leaflet 1, September 1993.
14. Ancestor of Kathleen Hollingsbee.

15. Chalklin, C.W., *Seventeenth Century Kent*, p.24.
16. See Appendix 16 for Henry Jelly's will.
17. St Mary's, Dover, Churchyard Monumental Inscriptions.
18. Kent County Record Office, Dover Apprenticeship Enrolments.
19. St James's Monumental Inscriptions, Dover Library and D. Welby's *A Tidy Ruin*.
20. See Appendix 17.
21. PRO Inland Revenue Vols. for Kent 1763-74.
22. Kent Poll Book 1754.
23. Dover Borough Records Apprenticeship Enrolment–Indentures 1673-1788, Kent Archives Service, Maidstone.
24. Dover Borough Records Apprenticeship Enrolment–Indentures 1673-1788, Kent Archives Service, Maidstone.
25. *Kentish Gazette*, 13 January 1786, p.4, col.2.
26. *Kentish Gazette*, 23-7 April 1790, p.1, col.3.
27. Also spelt Affrey and Affra.
28. See chapter on Jelly family.
29. Jones, John Bavington, *op. cit.*, p.337.
30. Kentish Poll Book, 1754.
31. Minute Book of Dover Court of Lodemanage.
32. *Kentish Gazette*, 12-15 January 1790, p.4, col.4.
33. Green, Ivan, *The Book of the Cinque Ports*, p.110.
34. Original indenture in possession of the author.
35. Jones, John Bavington, pp.250-2, 277-8.
36. Dover Borough Records Apprenticeship Enrolment–Indentures 1673-1788, Kent Archives Service, Maidstone.
37. St Mary the Virgin, Dover, Monumental Inscriptions.
38. *Dover Telegraph*, 17 February 1838, p.1, col.2.
39. Dover Apprentice Enrolments, Kent County Archives Office & Inland Revenue records at Public Record Office, of which Kent apprenticeships 1763 to 1774 are on Kent Family History Society microfiche.
40. Ireland, *County of Kent*, 1829, Vol. II, p.509.
41. *Kentish Gazette*, 3 March 1801.
42. Ledger, G., *A Sketch of Dover*, 1799, p.171.
43. *Lydden–A Parish History*, pp.53-4.
44. A Knight's Fee was land held by a knight for which he provided military service to his immediate overlord.
45. *Dover Telegraph*, 19 September 1846, p.1, col.3.
46. Dover Apprentice Enrolments, Kent County Archives Office.
47. Squibb, G.D. and Wagner, A.R., *Papworth's Ordinary of British Armorials*, London, 1874, p.380 and Burke, Sir Bernard, Ulster King of Arms, *The General Armory of England, Scotland, Ireland and Wales*, London, 1878, p.540.
48. *The Dover Chronicle*, 19 May 1838.
49. 1839 *Dover Directory*–Miscellaneous Trades: Jennings, George Finch, Woolstapler, Eastbrook Cottage, Dover.
50. Dover Apprentice Enrolments, Kent County Archives Office.
51. *Kentish Gazette*, 5-9 February 1790, p.1, col.3.
52. From Temple Ewell, near Dover–plaque in interior of church.
53. *Dover Telegraph*, 5 November 1836, p.8.
54. 1871 census, River Parish (Crabble), Ref.29.
55. *Dover Telegraph*, 2 October 1847, p.8, col.4.
56. 1851 census.

Abbreviations

ADM	Admiralty
A.I.F.	Australian Infantry Force
b.	born
bap	baptised
bur.	buried
c.	circa, about
C.B.	Companion of the Order of the Bath
C.B.E.	Commander of the Order of the British Empire
CCL	Canterbury Cathedral Library
C.I.E.	Companion of the Order of the Indian Empire
C.M.	Master in Surgery
C.M.G.	Companion of the Order of St Michael and St George
d.	died
Dip. F.H.S.	Diploma in Family Historical Studies
diss.	dissolved
div.	divorced
Eng.	England
F.R.G.S.	Fellow of the Royal Geographical Society
F.Z.S.	Fellow of the Zoological Society
F.R.S.	Fellow of the Royal Society
F.S.A.G.	Fellow of Society of Australian Genealogists
HO	Home Office
K.C.V.O.	Knight Commander of the Royal Victorian Order
LDS	Church of Jesus Christ of Latter Day Saints
L.F.P.S.	Licentiate of the Faculty of Physicians and Surgeons
Lieut.	Lieutenant
L.M.	Licentiate of Medicine/Midwifery
L.R.C.P.	London Royal College Physicians
L.S.A.	Licentiate of the Society of Apothecaries
m.	married
M.M.	Military Medal
M.A.	Master of Arts
M.D.	Doctor of Medicine
M.R.C.S.	Member of the Royal College of Surgeons
N.C.O.	Non Commissioned Officer
NZ	New Zealand
N.Z.R.N.	New Zealand Registered Nurse
O.B.E.	Officer of the Order of the British Empire
PRO	Public Record Office
R.A.M.C.	Royal Army Medical Corps
R.N.	Royal Navy
R.S.A	Royal Society of Arts
Q	1st, 2nd, 3rd or 4th quarter of year stated
sic	as recorded in the original
SLC FHL	Salt Lake City Family History Library
St M.	St Mary the Virgin, Dover
WWI	World War I
WWII	World War II

Bibliography

Algar, F., *Colonial Handbook*, Auckland, N.Z. (1870)

An Ancient Freeman, *Dover; A Reminiscence of its History Past and Present*, Ouzman & Malyon, London (1903)

Allan, Ruth, *Nelson, A History of Early Settlement*, A.H. & A.W. Reed, Wellington (1965)

Atton, Henry and Holland, Henry Hurst, *The King's Customs*, Vols. I & II, John Murray, London (1910)

Black, Adam and Charles, *Who's Who*, London (1947)

Bonython, William, *Bonython's Dover Guide*, William Bonython, Apollo Library, Dover (1823)

Brett, Henry, *White Wings, Immigrant Ships to New Zealand 1840-1902*, A.H. & A.W. Reed Ltd, Wellington, N.Z. (1984)

Broad, Lowther, *A Jubilee History of Nelson*, Bond, Finney and Co., 'Colonist' Office, Nelson, N.Z. (1892)

Buckingham, Christopher, *Lydden—Parish History*, Thomas Becket Books, Lydden, Dover, Kent (1967)

Burke, Sir Bernard, *The General Armory of England, Scotland, Ireland and Wales*, Harrison, London (1878)

Chalklin, C.W., *Seventeenth Century Kent*, Longmans Green & Co Ltd, London (1965)

Chapman, Henry Stephen, *Deal: Past and Present*, Reeves & Turner, London (1890)

Chatterton, E. Keble, *King's Cutters and Smugglers*, George Allen & Co., London (1912)

Dickens, Admiral Sir Gerald, *The Dress of the British Sailor*, Trustees of the National Maritime Museum by Her Majesty's Stationery Office, London (1977)

Douch, John, *Smuggling Rough, Rude Men*, Crabwell Publications/Buckland Publications Ltd, Dover (1985)

Elkington, George, J.P., *The Worshipful Company of Coopers with notes and recollections 1873-1930*, W.J. Parrett Ltd, Printers, Margate (1930)

Ellis, M.H., *Lachlan Macquarie his Life, Adventure & Times*, 3rd edition, Angus & Robertson, Sydney, Australia (1958)

FitzHugh, Terrick V., *The Dictionary of Genealogy*, Alphabooks, England (1985)

Green, Ivan, *The Book of the Cinque Ports*, Barracuda Books Ltd, England (1984)

Hankinson, C.F.J., *Debrett's Peerage, Baronetage, Knightage & Companionage*, 145th year, Odhams Press Ltd., London (1947)

Hasenson, Alec, *The History of Dover Harbour*, Ayrum Special Editions, London (1980)

Hasted, Edward, *History of Kent, England*, 4 vols. (1778-1799)

Hicks, Sir Henry, *The Poll for Knights of the Shire to represent the County of Kent*, printed for Stephen Austen, Bookseller at the Angel & Bible in St Paul's Churchyard (1734)

Houlbrooke, Ralph A., *The English Family 1450-1700*, Longman Group Ltd, London & New York (1984)

Hull, Dr. Felix, *Ordinance Survey Historical Guides Kent*, George Philip & Son Ltd, London (1988)

Jessup, Frank W., *A History of Kent*, Phillimore & Co Ltd, England (1974, 1987, 1995)

Jones, John Bavington, *Dover—A Perambulation of the Town, Port and Fortress*, Dover Express Printing Works, Dover (1907)

Jones, John Bavington, *Dover*, Dover Express, Dover (1907)

Jones, John Bavington, *Annals of Dover*, 2nd ed., Dover Express, Dover (1938)

Jones, John Bavington, *The Cinque Ports*, 2nd ed,. Dover Express & East Kent News, Dover (1937)

Jones, John Bavington, *The Records of Dover Charters, Record Books, & Papers of the Corporation with the Dover Customal*, Dover Express Works, Dover (1920)

Keyes, Robert, *Dover; A Reminiscence of the Past, by an Ancient Freeman* (1904)

Leather, John, *Spritsails and Lugsails*, Adlard Coles, London (1979)

Ledger, G., *A Sketch of Dover* (1799)

Lewis, Samuel, *A Topographical Dictionary of England*, originally published in four volumes, London (1831), reprinted by Genealogical Publishing Co., Inc., Baltimore, MD, U.S.A. (1996)

Lewis, W.J., *'A Fashionable Watering Place' Aberystwyth*, The Cambrian News Ltd., Aberystwyth (1980)

Lord, Peter, *Artisan Painters*, National Library of Wales (1993)

Lyon, John, *A History of the Town & Port of Dover & Dover Castle* (1965) (SLC FHL Reel 477363, item 2)

March, Edward J., *Inshore Craft of Britain in Days of Sail and Oar*, Vol. 2., David & Chailer (1970)

Meredith, Mark, *Who's Who in Literature*, Literary Year Book Press Ltd., Liverpool, England (1932)

McLintock, A.H., *An Encyclopaedia of New Zealand*, R.E. Owen, Government Printer, Wellington, N.Z. (1966)

Miller, F.W.G., *Golden Days of Lake County*, Whitcombe & Tombs, Christchurch, N.Z. (1949)

Mowat, R.B., *Britain*, Oxford University Press, England (1923)

Mowll, John H., *Royal Visitors at Dover*, St George's Press, Dover (1937)

O'Byrne, William, *R.O'Byrne's Naval Biography*, John Murray, London, Publisher to the Admiralty (1849)

Philpot, John, *Roll of the Constables of Dover Castle, & Lord Wardens of the Cinque Ports* (1627) (SLC FHL Reel 0973133, item 5)

Plumb, J.H., *The First Four Georges*, B.T. Batsford Ltd, England (1956)

Reid, J.C., *A Book of New Zealand*, New Zealand (1964)

Richardson, John, *The Local Historian's Encyclopedia*, Historical Publications Ltd, Great Britain (1974)

Rodger, N.A.M., *Naval Records for Genealogists*, Her Majesty's Stationery Office, London (1988)

Rose, Jack & Lees, Hugh D.W., *Lowestoft Then and Now (A Walk in the Past)*, Lowestoft Archaeological and Local History Society, Lowestoft (1973)

Scholefield, G.H., *Newspapers in New Zealand*, A.H. & A.W. Reed, Wellington, N.Z. (1958)

Smith, Frank, *The Lives and Times of our English Ancestors*, Vol. II, Everton Publishers, Utah, U.S.A. (1980)

Smith, Graham, *Something to Declare—1000 Years of Customs & Excise*, George G. Harrop & Co. Ltd, London (1980)

Squibb, G.D. & Wagner, A.R., *Papworth's Ordinary of British Armorials*, reproduced from the original version 1874, Tabard Publications Ltd., London

Trevelyan, G.M., *English Social History*, Book Club Associates, London (1973)

Vivian, Lieut-Col. J.L., *The Visitations of the County of Devon*, comprising The Heralds' Visitations of 1531, 1564, & 1620, Henry S. Eland, Exeter (1895)

Watts, Christopher T. and Michael, J., *My Ancestor was a Merchant Seaman*, The Society of Genealogists, London (1986)

Welby, Douglas, *Dover's Tidy Ruin*, published on behalf of the Dover Archaeological Group, Dover 1976.30

Winbolt, S.E. & Ward, Winifred, *Kent*, G. Bell & Sons, Ltd, London (1930)

Worthington, Lieut. B., *Proposed Plan for Improving Dover Harbour by an Extension of the South Pier Head, &.*, W. Batcheller, Dover (1838)

Worthington, Philip M., *The Worthington Families of Medieval England*, Phillimore & Co Ltd, England (1985)

Archaeologia Cantiana, Vol. 47

Dover Borough Records Apprenticeship Enrollment—Indentures 1673-1788, Kent Archives Service, Maidstone

Dover Lodemanage Book, Minute Book of Dover Court of Lodemanage 1763-1808 (SLC FHL Reel 6341990).

Historical Records of Australia, William Applegate Gullick, Government Printer, Sydney, 1920.

The Concord Desk Encyclopaedia, Presented by Time, Concord Reference Books, New York, 1982

Index of Persons

General Index